Latin American Migrations to the U.S. Heartland

T0384046

Latin American Migrations to the U.S. Heartland

Changing Social Landscapes in Middle America

Edited by

**LINDA ALLEGRO AND
ANDREW GRANT WOOD**

**UNIVERSITY OF
ILLINOIS PRESS**
Urbana, Chicago, and Springfield

First Illilnois paperback, 2019
© 2013 by the Board of Trustees
of the University of Illinois
1 2 3 4 5 C P 5 4 3 2 1
∞ This book is printed on acid-free paper.

The Library of Congress cataloged the cloth edition as follows:
Latin American migrations to the U.S. Heartland :
changing social landscapes in Middle America /
edited by Linda Allegro and Andrew Grant Wood.
pages cm. — (The working class in American history)
Latin American migrations to the US heartland
Includes bibliographical references and index.
ISBN 978-0-252-03766-5 (cloth : acid-free paper)
ISBN 978-0-252-09492-7 (ebook)
1. Hispanic Americans—West North Central States—Social
conditions. 2. Latin Americans—West North Central States—
Social conditions. 3. Immigrants—West North Central States.
4. Foreign workers—West North Central States. 5. Social
change—West North Central States. 6. West North Central
States—Social conditions. 7. West North Central States—
Ethnic relations. 8. West North Central States—Economic
conditions. 9. Latin America—Emigration and immigration.
10. West North Central States—Emigration and immigration.
I. Allegro, Linda. II. Wood, Andrew Grant, 1958–
F358.2.S75L36   2013
305.868'077—dc23   2012048319

Paperback ISBN 978-0-252-08435-5

To my children, Cyrus and Roma Belle,
who are growing up Okie, and to my maternal kin
in Granada, Nicaragua, who have resisted emigration.
~ Linda Allegro

To Mary Allison "Wendy" Wood (1936–2006),
Canadian migrant, sun worshipper,
and disability rights advocate.
~ Andrew Grant Wood

Contents

Preface

We began conceptualizing this project in 2007 when Oklahoma lawmakers—concurrent with other legislators elsewhere in the country—passed a draconian law attempting to expunge the undocumented population from the state. As Latin Americanists educated in New York and California, we were disturbed by the many inaccuracies disseminated about immigrants, the scapegoating of people of Latin American heritage, and the countless diatribes about "illegals" in the media. Before long, this new wave of anti-immigrant fervor had crystallized into an angry narrative alleging an "unworthiness"—and possibly even criminal intent—on the part of nearly all Latin American immigrants. Over and over we heard people ask: Why were they here? What public services were they taking advantage of? Why didn't they speak English? What part of illegal don't you understand?

From our perspective, the prevailing public discourse that so dehumanized border crossers stood in sharp contrast to the hardworking and morally grounded individuals and families we knew. Miguel, a talented corrido songwriter from Michoacán, worked as a landscaper tending the lawns of individuals who barely knew of his existence. As a day laborer, his full life as a musician, father, and friend remained unknown. Juan's daughter, Amanda, with undocumented status, actually supported her unemployed American husband working as a nanny. Antonia, having buried a husband and leaving seven children behind in Guatemala, followed a cousin's path to rural Oklahoma where she worked in a cafeteria kitchen and sent her paychecks home. The determined work ethic of these people, as far as we could see, ran contrary to the often prejudicial, two-dimensional portrayal of "Hispanics." Given these and many other similar situations, we felt inspired to render a more humane depiction of Latin American migrants in the U.S. Heartland.

As we explored the immigration dynamics taking place in Middle America, we uncovered an emerging body of literature that explained the hard economic times many rural heartlanders have experienced in recent years under the prevailing market-fundamentalist paradigm. From the farm crisis of the 1980s, to the boarding up of mom-and-pop shops on Main Street making way for the onslaught of big-box stores that followed, to the chipping away of labor protections codified in right-to-work (RtW) laws, the emerging history of the region revealed tales of corporate greed and social-psychological devastation. The more we uncovered from the wreckage of the U.S. rural Heartland, the more it resembled the story of rural restructuring in Mexico and other Latin American nations.

Since the 1990s we have observed the impact that the General Agreement on Tariffs and Trade (GATT) and the North American Free Trade Agreement (NAFTA) have had on the corn industry of Mexico, the systematic erosion of labor and environmental laws in the privatization of once-nationalized industries, the reorientation of domestic manufacturing to export processing exemplified in the maquiladora model, and the resulting migratory networks that have emerged as individuals have been forced to deal with the restructuring. More recently, however, we connected this south-of-the-border history with works such as *Broken Heartland: The Rise of America's Rural Ghetto* (1996), *Deer Hunting with Jesus: Dispatches from America's Class War* (2007), *Any Way You Cut It: Meat Processing and Small Town America* (1995), and *Agrarian Socialism: Marx, Jefferson and Jesus in the Oklahoma Countryside* (2002)—all works that recount the trials of working-class folks in rural America who have tried to keep afloat while their communities and livelihoods have sunk under a sea of neoliberal corporate expansion.

Academically, the fields of Latin American migration and U.S. Heartland studies have not typically been linked. Indeed, in an age of growing multiculturalism under globalization, the bridging of the predominantly white working class with foreign migration and labor has often been at odds. While we note some obvious commonalities particularly in regard to issues related to family life, religion, and labor, others argue that the social identities of heartlanders and Latin Americans are primordially different. Class solidarity has been displaced by a new ideological discourse about "race" and ethnicity under the aegis of a purportedly rational state apparatus. Distorting the potential for more cross-class analysis, the project of nationalism and its accompanying neoliberal agenda presents obstacles to building mutual respect.

Our volume is an attempt to understand intraregional developments in the U.S. Heartland by presenting the distinctly unique characteristics of place while at the same time contextualizing this geographic area into a larger globalized world. By uncovering collective traumas and stories of resilience, we hope to point out commonalities upon which mutually beneficial and sustainable solutions can be constructed. Fairly recently integrated into the global economy, we believe the U.S. Heartland is a fertile place upon which to plant seeds of a new vision of sustainability and cooperation. Heartlands tend toward the bread and butter. As one labor organizer recently put it, "There is real potential here for class-based solidarity because the Heartland has not been entirely co-opted by liberal consumerism as a way to address social and economic inequality." Most of the authors in this volume are in fact heartlanders—individuals who come from the very places they tell us about. Many have traveled—like the individuals and families they study—across borders and back. We hope the many rich insights offered in the present volume will be appreciated as a helpful and genuine contribution toward real social renewal and grassroots solidarity.

Acknowledgments

The authors would like to thank the University of Tulsa Office of Research and Sponsored Programs for financial support. Special thanks to Justin Hobbs for creating the Heartland map. We also wish to express our gratitude to our editor, Laurie Matheson, for her support and vision.

Introduction

Heartland North, Heartland South

LINDA ALLEGRO AND
ANDREW GRANT WOOD

The neoliberal restructuring of the international economy since the early 1970s has changed the world to an extent perhaps not seen since the late nineteenth century. Coupled with revolutionary developments in technology and communication, the mobility of capital has accelerated following the deregulatory dictates of the World Bank, International Monetary Fund, and U.S. policy-centered Washington consensus. Not surprisingly, this global transformation has been accompanied by a substantial increase in the movement of labor and populations in general. For the well-positioned few, it has proved a time of great optimism and reward. In contrast, millions of ordinary people have been dispossessed of their livelihood and forced to find a way to survive in an era where the odds are dauntingly stacked against them.

Political and financial crises across the Americas since the 1970s have uprooted millions. Bolivians travel to Argentina in search of employment, Nicaraguans depart for neighboring Costa Rica, Haitians to the Dominican Republic, and so on. Migration is indeed a hemispheric phenomenon. Farm families in North America have seen their rural way of life overtaken by corporate agriculture and replaced by China-supplied Wal-Marts driving depopulation. In Latin America, debt defaults brought the imposition of structural adjustment policies (SAPs) that pushed privatization and the elimination of social programming. Ensuing state economic policy then prompted the abandonment of the working and middle classes while privileged elites profited (Harvey 1989; 2000). Millions of jobs have been eliminated, deskilled, downsized, or relocated. And wherever big money and jobs go, so necessarily go people in search of work.

The Americas is a hemisphere developed in the modern era as an assortment of settler societies. Somewhat contrary to the mythic "nations of immigrants," this distinction allows for recognition of the many ensuing waves of people who migrated in search of work (Dunbar-Ortiz 2008). Here we can—and should—acknowledge a common history among the many different ethnic groups throughout the hemisphere as they encountered changes in the global economy and relocated (sometimes by force) as a result.

As thousands in more recent years from Asia and Latin America—particularly Mexico, Central America, and the Caribbean—have come to the United States in search of work, they have helped shape yet another major period of economic restructuring and labor recruitment. Along with the influx of thousands to more traditional immigrant-worker "receiver" areas, one of the most interesting trends in the contemporary era is not only the sheer number of people on the move but also the new settlement patterns to destinations that extend far beyond coastal, gateway areas to locations in the U.S. South, Midwest, and Heartland states.

Since the mid-1990s, the number of Latin American migrants to what we define as the U.S. Heartland (Oklahoma, Kansas, Nebraska, Arkansas, Missouri, and Iowa) has also grown significantly. Although well below the population numbers of Latin Americans in large urban, coastal cities, their demographic growth rates have expanded considerably, often doubling, even tripling, in the last decade. This is a dynamic situation that interestingly brings together a transnational mix of working people largely from traditionally rural areas and small towns throughout the hemisphere. Hence our concern with those we term "heartlanders" both north and south of the U.S.-Mexico border.

Global Encounter(s) in the Heartland North

The U.S. Heartland is often represented as a homespun, rural-based society where gun and doll shows, rodeos, livestock fairs, and country music festivals are common. The long-standing presence of African American and Native American minorities notwithstanding, the region is thought to be predominantly a white Anglo-Saxon Protestant stronghold in contrast to the more diverse "fly-to" coastal areas or the traditionally Hispanic southwestern border states. Considered part of the nation's "Bible Belt" because of the seeming omnipresence of churches—especially of Evangelical/Baptist denominations—the Heartland and its people have largely been thought of as Jesus loving, deeply conservative, and fearful of foreigners. The region is often romanticized as an archetypical [Norman] Rockwellian, Main Street, USA. It is a metaphoric place in the national imagination believed to be

The Heartland Six

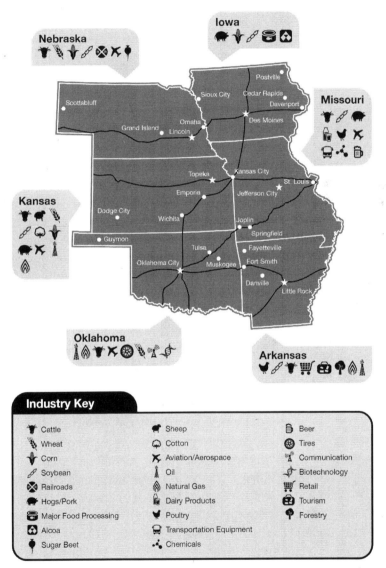

Iowa

Nebraska

Missouri

Kansas

Oklahoma

Arkansas

Postville
Sioux City
Cedar Rapids
Davenport
Scottsbluff
Omaha
Des Moines
Grand Island
Lincoln
Topeka
Kansas City
St. Louis
Emporia
Jefferson City
Dodge City
Wichita
Joplin
Guymon
Springfield
Tulsa
Fayetteville
Oklahoma City
Muskogee
Fort Smith
Danville
Little Rock

Industry Key

Cattle	Sheep	Beer
Wheat	Cotton	Tires
Corn	Aviation/Aerospace	Communication
Soybean	Oil	Biotechnology
Railroads	Natural Gas	Retail
Hogs/Pork	Dairy Products	Tourism
Major Food Processing	Poultry	Forestry
Alcoa	Transportation Equipment	
Sugar Beet	Chemicals	

Map Illustration by Justin Hobbs | hobbsbranding.com

largely untouched by the vast transformations wrought by globalization witnessed in the coastal megacities.

The Heartland has been significantly restructured under globalization. High suicide rates have been noted among farmers who lost their land in the farm crisis of the 1980s (Davidson 1996). Huge corporate enterprises have come to dominate the region, including an array of massive agricultural, poultry, cattle, and hog processing firms such as Tyson (Springdale, Arkansas), Monsanto (St. Louis, Missouri), and ConAgra (Omaha, Nebraska), not to mention the world's biggest retailer, Wal-Mart (Bentonville, Arkansas). The area plays host to a people painfully aware of the economic troubles brought on by outsourcing and subcontracting. Making things worse, the region's middle and working class have been betrayed by both arrogant conservative and liberal politicians. In the past few decades, Republican elites have effectively manipulated ordinary Americans with their discourse of "family values" while at the same time successfully promoting procorporate policies that have left many Heartland communities economically bereft. In the meantime, the same midcontinent working- and middle-class individuals have largely been shunned by coastal liberals who find themselves fearful of the contradictions and sometimes outright stubbornness of ordinary folk in what they see as a vast, unchangeable sea of electoral-map red.

Interestingly, it is not difficult to notice a striking sense of cultural—or at least aesthetic—commonality between the new Latin American migrants (many from rural backgrounds) and their down-home, working-class white, black, and "red" brethren. European Americans, American Indians, and African Americans—along with their "Latino" neighbors in the Heartland—demonstrate a preference for cowboy apparel (hats, boots, jeans, etc.) and penchant for oversized U.S.-brand pickup trucks with either various Mexican adornments such as large, red, white, and green Virgin de Guadalupe glass decals or front license plates advertising "Beef" and "Jesus Saves." Expatriate blogger Joe Bageant refers to Latino rednecks as constituting the same stock of loggers, cowboys, Poles, and Germans who constitute the American working class today. In the words of Bageant, "Do you think beer and low riders and macho sports aesthetic of Latinos, the heterosexual, patriotic Jesus focused Catholic is that much different from their Jesus focused Baptist Dixie and Midwestern counterparts?" (Frank and St. Clair 2008). At flea markets and in microeconomies off the grid in small towns, it is not uncommon to witness a multiethnic exchange of peoples and commercial and consumer practices, dispelling the myth of their "natural" incompatibilities. Moreover, it is not uncommon for heartlanders to have traveled on religious missions to Latin America, paving the way for interregional exchange. For many Latin

Americans who come to rural North America, gravitating to church life constitutes a comfort and familiar zone. With names like Cuts and Bruises Ministry, Ministerio Hispano de Victory, and Guts Church, the Heartland similarly resonates with the pronounced religious familiarity found in small-town Latin America.

Significant demographic shifts are taking shape today in this U.S. geographic center. The population totals are not as massive as one sees in the traditional receiving coastal/borderlands areas, but what is happening in the middle of the country is just as important and even more dramatic in relative terms. Small towns and rural areas throughout the Heartland are undergoing economic, social, and cultural restructuring as Latin Americans rapidly become a growing population within otherwise traditionally bifurcated "white" and "black" (as well as to some extent "red" or Native American) communities. In other words, the Heartland is no longer a quaint, traditional "American" political, economic, and social backwater but a complex, rapidly changing realm being transformed by globalization and the related process of international migration.

To highlight some of the most interesting demographic changes, one can note that although Guatemalans and other Central Americans are growing in number, the vast majority of Latin American migrants in the U.S. Heartland are Mexican nationals. Given the historic, geographic, and territorial ties of the region to Mexico as well as to the economic restructuring brought on by more recent regional trade agreements, the distinctly Mexican presence in the U.S. Heartland is profound.

Further, many first-generation Latin Americans residing in the Heartland are young, working-age adults. According to U.S. census data, the median age is thirty-five years old. Not surprising, this demographic reinforces the idea that migrants have workforce participation rates higher than national levels. Also significant are the relatively even numbers of males and females in the immigration pool, indicating that families are on the move and more likely to settle. In step with migratory trends in other parts of the nation, the increase in female migration in recent years is an indication of the restructuring of work and family patterns in the home nation that are compelling women to find work internationally. It also speaks to the way restrictions in immigration policy have curtailed previous male circular migration streams and replaced them with a fairly unidirectional movement of families, particularly when family members are undocumented and not afforded the ability to traverse borders. Resulting from the militarization of border enforcement, undocumented male breadwinners are less likely to return to their home towns, instead opting to bring their families with them to their new destinations.

The Failure of U.S. Immigration Reform and the Discourse of National Security

Latin American migrants to Middle America have created a variety of economic and social opportunities for themselves. Overall, many heartlanders have welcomed the new arrivals by establishing community and religious-based initiatives and various partnerships to accommodate them. At the same time, however, others less tolerant have crafted exclusionary and restrictive laws that have marginalized immigrants, while stalled reforms at the federal level have obstructed nearly all legitimate, documented paths to legal residency and potential citizenship. As a result, migrants have continued to pursue economic and social opportunity but in a manner that has made them all the more vulnerable to unscrupulous employers and hate groups who are wont to characterize them as criminals.

The accelerated entry of Latin American migrants to the Heartland comes at a distinct moment in North American and world history. Added to the rapid pace of capitalist economic incorporation, new national security concerns since September 11, 2001, have further heightened concerns about transnational border crossers despite the persistent and highly contradictory rhetoric of neoliberal free trade.

At the local, state, and national levels, opportunistic politicians and pundits have deployed hateful portrayals of migrants from Latin America, characterizing "them" as an economic menace ("they take our jobs"), security risks ("potential terrorists and drug dealers"), and a cultural threat ("Hispanics aren't assimilating"). In late 2005, for example, U.S. Representative James Sensenbrenner (R-WI) drafted legislation targeting undocumented migrants. His idea was to classify these immigrants as felons, automatically making them subject to deportation and forever disqualifying them from gaining legal status. With the passage of Sensenbrenner's HB 4437, officially known as the Border Protection, Antiterrorism, and Illegal Immigration Control Act, a Republican-dominated House of Representatives made a somewhat hollow yet nevertheless potent rhetorical appeal for restricting and removing undocumented migrants.

Conflated with anxieties about terrorists, foreign invaders, and lawbreakers, Sensenbrenner's legislation explicitly branded Latin American migrants as "illegals." In this analysis, the legislator from Wisconsin was only partially correct, for the fact is that not being officially authorized to reside in the United States is a civil violation, like a traffic infraction; it is not a criminal act. Tellingly, when Sensenbrenner was later reminded that criminalizing undocumented migrants would entitle offenders to a lawyer and a day in court, he backed off (Riley 2008).

The U.S. Senate, in turn, proposed a more moderate version of immigration reform, including a plan for earned legalization. Unable to arrive at a compromise, the whole legislative process was jettisoned by the end of the 2005–2006 congressional session. A substitute bill, the Secure Fence Act of 2006, was consequently passed and signed by then President George W. Bush. This measure, however, received only negligible funding from the subsequently Democratic-dominated Congress in late 2006. In turn, many state, municipal, and local governments responded with immigrant-restrictive laws and ordinances seeking to address perceived federal failures. In the meantime, anti-immigrant advocates nevertheless called for upgraded border security, enhanced workplace enforcement, and bolstered efforts to identify and repatriate undocumented migrants.

Engendered in the post–September 11 climate of homeland security and the war on terror, concern over undocumented migrants became, for some conservatives such as a number of self-appointed television pundits like Lou Dobbs, a personal obsession. Dobbs's "Latino threat narrative" joined what anthropologist Leo Chavez has identified as "the grand tradition of alarmist discourse about immigrants and their perceived negative impact on society" (Chavez 2008: 3). Whether legal or undocumented, people of Latin American heritage, including U.S. citizens, have found themselves increasingly profiled and accused of being "illegal aliens" despite their dynamic social contribution as laborers. In some cases, legal residents and U.S. citizens who simply came in contact with undocumented migrants have been accused of "harboring illegals" and hence breaking the law. These provisions are obviously intended to discourage any form of legitimate association with individuals connected to migrant-related activities (De Genova 2002).

Many pushed back against the restrictive measures. Demonstrations across the country in spring 2006 called for basic human and civil rights for migrants. The film *A Day Without an Immigrant* became a rallying cry of pro-immigrant groups advocating for much-needed national immigration reform and legalization. Newer organizations such as the Center for New Community, Progressive States Network, and the Immigration Policy Center are working to counter the rising anti-immigrant tide. In the meantime, Washington lawmakers fail to produce even the most moderate immigration-reform legislation. In delaying indefinitely, they defaulted to individual states on the immigration issue. With this, conservative anti-immigration groups and opportunist politicians seized the opportunity.

Anti-immigrant efforts became more emboldened through the funding sources of John Tanton, the founder of the Orwellian-termed Federation for American Immigration Reform (FAIR), State Legislators for Legal Immigration (SLFLI), and Numbers USA (DeParle 2011). Also significant have been the mobilizing efforts of the Center for Immigration Studies, which helped defeat the Dream Act, a legalization bill for undocumented children and youth. Kris Kobach, a former member of John Ashcroft's Justice Department team, helped develop the legal framework that growing numbers of state and local officials have used to justify anti-immigrant proposals, including the Arizona law (SB 1070) in 2010 (Khimm 2010). Hate speech and related crimes directed at Latin Americans have risen sharply in recent years as documented by organizations such as the Southern Poverty Law Center. Scapegoated and held responsible for everything from plant closings, layoffs, union busting, poor public education, drug dependency, and failing state and local budgets to an amorphous "decline" in the moral fabric of the nation, people of Latin American descent experienced a surge in anger and resentment directed at them. Of course, this is nothing new in the history of the United States or, for that matter, many nations across the hemisphere, as wave after wave of migrant workers have been blamed (most often by those who immediately preceded them) for the assorted "social evils" experienced at any number of key historical moments (Suarez-Navaz 2004).

Latin American Migration in the Last Half Century: A Review of the Literature

The literature on Latin American migration to the United States in the last half century can be marked by distinct structural features and themes. In this section we divide the last half century into four periods corresponding to different social, economic, and political forces that shaped the movement of Latin American peoples to the United States. These eras do not represent tightly marked historical moments. Rather, they signify general trends and patterns in the relatively nascent field of migration studies highlighting distinct characteristics of the new (read post-1965) international migration from Latin America. We organize the literature to account for the various ways in which these populations have been managed, controlled, incorporated, and represented. Drawing on a selection of leading texts in the study of Latin American immigration, we offer a portrait of a peoples and their encounters as they enter the United States into the early part of the twenty-first century.

THE POST-BRACERO ERA (1964–1994)

We refer to the first period of contemporary Latin American immigration as the post-Bracero era, beginning with termination of the Bracero Program in 1964 and extending until the enactment of the North American Free Trade Agreement (NAFTA) in 1994. Some of the pioneering works on Latin American migration in this period position immigration within a context of a world system in which the movement of capital from the financial global centers of New York City, Houston, Miami, and Los Angeles shaped the directionality of labor flows. In her epic work *The Mobility of Labor and Capital,* Saskia Sassen (1988) makes the compelling argument that immigration to the United States has not happened randomly or been preconditioned by poverty alone but instead has been shaped by the investment of financial capital in particular sites in Latin America, including Mexico, Colombia, Puerto Rico, and the Dominican Republic. These incursions of capital in turn triggered labor migrations to urban financial metropolises. These movements also correspond to U.S. foreign-policy interests and military activities in the region; the liberalization of U.S. immigration policy, such as the Immigration and Nationality Act of 1965; and the internationalization of production. The framing of immigration as a structural feature of globalization characterized by expanding capitalist encroachment into less developed regions set the stage for subsequent work on labor mobility and migratory patterns.

Most emblematic of this era are the works advanced by Alejandro Portes, Manuel Castells, Wayne Cornelius, Patricia Fernández-Kelly, and others who drew attention to the changing ethnic composition of immigration to the United States from a once predominantly European migration to one replaced with immigrants from Latin America and Asia. Subsequent settlement patterns of these migrants led to increased scholarship in host urban centers of the traditional growth states: New York, New Jersey, California, Illinois, Florida, and Texas. With the exception of studies in farmworker and agricultural relations, much of the literature was shaped within a context of urbanization and urban poverty. Also informed by the growing fields of ethnic studies, particularly black, Chicano, and Puerto Rican studies, new insight into the complexity of race and class was presented centering the analysis on underrepresented communities, referred to as the underclass of the inner city. The emerging literature in the nascent field of Latino studies reflected interdisciplinary perspectives tackling theories of incorporation and identity for distinct national origin groups.

With the beginning of the deindustrialization of metropolitan areas in the 1980s, the literature grew to encompass postindustrial studies as the economy in the traditional growth states shifted to service-sector work and expanding activity in the informal economy. The outsourcing of production, the expansion of free-trade zones, the elimination of collective-bargaining rights, the growth of subcontracting industries, and the deregulation of particular industries, especially construction, apparel, electronics, hotel and hospitality, and other industry further shaped patterns of international migration. Furthermore, the outsourcing of manufacturing jobs to newly created free-trade or export-processing zones drew attention to emerging gendered work practices as new ethnic, racial, and gendered divisions of labor changed spatial patterns of work and residence. Women and families entered the migration pool joining predominantly male migration circuits.

THE ERA OF NAFTA (1994–2005)

The nascent and soon to be vast literature on migration patterns in the NAFTA era focused less on global cities and moved the center of analysis to the U.S.-Mexico border. The focus has been on the burgeoning manufacturing and later postindustrial service economy of the encroaching neoliberal model shaping the borderlands region. Through the study of regional free-trade agreements, particularly NAFTA and the Dominican Republic–Central America Free Trade Agreement (CAFTA-DR), research advanced the study of mobility processes and new geographies of settlement both intraregionally and internationally. The 1990s opened the gates of neoliberalism. With it came brands, products, and policies of deregulation to facilitate the thrust of privatization. As corporations dictated the terms of free trade by establishing the precedent of capital border crossing, labor followed suit.

An accompanying process has been the expansive and highly fortified law enforcement strategies along the U.S.-Mexico border to contain transborder migrant flows. Research here produced a wealth of information on U.S.-Mexico border studies, including the framing of a new language for conceptualizing a distinct borderlands region. Significant in this research is the way the fortified entry points on the U.S. southern border diverted historic border crossings through new migratory corridors extending beyond historic gateways to new entry points east of the California state line into dangerous and deadly areas in the Sonoran/Arizona desert. The expansion of the predominantly Mexican undocumented population in the United States resulted in part from changes in U.S. immigration and border policy that greatly reduced legal avenues of entry, thwarting circular and seasonal migration patterns that had characterized migration practices in the region.

Growing visibility of Latin Americans along the North Atlantic seaboard and in the U.S. South and Midwest led to research dedicated to exploring various "new destinations" of Latin American migrants. With this emerging trend, studies illuminated socioeconomic developments outside the traditional growth states. Particular attention has been paid to the relationship of Latin American migrant labor to the expanding agricultural industry and its corollaries, given the very internal restructuring of U.S. agriculture. With ethnographic work on the division of labor in meat-processing industries, for example, a numbers of scholars spoke to the way corporate strategies dictate the terms, wages, recruitment, and nature of that work. Not surprising, the benefits to the firm far outweigh those of the workers, who are often subject to poor pay, worker injury, discrimination, and health risks. With this literature, there has been a renewed interest in the study of rural destinations and agricultural-related work.

THE STRATEGY OF INTERNAL POLICING AND ERA OF ENFORCEMENT (2005–2008)

Building on this, we mark a third period beginning with developments following 2005, the year the U.S. House of Representatives passed HR 4437, the Border Protection, Anti-Terrorism, and Illegal Immigration Control Act (commonly known as the Sensenbrenner bill), to the Wall Street crash of 2008. What is distinct about this period is the expansion of interior law enforcement strategies aimed at curtailing undocumented migration through internal policing. Work-site raids, new Immigration and Customs Enforcement (ICE) operatives, 287(g) Memorandums of Agreement (MOA) deputizing local police on immigration matters, new eligibility requirements for accessing social services and health care, and other local and state laws targeting migrant communities heightened everyday "deportability." By drawing in new sites for monitoring legal status, including schools, local police stations, clinics, and apartment complexes, the range of immigration control was deeply broadened.

Resulting from the absence of federal immigration reform, a patchwork of internal border-control strategies emboldened the rhetorical claims about the immigrant "threat." Expanded powers granted to state and local governments to manage what essentially is a federal issue created incongruous laws with selective enforcement procedures and an unfortunate era in immigration history. While employer sanctions, work-site raids, and deportation strategies have long been carried out, the new involvement by state and local officials in the policing strategies of immigrants marked a distinct moment in immigration history. The detention sites now moved beyond the border to highways, parks, roadsides, and parking lots where apprehensions for traffic violations became routine. Working within their state jurisdictions and often testing what they can and can't do within their constitutionally bound place under federalism, states and local governments have introduced a number of new, often confusing laws regarding immigration. For example, Iowa (2002) and Kansas (2007) passed legislation to make English the official language of their states. Others imposed new requirements for undocumented students to obtain financial aid. Many states passed driver's license restrictions requiring new residency identification for driving. Since 2005, sixty-two local and county-level police and sheriff departments have active 287(g) agreements with ICE to control immigration. Other ordinances relating to housing and health care access have also come under the purview of immigration control. The post-2005 era represents a distinct moment in the history of Latin American migration as it is characterized by the failure of national immigration-reform legislation and a corresponding attempt by local and state governments to manage it.

The era also engendered a heavy legal discourse in which a language of criminality appeared to naturalize the condition of being "illegal." The presentation of transborder crossings in alarmist terms, including the referencing to the movement of peoples as swarms, floods, waves, and spreading cancers, further justified the need for drastic solutions, including expanding detention and deportation approaches for expunging this "unworthy" population. Presenting the issue in alarmist terms has negated the possibility of proposals that seek to manage the transborder movement of peoples in a more orderly and humane way.

THE POSTGLOBAL FINANCIAL CRISIS ERA (2008–PRESENT)

Once the federal government shelved the discussion over paths to legalization for 12 million undocumented immigrants, the fever pitch about "illegals" reached center stage as the media flocked to cover stories about Minutemen, Maricopa County and its zero-tolerance sheriff, and anti-immigration laws in Oklahoma; Arizona; Alabama; Hazelton, Pennsylvania; Cobb County, Georgia; and Farmers Branch, Texas. With the election of the first African American president and his inherited financial crisis, public attention shifted away from immigration toward health care reform, the emerging Tea Party movement, and the bipartisan divide. Caught up in legal challenges, immigration supporters and opponents waited out the decision by the high courts on the legalities of state and local jurisdictions to control immigration. For the nearly 12 million migrants residing in the United States without documentation, there is presently no coherent policy reform being considered in Washington. While the Obama administration passed an executive order known as Deferred Action for Childhood Arrivals (DACA) in summer 2012, the application process is cumbersome and limited in that it addresses only a small component of the undocumented population residing in the United States. In a climate of hyperpartisanship in Congress, there is little political will for taking on immigration reform despite, as Linda Bosniak and others have noted, that our national failing to secure basic civil and social rights to undocumented individuals (effectively stigmatizing them as second class "pariahs") "harms everyone [while also] violat[ing] our deepest principles" as a democracy (Bosniak 2009).

Redrawing Boundaries?

What should be done about undocumented migration? Some, like Joseph H. Carens, have argued for legalization of undocumented migrants who have settled in the United States. According to Carens, "time erodes the state's right to deport," and over time, most migrants have achieved a sufficient degree of "social membership" in local communities. Following a residency of, say, five years, during which migrants establish themselves and contribute to society in various ways, Carens (2009) argues that they ostensibly come to recognize their new country as "home." Failure on the part of the state to acknowledge this connection and all that it entails, Carens argues, "is cruel and unjust."

In the same 2009 *Boston Review* forum, Douglas S. Massey notes that in 1965 when the U.S. Congress ended the temporary guest-worker arrangement with Mexico and added new limits on immigration levels within the Western Hemisphere, the stage was set for the current crisis. Whereas the previous number of visas allotted to Mexicans for permanent residence in the United States was unlimited and the number for guest workers totaled approximately 450,000 each year, Massey observes, after 1965 these figures were significantly reduced to a slim 20,000 visas for permanent residence and no visas for temporary workers. The 1986 Immigration Reform and Control Act (IRCA) attempted to address the severe lack of official avenues available for Mexican migrants to enter the United States by declaring an amnesty for those then residing in the United States. At the same time, however, federal agents were increasingly militarizing the border in an attempt to further limit transnational flow northward, while politicians and anti-immigrant groups heightened their call for criminalization of undocumented workers. Ensuing free-trade legislation has only exacerbated this fundamental situation in recent decades as U.S. policy makers have provided no practical, legal avenue for people to legitimately cross the border. "Mexico is our second largest trading partner," Massey rightfully points out, "yet in terms of immigration policy we . . . allocate . . . the same number of visas as to Botswana or Nepal." Given this massive contradiction in immigration policy, is it any wonder there are many undocumented in the United States?

The literature on transnational citizenship is gaining more theoretical attention and legitimacy as the empirical reality of new transnational lifeways is becoming more commonplace in the Americas. In the same way that the notion of nationalism was an ideal of centuries in the making, is the notion of transnational citizenship what we should be thinking about as we enter the twenty-first century?

We endorse new constructs that consider various ways to guarantee transnational workers basic civil rights. Surely government lawmakers who so carefully worked out the details of various free-trade deals in the past can creatively conceive of an inclusive, hemispheric notion of citizenship in the Americas. It is a matter of priorities and political motivation. If the United States is to achieve more than another temporary fix in terms of immigration, we need to move beyond simply settling for another temporary fix accompanied by an additional wasting of millions of taxpayer dollars spent further erecting a twenty-first-century Berlin Wall along the U.S.-Mexico border. Instead, we must provide for a legal, workable path for people to migrate and in such a way ensure that their civil and human rights are respected. It is the "American" thing to do. It is the right and humane thing to do, and it is high time that such kind of immigration reform be achieved.

We do not wish to advocate a purely libertarian, free-market approach, but rather question the logic of neoliberalism's agenda, whereas "capital leads and people follow." Economies, markets, and human ecologies are socially constructed, not the other way around. For decades it has been a scant minority of international corporate elites who have called the shots, and the results have been disastrous. We believe that local communities need to reclaim themselves in such a way so as to prioritize people and sustainability rather than what appears today as a ruthless, wasteful, and seemingly endless downward spiral in search of profit. Workers should be able to find employment in their own communities, and in the words of the resounding voices of migrant laborers from Buenos Aires to Oaxaca and beyond, *tenemos el derecho a No migra* (we have the right NOT to migrate) (Bacon 2008). Built, therefore, into the very heart of migration studies should be an analysis not only of how workers move and resettle but why they have to in the first (or second or third) place. How can local, regional, and national economies be better structured and invested in to avoid unnecessary and unwanted movement of people so as to truly improve the standard of living for the majority and not just a privileged few?

Outline of Volume

Our endeavor seeks to reveal the many ways in which identities, economies, and geographies are being reimagined in the Heartland as Latin Americans negotiate their new sense of work, home, and community. Part I of the volume begins with "Geographies in Historical Perspective." In the first chapter, "Mexicans in the United States: A Longer View," Andrew Grant Wood relays in broad terms the long history of European American settlement and subsequent Latin American migration—particularly undertaken by Mexicans—to the U.S. Heartland. Particular attention is paid to the capitalist-led development during the second half of the nineteenth century as the United States sought to build itself into not only a formidable industrial power but also a world power. In this, the chapter traces the vital role that immigrant workers—and specifically Mexican laborers—have paid in this process despite their often being treated as second-class citizens. According to the author, an appreciation of this history provides one with a clear sense of the neocolonial aspirations of U.S. enterprise—both governmental and commercial—as well as the many contradictory and timeworn Anglo rationalizations that exploit Mexican workers in the United States today.

The second chapter is entitled "*Betabeleros* and the Western Nebraska Sugar Industry: An Early Twentieth-Century History." Here, Tisa M. Anders discusses the newly founded and (soon to be) prosperous city of Scottsbluff in Western Nebraska as the chosen site for the first sugar factory in that region in 1910. Within a decade of its opening, Mexican and Mexican American migrant workers were the main group recruited for the fields. Finding that migrants successfully negotiated a variety of social, cultural, and economic challenges, this chapter considers how migrant workers and their families became part of the growing Scottsbluff community as the sugar industry developed. In addition to a variety of primary source materials, their labor and community-building efforts are brought to life through a series of oral-history interviews.

The third chapter in this section is titled "Latinos and the Churches in Idaho, 1950–2000." Errol D. Jones's essay examines the relationship between people of Mexican/Latin American descent and Idaho's established churches from the 1950s. A politically conservative state with an economy dominated by agriculture, mining, and forestry into the 1980s, Idaho attracted large numbers of Latino migrants who worked mainly in agriculture. Beginning in the 1950s, a progressive movement developed within the mainstream Protestant churches and the Catholic Diocese of Boise to reach out to migrants in an effort to mitigate their harsh conditions and welcome them into their churches. Supported by the National Council of Churches and the American Conference of Catholic Bishops, Idaho's religious leaders became catalysts of reform in the agricultural industry in the state and become brokers for the needs of migrants and those who sought to abandon migrant life and settle permanently in Idaho. With the growth of the mostly Catholic Latino population, the Boise diocese, despite some resistance, was compelled to change to accommodate their culture and to champion the need for social and economic reform.

In Part II, "Contesting Policy and Legal Boundaries," Sandy Smith-Nonini looks at farm labor in North Carolina. Her chapter 4 is called "Seeing No

Evil: The H2A Guest-Worker Program and State-Mediated Labor Exploitation in Rural North Carolina." Here she writes how the public discourse on the Mexican border focuses on immigrants transgressing legal boundaries of U.S. territory and on challenges to imaginary citizenship. Less attention is paid to the state's role enabling the flow of immigrants that aids private profit. Neoliberal privatization weakened state regulations and led to reorientation of government programs in ways that aid the elite. North Carolina's large H2A "guest-worker" program claimed to be an example of state intervention to mitigate farm labor abuses, but the program devolved into "government by proxy" during the 1990s, as the state delegated control of workers and oversight directly to a private broker representing growers, creating invisibilities and legitimizing abusive practices, not unlike the discredited Bracero Program. The 2004 Farm Labor Organizing Committee (FLOC) union contract with this H2A broker has contested these relations and introduced new immigrant agency. FLOC transgressed borders in the reverse direction, angering Mexican authorities (who sought to deport organizers) and H2A recruiters, charged by the union with extorting high fees from workers. Corrupt recruiters are suspected in the 2007 murder of a FLOC organizer. Current work to seek justice in this case brings international human rights, another transnational discourse, into the debate. This chapter discusses implications of "transnational" organizing and transborder solidarities as a counterpolitics to neoliberal exclusion.

Chapter 5 by Linda Allegro is entitled "On Removing Migrant Labor in a Right-to-Work State: The Failure of Employer Sanctions in Oklahoma." Her chapter explores the anti-immigrant bill known as HB 1804 in Oklahoma, which sought to criminalize undocumented labor after a decade-long corporate recruitment strategy that solicited migrant labor under the premise of right-to-work. Of particular interest is the emphasis on the weak policy controls the legislation placed on employers while disproportionately penalizing migrants and their families. In this way it disentangles the inconsistent position of the "anti-illegals" narrative that espouses draconian measures penalizing undocumented migrants but has an unenforceable strategy for controlling the workplace, arguably the greatest draw of migrant labor. Such selective application of the rule of law demonstrates the veiled racism of the anti-illegals narrative and the dishonest nature of the professed goal of holding all parties responsible for the increase in undocumented immigration. Resulting from these paradoxes has been an increase in local law enforcement disciplining migrant bodies and lives in public spaces.

Part III is entitled "Transnational Identities and New Landscapes of Home." In chapter 6, "Rooted/Uprooted: Place, Policy, and Salvadoran Transnational Identities in Rural Arkansas," Miranda Cady Hallett asks what happens when transnational migrant families own homes, plant trees, and establish businesses in small-town America but still lack a viable path to legal residency? In this chapter, based on extensive fieldwork in small, rural Arkansas communities with Salvadoran transnational migrants, the author explores the contradictory dynamics between a growing identification with local geographies and continuing legal exclusion. Most Salvadoran migrants are caught "betwixt and between" categories of national belonging; classified as either "illegal" or "temporary," they lack rights to political participation either in the United States or in El Salvador. These legal exclusions create a mobile space of exception around the body of the migrant, analogous to free-trade zones and corporate enclaves, which facilitate the exploitation of migrants' labor. Legal exclusion also contributes to social exclusion through the contradictory production of both invisibility (according to the census, most of the migrants are not there) and hypervisibility (racialized images of "illegal threat" contribute to scapegoating and police harassment). In spite of this, transnational migrants continue to put down roots in their new places of settlement, purchasing homes, holding down jobs, building churches, yard-saling, transforming the facade of Main Street, birthing children, dying, and being buried. Migrants' lives and subjectivities are infused with the contradictions between lived experience and legal status.

Chapter 7 is called "Contesting Diversity and Community within Postville, Iowa: 'Hometown to the World.'" Here Jennifer F. Reynolds and Caitlin Didier argue that beginning in 2000 different popular media accounts, from Stephen Bloom's book *Postville: A Clash of Cultures in Heartland America* to Nikki Tundel's documentary film *Postville: When Cultures Collide,* have raised and examined the following question: how do small-town middle Americans adapt to rapid cultural change that is more typical of big-city life? Postville, Iowa, was singled out for attention over all the other rural midwestern or southern towns that also house corporate beef, pork, or chicken food-processing plants. It had all the trappings of an "exotic" case study; the new owners of the meat-processing plant were city people, from Brooklyn, and they observed an orthodox form of Judaism, Hasidism. And despite the fact that the kosher meat-processing plant, Agriprocessors, was family owned and operated, it has been managed much like other notorious corporate firms that have relocated to rural places to cut costs related to unionized labor and the transportation of livestock. Management, moreover, recruited immigrant labor from the ex-Soviet republics, Asia, Israel, and Latin America. When ICE officials raided Agriprocessors on May, 12, 2008, it was further revealed to the nation that the majority of the workers were undocumented. Early popular accounts made much of the religious, ethnic, regional, and racial differences that divided the original residents from all the "newcomers," often at the expense of observing the political, economic, and legal dimensions that have played off of these differences. This chapter is based on ethnographic research, conducted at different points of time in the town's recent history. It draws upon a tradition of critical ethnographic inquiry into transnational circuits of migration and meat-processing communities to examine the particulars of how this place is a contested social field wherein different players struggle over macrosociological meanings of citizenship and belonging in locally specific ways.

Part IV is called "Media and Reimagined Sites of Accommodation and Contestation." In chapter 8, entitled "Humanizing Latino Newcomers in the 'No Coast' Region," Edmund T. Hamann and Jenelle Reeves reveal that in December 2006 and again in May 2008, the Midwest was the setting for large-scale ICE raids in rural meatpacking towns that drew national attention. In the first raids, concurrent sweeps in six different communities that hosted Swift plants, children and schools emerged as important and sympathy-generating themes as children were separated from detained parents and schools were left struggling to figure out what to do with those children. Both of these issues distracted from the intended law enforcement thrust of the raids, reducing their popularity and making them more controversial. In contrast, the May 2008 raid at a kosher meat-processing facility in Postville, Iowa, had the ICE enforcement agents querying their detainees about whether they had children and placing those who answered yes under house arrest. Although this, too, destroyed the former workers' chance at earning a livelihood (and thus materially punished families), it did not separate mothers from children, nor did it require schools to become emergency sanctuaries for frightened and marooned children. Thus two key sympathy-generating factors that could make the larger public dubious of ICE enforcement were bypassed. Invoking trope theory, this chapter looks at local and regional mainstream print media coverage of both raids to see how the imagining of children, school, transnationality, and workers in and by Middle America was changed between the two raid cycles, in turn changing the semiotics of how these raids were to be responded to.

Chapter 9 is "Immigrant Integration and the Changing Public Discourse: The Case of Emporia, Kansas" by László J. Kulcsár and Albert Iaroi. This study discusses the public discourse around the integration process of immigrant Latino workers in Emporia. It employs aggregate statistical analysis, media-content analysis, and key-informant interviews to examine how the public discourse has changed over time. Particular attention is given to the arrival of the Somali refugee workers that subsequently altered the discourse on immigrant-worker integration. Findings show that the community perception of Latin Americans shifted significantly once a culturally and ethnically less similar group arrived in town. Discussion includes the role of local actors in immigrant integration with an emphasis on their main employer, Tyson Foods. Contrary to the general challenges of immigrant integration, revolving largely around unauthorized migrants, in this case the difficulty had to do with integrating legal immigrants who had racial and religious differences from not only the mainstream community but from the dominant minority as well.

Part V looks at "Religion and Migrant Communities." In chapter 10, called "'They Cling to Guns or Religion': Pennsylvania Towns Put Faith in Anti-immigrant Ordinances," Jane Juffer writes that migration has become a central issue for the U.S. religious Right, which has joined forces with city councils, paramilitary border vigilante groups, and conservative politicians to proclaim that Latino migrants represent a threat to family values, the "law," and the so-called Anglo-Saxon, Protestant roots of the nation. This coalition has been particularly influential in areas of the country where there have previously been few Latino residents, such as small-town Pennsylvania. In addition to Altoona and Hazleton in this state, more than a hundred cities across the country have passed laws that make it illegal for employers to hire and landlords to rent to undocumented peoples. Though purportedly local in their ambitions, the ordinances are underwritten by national organizations with connections to the Christian Right and white supremacist groups; together, they have rallied people around an antiglobalization populism that claims the federal government is not doing its job policing the borders and maintaining national economic sovereignty. Conservative Christians in the United States seek recourse in nostalgic notions of family and community; by contrast, progressive religious groups have encouraged local churches to embrace undocumented migrants and reject the rule of law, appealing to the belief in a higher mandate that includes "welcoming the stranger among us." While Christian fundamentalist ideologies facilitate the mainstreaming of white supremacist practices, an ecumenical religious left challenges xenophobia and redraws the boundaries of community.

Part VI looks at "Demographics." In "Latin American Migrations to the U.S. Heartland: Demographic and Economic Activity in Six Heartland States, 2000–2007," Scott Carter offers a descriptive analysis of the demographic presence and economic activity of the Hispanic population in six core Heartland states (the "Heartland 6" or HL6). It is intended to give an overall view of the underlying trends in Hispanic demography, productivity, employment, and other relevant socioeconomic variables for the years 2000–2007. The results show that the HL6 experienced increased rates of growth in its Hispanic population, a trend consistent with evidence reported in the recent "new destinations" literature (Bump, Lowell, and Pettersen 2005; Zúñiga and Hernandez-León 2005). At the same time, traditional growth states vis-à-vis Hispanic presence report decreasing trends in their growth rate. This represents a diffusion, or convergence, of Latin American migrations throughout the United States. Economic performance, income distribution, employment, and the age-gender profile are also descriptively presented. Traditional data sources reported by the U.S. government are used, specifically the American Community Survey of the U.S. Census Bureau, the Bureau of Economic Analysis of the U.S. Department of Commerce, and the Bureau of Labor Statistics, as well as a few relevant state agencies.

In sum, we hope *Latin American Migrations to the U.S. Heartland* will contribute to a new generation of scholarship that combines economic, social, and cultural approaches to achieve a fuller understanding of our changing North American landscape.

References

Bacon, David. 2008. "The Right to Stay Home—Derecho de no migrar." New Report, *New American Media,* July 9.

Bosniak, Linda. 2009. "The Basic Rights of Short Term Immigrants Also Need Protection." *Boston Review,* May/June.

Bump, Micah N., B. Lindsay Lowell, and Silje Pettersen. 2005. "The Growth and Population Characteristics of Immigrants and Minorities in America's New Settlement States." In *Beyond the Gateway: Immigrants in a Changing America,* ed. Elizbieta M. Gozdziak and Susan F. Martin. Boulder, Colo.: Lexington Books.

Carens, Joseph. 2009. "The Case for Amnesty." *Boston Review,* May/June.

Carens, Joseph H. 2010. *Immigrants and the Right to Stay.* Cambridge, Mass.: MIT Press.

Chavez, Leo. 2008. *The Latino Threat: Constructing Immigrants, Citizens and the Nation.* Stanford, Calif.: Stanford University Press.

Cornelius, Wayne, et al., eds. 2004. *Controlling Immigration: A Global Perspective,* 2nd ed. Stanford, Calif.: Stanford University Press.

Davidson, Osha Gray. 1996. *Broken Heartland: The Rise of America's Rural Ghetto.* Iowa City: University of Iowa Press.

De Genova, Nicolas. 2002. "Migrant 'Illegality' and Deportability in Everyday Life." *Annual Review of Anthropology* 31: 419–47.

DeParle, Jason. 2011. "The Anti-Immigration Crusader." *New York Times,* April 17.

Dunbar-Ortiz, Roxanne. 2008. "Go Home, Red State Rebels!" In *Red State Rebels: Tales of Grassroots Resistance in the Heartland,* ed. Jeffrey St. Clair and Joshua Frank. Oakland, Calif.: AK Press.

Fernandez-Kelly, M. Patricia. 1983. *For We Are Sold, I and My People: Women and Industry in Mexico's Frontier.* Albany: State University of New York Press.

Frank, Joshua, and Jeffrey St. Clair, eds. 2008. *Red State Rebels: Tales of Grassroots Resistance in the Heartland.* Oakland, Calif.: AK Press.

Harvey, David. 1989. *The Condition of Postmodernity: An Enquiry into the Origins of Cultural Change.* Cambridge, Mass.: Basil Blackwell.

Harvey, David. 2000. *Spaces of Hope.* Los Angeles and Berkeley: University of California Press.

Khimm, Suzy. 2010. "The Man Behind Arizona's Immigration Law." *Mother Jones,* May 7.

Massey, Douglas. 2009. "Only by Addressing the Realities of North American Economic Integration Can We Solve the Problem." *Boston Review,* May/June.

Portes, Alejandro, Manuel Castells, and Lauren Benton, eds. 1989. *The Informal Economy: Studies in Advanced and Less Developed Countries.* Baltimore: Johns Hopkins University Press.

Riley, Jason L. 2008. *Let Them In: The Case of Open Borders.* London: Gotham Books.

Sassen, Saskia. 1988. *The Mobility of Labor and Capital: A Study in International Investment and Labor Flow.* New York: Cambridge University Press.

Stein, Judith. 2010. *Pivotal Decade: How the United States Traded Factories for Finance in the Seventies.* New Haven, Conn.: Yale University Press.

Suarez-Navaz, Liliana. 2004. *Rebordering the Mediterranean: Boundaries and Citizenship in Southern Europe.* New York: Berghahn Books.

Zúñiga, Victor, and Rubén Hernandez-León. 2005. *New Destinations: Mexican Immigration to the U.S.* New York: Russell Sage.

PART I

Geographies in Historical Perspective

CHAPTER I

Mexicans in the United States

A Longer View

ANDREW GRANT WOOD

> Here is not merely a nation but
> a teeming nation of nations.
> —Walt Whitman, *Leaves of Grass*

> Like the Indians,
> the Mexicans "were here first."
> —Carey McWilliams,
> *North from Mexico*

The making of the United States as a modern nation was realized through a creative combination of violence, primitive accumulation, diplomacy, and engineering undertaken by powerful elites headquartered in eastern cities. During the first half of the nineteenth century, those directing the fate of the United States set out to incorporate vast tracts of middle and western North America into its national territory. In this process, areas formerly claimed by French, British, Russian, and Spanish (and then Mexican) authorities gradually gave over to Anglo-American conquest. The year 1845, for example, saw the young nation add the breakaway Republic of Texas as a state. A year later, the United States and Mexico went to war. The resulting Treaty of Guadalupe Hidalgo caused Mexico to cede approximately half its national possession to the American juggernaut.

War between Europeans and Native American groups over the next three decades brought to a conclusion a long process that cost aboriginal peoples much of their land and way of life. "The Indians were victims not only of American avarice," wrote historian Ray Allen Billington years ago, "but of the age in which they lived [for] with the momentum of expansion well established and, with the nation's 'Manifest Destiny' to control the continent clear, all who stood in the way of white conquest were doomed" (Billington 1974: 578).

Yet this making of "America"—decimation of native peoples notwithstanding—proved perhaps not as dire as Billington suggests. Nevertheless, it was a process realized largely under the aegis of Anglo conquest and neocolonialism such that those "who stood in the way of white[s]" were indeed forced to come to terms with Anglo power and privilege (namely, accept second-class, marginal classification) or face extinction. Then, as today, people of color—including those of Mexican descent—suffered a similar fate at the hands of unsympathetic law enforcement, immigration officials, individuals, and groups ignorant of our highly contested continental history.

Colonial Conquests

In light of our Anglo-dominated media and political power structure, it is an ironic fact that it was the Spanish who proved the first European colonizers who asserted claims (however tenuous) over much of North America during the sixteenth and seventeenth centuries. As is well known, their colonizing efforts reached to the southernmost tip of South America and north above the Sonoran Desert and well beyond. For more than one hundred years before any rival European power mounted colonial challenge, the Spanish had staked out their territorial ambitions by establishing presidios (military outposts), towns, ranches, and missions.

Life was rustic at best on the frontier as northernmost New Spain was populated by only a modest number of settlers. In the seventeenth century, the most important settlement was the New Mexican town of Santa Fe, which had been founded in 1610. Then, after much delay, the eighteenth century saw the rise of several new centers, including Albuquerque (1706), Nacogdoches (1716), San Antonio (1718), San Diego (1769), Tucson (1776), San José (1777), and Los Angeles (1781). Still, New Spain's periphery remained underdeveloped for most of the colonial period, and it was not until the late 1770s when the Bourbon Reforms served to intensify commercial relations in the north. Increasingly, those living in the frontier area gained access to foreign trade from the growing French Louisiana territory and points east where Spain's rivals the English had insinuated themselves along the eastern littoral, taken part in a revolutionary war, and gave birth to a new, independent republic. Before long, open contest for control of North America would play out between these three European powers and their social and cultural inheritors.

For their part, Anglo-American expansionism into middle and western North America accelerated significantly with the 1803 Louisiana Purchase.

Ensuing treaties such as the U.S.-Spanish Adams-Otís accord of 1819 ceded Florida to the Americans while at the same time designated a boundary between (rapidly weakening) Spanish and U.S. claims after several years of heated dispute. Two years later, Mexico—after nearly a decade of struggle—finally gained independence from Spain in 1821. Shortly thereafter, U.S. President James Monroe's foreign policy deliberations crystallized into what would eventually become known as the Monroe Doctrine. Monroe's statement made in December 1823 laid out U.S. neocolonial designs in the hemisphere by stating "that the American Continents, by the free and independent position which they have assumed and maintain, are henceforth not to be considered as subjects for future colonization by any European power" (quoted in Sellers 1994: 184). In other words, further European incursion into North America—whether by the British, French, Russians, or Spanish—would not be tolerated.

Political ambition went hand in hand with dynamic economic growth. As historian Charles Sellers writes in characterizing the rapid expansion of capitalist economic relations, "by 1815, market revolution was . . . dissolving deeply rooted patterns of behavior and belief for competitive effort, it mobilized collective resources through government to fuel growth in countless ways . . . [e]stablishing capitalist hegemony over economy, politics, and culture, the market revolution created ourselves and most of the world we know" (Sellers 1994: 5). Fundamental in its force and critical to the success of the young republic, economic liberalism ran concomitant with Anglo notions of "racial" superiority and the young American republic extended westward.

Expanding communication and transportation infrastructure soon cut across the continent. Headquartered in New York, Boston, Philadelphia, and other urban centers, the network facilitated capitalist enterprise as it consumed distance and shortened time. Satellite cities such as Albany, Buffalo, Pittsburgh, Cleveland, Detroit, Chicago, Nashville, Louisville, Cincinnati, St. Louis, and New Orleans articulated rapid growth (Pred 1966). Ensuing U.S. consolidation over the next century would give rise to one of the most dynamic periods of capitalist economic expansion in history. This political and economic transformation came at great cost, however. As long-standing ecological and social paradigms shifted, many found themselves tragically excluded from an often violent and unforgiving new economic order.

In fateful contrast, Mexican rule in North America meanwhile encouraged the establishment of new east-west land routes. What developed would soon add to earlier access points farther to the south (i.e., from the now U.S.-controlled port of New Orleans) as well as new pathways west farther to the north where—to varying degrees of success—U.S. government-sponsored adventurers such as Lewis and Clark, Zebulon Pike, and others had begun to chart portions of French-controlled Louisiana and Spanish, British, and

Russian territories west. Yet if by 1820 official Anglo mapmaking expeditions had left much to be desired, fur traders—especially along the northwest frontier—picked up the slack. By 1840, as one historian has noted, "adventurous frontiersmen [had] penetrated into every nook and corner of the Far West [and in so doing] spied out [its] secrets, plotted the course of its rivers, discovered the passes through its mountains, and prepared the way for settlers by breaking down Indian self-sufficiency" (Billington 1974: 379).

The opening of the Santa Fe Trail in 1820–1821 significantly facilitated Anglo-American westward expansion. Settlers of Spanish American heritage living in the far northern provinces of the soon to be Mexican nation had increasingly benefited from trade with Anglos based in the Mississippi Valley. Rather than risk the long and tortuous fifteen-hundred-mile journey to Mexico City, settlers figured they could exchange furs, precious metals, and other items in exchange for Anglo-manufactured goods. Spanish colonial authority, however, thought otherwise and sought to keep trade to a minimum.

With the dawning of the Mexican era, new laws regarding foreign activity allowed for a liberalization of commercial trade. Over the next two decades, annual treks amounting to approximately nine hundred miles each way every spring originated from Independence, Missouri, and made their way through Indian Territory into New Mexico. The resulting exchange proved prosperous for both *hispanos* and Anglos (Reséndez 2004: 93–123). Although the total volume of trade did not prove especially significant to the budding U.S. national economy, practical knowledge relative to the way in which Anglos could travel and survive passage into Mexican lands proved invaluable (Billington 1974: 388–91).

Settlement schemes offered by the Mexican government reversed previous Spanish mercantile policy and subsequently invited foreigners into the northern provinces of Texas, New Mexico, and California. As long as newcomers paid taxes to the government based in Mexico City, their presence and commercial activity were allowed. During this formative period, a number of Anglos went west. Traders captured mustangs in East Texas and the soon to be Oklahoma territory while also exchanging goods with indigenous peoples. Contraband trade in guns, ammunition, furs, horses, mules, cattle, and other stolen goods between native groups and Anglos, for example, slowly began to undermine Hispanic autonomy. Indian raids on *ranchos,* according to one observer, "cannot be understood as the idiosyncratic activities of 'hunters and gathers' [but] [r]ather . . . an important, and perhaps the major, covert instrument of American expansionist policy and an encroaching capitalist economy" (Vélez-Ibáñez 1997: 61).

In more firmly established Spanish American areas, some Anglos converted to Catholicism and married into existing Tejano and *nuevomexicano* families.

In so doing, they helped cement cross-cultural alliances that proved mutually favorable to nearly everyone involved. As historian Andrés Reséndez writes, "Anglo Americans could make the introductions and pave the way for their Hispanic counterparts with suppliers in Missouri and Louisiana [while] Hispanic [sic] traders could reciprocate [by] helping out their Anglo American colleagues with Mexican customs officers and other authorities" (Reséndez 2004: 104).

Yet despite a relatively small handful of sympathetic forebearers, Anglo-American movement into Mexican territory increasingly tipped the balance of power. The market revolution brought a political-economic realignment tilted in favor of the rapidly growing U.S. economy. This, however, did not mean that Mexicans in the far northern provinces turned against Anglo entrepreneurs. The reality proved to be quite to the contrary. Instead, it was federal officials in Mexico City who most zealously sought to guard the border. Articulating concern about the growing tide of Anglo migration into their territory, Mexican representative to Washington Manuel Zozoya had worried in late 1822 that "the haughtiness of these Republicans, does not permit them to look upon us as equals . . . their conceit extends itself in my opinion to believe that their capital will be that of all the Americas" (quoted in Weber 1994: 301).

Soon concerning themselves with "the Texas question," a Mexican law forbidding further Anglo-American immigration into that province took effect on April 6, 1830. Anglo settlers continued to come anyway, figuring they could avoid confrontation with Mexican authorities. Ensuing conflict over control of the frontier eventually proved that the Mexican government could not turn back the tide of northern regional development, which had, by and large, created new economic opportunities for Indians, Hispanics, and Anglos. Anglo incursions into Texas so discouraged some, including longtime loyal Mexican observer and important advisor to the central government on Texas affairs, General Manuel de Mier y Terán, that he decided to commit suicide. On July 3, 1832, he dramatically took his life by falling on his sword on the grounds of San Antonio Church in Padilla, Tamaulipas.

The emerging situation in Texas and elsewhere in the trans-Mississippi west largely favored U.S. interests. Northern Mexican provincials found themselves torn between the lure of advancing commercial forces from the east and Mexican government admonitions coming from Mexico City. For their part, those in the Mexican capital had come to view their northern cousins who associated with the gringo economy as not merely lacking in patriotic allegiance but even potentially "secessionist" (Reséndez 2004: 123).

Pursuant to these concerns, in 1835 the Mexican government significantly limited states' rights and centralized power in Mexico City. A number of regional revolts soon erupted in response in Yucatán, Zacatecas, California, and, perhaps most notably, Texas, where on December 12, 1835, Sam Houston declared a rebellion against Mexico. Mexican President Antonio López de Santa Anna responded quickly and led troops to confront the rebel Texans. War ensued, and the Mexicans were defeated. The breakaway Republic of Texas was subsequently established.

In the wake of the Texas rebellion, elaborate rationalizations of Anglo "racial" superiority—many of them still employed today—were increasingly employed to justify the young nation's expansionism and ensuing wars of conquest. In the early 1840s, U.S. expansionism continued apace, and soon conflict with Mexico was considered inevitable despite the fact that the fate of North America still clearly lay in the balance.

President James K. Polk's four years in office would see the United States grow by an amazing two-thirds. Elected in 1844, his relations with the Mexican government turned cold when they refused to sell California and New Mexico.[1] Upon taking office, Polk put U.S. Navy personnel stationed in the Pacific on alert if war broke out between the two republics. Through the U.S. consul in Monterey, California, Polk encouraged anti-Mexican sentiment among Anglo settlers in fall 1845. Taking the message to heart, U.S. Army Capt. John C. Frémont soon organized an uprising in the Sacramento area and subsequently proclaimed an independent ("bear flag") republic in mid-1846.

To provoke outright conflict to the south, Polk had meantime sent U.S. troops headed by Gen. Zachary Taylor in September 1845 to occupy an area near Corpus Christi. The following January 1846, the army moved to an area along the Rio Grande just across from the thriving Mexican port of Matamoros. Conflict became immanent, and in early May 1846 the U.S. Congress declared war. Military victory followed military victory as U.S. forces took Santa Fe, New Mexico, in August 1846 and then quieted Mexican resistance in California by the end of January 1847. Over the next few months, U.S. troops coming from the north and east eventually converged on Mexico City and forced the Mexicans to surrender. Ensuing diplomatic and political negotiations produced the Treaty of Guadalupe Hidalgo, which was approved by the U.S. Senate in February 1848 and set the new international boundary at the Rio Grande and designated New Mexico and Upper California (present-day California, Nevada, Utah, much of New Mexico, Arizona, and one-third of Texas as well as parts of Oklahoma, Colorado, and Wyoming) as part of the United States. In return, Mexicans received payment of $15 million and the taking over of Mexican debts owed to U.S. citizens (McPherson 1988: 47–50).

For the approximately 80,000 Mexicans living in the uppermost reaches of northern Mexico, the aftermath of the war abruptly brought them under

U.S. control. Elaborate promises were made to those of Spanish/Mexican heritage in the ceded territories: namely that land claims and individual rights would be respected. This proved not to be the case, by and large, as Anglo merchants, lawyers, and settlers collaborated to gradually gain control of Hispanic claims (Limerick 1987: 235–43; Montejano 1987: 42–47, 50–53).

In Texas, "Mexicans . . . lost considerable land through outright confiscation and fraud [so that] by 1900 the Mexican upper class would become nonexistent except in a few border enclaves" (Montejano 1987: 50). Where extralegal measures did not come into play, sheer economic advantage generally favored Anglos through their better connections to external markets and access to credit. Some Mexicans took to the more aggressive economic approach favored by incoming U.S. business and government agents. Many did not, however, and were pushed aside by the economic revolution steadily moving across the continent.

Wanted: Wage Laborers

Industrial growth and territorial expansionism continued through the difficult American Civil War years as creative destruction wrought by armed conflict paved the way for new economic opportunities. As the second half of the nineteenth century unfolded, the market revolution continued to gain momentum as northern financial and industrial interests (generally associated with the Republican Party) increasingly directed the course of empire.

Perhaps most emblematic of this process at midcentury was massive railway expansion. In the 1850s, total track mileage went from 9,000 to 30,000. Some twenty-five years later, the growing time-space compression afforded by ever-expanding railroad networking had become so pervasive that the transport companies invented standard time and designated four time zones stretching across the continent (Cronin 1992: 69, 79). "Space," as one preeminent nineteenth-century German economic theorist and historian once put it, was seemingly being "annihilated by time."

Inland areas still yet officially unaffiliated soon joined the United States in relatively rapid succession: Minnesota, 1858; Oregon, 1859; Kansas, 1861; Nevada, 1864; Nebraska, 1867; Colorado, 1876; North Dakota, 1889; South Dakota, 1889; Washington, 1889; Montana, 1889; Idaho, 1890; Wyoming, 1890; Utah, 1896; Oklahoma, 1907; Arizona, 1912; and New Mexico, 1912. By the onset of World War I, the nation truly extended from California to "the New York Island" and nearly all that lay in between.

Having captured vast tracts of North American geography and supposedly "closed the frontier," it was time for eager capitalists to harness newly incorporated social forces and natural resources. Following close on the heels of territorial conquest through violence, U.S.-based technological, organizational, and financial innovations would turn the United States into a rapidly growing urban and industrial power. Realization of such a feat, it should always be remembered, took shape thanks in large part to millions of anonymous workers across the recently consolidated national territory.[2]

Yet with slavery abolished by the mid-1860s and native peoples increasingly devastated by disease, conquest, and outright war, a significant need for available workers arose.[3] Illustrating the growing demand for industrial and related work in rapidly growing cities, nearly 9 million made their way from rural to urban areas during the late nineteenth century (García 2004: 4). Added to this demographic shift were thousands of immigrants from Europe, Asia, and the Americas who came to the United States in search of employment.

For the period between 1821 and 1932, a whopping 32,244,000 came to the United States. One of the heaviest immigration decades proved to be the 1880s, when the number of immigrants jumped from 2.8 million to 5.1 million. Subsequent highs came during the 1900s (8.8 million), the 1910s (5.7 million), and then the 1920s (4.1 million), until restrictions imposed during the early 1930s brought the number down to a half million during that later decade (Míguez 2003: xiii).[4]

During the late nineteenth century, immigrants—particularly Irish and Germans followed by others from eastern and southern Europe—played a significant part in developing urban manufacturing as well as filling the ranks of various services in a number of cities. In New York, Boston, Chicago, Detroit, Cleveland, and San Francisco, for example, the number of immigrants amounted to around 35 percent of the total population in 1900 (Pred 1966: 132–34).[5] European immigrants moved to other major areas such as St. Louis, Milwaukee, Minneapolis, and Kansas City to fill industry jobs.

In neighboring Mexico, a variety of influences conspired to push a growing number of Mexicans into the United States during the three-decade regime of President Porfirio Díaz. Economic restructuring generally enriched large landowners and foreign investors as agriculture became increasingly mechanized and commercially oriented. Cash crops (i.e., sugar, cotton, wheat) took priority, while production of basic foods (corn, beans) dwindled. In many cases, conditions became extreme as entire communities lost their land to powerful, privatizing interests. Economic growth occurred, however, without a corresponding social development. As a result, migration to cities in the United States ensued (Coatsworth 1981).

Many who came north found work in southwestern mining, agriculture, and construction. Their collective movement northward opened a new, transnational era. Aiding this process was the construction of railroads connecting

Table 1.1. Mexican immigration to the United States, 1900–1940

Years	Immigrants	Percentage of all immigration to U.S.
1901–1910	49,642	0.5%
1911–1920	219,002	3.8%
1921–1930	458,287	11.2%
1931–1940	22,319	3.9%

Sources: U.S. Department of Commerce, *Historical Statistics of the United States,* cited in Daniels, *Guarding the Golden Door,* 62; Massey, Durand, and Malone, *Beyond Smoke and Mirrors,* 31–33.

Mexico and the United States. As the migrant stream gathered momentum, a growing number of Mexicans journeyed to Los Angeles, San Francisco, Denver, Tucson, Phoenix, El Paso, San Antonio, Dallas, and Houston. Nearly all came to rely on previously established family and community contacts. Still others set out for lesser-traveled territories in the Pacific Northwest, Midwest, Southeast, Northeast, and Heartland states. In countless rural areas, towns, and smaller cities scattered across the United States, Mexicans developed new social networks and various cross-cultural relations.

The outbreak of the Mexican Revolution in 1910 further accelerated the flow of migrants both to urban areas as well as north into the United States. As anthropologist Manuel Gamio and economist Paul S. Taylor documented, people came not simply to escape the ravages of the Revolution but also to try their luck in a foreign land (Gamio 1931: 1–28; Taylor 1929–1933).[6] Their migration northward across the thousand-mile southern international border paralleled that of people coming to the United States from Europe and Asia.

Yet both before and immediately after World War I, U.S. officials sought to greatly reduce immigration flows from Asia and Europe (Daniels 2004: 46). Conversely, they sought to speed the process for those coming north from Mexico. The U.S. Congress waived literacy tests and head taxes for Mexicans. Further, border-town recruiters (dubbed *enganchistas* or literally "hookers") enhanced, often by dubious means, the migrant flow. Many of those who crossed did so at Ciudad Juárez/El Paso and signed work contracts as temporary laborers. Others came without papers, sometimes with the help of smugglers (*coyotes*).

During the early twentieth century, the greatest concentration of Mexicans residing in the United States lived in Texas, California, Arizona, Illinois, and Kansas, respectively. Significant numbers of Mexicans could increasingly be found residing in Indiana, Michigan, and Missouri. A preliminary bracero (field hand) program administered by the U.S. government between 1917 and 1921 brought temporary (on six-month contracts) workers to the fields. Although limited, this practice afforded officials a test run for what would later become a full-fledged government labor-recruitment scheme. For their part, Mexican participants gained firsthand information about conditions in the United States, which they shared with relatives, friends, and townsfolk back home. During these early years, many Mexicans labored part of the year for a recruiting company—such as a particular railroad line—and then transitioned to seasonal agricultural work (García 2004: 7–8).

The sugar beet industry drew the first significant Mexican migrants to the U.S. Midwest and Heartland states. Following the hiring of a small number of workers by the Sugar Beet Company in Garden City, Kansas, after the turn of the century, the industry soon grew to represent the largest employer of Mexican labor in the United States during and after World War I. Realizing that Mexican labor could be successfully recruited to the Midwest by paying workers a slightly better wage as well as their transportation costs, companies, in essence, provided for both the initial contracting and then, according to Paul S. Taylor, the "continued presence of *Mexicanos* in the Midwest" (quoted in García 2004: 10). Seeking to keep their growing agricultural labor force in the region year-round, sugar beet employers also began to encourage workingmen to bring their families. Still, one should not overestimate the hospitality afforded Mexicans by the beet companies and their recruiters stationed along the border or working illegally inside Mexico. Many laborers found that once they set to work in the fields, employers often went back on their promises (García 2004: 21–24).

As the general population figures reveal, Mexicans nevertheless continued to come north. Starting in the early years of the century and continuing until the onset of the Great Depression, trainloads of workers arrived every year. By 1927, approximately 20,000 Mexicans, for example, had taken work in Michigan, representing 75 percent of the total number of beet laborers in the state (García 2004: 14; Balderrama and Rodríguez 1995: 21–25). Others obtained employment in Minnesota, Ohio, and Missouri as well. Significant beet operations also took shape in the Heartland and Great Plains regions as Mexicans came to Iowa, Nebraska, South Dakota, Montana, Wyoming, and Colorado.[7]

Toiling in the beet industry proved exhausting and did not pay well. Unscrupulous recruitment and contracting practices of the companies left many feeling bitter and betrayed. Some complained to Mexican consular officials. Others simply left, and turnover proved high as many made their way south toward the border states or even back to Mexico. Despite high attrition rates, a small nucleus of laborers and their families nevertheless made a place for themselves. Some gravitated to emerging urban *colonias* in places such as Omaha, Nebraska; Topeka and Emporia, Kansas; Oklahoma City and Tulsa, Oklahoma; Davenport, Iowa; and Kansas City, Missouri. Mexicans took to railroading, meat processing, and a variety of other nonagricultural types of work. Mexican communities in each of these cities grew fairly rapidly. The same proved true for industrial midwestern centers such as Detroit and Chicago. Soon, however, a severe economic downturn in 1921–1922 caused between 200,000 and 400,000 Mexicans to return to their native land as businesses either slashed their labor forces or closed altogether.[8]

Foreshadowing the larger and longer depression that would come less than ten years later, many workers in the 1921–1922 crisis endured wage cuts in order to keep their jobs. Countless others left near destitute by the depression appealed to Mexican officials (consuls both in the United States and back in Mexico City) for help. Responding to the dire need for assistance, Mexican consuls teamed up with local charitable agencies and mutual aid societies (*sociedades mutualistas*) to help with food donations. These organizations also pooled resources to repatriate Mexicans as well (García 2004: 40–48).

Gradually, however, agricultural interests—and the sugar beet industry in particular—would again call upon Mexican laborers. One historian writes, "[T]he seasonal nature of industrial work, and the precariousness of finding steady employment in industry provided beet companies with a sizable and self-perpetuating labor pool. . . . [By then] beet companies [had] also learned that Mexican workers were easy to exploit because they were isolated and poorly organized" (García 2004: 47). Given this, industry heads would derive significant profits. In robust economic times, laborers would be called to task. In slack periods, workers were simply laid off.[9] Soon, however, economic crisis and the ensuing repatriation program of the 1930s would reduce this figure by half (Balderrama and Rodríguez 1995: 98–122).[10] At the time, Carey McWilliams reflected on the process by writing, "What of the Mexican himself? He never objected to exploitation while he was welcome, and now he acquiesces in repatriation. . . . He has cooperated . . . with the authorities. Thousands have departed of their own volition. In battered Fords, carrying two and three families and all their worldly possessions, they are drifting back [to Mexico]. . . . The Mexican can be lured back, 'whenever we need him'" (McWilliams quoted in Vargas 1999). By the early 1930s, the pattern had been set. When U.S. concerns faced labor shortages, they called upon Mexico to help remedy the situation. When economic times turned slack, Mexicans were laid off, left to their own devices, and sometimes even forcibly sent back south.

Not everyone acquiesced to the new economic order. In fact, a number of labor strikes broke out during the Great Depression years that significantly challenged propertied elites. California saw a number of worker mobilizations, including the 1933 San Joaquin Valley cotton strike when thousands of Mexican and Mexican American laborers—many of them women—walked off the job (Weber 1994). Other struggles took shape elsewhere in the United States during the tumultuous 1930s.

With the outbreak of World War II, demand for workers in industry, agribusiness, and the service sector again increased. The 1942 Bracero Program provided for an influx of Mexican immigrants to the United States (Galarza 1965). Over its nearly two-decade history, approximately 5 million contracted individuals had been brought to labor largely in southwestern agriculture. Others were assigned to different sectors, including railroad, mining, and other nonfarm work. While providing opportunities for Mexicans willing to work for low wages performing demanding physical labor, the binational accord ostensibly furnished capital interests with a ready and seemingly pliant labor force that could be exploited for maximum profit (Kushner 1975: 95–114).

Undocumented in the United States

Following World War II, Mexico's economy entered what observers would later term the "Mexican Miracle." Beginning during the presidency of Miguel Alemán (1946–1952) and stretching into the early 1970s, investment in manufacturing, public works construction, and tourism provided stimulus for significant GDP growth. Commercial agriculture also flourished while export revenue soared following a 1954 peso devaluation aimed at curbing inflation (Bethell 1991: 324).

Throughout this period, labor remained at a surplus, however, despite significant land-reform efforts enacted by President Adolfo López Mateos (1958–1964).[11] Mexico was urbanizing at an unprecedented rate. And while many of those who came to the cities from the countryside found a place for themselves, others did not fare as well and ended up in sprawling shanty towns on the urban periphery.

Those Mexicans motivated and capable of enduring the trek north to the United States did so in increasing numbers. Since the late 1930s, the U.S. economy had experienced robust growth because of its highly technical capability, heavy industrial base, and avoidance of wartime destruction. By the end of the Korean War in mid-1953, the pace began to slow, however. By the end of the decade, growth rates had fallen, especially in manufacturing. Not surprisingly, unemployment rose. But at the same time, wages for unionized workers remained stable (Brenner 2006: 52–57).

It is estimated that more than 500,000 people of Mexican descent living in the United States served during World War II (Santillan 2001). Many others benefitted from the wartime boom, taking up employment in service, retail, government, professional, and manufacturing. Soon, however, immigrant labor from Mexico searching for work in the United States during the 1950s became increasingly unwanted. Low-paid farm labor continued to benefit agricultural interests and consumers, of course, but in shrinking numbers as the economy contracted once again. Further, fear that undocumented immigration was driving down wages and costing "Americans" jobs sparked public debate, political maneuvering, and eventually the creation of a new deportation drive.

The Department of Labor termed the 1954 campaign "Operation Wetback" and called upon the Immigration and Naturalization Service to carry it out. Targeting undocumented individuals, millions were rounded up and sent south. Similar to the repatriation effort two decades earlier, empathetic souls such as activist, professor, and poet Ernesto Galarza as well as groups such as the Asociación Nacional México-Americana (ANMA) organized to resist these practices. Still, their voices were shouted down by those dedicated to "rooting out" "illegals" and "securing the border." More than 3 million undocumented Mexicans found themselves headed south in the years between 1951 and 1953 alone (García reprinted in Vargas 1999: 358). Work situations formerly occupied by Mexicans forcibly removed were filled with braceros whose tenure in the United States was controlled by propertied interests (Galarza 1965). Wages stagnated where bracero labor took hold, so much so that farmworkers in 1955 received less for their efforts that year than they had in 1950. Still, labor in several sectors resisted when possible. Overall, the Bracero Program, as one observer has noted, proved "a grower's dream" (Calavita in Vargas 1999: 375). After increased scrutiny and criticism, it officially ended in 1964 and was fully phased out by the end of 1967.

Conditions soon improved as heavily regulated labor recruitment ended. In the meantime, organizing efforts among farmworkers had taken hold. In September 1965, organizers—including César Chávez and Dolores Huerta, among others—staged a strike for higher wages among grape workers in the San Joaquin Valley town of Delano, California. Theirs would prove a heroic struggle that would significantly change perceptions of farm labor in the United States. Increasingly visible as a workforce to be reckoned with because of a series of collective actions, agricultural workers in the late 1960s and 1970s gained key support from working- and middle-class consumers as well as a handful of powerful elites such as Robert Kennedy. Thanks to the aid of sympathetic Mexican American assertiveness in cities, organizing in the fields won critical victories. Still, macroeconomic forces encouraged by powerful advocates of neoliberal economic policy beginning in the 1970s would significantly change the global political and cultural landscape

(Harvey 1989). For workers, these forces would do much to roll back gains made in the previous decades. Nevertheless, ensuing economic crisis in the 1980s would give rise to an unprecedented wave of mass migration to the United States from Mexico, so that in recent years more than 10 percent of Mexico's population lives in the United States, between 15 and 20 percent of its workforce labors in the United States, and approximately one in seven migrate north at one time or another, a pattern replicated in many ways among Central Americans as well.[12]

Conclusion

Over the long course of North American history, Mexicans (and those before them of Spanish American descent more generally) have figured as one of several key migrating groups to occupy the continent. As the southern neighbor to the United States, Mexican conquest and colonization of North America played out in such historic and substantial fashion so as to throw into question the notion that Mexicans are, in fact, even to be considered "immigrants" to the United States. Certainly the early colonial history of North America calls into question shortsighted assuredness of individual nation-state geographies. The historical reality demonstrates otherwise as in fact territories presently claimed by the United States were once settled and administered by Spanish-speaking peoples.

For some, the past may hold little relevance. Yet when taking account of the number of people of Mexican heritage, estimates figure that by 1940 well over 2 million Mexicans resided in the United States. Presently, estimates of the number of foreign-born Mexicans in the United States stands at approximately 12 million (Batalova and Terrazas 2010). Central Americans total around 3 million (Terrazas 2011). Mexican and Central American presence is clearly then to be observed not only in traditional receiving states across the southwestern borderlands, Texas, Illinois, and California but also in Midwestern and Heartland areas. It is there, along with much of the rest of the country where "the future speaks Spanish."[13]

Notes

1. Polk came to office after making a call for the incorporation of the Oregon Territory to 54 parallel 40' north as well as all Mexican lands north of 31 parallel and the 1845 annexation of Texas (whose southern boundary was to be fixed at the Rio Grande). In contrast to his dealings with Mexican officials, Polk saw fit to compromise with Britain in settling on a boundary at 49 parallel.

2. Further elaborating the dictates of Manifest Destiny, the engineers of U.S. power also turned to consider various offshore neocolonial projects (i.e., the Philippines,

Cuba, and Puerto Rico). In this quest, not only military might but also the fundamental power provided by human labor would be essential; see Paul A. Kramer, *The Blood of Government: Race, Empire, the United States and the Philippines* (Chapel Hill: University of North Carolina Press, 2006); Caesar J. Ayala and Rafael Bernabe, *Puerto Rico in the American Century: A History since 1898* (Chapel Hill: University of North Carolina Press, 2009); and Louis A. Pérez, *Cuba in the American Imagination: Metaphor and the Imperial Ethos* (Chapel Hill: University of North Carolina Press, 2011).

3. One estimate figures that in California alone, aboriginal population sharply declined from around 150,000 in 1840 to somewhat less than 30,000 in 1870; Ward, *The West*, 157.

4. This influx far exceeds the number of arrivals for the same period in every other nation in the Americas, including runners-up Argentina (6,405,000) and Canada (5,206,000); Míguez 2003: xiii.

5. Twelfth Census of the U.S. Population, part 1, quoted in Pred 1966: 132–34; Daniels, *Guarding the Golden Door*, 10.

6. On the work of Gamio and Taylor, see, for example, Devra Weber, Juan Vicente Palerm, and Roberto Melville, eds., *The Mexican Immigrant: The History of His Life. Complete Interviews, 1926–1927* (Mexico City: Editorial Porrua, CIESAS/UC MEXUS, 2002); and Abraham Hoffman, "An Unusual Moment: Paul S. Taylor's Mexican Labor in the United States Monograph Series," *The Pacific Historical Review* 45, no. 2 (May 1976): 255–70.

7. *Sugar Beet Culture in the Northern Great Plains Area,* U.S. Department of Agriculture, Farmer's Bulletin #2029, October 1951, 2, University of North Texas Digital Collection, http://digital.library.unt.edu/permalink/meta-dc-1503 (accessed September 13, 2012).

8. On the Mexican community in Detroit, see Zaragosa Vargas, *Proletarians of the North: A History of Mexican Industrial Workers in Detroit and the Midwest, 1917–1933* (Berkeley and Los Angeles: University of California Press, 1993). For Paul Taylor's pioneering work on Mexicans in the Chicago area, see Paul S. Taylor, *Mexican Labor: Chicago and the Calumet Region* 7, no. 2 (Berkeley: University of California Publications in Economics, 1932). For more recent work on Mexicans in Chicago, see, for example, Nicholas De Genova, *Working the Boundaries: Race, Space, and "Illegality" in Mexican Chicago* (Durham, N.C.: Duke University Press, 2005).

9. García 2004: 48.

10. Some population estimates read that approximately between 1.3 and 1.6 million people of Mexican descent lived in the United States between 1930 and 1940 despite repatriation efforts made during the decade; Daniels 2004: 63.

11. The reform efforts gave 11.4 million hectares to approximately 300,000 recipients, an achievement second only to that by former Mexican President Lázaro Cárdenas; Smith, in Bethell 1991: 353.

12. "Give and Take across the Border," *San Francisco Chronicle,* May 21, 2006.

13. William Grimes, "In This Small Town in Iowa the Future Speaks Spanish," *New York Times,* September 14, 2005, review of Dale Maharidge, *Denison, Iowa:*

Searching for the Soul of America through the Secrets of a Midwest Town (New York: Free Press, 2008).

Works Cited

Balderrama, Francisco E., and Raymond Rodríguez. 1995. *Decade of Betrayal: Mexican Repatriation in the 1930s.* Albuquerque: University of New Mexico Press.

Batalova, Jeanne, and Aaron Terrazas. 2010. "Frequently Requested Statistics on Immigrants and Immigration in the United States." *Migration Information Source* (December). http://www.migrationinformation.org/USFocus/display.cfm?ID=818 (accessed September 13, 2012).

Bethell, Leslie, ed. 1991. *Mexico Since Independence.* Cambridge: Cambridge University Press.

Billington, Ray Allen. 1974. *Westward Expansion: A History of the American Frontier.* New York: Macmillan.

Brenner, Robert. 2006. *The Boom and the Bubble: The U.S. in the World Economy.* London: Verso Press.

Chavez, Leo. 2008. *The Latino Threat: Constructing Immigrants, Citizens, and the Nation.* Stanford, Calif.: Stanford University Press.

Coatsworth. 1981. *Growth Against Development: The Economic Impact of Railroads in Porfirian, Mexico.* DeKalb: Northern Illinois University Press.

Cronin, William. 1992. *Nature's Metropolis: Chicago and the Great West.* New York: W. W. Norton.

Daniels, Rogers. 2004. *Guarding the Golden Door.* New York: Hill and Wang.

Galarza, Ernesto. 1965. *Merchants of Labor: The Mexican Bracero Story.* New York: McNally and Loftin.

Gamio, Manuel. 1931. *The Mexican Immigrant: His Life Story.* Salem, N.H.: Ayer.

García, Juan R. 2004. *Mexicans in the Midwest: 1900–1932.* Tucson: University of Arizona Press.

Harvey, David. 1989. *The Condition of Postmodernity.* New York: Basil Blackwell.

Kushner, Sam. 1975. *Long Road to Delano.* New York: International.

Limerick, Patricia Nelson. 1987. *The Legacy of Conquest: The Unbroken Past of the American West.* New York: Norton.

Massey, Douglas S., Jorge Durand, and Nolan J. Malone. 2002. *Beyond Smoke and Mirrors: Mexican Immigration in an Era of Economic Integration.* New York: Russell Sage Foundation.

McPherson, James M. 1988. *Battle Cry of Freedom: The Civil War Era.* New York: Oxford University Press.

McWilliams, Carey. 1990. *North from Mexico: The Spanish Speaking People of the United States.* New York: Praeger.

Míguez, Eduardo José. 2003. "Introduction: Foreign Mass Migration to Latin America in the Nineteenth and Twentieth Centuries—An Overview." In *Mass Migration to Modern Latin America,* ed. Samuel L. Baily and Eduardo José Míguez. Wilmington, Del.: SR Books.

Montejano, David. 1987. *Anglos and Mexicans in the Making of Texas: 1836–1986.* Austin: University of Texas Press.

Pred, Allan R. 1966. *The Spatial Dynamics of U.S. Urban-Industrial Growth, 1800–1914: Interpretive and Theoretical Essays.* Cambridge, Mass.: MIT Press.

Reséndez, Andrés. 2004. *Changing National Identities at the Frontier: Texas and New Mexico, 1800–1850.* Cambridge: Cambridge University Press.

Santillan, Richard. 2001. "Saving Private José: Midwestern Mexican American Men during World War II." Essay, California State Polytechnic University, Pomona. http://www.csupomona.edu/~jis/2001/Santillan.pdf (accessed September 13, 2012).

Sellers, Charles. 1994. *The Market Revolution: Jacksonian America, 1815–1846.* New York: Oxford University Press.

Smith, Michael M. 1980. *The Mexicans in Oklahoma.* Norman: University of Oklahoma Press.

Taylor, Paul S. 1929–1933. "Mexican Labor in the United States." In *University of California Publications in Economics,* ed. Carl Phehn, Ira Cross, and Melvin Knight. Berkeley: University of California Press.

Terrazas, Aaron. 2011. "Central American Immigrants in the United States." *Migration Information Source* (January). http://www.migrationinformation.org/USfocus/display.cfm?id=821 (accessed September 13, 2012).

Vargas, Zaragosa, ed. 1999. *Major Problems in Mexican American History: Documents and Essays.* Boston: Houghton Mifflin.

Vélez-Ibáñez, Carlos G. 1997. *Border Visions: Mexican Cultures of the Southwest United States.* Tucson: University of Arizona Press.

Ward, Geoffrey C. 1996. *The West: An Illustrated History.* New York: Little, Brown.

Weber, Daniel. 1994. *The Spanish Frontier in North America.* New Haven, Conn.: Yale University Press.

CHAPTER 2

Betabeleros and the Western Nebraska Sugar Industry
An Early-Twentieth-Century History

TISA M. ANDERS

The rolling plains of Nebraska are punctuated by the towering silos and buildings of the sugar factories: skyscrapers of the prairie by day, lighthouses of the land by night. These buildings and businesses arose in the early 1900s to meet the demand to extract sugar from a new plant introduced in the area: beets. From the beginning, the sugar beet industry never stood on its own as an American enterprise. The fields and sugar-manufacturing buildings located on U.S. soil were the exception. Just as this nonindigenous crop needed to be imported to the Heartland, so did the labor for the fields and factories. German Russians, the largest group of foreigners initially working in this arena, literally brought the knowledge and expertise with them from Europe. In the coastal regions and sparingly in Nebraska, Japanese laborers also took part in the early industrial development. In Western Nebraska, Mexican and Mexican American migrant workers joined the two groups and later replaced them.

As with any societal structure, the sugar beet industry grew and developed from a variety of decisions and decision makers, emerging from the support and participation of several societal sectors. In fact, as historian Dennis Nodín Valdés describes: "Despite the [small] size of these farms, the sugar beet industry was large-scale, modern and corporate" (Valdés 1989: 9). In her seminal work on the U.S. sugar beet industry, historian Kathleen Mapes similarly asserts, "What emerges is a history of the making of modern industrial America, one that is easily missed when the links between the countryside and cities, agriculture and industry, farmers and migrant workers, and foreign policy and domestic debates are overlooked" (Mapes 2009: 3).

Industry's targeting of Mexican and Mexican American workers for the fields was not an afterthought or happenstance. The entire production and growth of the sugar beet industry in the United States involved a very methodical and intentional process wherever implemented, including Western Nebraska. Once the lawmakers, financial institutions, community heads, and growers pulled together the various and sundry conditions required for start-up, securing adequate labor became necessary for the industry to succeed.

Businessmen and local leaders chose the newly founded and soon-to-be prosperous city of Scottsbluff in Western Nebraska for the first sugar factory in that region in 1910. Within a decade of the factory's opening, *betabeleros* (Mexican and Mexican American migrant workers) turned out to be the main group recruited for the fields. While their contributions were crucial to the growth and development of the industry, they were not allowed at the decision-making table. Fortunately, the prohibition did not have the last word. As agricultural economist Paul S. Taylor reports, "Hand labor had no share in making the decisions, but its place within the industry was shaped by them, and its participation was necessary to give them effect" (Taylor 1967: 19).

Often, this past and present participation of the *betabeleros* has been viewed by dominant Western culture as a passive, background existence. That is a false, ahistorical assessment. To begin, city leaders and the industry needed and, therefore, wooed the beet workers. Second, the laborers' hard work made the industrial expansion possible. Finally, even amid a culture of bigotry and racism, the migrant workers were active agents in their lives and that of their communities, whether in residence short- or long-term.

This chapter explores what that active agency meant for Mexican and Mexican American migrant workers, their families, and their communities in the context of the growth of the sugar beet industry in Western Nebraska. The factors leading to the early industrial growth, the labor itself, along with a presentation of core characteristics of the *betabeleros* in this Heartland region demonstrate many of the ways the workers moved beyond the passive existence assigned to them. Anders examines the *betabelero* experience through the lens of twentieth-century industrial development with a focus on the first four decades, 1900–1940. Oral interviews with former Mexican migrant workers supplement the historical analyses of primary and secondary source documents. Anders conducted seven interviews with former Mexican American migrant laborers specifically for this chapter: six persons worked the fields surrounding Scottsbluff; the seventh was a former beet worker in central Nebraska. Their labor in the fields took place in the 1940s–1970s, although some family members had involvement in earlier decades (Yow 2000).[1]

The chosen geographic location for this exploration is the western part of Nebraska and the community surrounding the city of Scottsbluff. Often referred to as the North Platte Valley or simply the Valley, this area comprises low lands that run along both sides of the North Platte River, the vicinity's primary water source. While the main discussion of the sugar industry primarily focuses on that city's factory, the experiences of Mexican migrant workers cover a larger three-county area: Scotts Bluff, Morrill, and Box Butte, all located in the south-central panhandle of this Heartland state. This area attracted the author for a variety of reasons. First, she grew up in Scottsbluff. Anders thus brings an insider focus to the topic. Additionally, scant scholarly attention has been paid to this region.

The majority of literature and historiography surrounding the sugar industry in Western Nebraska focuses on technique and technology. The primary works covering Mexican migrant workers center on sugar beets in Colorado, North Dakota, and Michigan or, when dealing with Nebraska, the meatpacking industry in the central and eastern parts of that state (Rowan 1948; Arrington 1967; Preston 2002; Donato 2007; Taylor 1928; Gouveia and Stull 1997; Gouveia, Carranza, and Cogua 2005; Mapes 2009; Norris 2009; Hamilton 2009). While Colorado borders Nebraska and many similarities exist between the two regions, different conditions warrant independent studies.[2] Consequently, delineating the successes and struggles of the Western Nebraska locale brings forth stories that heretofore have been largely unknown.

Although several characteristics remain idiosyncratic to this region, the sugar industry and resulting cultural evolution there provide an example of the larger national issues surrounding immigration and rural development. These local dynamics especially mirror the latifundista system in Latin America (Feder 1971: xv; Norris 2002/2003).[3] At present count, APC (Africa, Pacific Region, and Caribbean) Sugar's Web site refers to 110 nations in the world manufacturing sugar by beets or cane. Western Nebraska's history and contemporary reality thus grant a glimpse into the wider international context.

While the Latino population in general and Scottsbluff in particular encompass more than Mexican and Mexican Americans, this study highlights them due to their targeted recruitment by the sugar industry in Western Nebraska and their influence upon the Scottsbluff community. Valdés describes this group that made up the majority of the *betabeleros* (beet workers) in Nebraska: "The Mexican-descent workers originated in both Texas and Mexico. The former were largely children or grandchildren of Mexican immigrants who settled in Texas. The difference in earnings between Texas and the Midwest was great enough so that northern capitalists could recruit Mexican Americans as a low-wage labor pool. *Tejanos* frequently came north first as farm workers, deciding one or more seasons later to settle in the region" (Valdés 1989: 15).

Industrial Development

As with any institutional structure, the sugar beet industry grew and developed from a variety of decisions and decision makers. Examining the confluence of the various actions and actors provides the foundational matrix for the migrant laborers' work. It also demonstrates that the systematic planning and implementation along with the coming together of the many societal sectors similarly took place in the recruitment and retention of the Mexican and Mexican American migrant workers.

On a national level, the United States experienced a difficult depression in 1897, hitting western agriculture especially hard. One potential strategy to combat the economic downturn included trying out new crops. Businessmen, community leaders, and government officials noticed successful sugar beet districts such as in Eastern Nebraska. Since this experimental industry had assisted many towns in coming out of similar economic depressions in the previous decade, other local economies desired similar boosts. State and national levels expected affirmative ripple effects.

"A factory would assure the district of more employment, higher wages, a better market for its coal and limestone and other manufacturing materials, and higher and more stable farm income. Communities which had established factories had risen out of the slough and had achieved a desirable degree of prosperity," declares the economist and historian Leonard J. Arrington (Arrington 1967: 11). Additional reasons embraced their multipurpose character. Humans consumed the sugar. Animals ate the tops, pulp, and molasses. The deep roots remained in the soil to nurture it. Cecil Rhodes in the *Scotts Bluff Republican* on March 17, 1911, reported on studies conducted in Europe and the United States demonstrating yields from other crops increased when grown in appropriate rotation with beets.

Scottsbluff underwent incorporation as a village in 1900. In those early years, visionary business leaders began taking the steps to bring a sugar factory to their community. However, the actual edifice did not become reality until 1910. Preparation for the more expanded, permanent action required several building blocks and steps. To begin, the leaders wanted assurance that beets would flourish in the Valley. Next, industry growth called for the development of an irrigation system and further expansion of the railroad. After the accomplishment of these necessary precursors, the financial and legislative pieces needed to come together.

In the first decade of the twentieth century, beets had already been successfully grown on a limited scale in the Platte Valley. A 1920 (September 3) *Scotts Bluff Republican* retrospective underscored this feat: "The building of a factory here was no wild experiment, as the soil conditions were found as good if not better than obtained in Colorado, where the Great Western Sugar Company (GW) had really [sic] experimented through the building of the Loveland factory in 1901." Two factors limited further crop expansion: water and transport.

With no sugar-processing factory in Scottsbluff or even nearby, shipment by rail to Eastern Nebraska turned out to be necessary: 340 miles if the final destination was Grand Island; 500 miles if Leavitt (near Ames). The transport continued until the Leavitt plant closed in 1905; Grand Island, 1907. With the founding of the Great Western in Colorado and the building of factories there in select cities in the years from 1901 to 1903, the Western Nebraska beets also went to that state (Preston 2002: 388).[4] Again, the local newspaper, *Scotts Bluff Republican,* described the predicament on December 11, 1908: "At present the development of the industry is badly interfered with by the delays of shipping and the inability of the Colorado factory to take the beets as rapidly as they are supplied in the fall. In consequence of this failure this year a good many acres of beets were frozen in the ground during the recent cold weather."

Further expansion of the irrigation system provided the solution for the insufficient rainfall. In 1895, legislation passed in Nebraska allowing irrigation districts to be formed. The federal Reclamation Act of 1902 paved the way for the North Platte Project. This undertaking supplied several key components for the expansion of Western Nebraska's irrigation system: Pathfinder Dam on the North Platte River in Wyoming; Interstate and Gering-Fort Laramie Canal; and Whelan Dam near Guernsey, Wyoming. In order to catch the water from the Wyoming dams, a series of canals on farmland was constructed. Upon purchase of the land, ditches could be dug. Surplus water then became available for the fields along the canals. Utilization of hand labor, especially in the early decades, facilitated the digging of smaller ditches that moved the water from the canals into the fields (Preston 2002: 386–88; Lindsay 1924: 9; McMillen 2005; *Scotts Bluff Republican,* December 17, 1919).

The new irrigation system allowed sufficient acreage to be devoted to this new crop. Declares Carey McWilliams: "Irrigation was the magic key that unlocked the resources of the [Southwest] region. Irrigated farming is intensive farming: with high yields per acre, heavy labor requirements, year-round production, and crop specialization. . . . Throughout the region, the distribution of Mexicans in rural areas is largely determined by the location of irrigated crops. *Irrigation has had more to do with the economic growth of the Southwest than any single factor"* (emphases added; McWilliams 1948: 162–63).[5] His description equally fits Western Nebraska. Irrigation permitted more acreage for production of sugar beets. For example, in 1914, Scotts Bluff and Morrill Counties had 85,900 acres toward beets. This number grew to approximately 359,000 in 1923 (Anderson 1925: 380). "Sugar beet growing is destined to become a very important industry in the North Platte valley," reported the local newspaper. "There is a well organized movement on foot to secure a factory for the upper valley and when this hope of the country becomes an accomplished fact the acreage will be tremendously increased" (*Scotts Bluff Republication,* December 11, 1908).

Next, the people and products called for adequate transportation. As Jorge Durand, Douglas S. Massey, and Chiara Capoferro assert, "In the western United States, meanwhile, the arrival of the railroads connected agricultural and mining areas in the southwest, yielding sustained economic growth and rapid growth in labor demand." Scottsbluff began to get "hooked up" to the railroad lines early in the life of the community. In January 1900, the same year as the city's founding, the Burlington and Missouri Valley Railroad extended its line along the North Platte River. To begin, this brought the investors to Western Nebraska. The rails turned into a logical conduit to and fro for needed raw materials and products. Eventually, the railroad developed into a primary means for labor recruitment for the railroad itself as well as for other industries in the growing West, including the Nebraska Panhandle. The railroads also allowed Nebraska to serve as a secondary destination for many from Mexico who initially landed in California and other border states (Durand, Massey, and Capoferro 2005: 6, 7; Preston 2002: 386; Grajeda 1976: 58–59; Grajeda 1998: 16).

Industrial expansion mandated political clout and legal maneuverings. In the international realm, the United States in 1898 had recently fought the Spanish American War, gaining possession of the former Spanish colonies of Cuba, Puerto Rico, Guam, and the Philippines. While the conflict situated the United States as a powerful international player, the acquisition of the new colonies alarmed the beet sugar industrialists. The emerging beet sugar production within the United States came into stiff competition with the cane sugar industries of Cuba and the Philippines. Consequently, legislators enacted many tariffs to protect domestic beet sugar from the well-established international cane commerce. One such measure in 1897, the Dingley Tariff, imposed a high duty on imported sugar. Another example, the Platt Amendment of 1901, placed trade restrictions on Cuba. Throughout the decades of the twentieth century, the legislative lineup of protectionism contained similar taxes and/or restrictions (Johnson 1934: 73–96; Arrington 1967: 16; Reisler 1976: 87; Carranza 2008; Mapes 2009). In fact, in the midst of the plans to build Scottsbluff's first factory, a one-year delay of the contracts and construction occurred due to the federal government's failure to enact new tariff legislation. The *Scotts Bluff Republican's* editor, E. T. Westervelt, warned the farmers on December 4, 1908, that they needed to plant something other than beets because the community could not move forward with constructing a processing plant without the protective tax.

By January 1910, the protectionist legislation passed, giving Scottsbluff the green light to move forward with beet cultivation and sugar production. E. J. Burkett, one of Nebraska's senators at the time, wrote a letter to the local editor (*Scotts Bluff Republican,* February 4, 1910) explaining the value of the legislation and his vote on the sugar schedule:

> The sugar question is the most difficult one that every nation has to handle. In America it is particularly so because we have both cane and beet sugar production here at home, and in addition we have insular possessions whose future prosperity is almost wholly dependent upon the sugar industry. In addition to this it is the thing upon which we have always relied for a large part of our revenue. . . . I received petitions from two thousand of our Nebraska people, protesting against any reduction in the sugar schedule. We did reduce the tariff on all sugar schedules and five points on those coming from Cuba twenty percent, and admitted sugar from the Philipine [sic] Islands, Porto [sic] Rico and Hawaii free. I voted against further reduction.

Scottsbluff's community leaders did their part. The early growing successes of the beets convinced the local Chamber of Commerce of this industry's value. This entity selected two men to travel to Denver, Colorado, in 1908 with the express purpose of meeting with C. H. Mosey, president of the Great Western. GW had no interest in a new factory at that time. Competition with cane sugar from the Philippines and West Indies depressed the market and made that year bad timing for expansion. However, one year later with the adoption of protectionist legislation, GW sent A. V. Office to Scottsbluff to procure land for the new factory and to contract for 12,000 acres of beets at $5 per ton. The town provided the start-up capital of $27,800. In 1909, GW purchased the Leavitt, Nebraska, sugar factory and moved it to Scottsbluff. In an early-twentieth-century version of reusing raw materials, workers dismantled the buildings in Eastern Nebraska and then resurrected them on the opposite side of the state. Great Western incorporated the new business venture with the Nebraska secretary of state on August 7, 1909, with $1 million in authorized capital stock and under the name the Scottsbluff Sugar Company (Christensen 1999: 73–74; Arrington 1967: 13; Nebraska Department of Labor 1910, 1915, 1916).[6]

The community and company ensured Western Nebraska's first sugar-processing plant was up and running in time for the fall crop of 1910 (Christensen 1999: 73–74). The *Scotts Bluff Republican* (November 4, 1910) heralded the sugar factory's opening: "By the time this paper reaches all our readers the new sugar factory at this place will be running in full blast, turning out 1200 tons of sugar. On Wednesday morning of this week great clouds of smoke could be seen belching from the mammoth smoke stacks, while the ponderous wheels of the interior were put in motion and the mountain of machinery, that a few months ago was in a pile resembling scrap iron Was [sic] being tried out."

All the planning, bankrolling, and coordination paid off. The Valley did indeed thrive. Jack Preston describes the prosperity brought on by this campaign as the "white gold rush" (Preston 2002: 392). In Scotts Bluff County, the number of farms increased from 421 in 1900 to 1,391 in 1920. Additionally, the number of people per square mile in the county went up from 2.6 in 1880 to 28.8 in 1920. Esther S. Anderson reports on this significance: "The percentage of increase in the population in 1920 over that of 1910 was more than 147 percent, one of the highest percentage gains in county population in the United States" (Anderson 1925: 383). The town leaders' prediction that the community's success would be linked to that of the sugar industry proved true. Declared the local newspaper in 1920 (*Scotts Bluff Republican*, September 3): "[D]espite the success in the production of other crops the prosperity and growth of this valley has been and will be influenced by the sugar beet industry. As the industry has grown, so has the prosperity of this region grown, and the fact that it is estimated that some $10,000,000 will be paid to the farmers of this valley for this season's beet crop indicates why the prosperity is so tangible and so pronounced."

Labor Recruitment

Labor rose to the forefront as a critical component in the genesis and advance of the U.S. sugar culture. The movers and shakers of the industry in the early 1900s had four distinct options available to them. The first one focused on recruiting laborers from other countries with depressed labor markets. Option two limited the growing of beets to areas with a sufficient domestic labor supply and on smaller parcels of land. The third possibility relied on readily available cane sugar. Finally, the fourth alternative concentrated on allowing technology to develop, thereby lessening the heavy hand labor required each spring and fall. As Taylor describes, the industry gravitated to the first option: "To the sugar beet industry at the turn of the century, its own economic interest justified a decision to rely promptly upon immigrant laborers" (Taylor 1967: 20, 21).

With the determination to move forward with laborers from other countries, systematic recruitment efforts began. As Taylor further explains: "I[ndustry] promptly channeled its energy into well-staffed, organized recruitment programs to bring laborers to the beet fields for spring thinning and autumn topping" (Taylor 1967: 20). In Western Nebraska, the German Russians and Japanese started working the fields in the early years, followed by Mexican and Mexican American workers almost a decade later. Exploring the recruitment methods for the latter group demonstrates the methodical manner in which labor pursued the laborers.

Four distinct periods of Mexican migration to the United States are identified. *Betabeleros* in Western Nebraska have lived and worked there in each period. The Classic Era covered the nineteenth century through the 1920s with the placement of restrictive immigration policies. The Bracero Period of 1942–1964 took place during a time when the U.S. government sponsored a significant temporary-worker program. The Undocumented Era began at the end of the Bracero Period through 1986 when the United States passed the Immigration Reform and Control Act (IRCA). The fourth, current stage is the Post-IRCA Era, 1987 to the present (Durand, Massey, and Capoferro 2005: 1).[7]

Several characteristics of the Western Nebraskan *betabelero*-grower/industry relationship demonstrate that some of the dynamics of the Latin American latifundista migrated as well to the Heartland. Agricultural historian Jim Norris describes this paternalistic bond as *patronismo,* and it was a system in place in Mexico and southern Texas. Dennis Nodín Valdés places a similar structure in New Mexico and defines the midwestern counterpart as a padrone system. To create a more stable workforce, landowners in this configuration intentionally sought to form personal and cultural ties with their workers. Including entire families in the work system assisted in this goal. Additionally, without familial engagement, the laborers could not make ends meet since the latifundista system promulgated low wages. Landlords primarily employed oral agreements for the labor contracts with their rural workers (Norris 2002/2003: 203–4; Nodín Valdés 1990: 115–17; Feder 1971: 134–37). Mapes discusses the intended dependency of this inherited structure: "This family-based migratory labor system was supposed to ensure farmers a vulnerable, seasonal, and nonthreatening yet stable workforce; migrant family labor was not merely a labor but also a means for keeping workers in the fields and away from the local community in which they were only temporary residents" (Mapes 2009: 6).

In the late 1800s, the U.S. census recorded the number of foreign-born Mexicans living in Nebraska with double digits: 14 in 1880; 34 in 1890; 27 in 1900. This bumped up to the triple digits of 290 persons in 1910, swelling exponentially with a 110 percent increase by 1920 to 2,611 persons. In 1930, the numbers increased to 3,628 (Broadbent [1941] 1972: 13). The increased number of Mexicans in the state coincided with the decrease in German Russians working the beet fields due to their exiting the fieldwork and "passage of national-origin quota laws in the 1920s." Industry recruited approximately two thousand Mexican-origin workers for the fields each year in Nebraska during this time period. Dennis Nodín Valdés reports that by the late 1920s, Mexicans and Mexican Americans constituted 60 percent of the *betabeleros* (beet workers) in the Midwest (Gouveia, Carranza, and Cogua 2005: 26; Nodín Valdés 1989: 9). Miscellaneous newspaper articles about Mexicans and Mexican Americans demonstrate their presence in the community (*Scotts Bluff Republican,* October 14, 1919; July 27, 1920; August 20, 1920).

Just as the general development and growth of the industry needed federal legislation, ensuring an adequate labor supply during surplus and lean times required special immigration laws to keep the labor pipeline open between Mexico and the United States. For example, Harry A. Austin, secretary of the U.S. Sugar Beet Association, appealed to Congress to lift immigration restrictions in the 1920s:

> We feel justified in asking for this relief [in form of admission of seasonal laborers from Mexico] because our industry is primarily and fundamentally an agricultural industry. . . . Unless the farmer can secure the labor . . . he cannot inject the sugar beet into his cycle of rotation but must fall back one grant and other crops which require less labor and which are now surfeiting our markets. . . . [The sugar beet is] a cash-paying crop for which the farmer has a remunerative market in his own community [i.e., at the adjacent beet sugar factory] (Taylor 1967: 21).

In the first decades (1920s–1930s), factories took the lead in worker recruitment. Once the laborers arrived in Western Nebraska, growers agreed to provide adequate board and room as well as the fields and income for the work. The *betabeleros'* responsibilities included the work itself as well as negotiating within the confines of the system put in place by the others. Often these duties overlapped, such as when GW provided a certain amount of housing. The Scottsbluff community stepped in with a helping hand as needed.

The Great Western Sugar Factory appointed C. V. Maddux to the position of labor commissioner. References to his work especially appear in the 1920s and 1930s. Since GW's territory covered Colorado and Nebraska in those early years (GW expanded to Montana in 1906; Wyoming, 1916), their recruiting efforts pertained to both locations. Industry used a variety of propaganda and recruitment tools. To entice workers to appear in the farming communities by spring, the company offered special incentives, including free transportation. In attempts to entice them to remain, laborers received assistance in obtaining lots and building houses (Taylor 1967: 21; Donato 2007: 18–23; Hamilton 2009: xii).

Throughout the 1920s, Maddux's leadership team printed booklets, posters, calendars, and flyers in Spanish. GW utilized a print-media campaign in influential Spanish language newspapers. According to one estimate, the company distributed thousands of these print materials and contacted up to fifteen publishers. Portraying a romanticized version of a beet worker's life, another strategy encompassed "moving-picture shows." Taped in northern Colorado during this time frame and dubbed in Spanish, one film covered fieldwork, recreation, and cultural life such as celebrations for Mexican Independence Day. Explains Rubén Donato: "These films were influential. The company brought hundreds and thousands of Mexican and Hispano workers to Colorado's sugar beet districts." Upon the establishment of small communities, GW employees polled the Mexican and Mexican American residents for prospective names of their friends and family (Donato 2007: 6, 32; Reisler 1976: 88; Anderson 1925: 381).

Agents from GW went on six-week recruitment trips to Mexico and Texas each year in February. Placing one or two agents in charge, transporting labor to Nebraska by train turned into the next step. At each designated railway stop along the route, agents checked with the conductors to pay for any new passengers. The company provided meals of bread, meat, cheese, fruit, and coffee during the trip north to Nebraska. In 1926, GW utilized the services of fifty-five labor agents in the four states where GW had factories: Nebraska, Colorado, Wyoming, and Montana (Donato 2007: 32).

Pat and Carlotta Dominguez reported on the trainloads of Mexicans and Mexican Americans transported to the Valley to replace German Russians in the fields. As children, they arrived in Western Nebraska in the 1920s on one of these GW recruitment trains from Mexico. Husband and wife both vividly remembered their arrival scene. Pat described that fifteen or twenty families, all with children ranging in number from two to twelve, disembarked from each train. The workers stood in a line at the depot where growers met them, chose a family or families, and took them to the farms (Dominguez and Dominguez 2001).[8]

When the labor laws changed with the establishment of the Bracero Program (1942–1964), Great Western acquired licensing and bonding in Texas to contract with Mexican American workers living there. Up to twenty workers age fourteen and older could ride in the truck. Olga Olivares's maternal grandfather worked as a contractor for GW in the 1940s. He recruited hand laborers for the beet fieldwork and transported them in his "big trucks with tents." GW paid a certain amount per laborer. Upon arrival in Western Nebraska, he spread out the workers among farmers. He knew ahead of time the exact farms that needed field hands since the farmers worked very closely with GW. This often turned out to be the first step for the workers. Once they "had a foot in the door," they could negotiate and work directly with the growers at a later date (Ramsey 1999: 40; O. Olivares 2008).

In 1919, recruitment efforts drew 6,000 beet laborers to Colorado from Mexico, northern New Mexico, southern Colorado, and other southwestern states. This quickly became expensive. In 1921, GW reported the cost at $20.53 per person. The financial burden necessitated other recruitment and retention actions. Mark Reisler points out that GW started its recruitment of Mexican and Mexican American workers in 1915. By 1920, the company had spent $360,000 in its recruitment, food provision, and transport from Texas and Mexico for 13,000 workers (in comparison to 500 workers recruited in 1915 and 14,500 in 1926). The 1920 figures worked out to $27.69 per person. Due to this high cost, GW led the efforts in the 1920s to establish permanent colonies in the towns where the company had factories. Several goals undergirded this move: the ability to attract and keep good, permanent workers; improve yields; and boost profits for growers, the company, and stockholders. GW's grower magazine, *Through the Leaves,* documented many aspects of the colonization process, including the benefits, construction designs, and expenses (Reisler 1976: 88, 90; Donato 2007: 29–48).

Some workers received the option to build and purchase their homes under this GW plan. Beginning in the 1920s, the company sold small plots of land and the building materials to "qualified" families. Participation in the program required a recommendation from a grower, supervisor, or field man. Maddux also conceived a Certificate of Merit program, "Another Ton per Acre in 1925." The awardees distinguished themselves with excellent work in all aspects of the field labor: thinning, hoeing, weeding, and topping.[9] The Scottsbluff real estate available to *betabeleros* was and is bordered on the north by East Overland Avenue; south, South Beltline Road; east, 15th Avenue; west, 5th Avenue.[10] Rachel Gonzales spoke to this issue. On a little hill by the factory (in the parameters just reported), GW provided housing for workers. The families living there formed a small community, which is where Rachel grew up in the 1950s and 1960s (Donato 2007: 33; Gonzales 2008).

When GW first opened, the local newspaper (*Scotts Bluff Republican*) reported on March 11, 1910, that eight or ten cottages in town had been built "for the laborers on the beet crop." Later in September 1919 amid the prominence of Mexican and Mexican American workers, GW sent out a plea to the community. The company and the growers called for assistance in housing the seasonal workers coming to town for the harvest, laborers for both the fields and the factories. The area paper communicated the request along with an appeal for the residents to open their homes for roomers (September 23, 1919). In this manner, the homeowners would earn a bit of extra income while simultaneously aiding their community with housing the needed and wanted harvest workers. The community responded affirmatively. Two weeks later, the paper reported that the "question of rooms now seems solved" (October 7, 1919).

GW clearly conveyed their inability to house all of the workers. They complemented their own campaign with a supplemental one to encourage growers to also provide adequate housing and decent working conditions. Nodín Valdés suggests that by the mid-1920s, the Great Plains/Heartland states through GW housed about 10,000 families, only a third of the *beta-beleros*. The Chavez family in Scottsbluff typifies the not-housed-by-GW group. Initially drawn to the United States by work with the railroad and then a packinghouse in Kansas City, a GW field man recruited Mr. Chavez in 1919. They lived in a two-room labor house on a farm just west of Scotts-bluff. The residence sported an outhouse for bathroom facilities and a hand pump at the well. The family grew to eight girls and five boys. None finished high school due to their need to work in the beet fields (Ramsey 1999: 41). Pat and Carlotta Dominguez, the elderly couple who arrived on trains from Mexico as children in the 1920s, also fit in this category in that early decade. Carlotta remembered living in a beet shack located north of Scottsbluff during the time when she and her family worked the fields: "You could see light sifting through cracks in the ceiling and our meals were prepared on a coal stove" (Nodín Valdés 1990: 115; Christensen 1999: 169).[11]

The workers' social agency in this situation came alive in their desire to put food on the table for their families and to try to make a better world for their children, the dreams and goals for almost all Americans. Ralph Grajeda addresses this point: "These first immigrants during the first part of the twentieth century have done what all immigrants during the first part of the twentieth century have done: they have raised families; they have built communities; they have sent their sons and daughters to the schools to learn English. And they have sent their sons and daughters and grandsons and granddaughters to the nation's wars, and in substantial numbers sacrificed them to the purposes of this nation. They have endured" (Grajeda 1998: 18). In the early years of the sugar industry (1920s–1940s), the *betabeleros* accepted the travel arrangements and living accommodations available to them at the time. Additionally, the grower and worker negotiated the actual contract for the field work.

Contract labor constituted the primary employment category for the *betabeleros*. Workers, most often with their families, negotiated contracts to block, thin, and harvest beets for a certain amount per acre. McWilliams conveys that the contracts often had a "hold-back" provision, a stipulation that the workers had no choice but to remain from spring to fall to finish the harvest in order to get paid (McWilliams 1948: 166). It appears that the majority of negotiated contracts ended up as verbal agreements, although some written agreements did take place. For instance, the Farm and Ranch Museum in Western Nebraska recently discovered a Contract for Hand Labor for the Season of 1938 signed by growers E. E. Walker and George Iwata and primary beet worker Fortino Huerta (Preston 2009).

None of the families interviewed by the author recalled written arrangements. Their collective, multigenerational experiences cover the entire twentieth century in Western Nebraska. This happened despite national legislation in the 1930s requiring written contracts as well as labor recruiters in Texas mandated to comply with Texas state labor laws with a similar obligation (Norris 2009: 39–43; Norris 2002/2003: 197). In the 1920s, studies showed that beet workers in the Midwest earned an average of $340 to $436 annually. Taylor presents the minimum per-acre rate for the several years: 1909, $20; 1917, $20; 1918, 1919, $25; 1920, $30-$35; 1921, $22; 1922, $18; 1923, $21; 1924, $23; 1925, $22; 1926, $24; 1927, $24; and 1928, $23 (Taylor 1928: 142; Reisler 1976: 229).

Workers utilized a variety of ways to get matched up with farmers. As shown, GW and the farmers took the lead in initially placing workers in the 1920s. Obtaining that first season of employment and the beginnings of their own networking, laborers then possessed a better sense of who to work for the following year. Within families, sometimes the father negotiated the contracts; other times, the mother. In Dolores Wright's situation, her father brokered the contracts with local farmers during the 1920s and 1930s. She confirmed the verbal nature of those agreements. He received one paycheck for the entire family's contributions to the field work. While never cheated, she heard of others who experienced injustices. Often, those with disputes had no recourse for getting paid (Wright 2008).[12]

In contrast, Rachel Gonzales's mother negotiated the price and rates with farmers in the 1940s through the 1970s. She also determined how much work the family engaged in along with the number of laborers needed. Often, they worked year after year for the same grower. When securing a contract in fields worked by others in past years, Mrs. Salazar made sure to settle on an appropriate price. If the previous *betabeleros* had been somewhat sloppy in their weeding, the fields contained more weeds than the ones Rachel's family had worked the preceding year. In that case, her mother demanded a higher pay rate.[13]

Herminia Flores's family worked the fields with another family in the 1940s and 1950s. Her father negotiated the arrangements, received the paycheck, and then divided the monies. The payment rate depended upon how many rows and acres they worked.

Olga Olivares primarily worked for the farmers who hired her husband as a permanent, hired hand in the 1940s to 1960s. A few times they experienced unjust circumstances when unfamiliar farmers did not want to pay. She understood that growers had a rough time surviving, too. She also knew that some groups existed to "supposedly" defend agricultural workers. One time she had a dispute and made an appointment with an organization. She, unfortunately, received a letter regarding the meeting the day *after* it took place. Justifiably, the situation angered her. She intentionally let go and moved on. "That's how we survived," she declares.

Betabeleros and Beyond

Examining the labor itself provides a glimpse at what the *betabeleros* experienced on a daily basis and illustrates their foundational contributions to the community. Distinct features include mixed migrant-seasonal status, the multigenerational factor, the entire family's participation in the fields, the very difficult nature of the work itself, and a stepping stone to increased empowerment and advocacy.

Betabeleros comprised more than one type of agricultural worker. In fact, the majority of families involved in this sector encompassed a longtime mixture of migrants and seasonal workers. As itinerant migrant workers, they chased the crops throughout the year. Two types came under this category: "back-and-forth" workers (simply traveling from one state to another and then back home again) and "follow-the-crop" laborers (following crops from state to state to state). Texas to Nebraska, Nebraska to Texas illustrated the first variety. For Mexican Americans with home base in Texas, the follow-the-crop cycle consisted of Nebraska, North Dakota, Minnesota, and then returning home to Texas and the cotton fields. The seasonal workers maintained permanent residences in Western Nebraska and only worked the crops during the growing and harvest times from this home locale. These differentiations led to ramifications in overall lifestyle, such as temporary versus permanent residences, and legalities (Cobos 2009; O. Olivares 2008; D. Olivares 2008).

Legal standing defined employment status as well as worker eligibility for government and private programs. For example, as children on the follow-the-crop migrant cycle (1930s and 1940s), Olga Olivares's parents sent them to migrant schools in different states. However, when her children came along and her oldest daughter started elementary school in the mid-1950s, Olga pulled the family off the migrant cycle. She adamantly insisted they remain in Scotts Bluff County for school. Consequently, her daughter Dora and siblings did not qualify for youth activities in the fields or migrant school since they possessed a settled home.

For the Mexican and Mexican American beet workers, the contribution of father, mother, and every child was critical to the well-being of the entire family (this equally applied to the Russian Germans). Nodín Valdés reports: "It [Mexican beet labor] differed from urban employment because it depended on women and children as well as adult men. Women were central to survival strategies. They worked in beet cultivation and harvest, tended gardens and canned local produce for family consumption, and performed other tasks essential to the total subsistence of the family" (Nodín Valdés 1989: 9). When growers hired the adult workers, they knew the entire family came along. The title of an article by Jim Norris about the beet fields in North Dakota captures the heart of this characteristic: "Growing Up Growing Sugar" (Norris 2005).

All of the persons interviewed by the author toiled in the fields as children. Dora Olivares reported lack of free child care as one reason the entire family worked in the 1950s and 1960s. In fact, they never considered the option of not working. Queries Dora, "What would my mother have done in summer with nine kids and in [the small town of] Lyman? We would have made her life miserable."

A study conducted in 1923 provided a detailed accounting of child labor. That year, the National Child Labor Committee (NCLC), a private organization, commissioned a group to look into the labor conditions of children *betabeleros* in the North Platte Valley of Nebraska. In the 1923 season, out of the 355 families interviewed, 995 children under sixteen years of age labored in the beet fields. Their parents estimated that the kids worked 7,995.5 acres, averaging 8 acres per child and translating into 47 percent of the season's total acreage (16,984 acres). Children under age ten made up one-third of that group with the remaining two-thirds between the ages of ten and fifteen (Lindsay 1924: 14).[14]

Due to the extensive use of child labor and the arduous working conditions, the committee did indeed have concerns. They, however, did not advise the passage of new laws. Instead, they recommended the enforcement of current child labor legislation (Lindsay 1924: 14).[15] In Nebraska in 2012, child labor laws allowed children under age sixteen to work with their parents. Several conditions required adherence: the children could not work more than forty-eight hours per week, eight hours per day. Their work could not begin prior to 6:00 A.M. or after 8:00 P.M. Teens between the ages of fourteen and sixteen were not allowed to work after 10:00 P.M. (Nebraska Department of Labor 2012).[16]

Another familial factor has been the multigenerational character of the beet work. Rachel Gonzales's and her family's experiences in the agricultural sector exemplify this case. Born and raised in Scottsbluff (the same for both her parents), Rachel incarnates her family's third generation in the twentieth century. Her mother, born there in 1925, personifies the second cohort. The first generation included Rachel's maternal grandparents, migrant workers from Mexico, and paternal grandparents, field laborers from Texas in the 1900s and 1910s. The only child in her family of origin to do so, Rachel's mother remained in Scottsbluff. In 1939, she married early at age fourteen years to her twenty-year-old husband. As children and teens, Rachel and her eight siblings all joined their parents in the fields. Expanding the picture, additional *betabeleros* in the family consisted of Rachel's husband and his siblings (another third generation) along with their parents (second generation). In fact, at age five, her husband learned how to work the irrigation hoses. Rachel and her husband's children never toiled in the fields. Thus, the beet worker cycle stopped with this family's fourth generation, society's Generation X.[17]

Adults and especially the children endured significant difficulties in this harsh fieldwork. With the passing decades, new technology in the guise of modern equipment, seeds, and chemicals slowly but surely led to the diminished need for hand labor. Yet as long as the crop cultivation required hand labor, similar dynamics remained consistent throughout the twentieth century in three phases: thinning, weeding (cleaning), and topping (Lindsay 1924: 18–21).

March of each year started the new season rolling with planting. The beet seed in the early decades consisted of a ball full of numerous seeds placed in rows approximately twenty inches apart. Due to the nature of the seed, "plants c[a]me up so close together that they form[ed] a solid mass" (Lindsay 1924: 18). Thus, the first stage of hand labor consisted of blocking and thinning the beets. For this, the workers needed to "knock down" extraneous beets, leaving a five-inch space between the stand-alone beets. That length was just the size of a hoe, so easily measured. As the workers thinned, they also took out numerous weeds. As such, they also named this phase "the cleaning" (Lindsay 1924: 18; Gonzales 2008).

As the beets and weeds grew, the time soon arrived for the second cleaning. This usually took place in the summer around July. "My mother was very demanding that we did a good job—the *limpia* [cleaning]," reminisces Rachel Gonzales. In the late 1930s and even into the 1950s, the workers used short hoes for the cleaning. These had small handles and required people to get on their hands and knees to grip them properly. Herminia Flores conveyed that her aunt, after a full day with the short hoes, sometimes experienced such painful effects she could not even go to the bathroom. Fortunately, in the later decades, long-handled hoes replaced them. The new equipment made the work much easier, especially on a person's back. Whether long or short, the field labor necessitated sharp hoes. In Herminia's group, the men sharpened the adults' hoes and the children's implements at lunchtime as well as several times throughout the day. Rachel's family owned their own hoes, which they stored in the trunk of their car. Her dad sharpened them every night.

All the Olivares children, even the youngest, worked in the beet fields from the 1950s to the 1970s. Dora started at age eight or nine. The little ones took turns in the rows and relayed with the other kids, their first "internship." In the next year, they "graduated" to their own row. Hot weather produced particularly tough times in the fields. Frequently, the children developed bloody noses and passed out. Under those conditions, Olga took it easy on the kids. They could wait until 2:00 P.M. or 3:00 P.M. before going to the fields. By age ten, Dora engaged in some of the same work as her mother except the weeding. Her mother did three or four rows to each kid's one row. "It was work!" exclaims Dora. "I remember waking up and my hands were locked around the hoe. The first week was terrible. After the first few days, we adjusted."

During beet time, the Olivares family routinely worked five days per week with an occasional Saturday or Sunday tacked on. They started at 6:00 A.M. each day, took a one-hour lunch break at home, and then back to the fields to work until 6:00 P.M. The number of rounds needed in a field dictated the exact schedule of any particular day. A strict taskmistress, Mother Olga Olivares took immense pride in her and their work. If angered by what she considered a sloppy job, the kids redid the rows to get them right. Dora credited this trait in her mom and the labor in the fields as the context where she developed pride in her work, irrespective of earnings. Additionally, the family grew close in their daily work together.

The third phase in the beet field, harvest time in October and November, again required intensive hand labor. Using knives with hooks on them, which somewhat resembled machetes, workers cut the green leafy tops off the beets; hence, this stage's descriptor, "the topping." Dolores Wright described this process in the 1940s. A tractor lifted or loosened the beets from deep in the ground. The laborers, including the minors, picked up beets by the leaves and stacked them so they faced one way. They placed the beets in piles up to three or four rows. With their special hooked knives, workers cut the leaves off, thereby separating the leafy tops from the smooth beet roots. Laborers then forked the beets onto trucks for transport to the factories. The leafy tops were transformed into mulch or cattle food. Pete Vallejo remembered this stage and task as the most difficult. Often, the weather turned out to be very cold, even freezing. He and other workers frequently cut their legs with the machetes or beet knives. "Fortunately," declares Pete, "machinery now exists to do the topping."

While an organized voice does not appear to have emerged among the agricultural workers in Nebraska, some organizations and advocates have sprung up through the years. This includes *betabeleros* who, slowly but surely, gained the courage and conviction needed to speak for themselves and on behalf of others. For example, Geronimo Perez, originally from San

Pedro Apulco, Zacatecas, Mexico, immigrated to Colorado where he worked for the railroad. As a young man, he moved to Scotts Bluff County to work the beet fields. President of the local Beet Workers Association (Asociacion de Betabeleros) from 1930 to 1931, he assisted in problem solving between workers and growers. His daughter, Jennie Vostades, shares that he worked hard to do well in this critical position. Founded in Colorado in 1929, the Beet Workers Association was part of the Trade Union Unity League and the American Federation of Labor (AFL). At its highest point, 10,000 members and sympathizers associated with the organization, primarily from Nebraska, Kansas, Colorado, Wyoming, and Montana (Geil 1995: 1; Donato 2007: 41; Nodín Valdés 1990: 119).[18]

Pete Vallejo participated in fieldwork from the 1940s to the 1970s. He describes his younger self as naive and ignorant. That changed the longer he worked the fields. He soon learned about dishonesty when some of the farmers intentionally misstated the number of acres needed to work with a given job. In response, Pete became skilled at measuring a field. He recounts that many farmers took advantage of people who did not have that skill. Appearing as retaliation for his proactive stance, farmers often tried to cheat him. Fortunately, he received support from the sugar factory's field man, who backed Pete. Another way some growers attempted to deceive the *betabeleros* included telling them they had not done a good job and then refusing to pay the workers.

Rosa Cobos, a later-twentieth-century advocate, rose up from the beet fields. Her introduction to Scotts Bluff County came in the 1970s during her teenager years. At that time, she, her siblings, and their parents lived in Watsonville, California. They worked the fields in the agricultural sector in this "fruit and salad" valley. In 1970, Cesar Chavez and the United Farm Workers of America movement were in full swing there. Her parents refused to cross the California picket lines in the summers of 1971, 1972, 1973, and 1974. Instead, they courageously chose a more itinerant style of farm labor and traveled to Western Nebraska and the beet fields. With this inspirational, foundational background, Rosa moved to Scottsbluff as an adult in 1982. She returned to the fields in a very different manner: as the "Erin Brockovich of civil policy law for poor people and migrant workers."[19]

For almost two decades, Rosa emerged as a lone advocate for these groups in Western Nebraska. In 1987, she began working for Western Nebraska Legal Services (later to merge with other state legal aid groups as Legal Aid of Nebraska). By 1990, her organization appointed Rosa to the directorship of the Migrant Farm Worker project. The U.S. Civil Rights Commission selected her for service during the years 2000–2005. In like manner to Geronimo Perez's involvement in the Beet Workers Association, Rosa primarily mediated conflicts between growers and *betabeleros*. Her additional advocacy involved community legal education for workers and community profes-sionals.[20] Even though the work consisted of numerous details, required extensive involvement, and, at times, turned difficult, Rosa does not regret her activism: "I gave up my life [in those years] and lost a lot. It, however, was a good cause for humanity. The work was my fate, destiny. My parents taught me [that] when you come into the world, do not live in vain."[21]

Numerous changes have taken place in the sugar industry in its first century of existence. The Scottsbluff factory's first campaign in 1910 netted an average of 1,012 tons of beets for the "daily slice," compared to 5,000 tons per day in 1997. As mechanization improved and the use of chemicals increased (herbicides, fungicides, and insecticides), the necessity of hand labor simultaneously decreased. In the 1960s, the industry hired as many as 6,000 migrant laborers annually; in 1975, 5,000; by 1999, 500–1,000 workers (Western Sugar Company n.d.; Ramsey 1999: 40). The number of person-hours ("man-hours") required to produce an acre of beets also substantially lessened:

Year	Person-hours
1915	120
1930	100
1950	51
1980	19
2001	8

Source: (Fenster and Baltensperger n.d.: 17).

Ironically, this led the industry away from the option chosen at the begin-ning of the twentieth century: the need for *betabeleros*. The new alternative, on the table in the 1900s but not manifested until decades later, required the increased use of technology.

Conclusion

Industry's initial choice to focus on immigrant labor provided the platform for recruitment of *betabeleros*. The early-twentieth-century Mexican-origin migrants did not have a voice in the boardroom of the sugar industry in the Heartland's Western Nebraska. However, their very lives and powerful presence in the fields attest to their presence and active participation in the formation of the economic development in that state as well as in the southwestern United States. Herminia Flores, former *betabelera* and current journalist, describes this influence. Upon the occasion of her first visit to the Farm and Ranch Museum in Gering, Nebraska, she asserts, "The back room is packed full of yesterday's farm and ranch equipment. As I tried to visually absorb everything, I realized that I was seeing much more than old machinery. I was glimpsing the agonies, defeats, victories, and joys of working the Lord's land. . . . People's bodies were the most used and valuable machinery" (*Gering Courier*, June 5, 2008).[22]

Yes, the *betabeleros* spoke with their bodies. Initially arriving as sojourners in the migrant worker cycle, they brought along their familiarity of the latifundista system and its Texan and southwestern U.S. analogues. After many decades toiling in the fields, most became settlers by the family's third generation of beet workers.[23] Due to advances in the sugar industry's technology as well as increased educational opportunities for the *betabeleros* and their children, the majority of the family's fourth generation broke the field-worker chain. In doing so, they contributed significantly to the forging of America. And, thanks to them, the sugar beet industry grew into one of the most prominent and prosperous trades in Western Nebraska throughout the twentieth and into the twenty-first centuries. This regional story provides a glimpse of the global sugar-industrial narrative and places it alongside the myriad other local sugar cultures throughout the world.

Notes

1. Purposive sampling was utilized in selecting narrators based on the author's personal connections as well as recommendations by one of the Latina leaders in the community. Interviews were conducted in sites chosen by the interviewees, i.e., private home (2), workplace (2), public restaurant (2), and telephone (1). The discussions, overall, were extemporaneous, allowing the interviewees to guide the sessions. Additional questions from the author's prepared research guide about the beet work itself along with the family's involvement with the growers and sugar factory supplemented the dialogue if not covered in the free-flowing portion of the interview.

2. An example of a commonality is that the primary sugar factory in Western Nebraska throughout the twentieth century, Great Western, also owned the main sugar factories in Colorado. One instance demonstrating regional differences is that Nebraska is part of the Midwest; Colorado, the West.

3. The latifundista system refers to the landholding system in Latin America. A latifundio is a farm with enough land to provide employment to more than the owner's family, e.g., over twelve workers.

4. The Colorado cities were Loveland, Greeley, Eaton, Fort Collins, Longmont, and Windsor.

5. McWilliams also reports that the use of irrigation actually had its beginnings with Spanish and Mexican efforts. They established the significance of irrigation and had cultivated a comprehension of its procedures when the territory was under Spanish and Mexican rule. Their precursive utilization of irrigation knowledge and techniques is a powerful cultural contribution and connection between the early Spanish and Mexican settlers in the old Spanish borderlands and the twentieth-century *betabeleros*.

6. While the Great Western Sugar Company's jurisdiction started in 1909, this first factory in Western Nebraska incorporated as the Scottsbluff Sugar Company with its place of business listed as Denver. The Scottsbluff community commonly referred to the factory by that name in its first year. After that initial time, even though no legal name change happened until 1916, the industry became known as GW in Nebraska. In 1916, the GW officially appointed an agent on February 24; the Scottsbluff Sugar Company publicly withdrew on July 25. Henry T. Johnson, in his master's thesis, reported the change resulting from a "few kinks in the law."

7. For more details about these periods and immigration patterns, see the volume's Introduction.

8. Pat and Carlotta Dominguez both lived into their nineties, passing away in late 2008 in Scottsbluff, Nebraska.

9. Coincidentally, the certificates also supplied supplemental information such as height and weight of the worker and number of family members.

10. This neighborhood remains predominantly Latino in the twenty-first century.

11. In addition to the taped interview for the video documentary, the Dominguezes were interviewed for Christensen's centennial history of Scottsbluff.

12. Dolores's situation was unusual as she was both German Russian (maternal) and Mexican (paternal). Very few biracial marriages took place, especially in the 1920s when her parents wed. Sadly, she died in October 2008, just a few months after the interview.

13. While Rachel's mother and the children worked the beet fields, Rachel's father had additional positions in the agricultural sector. For example, he worked in the granary as well as a slaughterhouse. During the October harvest campaigns, the sugar factory employed him as a shift worker.

14. For this 1923 report, Miss Robie O. Sargent and other "workers" in Nebraska assisted primary investigator Miss Sarah A. Brown. Still alive and well in 2009, the National Child Labor Committee (NCLC) is a private organization founded in 1904 and incorporated by an act of Congress in 1907 to promote child welfare in relation to work and working (http://www.nationalchildlabor.org).

15. In the existing laws at that time, no contract work was allowed, even with a parent, for a child under twelve years of age. Children aged twelve and older were prohibited from working more than eight hours per day. The NCLC urged the implementation of compulsory school attendance.

16. These laws were current through the 2008 legislative session.

17. The baby boomer generation includes persons born between 1946 and 1964; Generation X, 1968 to 1979. With all of the former laborers whom the author interviewed, the baby boomers were primarily third-generation *betabeleros*.

18. *Sweet Memories* (Geil Third Grade Class 1995) includes a written account of an oral interview with Jennie Vostades. An image of her father's Beet Workers Association card is included. Mr. Vostades's union card was issued from Fort Lupton, Colorado. He and his family lived near the town of Bayard, Nebraska. The Trade Union Unity League was an umbrella labor organization under the Communist Party of the United States and only in existence from 1929 to 1935. Donato (2007) reports that in 1935, the beet workers who had been involved with the American Federa-

tion of Labor associated with the AFL's new organization, the Agricultural Workers Union (AWU). The new state organization that formed as a result was the Colorado Conference of Beet Field and Agricultural Unions. The new group's relationship to Nebraska workers is not known to this author. Thus, *betabeleros'* interactions with unions, direct and indirect, make up a verdant area for further exploration.

19. Erin Brockovich, in her first advocacy campaign, was a lone advocate fighting an industrial-poisoning cover-up by the Pacific Gas and Electronic Company (PG&E). These efforts were communicated in film through a 2000 docudrama with Julia Roberts portraying Ms. Brockovich.

20. Rosa hosted Spanish-language radio spots for workers to know their rights. She also went to places where the migrant workers were, such as migrant clinics, Panhandle Community Service Agencies, and churches, to talk with workers directly. When possible, she worked with the town's social workers and other professionals to educate them on the unique context of the migrant workers.

21. Rosa shares that the most common problem she encountered was wage disputes, such as shortchanging the workers on acreage; for example, paying for 80 acres when 100 acres were actually worked. Another difficulty was growers treating the farmworker as an independent contractor. This meant that the laborers had the tax burden rather than the farmer. Also, often just one check would be cut for an entire crew. The designated person would then be required to cash it and distribute the funds to his or her colleagues. This action contained a double injustice: The amount was often large and counted against the wage holder for needed family benefits such as food stamps. Second, none of the other workers had a written record of their wages or work history. As such, the majority of Rosa's negotiations were requests to growers to cut individual checks for each worker.

22. Gering is the seat of Scotts Bluff County and is situated directly across the North Platte River from the city of Scottsbluff.

23. I am indebted to Dennis Nodín Valdés for coining the terms *sojourner* for workers of the *betabelero* migrant cycle and *settler* for families who maintained permanent homes in the communities where they worked the fields.

Works Cited

Anderson, Esther S. 1925. "The Beet Sugar Industry of Nebraska as a Response to Geographic Environment." *Economic Geography* 1, no. 3: 373–86.

Arrington, Leonard J. 1967. "Science, Government, and Enterprise in Economic Development: The Western Beet Sugar Industry." *Agricultural History* 41, no. 1: 1–18.

Broadbent, Elizabeth. [1941] 1972. "The Distribution of Mexican Population in the United States." PhD diss., University of Chicago; reprint, San Francisco: R and R Research.

Carranza, Miguel. 2008. Interview by Tisa M. Anders. Tape recording. May 30. Lincoln, Neb.

Christensen, Donald E. 1999. *Coming Home to Scottsbluff, Nebraska: The First One Hundred Years*. Virginia Beach, Va.: Donning.

Cobos, Rosa. 2009. Phone interview by Tisa M. Anders. February 13. Scottsbluff, Neb.

Dominguez, Pat, and Carlotta Dominguez. 2001. Interview in *La Vida: A Journey of Latinos throughout Nebraska*. VHS. Lincoln, Neb.: University of Lincoln Television at the NE-ETV Network.

Donato, Rubén. 2007. *Mexicans and Hispanos in Colorado Schools and Communities, 1920–1960*. Albany: State University of New York.

Durand, Jorge, Douglas S. Massey, and Chiara Capoferro. 2005. "The New Geography of Mexican Immigration." In *New Destinations: Mexican Immigration in the United States*, ed. Victor Zuñiga and Rubén Hernández-León, 1–20. New York: Russell Sage Foundation.

Feder, Ernest. 1971. *The Rape of the Peasantry: Latin America's Landholding System*. Garden City, N.Y.: Doubleday.

Fenster, C. R., and D. D. Baltensperger. n.d. *Breaking the Ground: The Evolution of Farming in the Panhandle of Nebraska through 2002*. Lincoln: University of Nebraska, Panhandle Research and Extension Center.

Flores, Herminia. 2008. Interview by Tisa M. Anders. Tape recording. May 16. Scottsbluff, Neb.

Geil Third Grade Class. 1995. *Sweet Memories: Our Heritage through Sugar Beets*. Mitchell, Neb.: Western Plains Business Forms.

Gonzales, Rachel. 2008. Interview by Tisa M. Anders. May 19. Scottsbluff, Neb.

Gouveia, Lourdes, Miguel A. Carranza, and Jasney Cogua. 2005. "The Great Plains Migration: Mexicanos and Latinos in Nebraska." In *New destinations: Mexican Immigration in the United States*, ed. Victor Zuñiga and Rubén Hernández-León, 23–49. New York: Russell Sage Foundation.

Gouveia, Lourdes, and Donald D. Stull. 1997. *Latino Immigrants, Meatpacking, and Rural Communities: A Case Study of Lexington, Nebraska*. Research Report No. 6. East Lansing, Mich.: Julian Samora Research Institute.

Grajeda, Ralph. 1976. "Chicanos: The Mestizo Heritage." In *Broken Hoops and Plains People*, 47–98. Lincoln: Nebraska Curriculum Development Center.

Grajeda, Ralph. 1998. "Mexicans in Nebraska." In *Our Treasures: A Celebration of Nebraska's Mexican Heritage/Nuestro tesoros: Una celebración de la Mexicana de Nebraska*, 15–23. Lincoln: Nebraska State Historical Society and Mexican American Commission.

Hamilton, Candy. 2009. *Footprints in the Sugar: A History of the Great Western Sugar Company*. Ontario, Ore.: Hamilton Bates.

Johnson, Henry Theodore. 1934. "History of the Beet Sugar Industry in Nebraska." Master's thesis, University of Nebraska.

Lindsay, Samuel McCune. 1924. *Children Working in the Sugar Beet Fields of the North Platte Valley of Nebraska*. New York City: National Child Labor Committee.

Mapes, Kathleen. 2009. *Sweet Tyranny: Migrant Labor, Industrial Agriculture, and Imperial Politics*. Urbana: University of Illinois Press.

McMillen, Becky. 2005. *Sweet Success—The Growing Season* (DVD). Scottsbluff, Neb.: Insight Creative Digital Video Production.

McWilliams, Carey. 1948. *North from Mexico: The Spanish-Speaking People of the United States.* New York: Praeger.

Nebraska Department of Labor. 1910, 1915, 1916. Secretary of State Records. http://nebpubdocs.unl.edu/ (accessed October 26, 2012).

Nebraska Department of Labor. 2012. Child Labor Law. http://dol.nebraska.gov/resources/Statutes/Child%20Labor%20Law.pdf (accessed October 27, 2012).

Nodín Valdés, Dennis. 1989. "The New Northern Borderlands: An Overview of Midwestern Chicano History." In *Perspectives in Mexican American Studies in the Midwest,* vol. 2, ed. Juan R. García, 1–28. Tucson: University of Arizona Press.

Nodín Valdés, Dennis. 1990. "Settlers, Sojourners, and Proletarians: Social Formation in the Great Plains Sugar Beet Industry, 1890–1940." *Great Plains Quarterly* 10, no. 2: 110–23.

Norris, Jim. 2002/2003. "Bargaining for Beets: Migrants and Growers in the Red River Valley." *Minnesota History* 58, no. 4: 196–209.

Norris, Jim. 2005. "Growing Up Growing Sugar: Local Teenage Labor in the Sugar Beet Fields, 1958–1974." *Agricultural History* 79, no. 3: 298–320.

Norris, Jim. 2009. *North for the Harvest: Mexican Workers, Growers, and the Sugar Beet Industry.* St Paul: Minnesota Historical Society.

Olivares, Dora. 2008. Interview by Tisa M. Anders. Tape recording. May 17. Scottsbluff, Neb.

Olivares, Olga. 2008. Interview by Tisa M. Anders. Tape recording. June 1. Lincoln, Neb.

Preston, Jack. 2002. "Heyward G. Leavitt's Influence on Sugar Beets and Irrigation in Nebraska." *Agricultural History* 76, no. 2: 381–92.

Preston, Jack. 2009. "Contract for Hand Labor for the Season of 1938." Unpublished document, Farm and Ranch Museum Archives, Gering, Neb.

Ramsey, Jane Barbour. 1999. *Scottsbluff: Evolution of a City, 1900–2000.* Estes Park, Colo.: Alpenaire.

Reisler, Mark. 1976. *By the Sweat of Their Brow: Mexican Immigrant Labor in the United States, 1900–1940.* Westport, Conn.: Greenwood.

Rowan, James E. 1948. "Mechanization of the Sugar Beet Industry of Scottsbluff County, Nebraska." *Economic Geography* 24, no. 3: 174–80.

Taylor, Paul S. 1928. *Mexican Labor in the United States: Valley of the South Platte, Colorado.* Vol. 1, no. 2. Berkeley: University of California Press.

Taylor, Paul S. 1967. "Hand Laborers in the Western Sugar Beet Industry." *Agricultural History* 41, no. 1: 19–26.

Vallejo, Pete. 2008. Interview by Tisa M. Anders. Tape recording. May 16. Scottsbluff, Neb.

Western Sugar Company. n.d. *Process Information. Welcome to Western Sugar: Nebraska Region.* Scottsbluff, Neb.: Western Sugar Company.

Wright, Dolores. 2008. Interview by Tisa M. Anders. Tape recording. May 31. Omaha, Neb.

CHAPTER 3

Latinos and the Churches in Idaho, 1950–2000

ERROL D. JONES

With its headwaters tumbling out of the snowcapped Teton Mountains strad-dling the Idaho-Wyoming border to the east, the Snake River churns across the southern Idaho plains, then turns northward before reaching the Oregon border, where it forms the boundary between the two states. An army of engineers descended upon the Snake and its tributaries in the twentieth century, damming its waters for agriculture and industry, building canals, and pumping water onto its arid expanses. Sage-covered plains and valleys yielded to expansive farms that produced an abundance of potatoes, sugar beets, onions, alfalfa, peas, hops, fruit trees, and, more recently, grapes. Sugar beets and potatoes dominated crop production in the first half of the twentieth century, creating a demand for seasonal labor unfulfilled by resident farm families. As early as 1904 with the construction of the first sugar beet rendering plant in southeastern Idaho, plant owners sent recruiters to the Mexican border to entice workers to make the long journey to the state and work in the beet fields. Railroad companies pushed their lines into Idaho, opening up more land to agriculture and commerce and providing work for Mexican and other immigrants. From that time to the Great Depression, Mexicans and Mexican Americans trekked into southern Idaho for the agricultural season, mingling culturally with small permanent Mexican communities in the region's farming towns.

Even before statehood in 1890, Mexican and a few other Latino pioneers settled in Idaho, drawn to the remote region out of curiosity or to exploit its natural resources. These early pioneers plied various trades: mining, cattle ranching, mule packing, saddle making, farming, and homemaking. There weren't many, but some made significant contributions to the early economic development of the state. This generation introduced "a wide spectrum of Mexican American culture, from traditional values, social and spiritual practices, music and food" (Gamboa 1992: 7) and laid the foundation of today's Mexican American communities in Idaho. Haltingly, even during the Great Depression, these communities grew, so that today the state's Mexican American/Latino population makes up more than 11 percent of the total.

Idaho is not known as a state with a significant Latino presence, but people from Latin American countries, mostly from Mexico, have called Idaho home since the mid-nineteenth century. Few in numbers until the 1970s, they nevertheless created small communities in the southern agricultural region of the state and put pressure on the dominant society to recognize their unique cultural differences. This chapter will examine the relationship between people of Mexican/Latino descent and Idaho's established churches from the 1950s into the twenty-first century. The story that unravels does not appear to be unique to Idaho in that it evokes similarities to other Pacific Northwest states, but it differs significantly from Mexican American's religious history in the border states of Arizona, California, New Mexico, and Texas, where their numbers were greater and their history richer and more complex.

Until the 1980s, Idaho was overwhelmingly rural and small-town, whose economy was dominated by agriculture, mining, and timber extraction. The mainstream population of white Euro-Americans embraced rural values of family, community, and faith. They distrusted government, were wary of strangers, fostered conservative and traditional ideals, and expected others to conform. Most of these people had migrated to Idaho from America's Heartland states of Oklahoma, Kansas, Arkansas, Missouri, Nebraska, and Iowa. More so than in its northwestern neighbors of Montana, Oregon, and Washington, religion played a larger role in the daily and community life

Table 3.1.

	Latino population of Idaho		Total population
1870	60	0.3%	22,000
1920	1,215	0.3%	431,866
1950	2,365	0.4%	588,637
1960	3,341	0.5%	667,191
1980	36,560	3.9%	944,000
1990	53,000	5.3%	1,004,000
2000	101,690	7.9%	1,293,953
2010	175,901	11.2%	1,567,582

of Idaho's citizens. For Mexican nationals and Mexican Americans who migrated to Idaho during most of the twentieth century, religion, family, community, and traditional values dominated their lives and made them feel at home in their new state. With the exception of the period since the 1980s, most Latinos who migrated to Idaho came either directly from small villages and towns in Mexico or from the Rio Grande Valley or other small Texas farming towns. Except for the small numbers of Native Americans, almost all of Idaho's people migrated from the American and Mexican heartlands.

Migrant Farmworkers and Idaho's Churches, 1950s and 1960s

Despite some values held in common, migrants of Mexican heritage who came to Idaho to stay permanently or to work seasonally and move on carried with them religious and cultural attributes markedly different from those of the dominant culture. Excepting Native Americans, quickly dispatched to reservations, most Idahoans descended from western Europeans. Of those who professed a religion, the Church of Jesus Christ of Latter-day Saints (Mormons) dominated the Snake River basin, or southern half of the state, followed by Protestants, and Catholics.[1] Not until after World War II did any of the established churches, with few exceptions, make significant efforts to proselytize or welcome into their congregations the increasing number of Mexican and Mexican American newcomers, most of whom were nominally Catholic. In the 1950s, however, southern Idaho's religious establishment awakened to the presence of a growing number of people of Mexican descent in their midst and took action to learn about them, help them with their social needs, and draw them into their congregations. From March to November in the 1950s, Idaho farmers could count on about nine thousand migrant laborers bringing their families to the farms and labor camps of the Snake River Valley. They were mostly Mexican Americans from the rural Rio Grande Valley of Texas, and migrancy for many had become a way of life, following the crops year after year. Working in a chaotic and unprotected labor market, migrant farmworkers had little or no education. Often abused, cheated of their wages, injured on the job, and housed in filthy, dangerous, unsanitary labor camps, no national or Idaho laws existed to protect them. The National Labor Relations Board offered no protection. Grievances, if voiced, fell on deaf ears. The federal Fair Labor Standards Act of 1938 did not apply to farmworkers.

Paradoxically, while Idaho agriculture depended for its success on migrant labor, the migrants and their families engendered community resentment. Often living in insufferable and unsanitary conditions, the migrants found it difficult to keep clean. They drove broken-down jalopies and pickup trucks, if they had a vehicle. Their dark skin and unkempt appearances, their inability to speak English well, if at all, and their practice of hauling their kids out to the fields to work or to keep an eye on them caused anxiety among many Idahoans glad to see them go at the end of the harvest season. Some thought migrants a drain on community resources, and still do, causing taxes to increase if they sent their children to school or had to use county health facilities. Few Idahoans realized the perils of migrancy. Migrants endured haphazard and irregular schooling for their children. They lacked decent, affordable, and sanitary housing and struggled to maintain wholesome family relationships. The migrant life robbed them of voting privileges, stable incomes, and health and welfare services available to local residents. "Time and again the cumulative negatives surrounding migrancy break through to fascinate and appall the public conscience," wrote an expert observer. "The thorny questions they raise generate strong feelings. Faced with pressures from powerful farm groups and dwarfed by larger issues, they simply stay lost" (Shotwell 1961: 37).[2]

But they would not "stay lost" for long. Changing economic conditions in Idaho's agriculture sector and stirring consciences among religious groups came together to help improve somewhat the lives of migrants in the 1950s and 1960s. Much of this was owed to national political, economic, and social occurrences that had a transforming effect in Idaho. To meet the pressing need for migrant housing, the federal Farm Security Administration (FSA) during the Great Depression began construction and operation of a series of model farm labor camps, two of which were built near the Snake River in Twin Falls and Caldwell, Idaho. Unfortunately, there were never enough. Migrants not so fortunate to find a place in one of those camps had to settle for whatever was available at the price they could afford in other areas. Oftentimes that meant sleeping in a car, in farmers' sheds or chicken coops, or in tents pitched at the edge of a field. In the late 1940s, the federal government closed some camps and sold the rest to local governments (like the Twin Falls and Caldwell camps) or to private farmers' associations. In nearly all cases, federal housing and sanitation standards, clinics, schools, and recreational facilities were tossed along with self-governing camp councils.

President Harry Truman's 1950 Commission on Migrant Labor made recommendations on housing, transportation, health, welfare, child care, education, working conditions, and labor-management relations but secured no concrete gains. Four years later, President Dwight D. Eisenhower appointed the cabinet-level President's Committee on Migrant Labor. The new committee extended Social Security coverage to farm labor and migrants in 1955. It also authorized the Interstate Commerce Commission to regulate the transportation of farmworkers over seventy-five miles and across state lines in privately owned trucks and buses. By 1960, twenty-eight states, including Idaho where agriculture was the number one industry, had migratory labor committees on the federal pattern. These in turn stimulated a variety of legislative measures relating to migrant labor.

Nudged by the President's Committee, pressured by Idaho's Protestant churches affiliated with the National Council of Churches Migrant Ministry (NCCMM), the Catholic Church's Boise Diocese, and various labor organizations, the Idaho legislature created the Governor's Migratory Labor Committee in 1955. It oversaw modest attempts to improve housing conditions and issued annual reports. The best camps (Twin Falls and Caldwell) provided adequate housing but others were intolerable, with little or no running water and dangerously unsanitary conditions. Some dated from the early part of the century when sugar companies built one- and two-room wood-frame houses for migrants near rendering plants. Individual farmers and farmers' associations provided space for tents and sometimes built shacks for the workers. But these poor dwellings repelled migrants and attracted widespread criticism from state officials, the press, and religious groups.

The Southern Idaho Migrant Ministry

Most migrants of Mexican heritage considered themselves Catholics, and since 1949 some parishes in Idaho made modest efforts to minister to their spiritual needs. Others gravitated toward Protestant (some Pentecostal) churches. Several mainline Protestant churches in the early 1950s, primarily in the Minidoka area of southern Idaho, peppered the NCCMM with requests to establish a migrant ministry in their area. After four years of solicitations, the NCCMM carried out a demonstration project in the Caldwell labor camp in southwestern Idaho. Local migrant ministry programs experimented in other areas of southern Idaho during the summer of 1955. Under the direction of Betty Whitaker from the NCCMM, who also had jurisdiction over the Oregon Migrant Ministry, several southern Idaho churches organized committees during the 1956 migrant season and late that fall united in Boise as the Southern Idaho Migrant Ministry (SIMM).

Two fundamental objectives underlay SIMM's mission. The first sought to alleviate the unfortunate conditions migrants endured in their daily lives by promoting labor camp improvements, public health advances, day care centers, and remedial education for adults and children alike and to mobilize community resources and attempt to convert the community from "indifference and hostility to acceptance and welcome" (SIMM 1968). The second objective aimed to bring about political and economic structural change that would remove problems responsible for the plight of migrants. By far the biggest challenge, this latter goal brought Idaho's progressive church leaders up against entrenched political and economic groups that regarded structural change a threat to their vital interests. SIMM leaders sought basic economic and social readjustments designed to empower migrants and help lift them out of poverty. For example, they believed that farm labor under supervision of the National Labor Relations Board should have the right to organize and bargain collectively. Social services should be extended to them without traditional residence requirements that "tend to deny to this class of worker the privileges that most other citizens enjoy" (SIMM 1968). Moreover, SIMM lobbied for a litany of legal reforms, such as elimination of Public Law 78 that extended the Bracero Program enabling growers to bring contract labor into the United States from Mexico and removing agriculture's exemption from carrying workers compensation insurance. In the end, attacking symptoms of migrant poverty proved far easier for SIMM than removing obstacles that kept migrants in poverty. But in its efforts, SIMM demonstrated to the migrants that they had friends who welcomed them into their communities and cared about them as people making an important contribution to society.[3]

A primary concern for SIMM member churches was to improve living conditions in the labor camps and to put pressure on the Governor's Migratory Labor Committee to draw up and enforce health regulations for migrant camps. After a four-year study, the committee called a public hearing on April 30, 1959, to review its new migratory labor camp health and sanitation regulations. Documents from that hearing revealed that Idaho's migrant agricultural workers, besides living in squalor, faced ignorance, prejudice, fear, and a preoccupation with cost over human needs. Despite objections raised in the hearing, many of which were absurd and racist, the new health and sanitation regulations went into effect that year.[4]

After that date, the Governor's Migratory Labor Committee annually conducted on-site inspections of the camps and issued public reports. With insured loans provided by the federal government under the 1961 Housing Act, many farm labor camp associations had complied with state health regulations by 1965 and the committee reported that most of the seventy-three camps inspected "have a healthful atmosphere, and the buildings are generally well constructed and properly maintained" (Idaho Advisory Committee to the U.S. Commission on Civil Rights 1980: 12). Conditions at a few, however, continued to be unbearable. After repeated citations of the American Falls labor camp, inspectors recommended either tearing it down for rebuilding or closing it altogether. When camp owners stalled, a frustrated official lamented that it was like "butting your head against a stone wall" (*Boise Intermountain Observer* 1969).[5]

Unfortunately, the governor's committee stopped functioning after 1969. Migrant camp standards lapsed, and the State Department of Health ceased to enforce health standards in the camps, leaving it to regional health districts whose oversight was limited to water and sanitation. As a recruiter for out-of-state migrant farm labor, the State Department of Employment was to "guarantee adequate housing and healthful labor camp conditions at the job site" (Idaho Advisory Committee to the U.S. Commission on Civil Rights 1980: 12), but by 1976 it no longer inspected camps. The Idaho Migrant Council, a private nonprofit organization formed in 1971, took up migrant housing problems and made efforts to improve and advocate for adequate health standards in the camps. From then on, except in the case of workers brought to Idaho under the H-2A temporary agricultural labor visa, the state abdicated its responsibility to regulate and inspect migrant camps to the Migrant Council, local communities, and the owners of private labor camps.

In 1958, two years after its formation, SIMM leaders, both lay and religious, concluded that effective action on behalf of migrants and long-range financial support depended on the creation of a state council of churches. Migrant Ministry leaders felt that their program was only one of several that demanded the formation of such a council. Therefore, SIMM's executive committee drew up a constitution for a state council of churches with SIMM, an agency or committee under the council's jurisdiction, apparently the only migrant ministry in the country out of which grew a state council of churches rather than the other way around. Meanwhile, SIMM continued to function, now under the direction of Sarah Hall Goodwin, who became its director in 1958 when Betty Whitaker transferred to Texas. An effective leader of SIMM and the Oregon Migrant Ministry for the next six years, Goodwin also shared major responsibility with the executive committee and others for putting the Idaho Council of Churches (ICC) into operation. On January 18, 1965, almost a full decade after the migrant ministry's creation, the requisite number of denominations accepted the constitution and the ICC began to function. The Roman Catholic Diocese of Boise joined as an active participant in the ICC's social outreach programs, which were composed primarily of Protestant churches like Lutherans, Presbyterians, Episcopalians, and Methodists. Mormons, the largest single denomination in the state, however, did not join the council or participate in the Migrant Ministry.

Mainline Protestant church leaders involved in the Migrant Ministry from its inception realized the majority of Mexican American migrants were Catholics and that the Roman Catholic Diocese of Boise had, in parishes with large numbers of migrants, urged its priests to visit labor camps and offer sacraments to the faithful. To avoid conflicts with their Catholic collaborators, Protestants offering social services in the camps made a point of not proselytizing. At times this created dissention within local committees like

Caldwell's where the Salvation Army balked at offering social services without attempting conversions. The Catholic Church in Idaho had expressed
particular concern about Mormons and Protestants making conversions
among traditionally Catholic Mexicans and Mexican Americans. Although
local SIMM committees refrained from proselytizing, Mormons and Pente-
costals sent missionaries among the migrants and lured some away from the
Catholic Church. Mormons did not achieve great success within the migrant
and ex-migrant communities despite Catholic fears and claims. By 1996, only
eight small Mormon Spanish-speaking congregations existed in the state.

Over the course of SIMM's initial decade, migrant programs gradually
changed in form and purpose. Education of migrant children became a
priority. The ministry encouraged school districts to integrate the migrant
children into regular classes and to provide summer school programs to help
them eliminate deficiencies. State legislation, after extensive SIMM lobbying, authorized local school districts to levy a small tax to support migrant
education programs, but few took advantage of the law. A major obstacle
was the lack of school personnel with the understanding of and sensitivity
toward children from the Mexican American migrant culture. Recognizing
this, the Migrant Ministry developed a program to bring volunteer teachers
from the border region of Texas to teach in their summer remedial program
at the Caldwell and other labor camps. Large numbers of volunteers and
Spanish-speaking college students worked the camps. But a sense of paternalism and noblesse oblige emerged among the Anglo volunteers who did not
have migrant backgrounds. Teachers' reports from the late 1960s lamented
the severe educational, emotional, and social disadvantages children suffered
on account of their migrant lives. Still, remedial and vacation Bible school
programs flourished and were extended. Recreational programs continued
to thrive, as did sewing classes, a traveling bookmobile, regular visits from
health care providers, and various service projects.[6]

In Twin Falls and other areas, local funding supported college student
summer services. Local funds fell short, however, in other regions and SIMM
used its scant resources to staff and run well-designed annual workshops
to train local volunteers. Always underfunded and reliant on volunteers,
SIMM's budget depended on contributions offered by its member congregations, one of which, the Mennonites, helped broker a deal with the Mennonite National Council in Elkhart, Indiana, to place a volunteer couple
year-round at the Caldwell labor camp. Living at the camp, the Mennonite
family integrated itself into the migrant community. They learned Spanish,
organized educational and social activities for adults and youths, taught in
the day care center, interpreted residents' needs to the churches, and served
as a liaison between migrant families in the camp and Caldwell's outside

community agencies. Moreover, they helped orient and establish another Mennonite couple at the Nyssa labor camp across the border in southeastern Oregon. There was a permanent Mennonite presence in the Caldwell camp throughout the 1960s.

In 1960 the National Migrant Ministry initiated a series of annual meetings of state migrant ministries to advance common long-range goals, create a more flexible organization to meet the changing needs of migrants, and develop a unified instrument for social change. SIMM sent representatives to all of these meetings. Consequently it was drawn more deeply into the national organization's unwavering focus to craft policies and legislation at the national level that would enable migrants to live dignified lives and achieve permanent solutions to migrancy and poverty. Rather than simply alleviate unfortunate local conditions, SIMM and its leaders came to consider the broader aspects of the migrant situation in the wider context of the farm problem in its entirety. Progressive leaders like Merle Wells, Mildred Liming, Sarah Hall Goodwin, Irwin Schweibert, and many others saw the need to educate Idahoans, specifically growers and processors, of the inevitability of changing the migrant situation. Hopefully, by preparing the entire community to accept and welcome some major and fundamental adjustments in the farm labor system, SIMM leaders wished to improve the migrants' situation. Aware of the tumultuous history of farmworker struggles in the United States and watching closely the unfolding conflict between César Chávez's United Farm Workers Union (UFW) and California's powerful agribusinesses, SIMM leaders concluded that unionization and collective bargaining would sweep the industry. Idaho would not be spared. Predicting future tension and conflict on Snake River Valley farms, SIMM wanted to show migrant workers that they had friends and supporters. Simultaneously, the ministry sought to interpret the need for change and help growers and processors understand and fear them less. For Idaho to adapt to the "solution of the migrant problem reasonably and with a minimum of friction and disorder" became a principal goal for the Migrant Ministry after 1965 (SIMM 1968).

Liberals' enthusiasm for civil rights reform promoted an agenda embraced by the Democratic administrations of John Kennedy and Lyndon Johnson that also included reforming the agricultural sector. Throughout the decade of the 1950s, the national Migrant Ministry urged Congress to end Public Law 78 (PL 78), a law that allowed U.S. farmers to bring Mexican contract labor into the country. Migrant Ministry leaders contended that huge agricultural corporations imported the labor as a way to keep wages down in their sector. Smaller family operations lowered wages as well in order to compete. Southwestern families reliant on farm labor for their livelihood could not survive on bracero wages and were forced to migrate to areas where braceros were not used and hopefully wages were higher. This pushed them permanently into the migrant stream, keeping them in poverty, and disrupting normal family life. End PL 78, critics claimed, and wages would rise and the migrant stream would dry up. SIMM activists understood that few braceros worked in Idaho, but if Congress overturned PL 78, fewer migrants would come to Idaho, raising wages for those who did and for locals attracted to farm labor by higher wages. They soon got their wish. In the 1961 congressional session, PL 78 supporters got another extension, but it was the last. Three years later, the bracero program came to an end.[7]

SIMM followed the lead of the national Migrant Ministry and pushed for other reforms as well. They championed the Health Services Bill that would provide funds to those areas where many migrants worked. It passed in 1962, but Congress failed to appropriate the money for it. They lobbied as well for a federal mandate to license labor contractors. Called crew leaders in Texas and the eastern United States, contractors were often heads of families that drew in distant relatives and friends. In many parts of the western United States, crew leaders were known as labor contractors. Oregon law distinguished between the two: crew leaders had to be registered with the state, and labor contractors needed to be licensed and bonded. The law defined crew leaders as spokesmen for a crew, working alongside them in the field, supervising and transporting them. Their compensation came from farmers. Labor contractors, on the other hand, signed contracts with growers or farmers' associations to provide workers at a predetermined sum. From that amount the contractor paid workers and provided them with transportation to and from the work site. The number of workers involved and the value of some of these contracts obligated labor contractors to obtain a state license to lessen the possibility of fraud. Some labor contractors had grown rich providing these services. It was big business. The interstate nature of some large labor contractors demonstrated the need for federal regulation. One contractor, for example, operated his business out of Washington with branches in Oregon, California, Idaho, and Texas. He had vehicles registered in several states and at times employed as many as twenty-two crew leaders, bringing him daily profits of $800 in 1960 dollars ($6,201.55 in 2012).

Worker complaints against contractor abuse in Idaho and the Pacific Northwest harked back to the beginning of the century and even before. Unscrupulous contractors were notorious for cheating workers of their wages, virtually enslaving them on farms. They beat and intimidated those who objected and who attempted to organize others. They further enriched themselves by making deals with grocers, who charged higher prices to workers and gave contractors kickbacks, and/or by monopolizing gambling, alcoholic beverages, and even prostitution. In part, contractor abuses pushed workers to strike Idaho farms on several occasions prior to the 1960s. Aware of such maltreatment, local SIMM committees urged passage of federal and state legislation forcing contractor bonding and licensing. Unfortunately for migrants and other seasonal farm laborers, SIMM and its allies failed to convince Idaho's legislature that such regulation was needed. Not until 2002 did Idaho adopt a rather weak Farm Labor Contractor and Bonding law that has not eliminated abuses.[8]

Social legislation that sparked so much controversy in the early 1960s had been championed by the national Migrant Ministry and its state affiliates since 1951 when they called for agriculture's inclusion under existing federal labor legislation, a minimum wage, and the aforementioned end to foreign labor importation. They urged Congress to adopt a federal housing code for migrant camps, to force growers to provide clean water and toilet facilities in the fields, and to extend health and welfare services to migrants regardless of residence. They also pushed for stronger federal child labor laws (children must be fourteen or older) for the agriculture sector.

Even before publication of Rachel Carson's *Silent Spring* exposed the dangers that came from increased pesticide use in agriculture, the Migrant Ministry warned of the harmful effects to farmworkers handling pesticides on a daily basis. Medical authorities cautioned workers to avoid the cumulative effects by showering with plenty of soap and hot water after exposure and washing work clothes thoroughly before using them again. In most labor camps, this was almost impossible. Parathion, a widely used and highly toxic insecticide, was so dangerous that breathing it could be fatal, demonstrated at the time by the death of six of twelve workers using it on a farm in Florida. Dangers to workers applying toxic chemicals escalated as agriculture in Idaho became more reliant on them to control pests and weeds. SIMM expressed concern about chemical use and hoped improved sanitation facilities in the labor camps would mitigate the problem.

After mining and construction, the National Safety Council rated agriculture the country's third most dangerous industry (by 1994 farmwork had the highest death rate and third highest injury rate of any occupation in the country). Yet only California, Hawaii, Ohio, and Puerto Rico had compulsory workers' compensation for agricultural workers similar to that enjoyed by workers in other industries. In 1961 three-quarters of all state workers' compensation laws explicitly exempted agricultural workers. Idaho was one of them. SIMM leaders argued against this exclusion with little effect in the Idaho legislature. It would take several tragic accidents, a broad-based coalition of farmworker advocacy groups, religious leaders, and heightened public concern before the exemption was overturned in 1997.[9]

Agreement on many of the issues pushed by SIMM was not universal, nor was there consensus about which legislation should be state and which should be federal. How aggressively should the churches work for legislative reform? Some farmers active in these congregations even served on local Migrant Ministry committees, like Elmer Teigs and his wife, Esther, who owned a farm in Nampa. If a committee took a public stand on an issue like housing, sanitation, or minimum wage, it always ran the risk of alienating members tied to farm interests. In some states, Migrant Ministry workers were locked out of farmers'-association-owned labor camps altogether. Owing to southern Idaho's conservatism, suspicion of federal and state government, antiunion bias, and elements of racism, all so common in other Heartland states, SIMM was perhaps the only group that could effectively promote social change. Given the circumstances, it is surprising that it even tried and met with the success it did.

The hard work of advancing social causes and supporting migrants paid off for the national Migrant Ministry and its affiliated state committees in 1964. That year federal funds became available with passage of the Economic Opportunity Act to support the work of community action organizations and to create a wide variety of programs focusing on the elimination of poverty. SIMM saw this as an answer to its perennial funding problem and its desire to expand its services to those it had been unable to help. Adult and children's educational offerings had special possibilities. Preschool classes for young children were very successful and met a particularly severe migrant need. Preschool programs, or Head Start, could be offered by nonprofit, nongovernmental agencies if they incorporated local poverty group participation in development and management functions. This would ensure that middle-class organizers worked side by side with disadvantaged recipients in a common effort. The objective was to give those benefiting from the program opportunities to learn new skills, have a stake in the planned outcome, and move out of poverty.

SIMM leaders recognized that an entirely new Idaho agency was needed to provide an effective community action program for migrant farm families. Rather than each local area with migrant workers developing its own separate and independent community action program, they decided that a single Idaho application for federal grant funds had a better chance of success. With the legal basis laid for the new Idaho Council of Churches in January 1965, church leaders created and organized on February 4 a nonprofit migrant community action program called Idaho Farm Workers' Services, Inc. (IFWS). Although winter in Idaho found most Mexican American migrant workers away in Texas, planners included them in corporation policy and management. "Hispanic participation sometimes was limited because much essential work had to be undertaken when they were off in other places," wrote the principle author of the document of incorporation. "But," he added, "Hispanic attitudes and values had to dominate program development and had to be respected for effective operation" (Wells 1995: 8).[10]

IFWS built upon the impressive work SIMM committees had done for over a decade. Its staff and board of directors, a few of whom were Mexican American former migrant farmworkers like Max Vargas, Jesse Berain, and others, still·had strong ties to SIMM. But out of this new federally funded organization grew a greater awareness among Anglo participants of the need for more migrant involvement, a basic tenet of Office of Economic Opportunity programs. For example, Jesse Berain, a migrant from the lower Rio Grande Valley of Texas in the early 1950s, worked with SIMM's summer programs for many years and now managed IFWS's projects in Twin Falls. Although IFWS assistant director Max Vargas regarded Berain as somewhat controlling and the "self-appointed leader" of the Twin Falls migrant community, he gave into Berain's insistence that migrant lifestyles emphasizing family unity and activities not be altered. Berain observed that offering education classes on the basis of segregating students into age grades failed. He urged offering classes to family groups regardless of the children's ages. It proved more effective, as Catholic Charities of Idaho realized in a similar program funded in 2007. Cultural gaps between poor local Anglo kids and migrant children, Berain emphasized, could be bridged more effectively by combining both groups into summer camping excursions. It helped the children understand one another's heritage. Berain's work in Twin Falls greatly helped to bring Mexican American migrant leadership to the IFWS program and led to greater reliance on Latino leaders in other migrant communities, even though doing so caused some tension between local migrant ministries and IFWS headquarters in Boise.[11]

IFWS initiated several inventive educational reforms that had a wide impact. Extending Head Start "opportunities from conventional kindergarten classes to cover migrant needs in Idaho, in fact preceded those of any other state," wrote one informed observer. It "was regarded nationally as a model for other communities" (Szasz 2000: 136). After 1965 IWFS's migrant activities found their way into local school systems in areas of growing Latino population, where they assisted local schools to move toward more ethnically diverse programs. Despite setbacks with adult education in some areas, IFWS's Vargas persevered. One migrant higher education project he promoted sent a group of twenty-one young people to live for a year on a college campus, where they worked to pass their high school equivalency exam and to take preparation courses for entering the university. This was the forerunner for the High School Equivalency (HEP) and College Assistance Migrant (CAMP) programs functioning on many college campuses in Idaho and other states today. Above all, progress was made toward acceptance of Mexican American participation and leadership among the more progressive elements of the dominant Euro-American society.[12]

Church leadership and control of IFWS ended for the most part in 1967 when Congress for a time eliminated educational and other grants to nongovernmental community action programs. IFWS's short life was over. But the programs created lived on and were soon picked up by various government agencies operating elsewhere in Idaho and Oregon. Julio Pérez, a seasonal farmworker and member of SIMM's board of directors, urged the board in 1968 to maintain adult education programs. Job training and placement were crucial to those ex-migrants who settled in southern Idaho. He revealed that many men had been attending night class for three or four years and wanted to continue. Their goal was to speak English, obtain a high school diploma, and train for a vocation or trade. Their desire to break out of poverty and improve themselves was strong, he confided, a force that had not been there before. Some liked farmwork and wanted to continue on a year-round basis but with the right to organize and bargain for better wages and working conditions. Some of these goals came to be realized, but not under the control of Idaho's churches.[13]

Treasure Valley Community College in Ontario, Oregon, took over most federally funded antipoverty programs for southwestern Idaho and southeastern Oregon. With leadership drawn primarily from Anglo college administrators, a struggle erupted when Mexican American community activists sought control of some of the programs. The conflict gave birth to the Idaho Migrant Council (IMC), created when Lucy Peña Hunt, Humberto Fuentes, Pedro López, and Tony Solis took over Migrant Education from college administrators. Fuentes and friends channeled Office of Economic Opportunity funds into the new Migrant Council, run by and for farmworkers. Incorporated in 1971, the IMC would spend the next forty years, most of that time with Fuentes at the helm, serving Idaho's poorer Mexican Americans in the areas of health, education, and housing. SIMM disbanded the following year and became the Department of Agricultural Concerns, functioning as a subcommittee of the Idaho Council of Churches. Into the 1970s and beyond as the IMC strengthened its position in the state's agricultural affairs, migrant farmworker issues diminished in importance for the Protestant members of the ICC. The Anglo community and Idaho's churches began to take note of a new spirit among Mexican Americans settling permanently in their state, one of proud independence and assertive self-determination.[14]

Latinos and the Roman Catholic Diocese of Boise

Mainline Protestant churches took up other issues in the 1970s and 1980s, but the Roman Catholic Diocese of Boise, whose jurisdiction covered all of Idaho, increasingly turned its attention to Mexican American migrants and ex-migrants whose numbers and influence increased at that time. Just as Idaho's Protestant churches took their cue on numerous matters from the

National Council of Churches, so too the Catholic Diocese of Boise followed the lead of the United States Catholic Conference (USCC). The Boise Diocese of the 1960s reflected a similar profile to that of the United States Catholic Church in ethnic and class makeup of the priesthood, hierarchy, and lay leadership: it was overwhelmingly white, middle class, Irish, and German. If few Mexican Americans or Latinos entered seminaries at the national level, there were almost none in Idaho and the Pacific Northwest. Calls for reform emanating from the Second Vatican Council (1962–1965) and the 1968 Latin American Bishops Conference in Medellín, Colombia, reverberated throughout the church and fell upon the receptive ears of Boise's Bishop Sylvester Treinen. Soon after his consecration as Boise's fifth bishop in July 1962, Treinen attended some of the Second Vatican Council's sessions. Small and slight in stature and almost elfinlike, he "looked like someone balancing a large basket" on his head when wearing the bishop's biretta. A self-described "cautious progressive," he projected a "warm, humble personality," and worried sometimes about his suitability to be a bishop (Schoenberg 1987: 659).

Regardless, bishop he was, and as such he felt deep concern about the poor and disadvantaged of his diocese, many of whom were of Mexican origin. In 1969 he commissioned Father Nicolas Walsh (the church's representative on the executive board of the ICC and the IFWS and later bishop of Yakima, Washington) to undertake a diocese-wide study to determine their plight so that the church could pursue a proper course of action. Walsh's definition of "disadvantaged" was broad, but it was obvious that the majority who fit it were migrants, farmworkers, and minorities, especially the state's Native American population. During the course of his investigation, he visited all but three parishes in the diocese. Federal, state, and local officials supported his study and helped with information. All priests and most parishioners welcomed his visits, but some questioned the need. One skeptic told him, "We didn't have any poverty or unemployment problems until you started looking around" (Walsh 1969). At the conclusion of his study, Walsh sadly noted that a rather large segment of Idaho's population remained convinced that there was no poverty or disadvantaged people in the state despite the fact that in some counties over 30 percent of the population could not meet minimum subsistence standards. His report to the bishop identified four principal problems that the church and civil society needed to resolve: health, housing, unemployment, and education, in that order. Nevertheless, of the 145 questionnaires returned to him, only 67 thought the diocese should set up a "charities office."[15]

In the same year, 365 miles to the northwest, Yakima's Bishop Joseph Dougherty dispatched Fr. José Ybarra to do a similar survey in eight parishes heavily populated by Mexicans and Mexican Americans. He found the situation there similar to Walsh's discoveries in Idaho. A decade earlier, Spokane, Washington's, Bishop Bernard Topel, described as a kind of "St. Francis of Assisi" who "lived in an old house with no heat, no phone and little or no food," visited Walla Walla, Washington, in 1958, where he observed the deplorable conditions of the Mexican workers living amid the prosperity of the wider community. Topel's observations convinced him of the "need for a socially active church." He wrote, "When I saw how bad these conditions are, I realized anew the necessity of unions" (Garcia 2005: 242–43). Topel's position was the same as SIMM's Protestant and Catholic leaders. As it turned out, these liberal, progressive approaches put the churches in the center of a cultural storm. For religious leaders to adopt such a stance and fight for the needs of the underprivileged, to draw people of Mexican heritage into the folds of the church with their distinctive and unique culture and lower-class status, risked loss of membership, support, and money from its more conservative, traditional, middle-class congregants.[16]

Armed with Fr. Nicolas Walsh's survey and well versed in the obstacles farmworkers in Idaho faced to live a decent, dignified life, Bishop Treinen courageously defended their rights to organize. He proclaimed, "There is no good reason why farm laborers should not receive the same protection as everyone else . . . [t]hey have as much right . . . to organize and bargain collectively" (Treinen 1970). Treinen's statement came in response to a strike farmworkers called in 1970 against Elmer Teigs's farm in Canyon County. It is ironic that workers chose the Teigs farm to strike. Active for years in the Migrant Ministry through their local Nampa committee, Teigs's wife Esther had been a dynamic member of SIMM's board in the 1960s.

Accounts differ as to the cause of the strike, but it is clear that local strike leaders sought to organize farmworkers into a union affiliated with César Chávez's United Farm Workers Union (UFW). When two UFW representatives showed up the third day of the strike, growers disingenuously characterized the organizing effort as "instigated by a bunch of outside" interlopers (O'Hallora 1970). It was obvious to those involved that strike leaders hailed from Caldwell.[17] Despite the local nature of the organizers and the clear desire of Mexican American farmworkers to have some say about their wages and working conditions, growers rushed to lobby state political leaders to pass a law preventing strikes during harvest season and to characterize "efforts to obtain safe working conditions as 'unfair labor practices'" (*Boise Intermountain Observer* 1971). A temporary Agricultural Labor law passed in 1971 and growers' letters to Governor Cecil Andrus and Senator Frank Church revealed their fear of yielding to farm labor. Worried one farmer to Senator Church, "I wonder how anyone can doubt the serious situation the subversives have planned for our nation" (Jeppeson 1971). The following year, Governor Andrus signed a compromise bill granting collective bargaining rights to agricultural workers but with restrictions on strikes and boycotts.[18]

Bishop Treinen's support of farmworkers' right to organize and to bargain for better wages and working conditions was cautious and based on his belief that farmers should be able to do the same thing to protect their economic interests. What was novel, if only for Idaho, was the bishop's call for farmers to organize and raise prices for their produce rather than exacting tribute from workers by lowering their wages. Consumers should pay more for the bounty of the land, Treinen reasoned, if it meant that lower prices came at the expense of the laborers who produced it. The bishop sought to reconcile differences between growers and their workers, but the growers would have none of it. To them, facing an organized workforce, especially one allied with Chávez's UFW, meant losing control and threatened their individual rights. While the bishop and some Protestant leaders saw the freedom to organize as a basic human right protected by law and enforced by government, Idaho farmers who controlled the legislature regarded it as a radical attempt to overturn private property rights. In the spirit of the Second Vatican Council, Bishop Treinen came down on the side of extending rights to those traditionally denied them.

Confronted in the 1970s with a growing population of people of Mexican origin who were nominally Catholic, the diocesan curia responded in ways akin to those taken earlier by Topel and other bishops in the Pacific Northwest facing even greater influxes of Mexican and Mexican Americans. At first, Bishop Treinen asked the Bishops Committee for the Spanish Speaking in San Antonio, Texas, to send Mexican and Mexican American priests to Idaho for the summer. Then several highly motivated priests in the diocese immersed themselves in Spanish language and Mexican American culture courses at the Mexican American Cultural Center in San Antonio. The chancery invited San Antonio's Bishop Patricio Flores, soon after his ordination as the first Mexican American bishop, to visit Idaho in 1971. Addressing in Spanish a crowd of 175 gathered at St. Paul's Parish church in Nampa, he told them (as he had told other groups of migrants many times before) that migrants should stay put and pressure their newly adopted communities to provide them with education, housing, and health care. As long as they migrate from place to place, he reasoned, nothing would change. "The monkeys in the San Antonio zoo have better places to live than the migrants in Texas or in Idaho," Flores lamented. The visiting bishop warned his audience that "even the Church will not begin to listen" until migrants and ex-migrants demand inclusion on an equal basis (Blough 1971).[19]

Part of that inclusion meant that the church in Idaho needed more Spanish-speaking priests or priests drawn from the ranks of the nation's Latinos. Moreover, the Second Vatican Council called for the liturgy to be offered in the vernacular, rather than Latin. To reach Idaho's Spanish-speaking Catholics, mass should be in Spanish. The civil rights movement of the 1960s and 1970s together with the influential Latin American Bishops Conference at Medellín in 1968 pushed the church to make a "stronger institutional commitment to social justice." To fulfill this special "option for the poor," the church would have to move away from its "identification with the economic interests of the middle and upper classes and the views of the political elite" (Sandoval 2006: 80). Clearly, Bishop Treinen was moving his diocese in this direction, albeit slowly, by insisting that seminarians from the diocese study Spanish intensively and by encouraging priests in parishes with significant Spanish-speaking populations to learn Spanish and study Mexican American culture.

Fr. Mauricio Medina, a priest of Mexican American background from San Luis, Colorado, came to the diocese in 1974 as its first priest of Mexican heritage. Medina, like so many clergy of Mexican heritage, was aware that his training and background caused him to reject his own culture. For that reason, before taking up duties in an Idaho parish with a large Mexican American population, he immersed himself in courses at the San Antonio Mexican American Culture Center. In Idaho he became co-pastor in an agricultural area home to a large and growing population of people of Mexican origin. Within a year ministering at St. Theresa of the Little Flower in Burley, Medina introduced bilingual services at one of the four masses offered. He also did bilingual baptisms and marriages with great success. More and more Spanish-speaking Catholics that had drifted away from the English-only church services began to attend and to become actively involved in the liturgy. The diocese's mission in Colombia, established in 1966, enabled Idaho priests who worked there to learn Spanish and gain an understanding of Colombian culture. Upon their return, they used this experience to good advantage in their work in Idaho's growing Latino communities. Over the years, several Colombian priests came to Idaho, some of whom remain to the present.[20]

Throughout the decades of the 1970s and 1980s, Bishop Treinen vigorously supported positive changes in the national church aimed at people of Latin American origin and demonstrated his commitment to serving the diocese's growing Latino membership. For example, in 1971 he created a new migrant laborer program and put the progressive priest Bill Wassmuth in charge. In 1974, recognizing his prior work in the diocese's mission in Colombia, his 1969 survey of Idaho's poor and disadvantaged, his keen intellect, and his ability to speak Spanish, among other attributes, Treinen named Fr. Nicolas Walsh the diocese's first vicar for Mexican Americans. This was only two years after the Mexican American Cultural Center was established with church support in San Antonio. Although Walsh held the post for less than two years before becoming bishop of Yakima, Treinen quickly filled it with another very capable Spanish-speaking priest, Thomas Taylor. Taylor dedicated himself to serving Mexican Americans and promoting their interests, but in 1977 he accepted a transfer to the diocese's mission in Colombia. The bishop then appointed Pocatello native Sr. Elisa María Martínez vicar for Mexican Americans, the first woman and Mexican American to hold that position. From 1977 until 1981, Sr. Elisa María tirelessly promoted increased Latino participation in the diocese before she took over the church's recently created regional Hispanic Ministry for the Pacific Northwest. Replacing her was Celine Caufield, executive director of the new Hispanic Ministry, a permanently funded diocesan entity. Having served the church in Guatemala, fluent in Spanish, and dedicated to the bishop's plan for Idaho's Latinos, Caufield guided the ministry until 1995, when she became the church's director of the National Migrant Farm Workers Network. Reflecting Idaho's changing ethnic diversity and growing refugee communities in the late 1990s and into the first decade of the twenty-first century, the Hispanic Ministry broadened its mission and changed its name to the Multicultural Ministry.

While vicar for Mexican Americans, Tom Taylor prepared a study, begun by his predecessor, that examined the needs and aspirations of Spanish-speaking members of the church and what the diocese should do about them. Taylor and other Idaho priests had used the cursillo to incorporate Mexican Americans into the predominantly white parishes. The cursillo, or "little course," brought priests and lay members together for intensive religious instruction and prayer for a short time. The goal was to train Mexican Americans into an active leadership cadre in the parish. It had proved very effective as a tool for involving Latinos as leaders in their parishes when Fr. Victor Briones introduced it in the Spokane Diocese in 1965. Taylor and other priests in Idaho and the Pacific Northwest used it successfully in much the same way.[21]

Taylor submitted the study committee's report in May 1976. In his weekly column in the *Boise Idaho Register,* Bishop Treinen thanked committee members for their hard work and told his readers of the challenges the church was prepared to accept in order to meet the needs of its more than twenty thousand Mexican American (then one-third of all Catholics in Idaho) parishioners. A principal goal for Idaho Catholics would be a growing awareness of the "felt spiritual and social needs of these people of another rich culture. This awareness is called for on the part of our priests and all non Mexican American Catholics." Catholics in Idaho, he emphasized, should reject the notion that it was the responsibility of Mexican Americans or any other ethnic group to conform to the majority culture. "Total integration of culture and language is not the answer," he stressed. "Such a dream is an affront to the Mexican Americans, just as it would be for other ethnic groups." He urged "understanding, respect, support, and love—all without paternalism." Catholics of all ethnic origins have to be willing to worship together without surrendering their "cultural and linguistic characteristics which helped to make them who they are" (Treinen 1976: 4). This marked a significant change for the Boise Diocese that since the 1920s expected immigrants to integrate into the dominant mainstream culture. Boise's large and influential Basque Catholic community found this turnabout particularly galling since their Basque chapel had been taken over by the diocese for the chancery office and they were incorporated into St. Johns English-speaking parish. "For years the dominant society and English prevailed in the parish and then along come Mexicans and with them mass in Spanish, the Virgin of Guadalupe, mariachis and piñatas," noted a prominent Basque leader. "Some wondered what had happened" (Bieter 2009).

The diocese's tentative steps taken earlier to embrace Mexican Americans in their midst became more deliberate and forceful as the Latino population swelled in the state and became a larger percentage of the Catholic community. To implement Fr. Taylor's findings, the church sought more bilingual and bicultural priests, sisters, and seminarians for those areas where Mexican Americans formed a significant portion of the population. Church personnel gave a higher priority to the study of the Mexican American culture and the Spanish language. Mexican Americans were more adequately represented on parish councils. Catechetical programs and liturgical celebrations were adapted to the needs of Mexican Americans. The diocese created special youth programs to bring talented young people into the church to encourage them in the vocations so that Mexican Americans would no longer think one had to be Irish to be a priest. The diocese encouraged base communities, made cursillos available, urged lay participation, and established a Mexican American permanent diaconate. To one degree or another, all of these things responded to issues made clear in Taylor's report and were in place by 1980. They also reflected and were in step with the growing influence and changes Latinos brought to bear on the national church.[22]

Idaho Churches Respond to National Events

The decade of the 1980s witnessed a steady growth in Idaho's Latino population. The demographic change brought increased pressure from Latino members that Idaho churches accommodate them and their unique cultural differences. But beyond internal institutional responses to this influx, other challenges arose that strained the cohesiveness of the society as a whole and of the churches in particular.

One of the issues that convulsed most of the decade was the Central American policy of the Ronald Reagan and George H. W. Bush administrations that saw the popular uprisings in El Salvador and Guatemala against repressive elite-dominated governments in Cold War terms. Reagan and Bush denounced the rebels as Communist surrogates manipulated by Cuba and the Soviet Union and asserted that the threatened governments needed U.S. support, military and otherwise, to stem the spread of Communism in the hemisphere. The Protestant National Council of Churches and the Roman Catholic United States Conference of Bishops saw the conflict differently and denounced U.S. government polices to fund counterrevolutionary forces attempting to overthrow the Sandinista government in Nicaragua and to support repressive Salvadoran and Guatemalan regimes at war against their own people. There is no evidence to suggest that Idaho churches actively engaged in the Sanctuary Movement to protect Guatemalan and Salvadoran refugees of the war (considered economic refugees or illegal aliens subject to deportation by the U.S. government), but religious groups sympathized with the refugees and angrily condemned the administration's actions. They sponsored workshops, invited speakers, organized protests, and sent delegations to Central America with the intention of changing government action. Not all churchgoers opposed the Reagan and Bush policies and regarded their fellow faithful as delusional and wrongheaded at best, as fellow travelers at worst. This decade witnessed an appreciable increase in Idaho of conservative, southern-based, Christian fundamentalist and Pentecostal churches that firmly supported the government's stance on Central America.[23]

A second closely related issue that dominated people's attention, church affiliated or not, was the national debate over immigration policy. Economic and political conditions in Mexico as far back as the 1880s had forced many Mexicans north. Now, in the 1980s, unemployment, underemployment, low wages, high inflation, and successive currency devaluations in Mexico spurred an unprecedented flow of migrants to the United States, most undocumented. The nature of being undocumented meant that only estimates could be made of how many entered each year and how long they stayed. Nevertheless, alarm and fear of a southern "invasion" gripped the nation, and polls showed that about 82 percent of Americans wanted the government to apprehend "illegals" and ship them back.[24]

Estimates of Idaho's undocumented population ran between 17,000 and 25,000, making the national debate charged with emotion and of particular interest in the state. Earlier when the churches tried to end the Bracero Program, they too opposed unauthorized immigration. By the 1980s, that position began to change. Violence against immigrants along the border, exploitation of undocumented workers afraid to speak out against fraud and other abuses, and official immigration raids that often split up families moved the churches back to a prior doctrine: the natural right of people to migrate when necessary. As the immigration debate intensified, most Idahoans believed the federal government should control its borders and enforce immigration laws. Church leaders agreed, but with this significant difference: immigrants, with or without documents, had rights too, and they must be protected. Idaho's Catholic leaders have steadfastly adhered to this position to the present day.

The 1986 Immigration Reform and Control Act (IRCA), a law nationally debated for five years, was the congressional solution to the problem. Catholic bishops were ambivalent about the law. On the one hand, they supported it because it provided amnesty and a path to citizenship to those who could prove they entered and worked continuously in the country prior to January 1, 1982. On the other hand, the law's primary intent, to stop the flow of unauthorized immigrants across the border, was misguided in the bishops' opinion because it ostensibly put the burden on employers, making it a criminal act to hire them. The bishops believed that employers, fearing fines and imprisonment if they employed undocumented workers, would indiscriminately fire anyone who looked Mexican and turn away Mexican Americans seeking work, solely on the basis of ethnicity. A former Immigration and Naturalization Services (INS) commissioner agreed that employer sanctions might "put into our employment practices a bias toward looking at people's foreignness that never existed before" (Hansen 1986: 19). Moreover, the bishops frowned on the law's expansion of a foreign "guest-worker" program and lamented that some positive measures failed to be included. To save the amnesty provisions of the new law, however, they supported it and hoped they could mitigate the damage they feared would come with employer sanctions.[25]

Answering the new archbishop of Los Angeles, Roger Mahony's, call to "assist as many as possible to win amnesty" and work to "change the law to include those . . . left out" (*Boise Idaho Register* 1987a), the Boise Diocese sprang into action. It obtained INS permission to set up authorized clearinghouses in several parishes with large Mexican-origin populations to help qualified undocumented workers apply for amnesty. It soon became clear to those involved in the legalization process that the law might become a vehicle for breaking up family units. Celine Caufield, the diocesan director of Hispanic Ministry, dejectedly explained that, "a family might have one parent with the requisites [for amnesty] and the other parent unable to remain in the country" (*Boise Idaho Register* 1987b). Another obstacle loomed large in the form of government fees, set at $185 for an individual and $420 for a family of four. Added to that were other necessary expenses such as medical examinations; notary, legal, and service fees; and document retrieval. The latter often meant applicants driving long distances to obtain affidavits proving work history in many states over several years. These were crushing burdens imposed upon the weakest and most exploited members of society. While the USCC protested in a lengthy letter to INS commissioners urging more lenient rules for legalization, the Boise Diocese conducted workshops to explain the law to farmers and farmworkers alike in parishes throughout southern Idaho.[26]

Applicants for amnesty had between May 5, 1987, and May 4, 1988, to complete the process. When the end of August 1987 approached, only two hundred applications had been processed at diocesan legalization centers. With the onset of the harvest season, they slowed to a trickle. Farmers in the Twin Falls area urged diocesan volunteers to come to their farms and help their workers apply. The director of the legalization team, Joanne Gouger, knew that many would not qualify and feared what would happen to them and their families. She also knew that many who were eligible simply found the process and cost too daunting. With the May 4, 1988, deadline approaching and so few applying in Idaho or nationally, the bishops supported an extension, ultimately killed in the Senate. Many blamed the INS for not publicizing and encouraging application for legalization and for making the rules so unreasonable and costly. Caldwell attorney and active member of St. Mary's Parish Camilo López, noting the high number of "illegal" workers estimated to be in Idaho, found it odd that with less than a month from the deadline, only 7,000 of a possible 25,000 had applied. He speculated that many who might have been eligible either had not been informed of the opportunity or "their mistrust of the INS is so great" that fear kept them away (Lopez 1988: 15). In the few weeks before time expired, hundreds more rushed to apply; the diocese processed almost 2,000 of the more than 9,000 in Idaho who sought amnesty, 10 percent of whom were denied legalization.[27]

Idahoans and Churches Reject Hate Groups

As the IRCA debate in Congress heated up, various Idaho communities experienced a racial backlash. A toxic brew of bigotry, ignorance, and hatred bubbled just beneath the surface in Idaho's history. Now and again it erupted through fissures opened by labor disturbances, economic downturns, and wartime tension and stress. In the 1980s, the increasing Mexican population in racially and ethnically homogeneous Idaho, coupled with the idea of granting amnesty rather than punishment to those who had flouted U.S. immigration law, reopened those fissures, just as they have today. A white supremacist group burned crosses on a farm near Jerome as part of their "crusade" to make five states in the Northwest an "all-white republic." Pocatello to the southeast also witnessed racist outbursts. In Rupert, the Catholic parish church was vandalized and desecrated, a message seemingly aimed at its Mexican American pastor. In September 1986, just a couple of months before IRCA was passed, a white supremacist group known as the Aryan Nations bombed the house of Fr. Bill Wassmuth, a noted and outspoken civil rights activist. The bombers struck other targets in the northern Idaho town of Coeur d'Alene where Wassmuth had his parish.

Shocked, angered, and frightened by these events, people all over the state gathered publicly to denounce the acts of intimidation. Earlier, Wassmuth had organized a Conference of Peace and Unity that attracted over a thousand people alarmed over the presence of the Aryan Nations in northern Idaho and denounced their racist doctrine. The bombing of Wassmuth's home no doubt was in retaliation for this meeting. Over 175 people packed the Guadalupe Center in Twin Falls to protest the cross burnings in Jerome and racist actions in Pocatello. Harry Massoth, leader of the Southern Idaho Peace Movement, chose the Guadalupe Center to express solidarity with the Mexican American community and to applaud the ethnic diversity of the Twin Falls area. Those who attended expressed disgust at the white supremacists and decried their "sickening" beliefs. One attendee expressed her fright and anger, "I'm frightened that the very idea that one race is greater than another exists in this day and age. I'm angry that the supremacists are trying to impose [the idea that] this part of the country be set aside for a superior race" (Bodey 1986: 1). Admittedly, the Aryan Nations proved a violent, racially extremist organization. It was eventually destroyed when the Southern Poverty Law Center won a judgment against them in September 2000, taking their twenty-acre complex in northern Idaho as settlement. But the same toxic brew of bigotry, prejudice, ignorance, and hatred still roils beneath the surface of Idaho's otherwise placid surface, spewing forth from time to time down to the present in the form of anger toward undocumented workers. This noxious mindset carries over to all people of Mexican origin in varying degrees of subtlety.[28]

Empowering Latinos in the Boise Diocese

Despite the tension and conflict over immigration and amnesty, Bishop Treinen regarded inclusion of Catholic Latinos as "prophetic" and their dynamic participation in the Boise Diocese a priority. Therefore he embraced the Encuentro movement and enthusiastically supported it. Begun in 1972, the Encuentro (Spanish for "encounter" or "meeting") movement was an attempt to develop a pastoral plan for Latinos. But it went beyond that to espouse the liberationist model of greater and more active Latino participation and inclusion in the church. This meant a rejection of assimilation for pluralism and respect of Mexican American culture and religious practices. Five years later, a second national Encuentro met in Washington, DC. Differing markedly from the first, hundreds of lay delegates recruited from Catholic activists at the local level assembled to discuss the future role Latinos should play in the church. In their workshops, the delegates tackled such problems as human rights, political responsibility, education, unity, and pluralism. Delegates committed to continue a "process of reflection" and spiritual growth within the Latino community, to form base Christian communities where Latino leaders could be nurtured, to "correct injustices both inside and outside the church," especially for migrant workers and undocumented immigrants (Sandoval 2006: 102–3). They resolved that Latino culture would be acknowledged in teaching the faith and emphasized the need for the church to encourage and train lay ministers.[29]

In 1983 the bishops called for a third Encuentro to meet again in Washington in two years. Preparations for this meeting affected the Boise Diocese deeply. Under Celine Caufield's energetic leadership, Mexican American members responded to a needs assessment survey and selected lay parish leaders to present them at a diocesan Encuentro held on March 16–17, 1985, in Twin Falls. There they analyzed and discussed the survey, hammered out their main concerns, and selected six delegates to represent them at a Northwest regional meeting where attendees would determine the priorities to be sent on to the national Encuentro in August. Idaho's Latino Catholics found that evangelization or a thoroughgoing process of inclusion concerned them most. Education, including the study of English, bilingual education, and religious education, must be addressed. Social justice, especially greater help for migrant workers and undocumented immigrants and those in need, figured prominently as an issue. More Latino members should be trained to serve on parish councils and be represented at all levels of diocesan decision making. The church, they stressed, needed to place greater attention on Latino youth problems and train adult leaders how to deal with them. Along with other northwestern delegates, they added another priority: the church must take a strong position against racism, a problem that affected Latinos in Idaho and elsewhere. At the national Encuentro, these interests were similar to those of Latinos throughout the church. The Encuentro process spurred Idaho's Latinos to demand an active role in their church; it heightened their awareness, raised their consciousness, and increased their confidence. Bishop Treinen and his successors supported the goals of the Encuentro movement and made implementing it a diocesan priority in the decade of the 1990s.[30]

If the Encuentro movement was regarded at first as divisive and rejected by some members of the national hierarchy, in Idaho, where the church was almost exclusively Euro-American until the 1970s, it encountered opposition in many parishes as noted previously with the Boise Basque community. Elsewhere, some objected to bilingual education and to the printing of posters and announcements in Spanish and complained about Spanish-language articles appearing in the *Boise Idaho Register* (*Idaho Catholic Register* after 1993). Rather than yield to criticism, the *Register* created a multipage section called "La Comunidad" containing bylines of local priests like Frs. Jesus Camacho and Enrique Terriquez. Others questioned the performance of mass in Spanish and the creation of a special ministry for Latinos that took scarce resources from programs they deemed more important. They decried the need of a separate ministry for Mexican American youth and succeeded in killing it for a time. Although the Encuentro movement in Idaho was less controversial and confrontational than in other dioceses like Colorado or Washington, for example, opposition to it did exist and still does.[31]

No doubt the unprecedented growth of Idaho's Spanish-speaking population has something to do with the tension and opposition to change within the church. It is also manifest throughout the rest of society. If Idaho's Latino population nearly doubled from 1980 to 1990, it almost doubled again the following decade. The 2010 census counted almost 176,000 Latinos, the state's largest minority at 11.2 percent of the population. Although the Boise Diocese does not have accurate demographic/ethnic data on its members and studies show that many Latinos and non-Latinos alike fail to register with any parish, the diocese estimates that Latinos make up more than half of Idaho's 166,000 Catholics. St. Jerome Parish in south-central Idaho had to build a huge addition to the old parish church that accommodated 350 worshippers so that it could seat the 1,250–1,500 Mexican worshippers who attend Saturday and Sunday mass in Spanish.[32]

Regardless of precise numbers, Bishop Michael P. Driscoll, like his predecessors Bishops Brown and Treinen, still puts immigrants and Latinos to the forefront of his concerns. A giant stride in that direction was the 2008 ordination of six new priests in the diocese, five of whom were Latinos. Under his leadership, the church established Catholic Charities of Idaho (CCI), which works with disadvantaged members of the Latino community, many of them immigrants. Armed with a grant secured in 2006, CCI expanded its literacy program statewide. Called Literacy as a Pathway to Economic Stability (LAPES), the program's goal is to improve "literacy skills across generations using a family strengthening model to increase Hispanics' economic and social participation in Idaho." The hope is to break the cycle of poverty through English-language proficiency and to "strengthen and sustain healthy individuals, families, and communities in Idaho" (Schlichte 2006: 9).

Bishop Driscoll's strong beliefs in social justice led him to lament the inability of the U.S. Congress to agree on a fair and sensible federal immigration policy in 2008 and to denounce government immigration raids recently accelerated in Idaho. He also appointed a part-time volunteer lobbyist to dissuade state legislators from passing laws aimed at unauthorized immigrants and the disadvantaged. Driscoll minces no words when it comes to stating his position on immigration. Prominently displayed on the diocese's online home page on April 15, 2009, he asked his readers to "pray for those immigrants in our country whose families are being torn apart, who are being denied the right to work and who live in fear of deportation because of the current unacceptable system." Knowing full well that many members of his church do not share his compassion for those arrested and deported, he rebuked them in a homily for failing to see the human dignity inherent in immigrants, regardless of their legal status. Catholics in Idaho must not rest, he reminded them, "until aliens in our land find justice and compassion" (Driscoll 2007).[33]

Conclusion

The thrust for social action in Idaho in the 1950s and beyond, especially where migrant farm labor was concerned, emerged from the state's mainline Protestant and Catholic churches. Given the fact that about 50 percent of the state's religious population was Mormon, their absence is significantly striking. Led by the Southern Idaho Migrant Ministry, these churches sought to alleviate the plight of migrants, most of whom were of Mexican heritage, and to act as cultural brokers for them in a society dominated by white Euro-Americans. Given the conservative, individualistic, antigovernment persuasion of most Idahoans, attitudes and values shared by other Heartland states, churches were perhaps the only institutions that could have successfully advocated progressive social change, however slight. The Migrant Ministry strove to alter socioeconomic and political structures that engendered migrancy and its attendant poverty. In both endeavors, the churches were aided by political changes at the national level that responded positively to the civil rights movement of the 1960s and that made federal funds available for economic and social improvements for migrants.

Idaho also underwent economic change that accelerated after the 1960s and enabled migrants to settle permanently and find year-round work. But the demand for migrants did not abate. Expanding economic opportunities attracted more people to Idaho after the mid-1980s. Latino Catholics made up a significant portion of that population growth, taking jobs primarily at the lower rungs of the economic ladder. Eager to participate as equals in their church and determined to improve their economic and social status and that of their children, they pressured civil institutions, churches, and especially the Roman Catholic Diocese of Boise to accommodate them. They expected the church to become an agent of social change. Despite resistance, both within the Catholic Church and outside it, the Latino culture of Idaho is making its presence felt. Allied with the bishop and other progressive groups, Latino leaders strive to play a positive role in the state's society and to win respect and appreciation for their cultural contributions in a nonthreatening way. Their means to achieving modest reforms, acceptance, and participation are through making alliances with the state's institutional leaders and demonstrating their adherence to the values and traditions of the Heartland.

Notes

1. According to a survey conducted in 2000, 50 percent of Idahoans claim some type of religious affiliation. Half of those religious adherents belong to the Church of Jesus Christ of Latter-day Saints (Mormons), a little less than a quarter of the population. Catholics make up the second largest denomination, 20 percent of religious affiliates, or 10 percent of the population. All Protestant groups together make up 31.5 percent of the state's religious adherents, 15.8 percent of the population; cited by Jill Gill, "The Power and the Glory: Idaho's Religious History," unpublished manuscript in author's possession, 2–3. There is little evidence to suggest that these percentages have changed significantly from the first half of the twentieth century.

2: Shotwell 1961: 30–39. Also, numerous interviews by the author with those who swam the migrant stream at some time in their lives: Jesse Berain, Maria Gonzalez Mabbutt, Amando Alvarez, Leo Morales, and Adan Ramirez to name a few. For more, see the interviews collected in 1990 and excerpted in Gamboa 1992. The taped interviews and transcriptions of these interviews are housed in the Idaho State Historical Society's Public Archives and Research Library, Boise, Idaho.

3. Southern Idaho Migrant Ministry, "Study Committee Report B," hereafter cited as SIMM, MS 99; Shotwell 1961: 181.

4. "Migratory Labor Camp Betterment Urged at Hearing," *News-Tribune*, April 30, 1959, 1; "Farm Labor Group Opposes Federal Action on Workers." *News-Tribune,* February 28, 1959, 1; Robin Peterson, "Idaho Migratory Labor camps, 1930–1980," (master's thesis, Boise State University, 2000), 39; Raymona Maddy, "Farmway Village, a Place to Call Home: A History of the Farm Labor Camp in Caldwell, Idaho, 1939–1997," in *The Hispanic Experience in Idaho,* ed. Errol D. Jones and Kathleen Rubinow Hodges (Boise, Idaho: Boise State University, 1998), 39–73; Veronica H. Martinez, "The Promised Land: Hispanics in Minidoka and Cassia County," in Jones and Hodges, *The Hispanic Experience,* 25–37.

5. Governor's Migratory Labor Committee report, 1965, cited in Idaho Advisory Committee to the United States Commission on Civil Rights 1980: 12; "The Scar at American Falls": 2. Richard Baker assessed conditions at the Caldwell and Wilder camps in 1990 in *Los Dos Mundos: Rural Mexican Americans, Another America* (Logan: Utah State University Press, 1995), 81, 135, 174, 178–90.

6. Idaho Farm Workers' Services, Inc., Archival Collection, MS 100, Box 9, Folder 2, Idaho State Historical Society Public Archives and Research Library, Boise, Idaho.

7. Shotwell 1961: 61–65; Richard B. Craig, *The Bracero Program: Interest Groups and Foreign Policy* (Austin: University of Texas Press, 1971), 150–97; Manuel Garcia y Griego, "The Importation of Mexican Contract Laborers to the United States," in *Between Two Worlds: Mexican Immigrants in the United States,* ed. David G. Gutierrez, (Wilmington, Del.: Scholarly Resources, 1996), 67–75.

8. Shotwell 1961: 118–19; Gunther Peck, *Reinventing Free Labor: Padrones and Immigrant Workers in the North American West, 1880–1930* (Cambridge: Cambridge University Press, 2000); Devra Weber, *Dark Sweat, White Gold: California Farm Workers, Cotton, and the New Deal* (Berkeley: University of California Press, 1994); Errol D. Jones and Kathleen R. Hodges, "A Long Struggle: Mexican Farm Workers in Idaho, 1918–1935," in *Memory, Community, and Activism: Mexican Migration and Labor in the Pacific Northwest,* ed. Jerry Garcia and Gilberto Garcia (East Lansing: Julian Samora Research Institute, Michigan State University, 2005), 54–72.

9. Jake Booher, "Will to Live Regained by Victim," *Boise Idaho Statesman,* October 15, 1973, 23; Dale N. Duncan Jr., "The Struggle for Equal Justice: The Battle for Workers Compensation in Idaho's Fields," in Jones and Hodges, *The Hispanic Experience in Idaho,* 135–55.

10. Wells 1995: Santos Recalde, "Migrants in Idaho Get Help from Head Start," *Boise Idaho Register,* July 17 and 24, 1970.

11. For Boise Diocese work with migrants, see *Boise Idaho Register,* July 15, September 16, December 23, 1960, July 5 and 26, October 11, 1963, June 26, October 23, 1964, February 12 and 19, April 16, June 4, 1965, January 14, February 4, July 1, 1966, and August 2, 9, 16, 23, and 30, 1968; Wells 1995: sec. 9; Wendell Peabody, IFWS Director, letter to the Board of Directors, August 16, 1967, MS 288, Series 2, Box 3, Idaho State Historical Society Public Archives and Research Library.

12. Szasz 2000: 135–38.

13. Julio Pérez, Southern Idaho Migrant Ministry, "Study Committee Report C."

14. Milton S. Jordan Jr., "A Movement Grows in Treasure Valley," *Boise Intermountain Observer,* November 28, 1970, 20; "The Migrant Education Tug-of-War," *Boise Intermountain Observer,* February 6, 1971, 6.

15. Nicolas Walsh, "Idaho's Underprivileged," *Boise Idaho Register,* April 4, 1969; see also Walsh's other reports in the *Register,* April 11, 18, 25, May 2, 9, 16, 30, June 6, 1969; Alice Dieter, "The Church as an Instrument for Social Reform," *Boise Intermountain Observer,* August 9, 1969.

16. Schoenberg 1987: 697–700; Garcia 2005: 242–43; Dieter, "The Church as an Instrument for Social Reform."

17. O'Hallora 1970: 3; Audra Green, "Union and Labor Organizing of Mexican Americans in Idaho: A Succinct History," seminar paper presented in Latinos in the U.S. history class, Boise State University, fall 2006; Stephen Hunt, "Historical Perspectives on a Treasure Valley Farm Labor Strike, 1970," seminar paper presented in Latinos in the U.S. history class, Boise State University, spring 2003; Treinen 1970: 1, 3.

18. "Fear versus Anger in the Legislature" 1971: 5; Marvin Jeppeson, to Senator Frank Church, March 1, 1971; Idaho Agricultural Labor Act, 1972, Idaho Code §§22-4101-22-4113; "New Farm Labor Law Spurs Demand for Potato Boycott," *Boise Idaho Statesman,* March 24, 1972, A8.

19. Celine Caufield, "History of the Hispanic Ministry of the Roman Catholic Diocese of Boise," May 1989, files of the Multicultural Ministry of the Roman Catholic Diocese of Boise, Box 8; Blough 1971: 8.

20. Sandoval 2006: 80; Mauricio Medina, "Fr. Medina Brings Unique Vantage Point to Idaho Mexican Apostolate," *Boise Idaho Register,* September 26, 8, October 3, 8, October 10, 8, October 17, 8, October 24, 8, October 31, 8, November 7, 1975, 8; Karin Richter Murdock, "The Missionary Work of the Boise Diocese in Cali, Colombia, and Its Effect on the Hispanic Community in Idaho," graduate paper prepared for History 580, Latinos in the U.S., Boise State University, 2002.

21. Garcia 2005: 244–48.

22. Pam Lyda, "Mexican American Diaconate Program Slated," *Boise Idaho Register,* September 10, 1976, 8; Garcia 2005: 248–49; Schoenberg 1987: 734–37; Sandoval 2006: 81–99.

23. Sandoval 2006: 142, notes that while Protestant ministers and parish priests providing sanctuary were punished by federal authorities, the Catholic Bishops Committee for Hispanic Affairs did not support them; Sr. Mary Ann Walsh, "Church Must Observe Law While Aiding Illegals," *Boise Idaho Register,* September 14, 1984, 15; Gill, "The Power and the Glory," 17.

24. Sandoval 2006: 138–39.

25. Stephanie Overman, "Hispanics, USCC React to Immigration Bills," *Boise Idaho Register,* June 29, 1984, 1; Hansen 1986: 19; Rita Glancey, "Church Can Help with Legalization, Says Idaho Hispanic Leader," *Boise Idaho Register,* January 30, 1987, 11; Eileen Putnam, "Employers to Get No Warning on Alien Fines," *Boise Idaho Statesman,* May 31, 1988, 10B; Sandoval 2006: 140–43.

26. "Idaho Reps Hear 'Discouraging' Words on Immigration Act," *Boise Idaho Register,* February 27, 1987; "New Legislation Rules Keep Aliens in Shadows, Says USCC," *Boise Idaho Register,* March 27, 1987, 15; Maria Salazar, "Immigration Bill Serves Agriculture," *Boise Idaho Statesman,* May 26, 1988, 10A; Laurie Hansen, "Church Leaders Criticize Immigration Rules as Deadline Nears," *Boise Idaho Register,* April 24, 1987, 15.

27. López 1988: 15; Laurie Hansen, "Church Urges Allowing More Aliens to Become Legalized," *Boise Idaho Register,* May 13, 1988, 15; Laurie Hansen and Colette Cowman, "Legalization Fraud No Problem in Idaho," *Boise Idaho Register,* December 9, 1988, 1.

28. "Sacred Hosts Desecrated at St. Nicholas, Rupert," *Boise Idaho Register,* August 3, 1984, 1; Bodey 1986; Nils Rosdahl, "Supremacy Problem Not Over," *Boise Idaho Register,* October 24, 1986, 1, 17; Tim Woodward, "A Little Tolerance Would Become Us All," *Boise Idaho Statesman,* May 14, 2008; "Boise—City of Bigots," *Boise Idaho Statesmen,* May 28, 2008.

29. Schoenberg 1987: 760; Sandoval 2006: 99–104; Garcia 2005: 252–55; Jesus

Camacho, "Pasado, presente, y futuro de los Hispanos," *Boise Idaho Register,* May 25, 1984, 11. Camacho, a Mexican priest who came to the Boise Diocese in 1981, started a Spanish-language radio program that still airs twice weekly. He wrote a regular column for the *Register* in the 1980s and is currently pastor at St Mary's Parish in Boise.

30. Celine Caufield, "Resultados diocesanos del Tercer Encuentro," *Boise Idaho Register,* April 19, 1985, 11; Garcia 2005: 255; Jesus Camacho, "Gracias por darnos la oportunidad de servirlos," *Boise Idaho Register,* August 31, 1984, 11.

31. Sandoval laments that in *Catholic New York,* the monthly of the Archdiocese of New York, where Hispanics are the largest group in New York City, there are only two pages of Spanish containing translated articles. There are no bylines or columns written by Latinos for Latino members; Sandoval 2006: 166.

32. Roman Catholic Diocese of Boise, "Idaho's Hispanic Community," Office of Education Ministries, 2003, Multicultural Ministry Office, file "Bishop's Correspondence," Box 4/409/8; author's interview with Fr. Ron Wekerle, August 9, 2011, Jerome, Idaho; Dixie Thomas Reale, "Priest Builds Cultural Bridges," *Twin Falls Times-News,* November 10, 2005, 16.

33. Michael Brown, "A Community Living in Fear," *Boise Idaho Catholic Register,* October 5, 2007; Michael Brown, "Bishop Calls Catholics to New Vision for Immigrants," *Boise Idaho Catholic Register,* October 19, 2007, 1, 3; Michael Brown, editor of the *Boise Idaho Catholic Register,* interview with author, March 3, 2009, Boise, Idaho.

References

Bieter, John. 2009. Interview with the author, Boise, Idaho, April 5.

Blough, Dorris. 1971. "The Monkeys Have It Better than the Migrants." *Boise Intermountain Observer,* August 7, 8.

Bodey, Judy. 1986. "Unity Gathering Held to Combat Racism." *Boise Idaho Register,* October 24, 1, 17.

Boise Idaho Register. "Idaho Reps Hear 'Discouraging' Words on Immigration Act." 1987a. February 27.

Boise Idaho Register. "New Legislation Rules Keep Aliens in Shadows, Says USCC." 1987b. March 27, 15.

Boise Intermountain Observer. "The Scar at American Falls: Despite Request That It Clean up or Close, Migrant Labor Camp Is Getting Worse." 1969. July 26, 2.

Boise Intermountain Observer, "Fear versus Anger in the Legislature." 1971. February 6, 5.

Driscoll, Bishop Michael P. 2007. "Welcome the Strangers." Pastoral Letter on Immigration Reform, June 15. http://www.catholicidaho.org/en/NewsEvents/Documents/Pastoral%20letter-6-15-07-Immigration%20Reform.pdf (accessed November 6, 2012).

Gamboa, Erasmo, ed. 1992. *Voces Hispanas, Hispanic Voices of Idaho: Excerpts from the Idaho Hispanic Oral History Project.* Boise: Idaho Commission on Hispanic Affairs and Idaho Humanities Council.

Garcia, Gilbert. 2005. "Mexicanos and the Catholic Church in Eastern Washington: The Spokane Diocese, 1956–1997." In *Memory, Community, and Activism: Mexican Migration and Labor in the Pacific Northwest,* ed. Jerry Garcia and Gilbert Garcia. East Lansing: Julian Samora Research Institute and Michigan State University Press.

Hansen, Laurie. 1986. "USCC Sees 'Unpalatable Options' in Immigration Bill." *Boise Idaho Register,* October 24, 19.

Idaho Advisory Committee to the U.S. Commission on Civil Rights. 1980. *A Roof over Our Heads: Migrant and Seasonal Farmworker Housing in Idaho.* Washington, DC: U.S. Commission on Civil Rights.

Jeppeson, Marvin, to Senator Frank Church. March 1, 1971. Farm Labor File, Senator Church Papers, Boise State University Special Collections, Boise, Idaho, Box 77, Folder 20.

López, Camilo. 1988. "Amnesty Extension Grow 'Critical' as May 4 Deadline Nears." *Boise Idaho Register,* April 29, 15.

O'Hallora, Danny. 1970. "The Chicanos Organize in Southwest Idaho." *Boise Intermountain Observer,* September 5, 3

Sandoval, Moises. 2006. *On the Move: A History of the Hispanic Church in the United States,* rev. 2nd ed. Maryknoll, N.Y.: Orbis Books.

Schlichte, Kristan. 2006. "CCI Receives Grant to Expand Services to Hispanic Community." *Boise Idaho Catholic Register,* November 17, 9.

Schoenberg, Wilfred P., S.J. 1987. *A History of the Catholic Church in the Pacific Northwest, 1743–1983.* Washington: DC: Pastoral Press.

Shotwell, Louisa R. 1961. *The Harvesters: The Story of the Migrant People.* Garden City, N.Y.: Doubleday.

Southern Idaho Migrant Ministry [SIMM]. 1968. "Study Committee Report B." January 1968, Southern Idaho Migrant Ministry Archival Collection, MS 99, Box 2, Folder 21, and Box 9, Folder 11, Idaho State Historical Society Public Archives and Research Library, Boise.

Szasz, Ferenc. 2000. *Religion in the Modern American West.* Tucson: University of Arizona Press.

Treinen, Sylvester. 1970. "Homily at Migrants' Mass." *Boise Idaho Register,* September 18, 1, 3.

Treinen, Sylvester. 1976. "Your Bishop Writes, 'A Significant Number.'" *Boise Idaho Register,* June 11, 4.

Walsh, Nicolas. 1969. "Idaho's Underprivileged." *Boise Idaho Register,* April 4.

Wells, Merle. 1995. "Hispanic Migrant Workers' Social and Educational Programs in Idaho." Idaho State Historical Society Reference Series #1092, Sec. 8.

PART II

Contesting Policy and Legal Boundaries

CHAPTER 4

Seeing No Evil

The H2A Guest-Worker Program and State-Mediated Labor Exploitation in Rural North Carolina

SANDY SMITH-NONINI

In the aftermath of the 2008 economic meltdown on Wall Street, we've seen renewed consensus on the vital role of the state in moderating capital flows and regulation of capitalist enterprises. This shift away from the Washington consensus that enjoyed hegemony since the mid-1980s invites a reevaluation of the period of neoliberal globalization. In the 1990s, many social analysts pointed out risks of nation-states losing power and sovereignty vis-à-vis the private sector, especially in the developing world. Yet studies of neoliberalism revealed many examples in which agents of the state, rather than simply withdrawing from economic regulation, reoriented their role to facilitate the mobility of private capital, often at the expense of the public interest (e.g., Goode and Maskovsky 2001; Harvey 2003). Thus it is important to view states as key institutions within which elites and other actors play complex roles manipulating access to power and resources on behalf of private interests. In few sectors, outside of defense, has the state taken such a central role as in U.S. agriculture, where subsidies have long been vital components of farm profits. Since the 1980s, as small farms have declined, the majority of government-subsidized agriculture has become corporate in nature, with less and less accountability to communities and consumers (Roberts 2008).

Labor relations are a paramount consideration in crop agriculture, a labor-intensive industry that is dependent on land—a nonexportable resource. The U.S. government has long regulated the supply of foreign farm labor on behalf of agribusiness, and that role became more critical as the industry restructured itself in the competitive neoliberal climate since the early 1990s. The H2A program, which permits quasi-private labor brokers to import Mexican "guest workers" for seasonal work on U.S. farms, expanded after 1990 into states in the mid-South, which was also experiencing new flows of undocumented immigrants. North Carolina, with one of the fastest growing Spanish-speaking populations in this period, also emerged as the state importing the most H2A workers.

This chapter draws on the case of the North Carolina Growers Association (NCGA), the state's large (and until 2004 its only) H2A brokerage, to examine the relationship between the neoliberal state and guest workers during the 1990s, a period of rapid economic growth.[1] My access to labor camps was facilitated through collaboration with nonprofit organizations working to defend farmworkers' civil and labor rights. I visited roughly twenty-six migrant labor camps in eastern and central North Carolina and conducted over one hundred thirty interviews of farmworkers, farmers and agribusiness representatives, state employees or officials, and representatives of nonprofit groups between 1998 and 2008. I also observed scores of meetings, educational events, and state conferences on farm labor.[2]

This study documents routine practices of the NCGA when the program was at its height. In 2004 the association underwent reforms due in part to lawsuits and to a new contract with the Farm Labor Organizing Committee (FLOC), a farmworker union, which won the right to organize workers inside the guest-worker brokerage. Until then FLOC was best known for its successful 1980s campaign to organize workers on farms supplying ingredients for Campbell's Soup in Ohio and Michigan (Barger and Reza 1994). FLOC began its campaign in 1998 targeting the Mt. Olive Pickle Company, the state's largest cucumber processor, to demand better working conditions on farms supplying its produce. Union organizers soon learned that three-quarters of the workers on these farms were provided through the NCGA. At the time, the prospects of a union victory seemed daunting given such a dispersed and itinerate workforce that lacked legal status, knowledge of English, or financial resources. In a historically antiunion state like North Carolina, it was difficult to build broad coalitions to support workers of any stripe. Much of the support for FLOC's boycott of Mt. Olive came from urban areas and was heavily based in churches and university communities.

The 2004 FLOC victory in North Carolina, discussed in more detail in the last section of this chapter, was historical in that it was the first time agricultural workers in the Southeast had gained official union recognition and was the first labor contract associated with an H2A program. Since FLOC later began monitoring recruitment of workers in Mexico, it also became the first transnational labor contract enforced on both sides of the U.S.-Mexican border.

The rapid growth in the U.S. guest-worker program can be traced to the years after the 1986 Immigration Reform and Control Act (IRCA), when despite the ostensible illegality of hiring undocumented aliens, employers were in fact relatively free to hire them without federal interference. In this atmosphere, private brokers of labor flourished. Heyman (1998) describes how post-1986 migrants increasingly became caught up in debt-peonage relationships with unscrupulous brokers, finding themselves forced into "double-edged, successful but entrapping conspiracies to violate the law." In contrast to the relatively unregulated labor market of most migrant farm labor, at first glance the H2A program would seem to be an example of strong state involvement in the market, both representing the interests of agribusiness employers by manipulating the labor supply and direct control of workers while offering federal oversight to mitigate abuses inherent to farm labor, such as subminimum wages, debt-peonage relationships with labor brokers, and substandard housing.

But this account will demonstrate that during the 1990s, the North Carolina H2A program morphed into a model of contractual labor relations that, rather than being an example of heavy-handed state intervention, actually represented a case of "government by proxy," not unlike other public-private partnerships formed in the neoliberal era (Holland, Nonini, and Lutz 2002). In this case, the state delegated responsibility for labor supply manipulation, control of workers, and regulatory oversight directly to private brokers who publicly represented and shared revenue streams with agribusiness growers.

Marginalized Workers by Design:
A History of Farm Labor Policy

Although the NCGA brokerage dates only to 1990, the current H2A program is part of a long history of government mediation in agricultural labor relations. State subsidies for American agriculture have always included either a tacit or official license to exploit the labor of marginalized populations. Antebellum North Carolina was less dependent on plantation agriculture than most southern states, yet the rural economy still relied heavily on slaves. Eastern tobacco-growing counties that employ the bulk of today's Mexican migrants were also the counties with the highest concentration of slaves prior to the American Civil War.[3] After the war, growers mobilized political support to revive "sharecropping," in which the landlord held legal control over distribution of the crop and African Americans often found themselves in long-term debt to the landowner (Wood 1986). Gradually, their legal and practical status became indistinguishable from that of wage laborers.

Wright (1996) notes that the poor wages and the irregular nature of farm-work favored those willing to migrate in search of the best situations. But this entailed costs, such as the inability to sustain a family or to obtain credit. Planters, who wished to guarantee availability of labor at harvesttime, found African American men's willingness to migrate for better wages threatening. In the 1930s, growers fought New Deal labor laws and convinced legislators to exclude farm labor from new minimum wage laws and from protections for unions offered by the National Labor Relations Act.

The federal Bracero Program, dating from 1942 through 1964, was prompted by a purported shortage of rural labor during World War II. Yet, as Hahamovitch (1999) showed, there was no evidence for a national labor shortage, rather, lawmakers responded to heavy lobbying by growers, who resisted paying more than Depression-era wages to workers. In addition, southern growers opposed federal efforts to redistribute U.S. migrant workers to address fluctuations in demand between crops. This set the stage for an agreement between the U.S. and Mexican governments to contract over five million braceros (literally "strong-arm men") to growers and ranchers mainly in California and Texas over a twenty-two-year period (Gonzalez 2006). During this period, the Immigration and Naturalization Service (INS) Border Patrol functioned as a "complaisant tool of agribusiness, which had entrenched power in the US Congress," controlling the movements of migrants (Heyman 1998). Today the Bracero Program prompts memories of "Harvest of Shame," the 1960 CBS documentary that exposed its widespread abuses and that, together with pressure from the United Farm Workers (UFW), led Congress to discontinue it. Despite contracts guaranteeing fair wages, decent housing, terms of employment, and even health insurance, these protections were poorly enforced and routinely circumvented by growers.

Federal immigration policy has historically been responsive to both the market and politics. During World War II and the 1990s economic boom, immigrants were welcomed, but in the late1960s, after the terror attacks of September 11, 2001, and in the 2008 recession, it became expedient to tighten border security. Revitalization of the H2A program (a successor to the much smaller H2 program) came about in response to the 1986 IRCA legalization process (with relatively lax requirements) for Mexican Americans living in the states and introduced employer sanctions for hiring new illegal immigrants. Interestingly, the sanctions proved largely symbolic, as the reforms inspired a flourishing underground business in selling immigrants false documents. In the booming 1990s, the INS made raids on workplaces a low priority (Heyman 1998; Griffith, Heppel, and Torres 2002; Martin 2004).

After 1986, many Mexican Americans abandoned migrant jobs for permanent work (Runsten and Archibald 1992).[4] Whereas before, farmwork as an occupation had been passed generation to generation, once legal status was achieved, the unstable and arduous life of farmwork did not compete well against jobs in other areas. As in the 1940s, from the perspective of growers, the decline of their ready supply of cheap migrant labor was seen as a "labor shortage." Rather than pay competitive wage rates, California and Texas growers lobbied Congress to gain approval for the H2A program. By the late 1990s, the H2A program was importing about 40,000 Mexican workers to the United States each growing season (Bacon 2001). Growers' claims of a labor shortage have remained in dispute. Federal studies found no national labor shortage in agriculture but noted that local shortages do occur (Commission on Agricultural Workers 1992; General Accounting Office 1997). Growers, however, disputed the federal statistics (Cleeland 1999). Delores Huerta, president of the UFW, has argued that what has been "in shortage" was not labor, but rather fair pay and safe working conditions.

In addition to farmwork, low-wage industries such as meatpacking, services, and construction work drew new immigrants east. North Carolina's Latino population quadrupled in fifteen years, reaching an estimated 379,000 by 2000, 65 percent of whom were from Mexico (2000 U.S. Census). By the late 1990s, an estimated 90 percent of all farm labor in the state was Spanish-speaking, as Latinos replaced an African American labor force that had moved into the growing service sector (Skaggs, Leiter, and Tomaskovic-Devey 2000). Service and retail jobs offered a more attractive alternative to the long hours and low pay of farmwork for young African Americans. The influx of Latino workers, coupled with new networks of labor recruiters, enabled growers to replace African Americans with a cheaper and more pliable workforce (Martin 2001: 4).

While the 1990s economic boom created opportunity for low-wage workers, new free-trade policies hurt prospects for both Mexican and U.S. small farmers. In interviews with new migrants to North Carolina, the constant refrain was that it was no longer possible to make a living wage in rural Mexico. They reported that unskilled and semiskilled jobs paid at best $2 to $3 per day in rural areas. The damage to Mexico's rural economy came in multiple blows, including the government's phaseout of rural farm subsidies, followed by the 1994 banking crisis and devaluation of the peso (Otero 1996). Increasingly, the North American Free Trade Agreement's (NAFTA's) rules, combined with the Mexican government's financial crisis, shifted power relations in Mexican agriculture to favor transnationals and U.S. brokers to the disadvantage of Mexico's agro-export industry and the small farmers on which the country had long relied for the maize used in tortillas, the population's dietary staple (Gledhill 1998; Raghavan 2000). New imports of cheaper U.S. corn and sugar into Mexico undermined domestic food producers. The plummet in local corn prices by nearly half in a three-year period after NAFTA rules took effect devastated hundreds of thousands of small farmers

(Audley et al. 2004). Migration became the principal strategy families used to cope. Illegal workers in the United States earning minimum wage received wages ten to fifteen times higher than what they could earn at home. Due to existing networks of U.S.-based farm crew leaders with ties to "coyotes," the easiest initial job for many new migrants to find was farmwork.

Immigration Reform and Rural Capitalism in the New South

One trend influencing the shift in U.S. agriculture to brokered farm labor has been increasing vertical integration, in which food processors gained more control over the pricing of produce and use of inputs on crops, a process that further pressured small farmers. The decline of small farms goes back to the 1980s in North Carolina. With its tradition of yeoman farmers, many of whom grew tobacco with federal price supports, the state had the highest number of farmers in the country in 1950 (Wright 1996). Poor farm families were seen by state elites as a resource for attracting northern textile factories (Wood 1986), and these policies of developing a rural industrial working class with one foot in agriculture facilitated the 1980s rise of meatpacking—mainly poultry and pig processing—which gradually replaced textiles as the dominant industry in many areas. The small family farms that used to dominate across the state have been rapidly disappearing as economics came to favor larger operators. Farms smaller than 50 acres declined by more than a third from 1982 to 1997, while the median size of farms grew by 24 percent in the same period, according to data from the North Carolina Department of Agriculture. During that period, the average tobacco farm actually doubled in size. Many large farmers benefited from sale of farmland by smaller farmers going out of business. Although total farm acreage has stayed relatively stable, surviving farms tended to be larger and more mechanized, often with new side operations such as on-site packing or processing facilities that boosted capital flows. By 1997 larger farms (with ten or more workers) had become the employers of two-thirds of the state's farmworkers, according to the Census of Agriculture.[5]

Processors and integrators captured a much larger share of the food income dollar from the mid-1980s, compared with growers, whose former 30 percent share declined. In the 1990s, the share of food dollars paying farm labor remained flat, at 8 percent to 9 percent since the mid-1970s, while farm wages had lost value due to inflation.[6] Increasing reliance on global trade, including imports of foreign produce (often grown abroad by U.S. companies), heightened competitiveness within the industry. New industry leaders tend to be companies that diversified, expanded their markets, and maximized production while minimizing labor costs—companies like Mt. Olive Pickle Company, the food processor targeted by FLOC when the union came to the state in 1998. Mt. Olive, based in the town of the same name in eastern North Carolina, grew to the second largest supplier of U.S. supermarket shelf pickles during the 1990s. The company expanded its market outside the South and began purchasing abroad in the winter season, emerging as one of the winners in the global trade game. Developing a national market and a network of international suppliers gave the company greater leverage in controlling prices paid to local growers for cucumbers. Mt. Olive was boycotted by FLOC from 1999 to 2004 for its suppliers' farm labor practices, although the company maintained in public that the boycott had little effect on its sales.

For most cucumber growers who sold to Mt. Olive, cucumbers were a side crop; the bulk of acreage supported tobacco. The appeal of growing cucumbers (and sweet potatoes, another side crop) was that they fit well into the tobacco growing season, providing additional income flows and sufficient demand for labor to keep their laborers occupied on the farm (as opposed to migrating for work) throughout the growing season. Mt. Olive wielded a great deal of influence over farm practices. The company offered detailed prescriptions for inputs for every phase of the cucumber production process, but the company's CEO, Bill Bryan, routinely distanced the company from the hiring and labor practices of its growers. Prior to the public scrutiny of its practices that resulted from FLOC's public campaign, however, Mt. Olive had been active in lobbying Congress on behalf of the local H2A program run by the NCGA, which supplied workers to most of the company's growers.

Effects of the Post-IRCA Shift to Brokered Farm Labor

Southern farmers squeezed by the neoliberal marketplace looked for new ways to cut labor costs. The turn to Mexican labor was facilitated both by INS policies of scaling back raids on farms (Martin 1997) and by the advent of new H2A programs in the Southeast. In addition, the rise of labor brokers for both H2A and illegal immigrants had radically transformed the nature of farmwork. Whereas in the 1980s most farmhands worked directly for growers, by the late 1990s, brokered farmwork with one of an estimated 1,200 quasi-legal farm contractors (*contratistas*) statewide had become the most common arrangement (representing ten times more farmworkers than enter through the H2A program). Gradually, shady middlemen replaced the farm owner as "patron," creating a system that, despite minimal reforms in pay and housing standards, continued to resemble the treatment of African Americans in the Jim Crow South.

Hubner (2000) reported that the typical small-scale broker attempted to maximize profits by paying workers poorly and by supplying new migrants everything from work gloves to fake Social Security cards—for a price. More unscrupulous brokers gouged workers on housing, transportation, and food and relied on intimidation to squelch complaints. One former undocumented worker in Duplin County recounted to me a saga of unpaid wages and broken promises experienced with no less than five different crew leaders in his first two seasons in the state (Smith-Nonini 2009).

A U.S. Department of Labor study found that farmworkers hired by middlemen earned 20 percent less than those hired directly by growers. Although reforms in North Carolina law set up minimum wages for farm labor in 1966, new migrant housing rules in 1986, and new pesticide regulations in 1993, farm labor advocates point out that the state has a poor record of enforcement. In interviews, undocumented farmworkers reported irregular workweeks, varying from no work at all early and late in the season, to periods with ten- to twelve-hour days and six- to seven-day weeks during harvests. By law, higher overtime pay is not required for farmwork, yet most workers do not object to the long hours because of the shortage of work between harvests (see Rothenberg 1998; Human Rights Watch 2000). A generous minimum wage exemption in North Carolina law allowed farmers who employed fewer than eight laborers on a full-time basis in any quarter to pay less than the federal minimum. State officials readily acknowledged in interviews that wage and hour oversight by the state was handicapped by a shortage of inspectors.

Farm labor critics charged that North Carolina's "complaint-driven" system was unresponsive to the realities of farm labor (Smith-Nonini 1999, 2005). For example, in 1998 only 16,000 (15 percent) of the state's estimated 126,000 farmworkers lived in inspected housing and standards were minimal; only one of the state's eight housing inspectors was bilingual, and inspectors relied primarily on interviews with farmers. Likewise, fines for farmer pesticide violations seldom exceeded $300, and the vast majority of the state's farmers using "restricted-use" pesticides could count on never seeing the face of a state inspector. Although pesticide training was offered at some migrant clinics, the realities of power relations in farm labor have meant that workers were often not in a position to adopt safe practices (Quandt et al. 1998). Most workers lacked multiple changes of clothes or facilities to wash work clothes on a daily basis (Smith-Nonini 1999).[7]

The Rapid Growth of North Carolina's
H2A Guest-Worker Program

While undocumented workers and Mexican American workers with green cards made up the majority of the state's farm workforce by the late 1990s, the decade saw the growth of a new phenomenon as the NCGA established a monopoly on the new pipeline of federal guest workers and gained new clients on many large eastern farms. Known by workers as "the *asociación*," the NCGA, which opened its doors in 1990, grew by two thousand new workers a year. By the end of the decade, the company brought in over 17,000 Mexicans a year, of which about 12,000 were supplied to association farmers in North Carolina; the remainder were sent to neighboring states through a separate company. Both operations were run out of the same warehouse by a former state employee, called Leroy Dunn in this account.[8] In press conferences, Dunn described himself as "a farmworker advocate" and called the NCGA a humanitarian alternative to unscrupulous labor brokers. He described the brokerage as "like a union," claiming that it offered "worker protections without labor union dues."

In contrast to undocumented workers managed by crew leaders, H2A guest workers are by contract entitled to workers' compensation coverage, free inspected housing, and transportation from Mexico. In the late 1990s, farms enlisted in the state H2A program accounted for more than three-quarters of all inspected housing in the state. To its credit, the H2A program created a degree of visibility for farmworker conditions and enhanced scrutiny of existing regulations on member farms. The program offers an opportunity for Mexicans to work in the United States legally, and this status is highly valued by the workers (Griffith, Heppel, and Torres 2002).

The rapid growth of the NCGA combined with lax state or federal oversight raised red flags for farmworker advocates. Legal-services lawyers and labor advocates encountered a steady stream of complaints from H2A workers, but most were afraid to file formal complaints when they encountered problems. Many critics also pointed to the potential for systematic fraud in the NCGA, given the ostensibly "nonprofit" program's vast revenue flow and poor federal or state oversight. Farmers paid the association $498 for each worker provided, on top of a $200 annual membership fee. At its height, the NCGA had a $5 million revenue flow, and by 2000 an inquiry by the Institute for Southern Studies showed that the company was paying taxes on its substantial income, despite its reported nonprofit status.

Potential problems with the program came to public attention in June 1998 when a group of guest workers fled secretly during the night from a farm in Lenoir County, in southeastern North Carolina. The men told news reporters and state agricultural agents that they had been worked for fourteen hours the previous day, with only short breaks, and were hounded by a foreman to keep up a rapid pace even after one worker got sick and vomited blood. They said the foreman refused to give out chips for each bucket of cucumbers picked, so they would have records of their production. They declined offers of legal help, citing fears of deportation, and only asked for work on another farm.[9]

On a visit to the area the next day with FLOC organizers, local workers said the grower, locally known as "El Diablo," had a reputation for harsh practices. In 2002 the state Department of Labor investigated a foreman from the same farm charged with ignoring a worker who fainted in the field. Mexican recruiters for the NCGA reported supplying a new crew each year to this grower because no experienced workers wanted to work there (Griffith, Heppel, and Torres 2002). Despite the farmer's bad reputation, the NCGA continued to assign him workers. Prior to the 2004 FLOC contract, the NCGA only rarely dropped growers over reports of abuses.

Recruitment of H2A workers was carried out by private Mexican firms that targeted agricultural areas such as Guanajuato and Michoacán. Until 2005 (when the policy changed due to a FLOC lawsuit), Mexican recruits paid an entry fee of up to $500 plus travel costs. Many took out loans at high interest rates to cover these fees. They were reimbursed for travel costs later and received a free trip home if they stayed until the end of their contract. The H2A workforce was almost entirely male, and as of this writing, the NCGA was fighting a lawsuit brought by the state's Farm Worker Legal Services over gender discrimination. Dunn denies that NCGA discriminates against women in hiring.

Recruited workers were bused to the Texas border, where NCGA agents arranged their seasonal visas, then they continued to the small town of Vass, in south-central North Carolina, where NCGA was based in a metal-walled warehouse on a wooded drive. By late spring, the program hosted orientation sessions of up to four hundred workers who crowded into a standing-room-only warehouse courtyard for orientation speeches and workplace assignments. One wall of the metal-sided enclosure featured a stucco facade of a Latin American hacienda with an altar to the Virgin Mary and a balcony on the second story with a Mexican blanket hung over the rails from which NCGA staff addressed the crowd of men below. A fountain and rustic furniture were visible behind teller-style windows where clerks processed workers' documents.

Farmers pay H2A workers by using either a piece rate or a set price for a share of production, which is not supposed to fall below an adjusted minimum wage rate slightly higher than the federal minimum—a provision intended to minimize the impact of foreign workers on domestic wages. To offset farmers' costs for the program, the federal government waived requirements for H2A employers to pay Social Security and unemployment taxes.

One of the worst times for farmworkers during my fieldwork was in 1999 when flooding in the aftermath of two hurricanes cut short the growing season in mid-September. When floodwater receded on one H2A farm in eastern Greene County, workers held a work stoppage, complaining that the many rotten sweet potatoes they dug up meant that their piece rate pay worked out to less than half minimum wage. In interviews, the men reported calling the NCGA office and being told they had to settle for what the farmer offered. They declined to file a formal complaint, citing fears of "consequences." Dunn later claimed the NCGA had no record of the workers' phone call.

The 1999 floods exacerbated a well-known problem within the H2A program: its unusually long contract period (ending in early November). Workers routinely encountered a shortage of work by mid-October, when an estimated 75 percent of all farmwork employment had ended. NCGA statistics showed that typically 25 percent to 35 percent of H2A workers abandoned their farms early from 1995 to 2002, thereby forfeiting reimbursement of their travel costs. The year 1999 stood out, with 60 percent of workers leaving early due to the floods (Yeoman 2001; Fann 2003). That fall, worker advocates and FLOC called on the NCGA to transport workers back home early since fall crops were ruined, but Dunn refused.

In theory, workers are compensated for slack periods. A clause in the H2A contract guaranteed workers pay for at least three-quarters of their days in the country. Yet interviews revealed that most were unaware of this right. Dunn reported that the NCGA only rarely paid out extra checks to comply with the three-quarters guarantee payment.

Blind Spots: State-Sanctioned
Forms of Intimidation

In interviews, workers reported that anyone who complained or who left their assigned farm without permission was "blacklisted" and lost the right to return with the program for one to three years. It is illegal for an H2A program to maintain a blacklist, and Dunn denied using a blacklist to punish workers. But evidence for the existence of the blacklist grew. The state's Legal Services program collected several affidavits from former H2A workers on their experience being blacklisted. Local filmmakers captured footage of a grower stating that "problem workers" lost the option of returning, and Dunn openly admitted that workers who left an assignment were not invited back. Some growers reportedly dealt with injured workers by simply putting them on a bus back to Mexico to avoid paying workers' compensation. Effects of this intimidation were made clear in tape recordings from the Legal Services telephone answering machines, on which H2A workers at different camps who had earlier filed complaints about abuses later left messages asking to withdraw the complaints, citing harassment by fellow workers (Smith-Nonini 2009).[10]

Some growers resorted to "No Trespassing" signs and sympathetic local sheriffs to keep unwanted visitors away from workers. An important omission in the H2A contract legitimized these practices by failing to recognize tenancy rights for farmworkers in employer-provided housing, effectively denying workers the right to invite guests onto the property. Labor organizers were arrested on at least three occasions between 1998 and 2004 while attempting to meet with workers. The cases were promptly dismissed, but such intimidation has a chilling effect on worker rights efforts.

Under Dunn's leadership, prior to 2004, the NCGA forbade student advocates, Legal Services attorneys, and FLOC organizers from attending worker orientations.[11] At these sessions, workers were actively warned against consulting federally funded Legal Services lawyers, who Dunn claimed were trying to destroy his program. In the company's Vass, North Carolina, warehouse, a large banner in Spanish on one wall read "Legal Services Wants to Destroy the H2A Program" and warnings not to trust Legal Services lawyers scrolled across a black electronic display in glowing red letters. On a videotape of one orientation, Dunn's associates told workers that Legal Services lawyers in Florida had put that state's guest-worker program out of business by harassing growers with frivolous law suits.[12]

Government Sanction: Both Mitigating and Enabling Exploitation

By the late 1990s, the hegemony that the NCGA had established as labor supplier to large farms had begun to impact state enforcement practices. There was no single state agency in charge of overseeing the H2A program, but rather, myriad subdivisions within agencies, which had inadequate budgets and lacked the capacity and political will for proper oversight. Although farmers were supposed to preferentially hire citizens or workers with green cards if available, state agricultural field agents told me they had stopped referring job seekers to H2A farms. There was little point, a former field agent said, since domestic workers "don't last more than a day on the job." He also complained that state workers encountered hostility from Dunn and his associates when they visited NCGA farms.

While it is one thing for small-time crew leaders to slip between the cracks of the legal system, when a large organization like the NCGA, with a federal license to import workers, wields this degree of economic and cultural power over a disadvantaged population, it creates the conditions for what Goode and Maskovsky (2001) have called a "regime of disappearance"—erasing poor and marginalized groups from public debates and visibility.

Clearly, while opening up some areas to public scrutiny, the association's H2A brokerage simultaneously created new invisibilities and legitimized forms of labor control that replicated many of the same abuses associated with non-H2A farm labor and the discredited Bracero Program. Like today's H2A system, the Bracero Program of the 1940s and '50s assigned workers to one employer who held the power to deport them and who penalized those who left the property. Both programs were plagued by charges of blacklisting, and both tended to entrap Mexican workers in debt as they paid fees and bribes to secure entry in the program. In another parallel with H2A., California and Texas growers during the Bracero era were able to count on ample support from state and federal authorities in defending the program and overlooking its abuses (Gonzalez 2006).

One way to make sense of the contradiction in the role of the state in the H2A program—which on the one hand supplies cheap workers, while on the other requires farmers to abide by housing regulations—is to pay attention to the interested private-sector constituencies that have historically shaped policy. In ongoing H2A debates in Congress, while proponents of the program argue that workers' rights are respected in the H2A contract, agribusiness representatives have pressed for legislators to remove the few worker protections that exist to make the program more user-friendly to farmers. They have proposed simplifying the process for farmers requesting workers, getting rid of requirements that farmers provide housing, and reducing the adjusted minimum wage rate. Today's agribusiness lobby to expand the H2A program has precedent in the lobby of growers that kept farmworkers excluded from New Deal labor protections.

While growers seek to streamline regulations that interfere with profitability, they show remarkable tolerance for bureaucratic irrationality in other areas, such as the lack of state appropriation of funds to enforce regulations and the U.S. Department of Labor's rubber-stamping of H2A work orders (99 percent of which are approved). Public criticism about these inadequacies frustrates employees in state agencies who prefer to talk about progress made since the 1970s, rather than the politicized nature of the program. Agency spokespersons insist: "We're doing the best we can with limited resources."

Interestingly, more frank criticisms of state policies come from Leroy Dunn, who complained in interviews that state inspectors rarely fined non-H2A farmers for substandard housing. And here Dunn has a point. For example, the 1,328 farms with inspected housing in 1998 accounted for less than a third of the migrant workers (H2A and non-H2A) hired by North Carolina farms. A former agricultural field agent told me it was common practice in the department to sidestep rules on inspected housing by registering undocumented migrants as day laborers, even though agents knew the farmer would rent them housing to make it feasible for them to work. Supervisors acknowledged those practices take place. Turf battles with the NCGA aside, state field agents and the NCGA both serve similar farmer clients, and neither have much incentive to enforce federal regulations that anger farmers, who wield political influence in the state legislature and have long enjoyed a level of immunity from public scrutiny.

These "regimes of truth" (Taussig 1992), where inconvenient policies become officially ignored, are equally vivid at those intersections where local practices on farms meet federal oversight. Despite receiving myriad complaints about the NCGA, the regional U.S. Department of Labor office in Atlanta declined to engage in any sustained investigation. Officials in Georgia likely recalled the debacle following the 1998 INS raids on the lucrative Vidalia onion harvest when federal agents were taken to task by state politicians who denounced the raids as threatening farmers' livelihoods. The local INS office was ordered to scale back surprise raids and to allow illegal workers to finish out the harvest and settled for a compromise allowing greater INS scrutiny of farmers' future hiring ("INS: Enforcement, Detention" 1998).

Although labor relations often take a back seat to trade in mainstream economic analysis, this study's focus on labor supply reminds us of Marx's (1967 [1867]) insights that labor is a fundamental denominator of value in the production of commodities and that the profits (capital) that make up economic growth are derived from surplus labor value (63, 75, 177–211). Free-trade accords such as NAFTA deregulated the flow of capital across borders, facilitating the leverage of bankers and transnational corporate actors; unlike European free-trade rules, however, the accord did nothing to liberalize laws on the flows of newly dispossessed human migrants on which U.S. agribusiness has come to depend for much of its profitability since the 1980s (Otero 1996; Sassen 1998). As a result, Mexico's marginalized rural workers have played a vital role in the restructuring of U.S. capitalism in the neoliberal period (Gledhill 1998). Access to cheap and pliable labor was essential to North Carolina's rise in status to the second most profitable agricultural state in 1990.

One way that programs like the H2A enable U.S. agribusiness to prosper is through selecting for able-bodied, young men (as opposed to families or women), facilitating a process in which the site of production (U.S. farms) is removed from the site of labor's reproduction, such as the impoverished families and villages of rural Mexico (see Burawoy 1976). Thus the infrastructure for labor's reproduction continues to be regarded as a "social problem" of the Mexican government. Historically, remittances from workers have failed to fill this gap in rural development (Gonzalez 2006).

This recalls Meillassoux's (1981) description of South African and French policies on migrant workers as "double labor markets" with two types of workers, (1) those who were integrated into a capitalist economy (and could not survive on wages offered migrants) and (2) migrant workers who only partially reproduced themselves within the capitalist sector. Strict legal restrictions on migrants were necessary to maintain this division; for example, France maintained lower wage scales for migrants, who were mainly hired for temporary jobs and endured arbitrary police harassment; South Africa's apartheid system used work permits, a pass system, rules against wives or children accompanying workers, and restrictions on long-term residence outside the "homelands."

Gonzalez (2006) also draws parallels between the Bracero and H2A systems and colonial systems of labor supply in British-ruled India, which in the late 1800s sent natives to the British West Indies to replace recently freed slaves, and in French-ruled Algeria where laws accommodated restricted immigration from colonized territories to ensure the labor needs of private enterprises (24–31). In both cases, the immigrant laborers were manipulated in ways that served the interest of capitalist employers, and they were denied full citizenship rights.

The U.S. "double labor market" is maintained in part through rhetorical sleights of hand that hide a contradiction in neoliberal ideology. On the one hand, the advantages of a "free" (unregulated) market for U.S. exports are touted as essential to recent (and future) profitability, hence NAFTA policies of pushing countries like Mexico to drop protectionist policies like tariffs on imported goods. On the other hand, while condemning protectionism abroad, lobbyists defend government protections of their own industry (in this case, to assure a steady flow of cheap labor to growers) as essential to profitability because of the heightened competition of the global market.

For example, in a March 2000 statement before Congress, an economist with the National Council of Agricultural Employers (NCAE) credited "global markets" and "the strong drive for freer trade" as responsible for the "dramatic growth" in profits for U.S. vegetable and fruit growers (for example, doubled receipts for fruits, tripled receipts for vegetables since 1980). He then went on to argue that growers could not afford the wages and benefits required by the H2A program due to their need to compete in the "global market place."[13] The rhetorical shift is a necessary concession to the

real existing double standard that neoliberal policies promote. Large growers argue in a principled manner against state regulations such as minimum
wage laws that impede profit making, but their zeal to roll back government
disappears when it comes to other state regulations (such as crop subsidies
or the H2A program), which facilitate profit making.

It is difficult to sustain such a contradictory logic through discourse alone.
Racism and xenophobia are also vital elements in the maintenance of a
"double labor market." In North Carolina, as in apartheid South Africa and
Rhodesia, the migrant labor market was reinforced by forms of violence and
an atmosphere of fear. As Meillassoux (1981) noted, "In this way employers
and governments take advantage of the contradiction which is forced upon
them by this type of overexploitation (whereby they simultaneously have
to attract and repel foreign rural-born workers)" (120).

Certainly ethnic difference, reinforced by the language barrier between
white farmers and Latino workers, helps to rationalize poor living conditions
and harsh strategies used to manage workers.[14] The informal labor arrangements encouraged for success in the competitive marketplace dovetail with
prejudices against centralized government in southern popular culture. In the
neoliberal ideal, government defines its function around facilitating market
contracts, with discourses of efficiency and freedom. By this value system,
the moral concept of government by "social contract" is abandoned, with
institutional responsibility shifted to contractual relationships with private
parties. No single government agency stood responsible for protecting immigrant workers, who lacked a public constituency in the electorate.

The irony is that the contract farming that many small- to medium-size
farmers have found themselves caught up in under new forms of rationalized, vertically integrated agriculture is also a form of flexible labor that
maximizes profits for processors.[15] The "struggling small farmer" as a lone
operator is increasingly a myth. The main employers of farm labor in eastern
North Carolina's tobacco belt have been large landowners for a long time,
but consolidation and vertical integration have concentrated ownership
even more since the 1980s. It is not incidental that these counties also tend
to have the fewest public services, lowest property taxes, and least public
infrastructure in the state (Hall 1986).

Thus, in spite of the anti-immigrant xenophobia that has emerged since
2006 and despite the post-2008 recession, the reality is that the U.S. economy
is more dependent on immigrant labor than ever. Given these labor relations, even such disparate parties as Wall Street bankers and labor leaders
acknowledge that the border is likely to remain porous. So it is not surprising
that many Democrats and most Republicans are sympathetic to the solutions
proposed by large growers, such as expanding the H2A program, loosening

its worker protections, and in some proposals even using it to create a lower-tier guest-worker status for the 10–12 million Latino immigrants who lack legal papers (Gonzalez 2006).

Grassroots Immigration Reform: A Transnational Labor Union

This study demonstrates how, in the absence of worker representation or regulatory oversight, neoliberal market pressures, exacerbated by ethnic discrimination, may take precedent in shaping labor brokerage programs, resulting in systems that resemble forms of indentured servitude. Given the stalemated condition of immigration reform, the recent successes of FLOC in its efforts to reform the NCGA through a labor contract deserve attention (see also Smith-Nonini 2009).

The multiparty contract, signed by the union, Mt. Olive Pickle Company, and the NCGA, came about a few months after North Carolina's Legal Services office filed a lawsuit on behalf of nine Mexican H2A workers, charging that the NCGA had maintained an illegal blacklist and had intimidated and extorted workers in violation of the state's Racketeer Influenced Corrupt Organizations Act.[16] The three parties signed two labor agreements: one allowed FLOC to organize within the H2A program and to have a voice in recruitment and oversight of contract provisions, and the other guaranteed 10 percent raises to workers for Mt. Olive growers over a three-year period and provided incentives for non-NCGA cucumber growers to cooperate with FLOC. Elimination of the NCGA blacklist was a condition of the contract. The signing led to more than 8,500 H2A workers and 600 undocumented workers joining FLOC, bumping North Carolina up to forty-ninth, instead of fiftieth, in the nation for union membership. Within a month, over a thousand grievances were filed with FLOC by workers, most dealing with the blacklist and recruiting irregularities. FLOC Vice President Leticia Zavala reported that resolved grievances in the first year gained workers over $4,000 in back wages and allowed 150 blacklisted workers to return in the H2A program. For the first time, workers gained unpaid sick leave, bereavement leave, and receipts for fees paid. The contract included a rapid grievance process and a system of seniority that gave priority to experienced workers in allotting the coveted H2A positions.

Despite improvements, there were also new insecurities for workers tied to gradual contraction of the NCGA, as the phase-out of federal price supports for tobacco led some growers to drop the crop. Also, some farmers have shifted to smaller nonunion H2A brokerages or to undocumented workers. Clearly the fact that most tobacco workers remain undocumented and without union protection threatens the gains of the union, and since 2005 the union has built a new campaign aimed at R. J. Reynolds Tobacco Company, demanding once again that a profitable corporation share responsibility for conditions on the farms that grow the crops it processes.

The most challenging aspect of the union's work since its 2004 contract has been FLOC's innovative efforts to work on both sides of the border. This arose in response to workers' reports of frequent scams by private Mexican recruiters hired by the NCGA who charged excess fees to prospective workers, sometimes in the thousands of dollars. In response, the union opened an office in Monterrey, Mexico, to educate workers about their labor rights and monitor Mexican recruiting networks. A FLOC lawsuit against the NCGA that was decided in FLOC's favor in 2006 required the brokerage to stop passing fees for transport and visas along to workers. The lawsuit disrupted a lucrative market in recruiting fees thought to be worth over $10 million.

Resentment by recruiters over the case may have motivated the unsolved April 2007 murder of FLOC staff member Santiago Rafael Cruz in his room above the Monterrey office. Cruz was tied up and beaten to death by unknown assailants in the middle of the night, and the brutal aspects of the crime suggested a political killing. The case was accepted by the Organization of American States (OAS) Inter-American Commission on Human Rights, which began requiring Mexican officials to provide protection for FLOC staff.

Clearly, FLOC's experience suggests that the transnational systems of graft serving private interests tied to immigrant pipelines cannot be resolved without organizing across borders. In the absence of socially responsive state policies, such organizing offers one path, however problematic, for reintegrating the "double labor market" that falsely separates economic production from the social processes that make life worth living.

But studies of labor history suggest that unions cannot succeed in a vacuum. UFW gains for farmworkers in California were undercut during the 1980s by failures in union leadership, California's hostile political climate (which led to business-friendly policies permitting the rise of crew leaders), and the lax rules of the IRCA amnesty law (which spurred further border-crossing, adding to a surplus workforce that the new brokers could exploit). Similarly, it is not incidental that the NCGA's willingness to negotiate with FLOC in North Carolina coincided with the decline in federal supports for tobacco farmers. In both cases, government interventions shaped the political environment for both agricultural profitability and conditions for farm labor.

Acutely aware of these power relations, FLOC has been a leader in campaigns for federal immigration reform. FLOC President Baldemar Velasquez argues against expansion of guest-worker programs as a solution to illegal immigration, favoring instead a system in which immigrant workers carry cards allowing them to work in the United States and to move freely between employers.

As long as the U.S. and Mexican economies are conjoined in a free-trade agreement like NAFTA that is highly leveraged against Mexican smallholders, most farm labor will remain vulnerable, trapped in illegal or quasi-legal contracting situations that lead to suffering and loss of life in the name of farm profit. As the current recession draws attention to the dangers of scapegoating, it is all the more clear that democratic efforts to broaden protections of labor laws and resist draconian immigration policies will be essential to creating conditions under which organized farmworkers can defend their gains and expand them.

Notes

1. From 1999 to 2000, I received support as a Mellon-Sawyer postdoctoral fellow through the University Center for International Studies at the University of North Carolina at Chapel Hill. I led a 1998–1999 Institute for Southern Studies documentary project on farm labor and from 1999 to 2005 was active with the Farmworker Action Team at the Eno River Unitarian-Universalist Fellowship (ERUUF) in Durham, North Carolina, which received funding from the Unitarian Universalist Funding Program to do public education about farmworker issues.

2. My visits to camps were often on weekends with a Unitarian-Universalist volunteer group, based in Durham. Visits often included recreational activities and a picnic lunch. Some seasons the group returned multiple times to the same camp so volunteers could follow experiences of workers throughout the season. I was a volunteer driver who transported workers to and from union meetings during the summers of 2005–2008.

3. Unpublished documentary materials compiled by Student Action for Farmworkers, Duke University, Durham, NC.

4. "U.S. Department of Labor Report to Congress: The Agricultural Labor Market—Status and Recommendations" (December 2000).

5. A comparison of ten eastern tobacco-growing counties with other counties revealed that they had an average farm size of 271 acres, or over 1.7 times the state average (158 acres), according to the 1998 North Carolina Agricultural Statistics Handbook. Farmers in these counties tend to grow labor-intensive vegetable crops that fit into the tobacco growing season.

6. North Carolina Agricultural Statistics, North Carolina Department of Agriculture, 1998.

7. The poor enforcement of regulations has consequences in human health. Researchers have found high rates of intestinal disease, skin diseases, and evidence of pesticide exposure among North Carolina farmworkers and their families. Most summers one or two farmworkers in the state die in the fields, usually due to dehydration and heat stroke. A 2005 study of heat-related fatalities in the state since

1977 found forty farmworker deaths, which was 45 percent of all occupational heat-related deaths (Mirabelli and Richardson 2005).

8. Leroy Dunn is a pseudonym.

9. Information from interviews with state officials in Agricultural Services, with a FLOC representative who visited the men, viewing of television footage of the incident, and reports in Ward 1999; Yeoman 2001; unsigned Associated Press articles in *Goldsboro News-Argus,* June 11, 1998, 2A, and in the *Raleigh News & Observer,* June 11, 1998.

10. The recordings (accompanied by translated transcripts) were played at a press conference held by a coalition of farmworker advocates shortly after the September 1999 floods.

11. For further documentation of controversies surrounding the H2A program in North Carolina, see Ward 1999; Schrader 1999; Glascock 1999; and Yeoman 2001.

12. The speech was videotaped and transcribed by an intern from Student Action with farmworkers who attended the orientation session and later shared the material with reporters attending a Legal Services press conference in fall 1999. The July incident was also witnessed by visitors to that orientation session who reported on it at a meeting of farmworker advocates.

13. Farm labor unions have pointed out this contradiction. Baldemar Velasquez, president of FLOC, sometimes argued that federal services for migrants such as health clinics and legal services are, in fact, subsidies to agribusiness. With the decline of the small farmer, such subsidies become harder to justify as serving a public good.

14. Although ethnic difference exacerbates the inequities migrants suffer, common ethnicity is no protection against exploitation; many unscrupulous non-H2A crew leaders are Mexicans or Mexican Americans (Hubner 2000), and these quasi-legal arrangements lead to overly "personalistic" labor relations in which *contratistas* call attention to "favors" they do for workers and seek to maintain a sense of obligation (Heyman 1998). Workers, lacking money, legal status, information, the ability to speak English, and transportation, often respond with quiet compliance.

15. Many farmers' Calvinist ethic of hard work and long-honed sense of persecution (by unpredictable weather and government bureaucrats) make for a kind of solidarity among farmers. Love of the land, traditions of self-reliance, and aversion to working under a boss are central to this romance (Mooney 1988; Barlett 1993). Whiteness and citizenship are unspoken assumptions about normalcy and carry a sense of entitlement (e.g., to public services, tobacco subsidies, hurricane aid) as well as exclusion (with immigrants taking a role previously held by blacks in being denied access to public goods). Many rural whites I interviewed were surprised to learn that illegal immigrants had any labor rights.

16. Also, that summer the United Methodist Church finally joined the many other U.S. churches in supporting the FLOC boycott of Mt. Olive, despite CEO Bill Bryan's efforts to defeat the proposal at the Methodist General Assembly. Bryan, a Methodist, had organized conservative church leaders to support the company and reportedly was demoralized by the loss. Around the same time, FLOC president Baldemar Velasquez began negotiating with two major supermarket chains about

removing Mt. Olive Pickles from their shelves. FLOC had already convinced Kroger stores in the area around the union's hometown of Toledo, Ohio, to drop the brand.

References

Arcury, Thomas, et al. 2005, "Organophosphate Pesticide Exposure in Farmworker Family Members in Western North Carolina and Virginia: Case Comparisons." *Human Organization* 64, no. 1: 40–51.

Audley, John J., et al. 2004. *NAFTA's Promise and Reality: Lessons from Mexico for the Hemisphere.* New York: Carnegie Endowment for International Peace.

Bacon, David. 2001. "Braceros or Amnesty." *Dollars and Sense* no. 238 (November/December).

Barger, W. K., and Ernesto Reza. 1994. *The Farm Labor Movement in the Midwest: Social Change and Adaptation among Migrant Farmworkers.* Austin: University of Texas Press.

Barlett, Peggy. 1993. *American Dreams, Rural Realities: Family Farms in Crisis.* Chapel Hill: University of North Carolina Press.

Bartra, Roger. 1993. *Agrarian Structure and Political Power in Mexico.* Baltimore: Johns Hopkins University Press.

Burawoy, Michael. 1976. "The Functions and Reproduction of Migrant Labor: Comparative Material from Southern Africa and the United States." *American Journal of Sociology* 81: 1050–87.

Commission on Agricultural Workers. 1992. "Report of the Commission on Agricultural Workers." Washington, DC: Commission on Agricultural Workers.

Ciesielski, Stephen, John Seed, Juan Ortiz, and J. Metts. 1992. "Intestinal Parasites among North Carolina's Migrant Farmworkers." *American Journal of Public Health* 82: 1258–62.

Cleeland, Nancy. 1999. "Immigration Policies Threaten U.S. Growth, Economy: A Decade of Restrictions Has Compounded Severe Labor Shortages in Many Fields." *Los Angeles Times,* April 11.

Compa, Lance. 2000. *Unfair Advantage: Workers' Freedom of Association in the United States under International Human Rights Standards.* Human Rights Watch Report. Commission on Agricultural Workers, Final Report, 1992, xxii.

Fann, Neal. 2003. Unpublished manuscript on H2A abandonments in North Carolina, prepared at the Sanford Institute for Public Policy, Duke University.

General Accounting Office. 1997. *H-2A Agricultural Guestworker Program Changes Could Improve Services to Employers and Better Protect Workers.* Report, HEHS-98–20.

Glascock, Ned. 1999. "Foreign Labor on Home Soil." *Raleigh News and Observer,* August 29, 1.

Gledhill, John. 1991. *Casi Nada: A Study of Agrarian Reform in the Homeland of Cardenismo.* Austin: University of Texas Press.

Gledhill, John, 1998, "The Mexican Contribution to Restructuring U.S. Capitalism." *Critique of Anthropology* 18, no. 3: 279–96.

Gonzalez, Gilbert G. 2006. *Guest Workers or Colonized Labor? Mexican Labor Migration to the United States*. Boulder, Colo.: Paradigm.

Goode, Judith, and Jeff Maskovsky. 2001. "Introduction." In *The New Poverty Studies,* ed. Judith Goode and Jeff Maskovsky. New York: New York University Press.

Griffith, David. 2006. "Rural Industry and Mexican Immigration and Settlement in North Carolina." In *New Destinations: Mexican Immigration in the United States,* ed. Victor Zuñiga and Rubén Hernandez-Leon, 50–75. New York: Russell Sage Foundation.

Griffith, David, Monica Heppel, and Luis Torres. 2002. *Guests in Rural America: Profiles of Temporary Worker Programs from U.S. and Mexican Perspectives*. Final report submitted to the Ford Foundation.

Hahamovitch, Cindy. 1999. "The Politics of Labor Scarcity: Expediency and the Birth of the Agricultural 'Guestworkers' Program." Center for Immigration Studies, *Backgrounder,* December.

Hahamovitch, Cindy. 2002. "Standing Idly By: 'Organized' Farmworkers in South Florida during the Depression and World War II." In *The Human Cost of Food: Farmworkers' Lives, Labor, and Advocacy,* ed. Charles Thompson Jr. and Melinda Wiggins. Austin: University of Texas Press.

Hall, Bob. 1986. *Who Owns North Carolina?: Report of the Landownership Project (Part II)*. Durham, N.C.: Institute for Southern Studies.

Harvey, David. 2003. *The New Imperialism*. Oxford: Oxford University Press.

Heyman, Josiah McC. 1998. "State Effects on Labor Exploitation." *Critique of Anthropology* 18, no. 2: 157–80.

Holland, Dorothy, Donald M. Nonini, and Catherine Lutz. 2002. "Social Landscapes of North Carolina, the South, and America as the Century Opens." In *Local Democracy under Siege: Public Interests and Private Politics,* chap. 2. New York: New York University Press.

Hubner, John. 2000. "Farm Workers Face Hard Times; Middlemen Maximize Profits by Paying as Little as Possible." *San Jose Mercury News,* July 7.

Human Rights Watch. 2000. *Fingers to the Bone: United States Failure to Protect Child Farmworkers*. New York: Human Rights Watch.

"INS: Enforcement, Detention." 1998. *Migration News* 5, no. 4 (April). http://migration.ucdavis.edu/mn/more.php?id=1489_0_2_0 (accessed September 25, 2012).

Martin, Philip. 1997. "Immigration and the Changing Face of Rural America." Paper in the series on Increasing Understanding of Public Problems and Policies, presented at the National Public Policy Education Conference. http://ageconsearch.umn.edu/handle/17709 (accessed September 25, 2012).

Martin, Philip. 1999. "California's Farm Labor Market and Immigration Reform." In *Foreign Temporary Workers in America,* ed. B. Lindsay Lowell, chap. 8. Westport, Conn.: Quorum Books.

Martin, Philip. 2001. "Farm Labor Policy Changes." Unpublished manuscript.

Martin, Philip. 2004. "Promise Unfulfilled: Why Didn't Collective Bargaining Transform California's Farm Labor Market?" http://www.cis.org/Unionization-CaliforniaFarmLabor (accessed October 24, 2012).

Marx, Karl. 1967 [1867]. *Capital: A Critical Analysis of Capitalist Production,* vol. 1. New York: International.

Meillassoux, Claude. 1981. *Maidens, Meal and Money: Capitalism and the Domestic Community.* Cambridge: Cambridge University Press.

Mirabelli, Maria, and David Richardson. 2005. "Heat-Related Fatalities in North Carolina." *American Journal of Public Health* 95, no. 4: 635–37.

Mooney, Patrick. 1988. *My Own Boss? Class, Rationality and the Family Farm.* Boulder, Colo.: Westview.

Otero, Gerardo. 1996. *Neoliberalism Revisited: Economic Restructuring and Mexico's Political Future.* Boulder, Colo.: Westview.

Quandt, Sara A., Thomas A. Arcury, Colin K. Austin, and Rosa M. Saavedra. 1998. "Farmworker and Farmer Perceptions of Farmworker Agricultural Chemical Exposure in North Carolina." *Human Organization* 57: 359–68.

Raghavan, Chakravarthi. 2000. "Mexico: NAFTA Corn Liberalization Fails Farmers, Environment." *South-North Development Monitor (SUNS).* http://www.twnside.org.sg/title/mexico.htm (accessed September 25, 2012).

Roberts, Paul. 2008. *The End of Food.* Boston: Mariner Books.

Rothenberg, Daniel. 1998. *With These Hands: The Hidden World of Migrant Farmworkers Today.* Berkeley: University of California Press.

Runsten, David, and Sandra Archibald. 1992. "Technology and Labor-Intensive Agriculture: Competition between Mexico and the United States." In *U.S.-Mexico Relations: Labor Market Interdependence,* ed. Jorge Bustamante, Clark Reynolds, and Raul Hinojosa Ojeda. Palo Alto, Calif.: Stanford University Press.

Sassen, Saskia. 1998. "America's Immigration 'Problem.'" In *Globalization and It's Discontents.* New York: New Press.

Schrader, Esther. 1999. "Fielding a Legal Team of Workers." *Los Angeles Times,* August 26.

Scott, James C. 1985. *Weapons of the Weak: Everyday Forms of Peasant Resistance.* New Haven, Conn.: Yale University Press.

Skaggs, Sheryl, Jeffrey Leiter, and Donald Tomaskovic-Devey. 2000. "Latino/a Employment Growth in North Carolina: Ethnic Displacement or Replacement?" Unpublished manuscript.

Smith-Nonini, Sandy. 1999. *Uprooting Injustice: A Report on Working Conditions for North Carolina Farmworkers and the Farm Labor Organizing Committee's Mt. Olive Initiative.* Durham, N.C.: Institute for Southern Studies.

Smith-Nonini, Sandy. 2005. "Federally-Sponsored Mexican Migrants in the Transnational South." In *The American South in a Global World,* ed. James L. Peacock, Harry L. Watson, and Carrie R. Matthews, 59–79. Chapel Hill: University of North Carolina Press.

Smith-Nonini, Sandy. 2009. "H2A Guest Workers and the State in North Carolina: From Transnational Production to Transnational Organizing." In *Global Connections and Local Receptions: New Latino Immigration to the Southeastern US,* ed. Jon Shefner and Fran Ansley, 249–78. Knoxville: University of Tennessee Press.

Taussig, Michael. 1992. *The Nervous System*. New York: Routledge.

Ward, Leah Beth. 1999. "Desperate Harvest: N.C. Growers' Trade in Foreign Farm Workers Draws Scrutiny." *Charlotte Observer*, October 31.

Wood, Philip. 1986. *Southern Capitalism: The Political Economy of North Carolina 1880–1980*. Durham, N.C.: Duke University Press.

Wright, Gavin. 1996. *Old South, New South: Revolutions in the Southern Economy Since the Civil War*. Baton Rouge: Louisiana State University Press.

Yeoman, Barry. 2001. "Silence in the Fields." *Mother Jones Magazine*, January/February.

CHAPTER 5

On Removing Migrant Labor in a Right-to-Work State

The Failure of Employer Sanctions in Oklahoma

LINDA ALLEGRO

> Some of us are illegal, and some are not wanted, our work contract's out and we have to move on; Six hundred miles to that Mexican border, they chase us like outlaws, like rustlers, like thieves.
>
> —Woody Guthrie, "Plane Wreck at Los Gatos" (1948)

> Soy mexicano señores. Me siento decepcionado. Soy vecino del pais de donde me han rechasado. Yo les trabajo barato y nunca lo han valorado. Con mucho orgullo lo digo que soy un hombre hispano. Vengo de mi linda tierra. Es el pais mexicano. Mi continente es el tuyo. También soy americano.

> I am Mexican, ladies and gentlemen. I feel deceived. I'm a neighbor of the country that has rejected me. I work for low wages and, yet, I am not much appreciated. But with much pride I say I am a Hispanic man. I come from my beautiful homeland, my Mexican nation. My continent is the same as yours. I, too, am American.
>
> —Juan Villaseñor, Michoacáno migrant laborer and songwriter living in Oklahoma, "La Nueva Ley de Oklahoma" (2007)

In February 2008, former Mexican President Vicente Fox spoke to a crowded auditorium in Tulsa, Oklahoma, advocating for further economic integration between the North American partnering nations.[1] As a free-market campaigner, Fox in his speech hailed the benefits of unrestricted free enterprise for the corporate benefits and jobs it creates. While his business-friendly and pro-immigrant audience gave him a standing ovation, a group of thirty or so anti-NAFTA protestors picketed the talk outside. Holding signs that read "Remember the Alamo" and "No to Amnesty and Open Borders," the demonstrators expressed discontent with NAFTA for the outsourcing and increase in Mexican migration the treaty spawned. The incident was noteworthy because Oklahoma had passed one of the toughest anti-"illegals" bills in the nation, known as HB 1804, which aimed to expunge the undocumented population from the state.[2] Emboldened by the highly charged restrictionist rhetoric of the bill, the protestors found a platform upon which to vent their frustrations over job loss and economic hardship, holding the migrants themselves responsible for the complexity of regional economic transformations.[3] The new language of "illegality" offered them a sense of racist deniability disguised in the name of the rule of law.

This chapter begins with a discussion of the goals proposed by The Oklahoma Taxpayer and Citizen Protection Act (HB 1804) passed by the Oklahoma legislature in early 2007. It analyzes the successful lawsuit filed by a consortium of chambers of commerce and business groups to nullify aspects of the bill that intended to penalize employers for hiring undocumented workers. Next it discusses the contradictory nature of attempts to discipline big business in a right-to-work state that has favored antiregulatory measures to entice firms to Oklahoma by, among other things, weakening labor protections. This, in part, paved the way for the influx of nonunion foreign workers. By offering a critical assessment of employer sanctions, this work unpacks how the post-Immigration Reform and Control Act (IRCA) regime has weakened labor rights of both foreign and domestic workers by dividing workers along legal-status categories, effectively weakening labor laws generally. Furthermore, the antiunion posturing of the business community translated into a proimmigrant position by default. This work raises concerns over the way this formula has led to the chipping away of worker rights more broadly. The concluding section looks at the new role of local law enforcement in disciplining migrant lives in public spaces (beyond the workplace) and to the implications this has for working people and their families.

Anti-immigrant Bill: HB 1804

On November 1, 2007, one of the nation's most far-reaching anti-"illegals" bills went into effect in Oklahoma. HB 1804 introduced a multipronged strategy for deterring and deporting undocumented migrants. The bill proposed reining in virtually every sector of society from social service agencies, businesses, students, to private citizens, for possible immigration inspection in the quest to expunge unauthorized migrants. Specifically, the bill sought to terminate the ability of undocumented migrants to get official government identification cards (including driver's licenses, ID cards, occupation licenses); end social services or entitlement benefits (including prenatal care); empower state and local law enforcement to enforce federal immigration law, including the ability to physically detain undocumented migrants until deported; impose requirements on employers to check the employment eligibility of all new hires as well as create legal and other financial sanctions on these employers who would knowingly and willfully employ undocumented workers; and make it harder for undocumented college students to get financial assistance in state colleges.[4]

Encouraged by high ratings after the bill was passed, the bill's author, Rep. Randy Terrill (Republican from Moore), proposed extending interior border control measures under what he called the "son of HB 1804." Here he proposed seizing the property of those who knowingly harbor and assist "illegal" immigrants, making English the official language of the state, increasing funding for local law enforcement agencies to train in federal immigration law, and denying U.S. citizenship to children born to undocumented mothers.[5] Of the wide range of enforcement provisions endorsed, this research focuses on the employer sanctions components of the bill. After all, if it wasn't for opportunities to work, would undocumented migrants endure the difficulties and harassment often associated with their presence in the United States? Clearly, any attempt to address "illegals" requires an assessment of the workplace, the leading magnet of migrant labor.

The measures addressing employer sanctions as proposed in HB 1804 are worth noting in detail. These measures included new compliance procedures for subcontractors to verify the immigration status of employees, a state tax on businesses that refuse to comply, and a cause for action against employers by citizens and lawful permanent residents if fired and replaced with an unauthorized worker. The employer sanctions provisions would not go into effect until almost a year after the enactment of HB 1804 as a way to offer employers time to prepare for new compliance measures. Hence from the outset, the bill offered leniency to employers to prepare for the new legal requirements before them. As will be explained later, a successful lawsuit was filed by a consortium of chambers of commerce and business groups virtually invalidating the employer sanctions provisions of HB 1804. Lessons from the roughly three-year span of events, from 2006 to 2009, indicate the highly symbolic nature of the employer sanctions rhetoric in an otherwise unenforceable approach to immigration control in the workplace, particularly for a right-to-work (RtW) state that has advanced a friendly-to-business climate.

The employer sanctions provisions of the bill proved to be bad public policy for a state that has promoted economic development by enticing corporations to relocate to Oklahoma. Indeed the rising growth rates of the Latino population since the mid- to late 1990s correlate directly with the economic expansion of key industries, such as animal processing, construction, and services that employ Latino workers (Barlett and Steele 2001). Due to declining population trends in much of rural America, a migrant workforce helped jump-start nascent economic development given the out-migration of working-age Oklahomans who left pockets of the rural Heartland a decade earlier as federal agricultural policy called on farmers to either "get big or get out" (Davidson 1996). Beginning in the late 1970s as the United States embarked on an ambitious program to vastly expand the country's agricultural export trade, food production became increasingly consolidated in the hands of a few corporations that took on virtually all aspects of agricultural production, packaging, distribution, and marketing (Davidson 1996). The growth of the Latino labor force in Oklahoma results, in large part, from macrostructural regional economic changes that encouraged and recruited Latin American migrants to work in expanding industrial agriculture and corollary industries (Stull and Broadway 2004; Barlett and Steele 2001; Stull, Broadway, and Griffith 1995). So if an ideological climate premised on deregulation and later embodied in the passage of RtW in 2001 propelled this new labor force to the state through the incentives it offered key industries, how was an anti-immigrant bill going to disaggregate segments from the newly constituted workforce?[6] Furthermore, how were employer penalties going to be enforced when chambers of commerce and business groups had worked to build support for making Oklahoma the twenty-second state to adopt RtW legislation? We turn next to Oklahoma's adoption of RtW laws in 2001.

Right-to-Work in Oklahoma

RtW laws are often used as a proxy for gauging a state's business-friendly climate (Dinlersoz and Hernandez-Murillo 2002). Indeed, much of the argument in favor of state RtW laws is that site selection of firms is based on whether business-friendly laws exist (Reed 2001; Dinlersoz and Hernandez-Murillo 2002). RtW campaigns are often accompanied by highly funded public relations schemes to support their goals (King and Catlett-King 2007). The origin of RtW begins with the Taft-Hartley Act passed by the U.S. Congress in 1947 affirming states' rights to decide labor practices. Taft-Hartley was a reaction to the National Labor Relations Act (NLRA), one of the hallmarks of the New Deal labor legislation of the 1930s that expanded the rights of organized labor by promoting the "closed shop" or prounion model as a key labor-management arrangement. Driven by a philosophy of free markets and limited government, a paradigm shift in labor relations began to unfold in the late 1940s seeking to erode the perceived legal privileges of organized labor (Clay and Larson 1998). At the cornerstone of the RtW philosophy is the notion that anything mandatory violates freedom, individual rights, and civil liberties. By invoking "freedom," the movement successfully crafted the notion that compulsory union membership is un-American (Leef 2005; King and Catlett-King 2007; Jacobs and Dixon 2006). For fiscal conservatives, collective bargaining by unions is viewed as an unwarranted restraint on free trade because it is perceived as a transgression on property rights (Jacobs and Dixon 2006: 123). In the decade following the passage of Taft-Hartley in 1947, twenty-one states, all in the South, Southwest, and Midwest, where labor organizing has been historically weak, adopted RtW legislation.

Organized labor euphemizes the term to "right-to-work-for-less," maintaining that dues-paying is a prerequisite for preventing the "free-rider" problem. In their view, RtW laws amount to union-busting measures that violate the right to association and undermine the ability of organized labor to bargain for better wages, working conditions, and other benefits (Cushman Wood 2004). Union dues are understood as the cost of union membership, helping fund the various activities the union engages in. The precipitous decline in union membership, especially in the private sector since the late 1970s, results, in part, from a capitalist offensive and hegemonic discourse that triumphed over all other alternative forms of structuring economic activity (Clawson and Clawson 1999: 101). With the implosion of the Soviet Union in the late 1980s and with it a dismissal of the efficacy of state-driven economics, neoliberal ideology obtained global acceptance and expanded its reach (Klein 2007). Corporate forces assumed a far more confrontational stance toward organized labor, dramatically changing the relationship between business and unions that had until then assumed a coexistence of sorts (Clawson and Clawson 1999: 96). Unions themselves also bear a great deal of responsibility for the top-down approach they enlisted that alienated rank-and-file members often remaining complacent by settling for contracts they increasingly lost (Moody 1988).

Oklahoma was a relative late adopter of RtW, achieving such status in 2001 through a statewide ballot. An RtW referendum was defeated in the mid-1960s and remained a nonissue for decades in step with a nationwide trend that had largely shelved the legislation.[7] RtW activists in Oklahoma attempted to resuscitate the legislation in 2000 on the claim that neighboring RtW states, such as Texas, Kansas, and Arkansas, were benefitting from economic productivity by favoring corporate incentives and outlawing compulsory unionism. Organized labor cautioned that RtW would cause wages to fall, eliminate jobs, reduce worker benefits such as health insurance and retirement packages, and thwart union recruitment efforts. In August 2001, a group of economists issued a briefing paper through the Economic Policy Institute warning against the passage of RtW in Oklahoma under the idea that bidding down the cost of labor to attract firms away from other states "depletes a state's resources for investing in real economic development" while imposing significant social costs (Economic Policy Institute 2001: 2, 4). Their research evidenced that such legislation shifts the distribution of income from wages to profits and sends a negative message to home-grown skilled workers that may intensify out-migration of state-educated, young, skilled Oklahomans (Economic Policy Institute 2001: 4–6).

With pro-RtW officials newly elected to statewide offices in 2000, the RtW movement gained steam with strong endorsements from arch-conservative and owner of the Oklahoma City newspaper *The Oklahoman* E. K. Gaylord as well as from Wal-Mart, Bama Foods, OneOk, Healthfirst, and others who together contributed $6.1 million to the RtW campaign (King and Catlett-King 2007). Not surprising, the State Chamber of Commerce and the Oklahoma City Chamber of Commerce also worked to build support in the business community to vote for Question 695 (Leef 2005: 222–27). In one of the most expensive political campaigns in the state's history and only a few weeks after the terrorist attacks of September 11, 2001, when the "late-breaking call of standing up for America and freedom resonated well," RtW won with 54 percent of the vote (King and Catlett-King 2007: 18).

Nationwide, union membership has dropped steadily since the 1980s. While private-sector union density stood at 15 percent in 1985, it now hovers around 7.2 percent. Union membership in Oklahoma falls below this national average (U.S. Bureau of Labor Statistics 2010). The movement toward RtW in Oklahoma is noteworthy considering that the state once was a bastion of progressive populism embodied in radical agrarian movements and home to Socialist Party and Industrial Workers of the World (IWW) sympathy throughout the 1910s and 1920s (Dunbar-Ortiz 1997; Sellars 1998; Bissett 1999; Wiegand and Wiegand 2007). Arguably, the early-twentieth-century populist ideology was more compatible with internationalist worker solidarity than the more nationalistic populist inclination a hundred years later. When Oklahoma became the forty-sixth state in 1907, its constitution featured broad labor protections representing the widespread populist culture of the time. After all, the state motto enacted at statehood read, "Labor omnia vincit" (labor conquers all). Almost a century later, Oklahoma shifted ideologically to favor corporate interests, representing one of the most entrenched neoconservative states of the union.[8] How, then, were employer sanctions under the professed "war on illegals" to be carried out after the passage of the anti-immigrant bill, HB 1804? What new penalties would be imposed on employers in compliance with efforts to expunge the undocumented population of the state who ostensibly were causing "economic hardship and lawlessness" (HB 1804: introduction).

Economic Impact of HB 1804

Given the dramatic tenor of the rhetoric surrounding "illegal aliens" in the months leading up to and following the passage of HB 1804, a significant portion of the Latino workforce left the state. In summer and fall 2007, news stories surfaced about apartment complexes being vacated, religious congregations shrinking, parents pulling their children from schools, and economic loses of a cross section of businesses as migrants retreated.[9] Estimates of the out-migration stood at around 25,000 in Tulsa County alone, and news stories reported the departure of Latino migrants to perceived friendlier neighboring states, such as Arkansas, Texas, and Missouri, with some return migration to Mexico (*USA Today,* January 10, 2008; *Chicago Tribune,* February 10, 2008; *Dallas Morning News,* February 13, 2008). Given the nature of mixed-legal-status homes in immigrant communities, the exodus represented members of the documented Latino workforce as well as U.S. citizens. The fear of deportation, family separation, and the general unfriendly (often hostile) environment compelled immigrant families to pack up and leave. In the wake of the migrant exodus, Rep. Randy Terrill boasted that self-deportations were precisely what the bill intended. He stated, "HB 1804 proves that attrition through enforcement works. All you have to do is enforce the law, deny them the jobs, deny them the public benefits, give state and local law enforcement the ability to enforce federal immigration law, and the illegal aliens will simply self deport.[10]

Feeling the tense social and racial fallout of the bill, much of the migrant workforce also retreated farther into their communities, with a noticeable drop in activity in shopping centers, parks, and restaurants, opting to "lay low" in their homes and reducing their spending and consumption. Restaurants, money transfer services, and auto dealerships reported revenue loses (Postelwait 2008). The repercussion of the exodus and the chilling effect it produced drew a great deal of local and national attention, particularly for a state that when the bill was passed held a relatively low unemployment rate of 4.5 percent. In the words of an Oklahoma cotton farmer who employs migrant labor, "I can't find U.S. workers to do this job. Even at a higher wage I am willing to pay, we just don't have enough workers."[11] Shortly after the bill went into effect, as evidence of a migrant exodus surfaced, opposition to the legislation from the business community began to mount. One of the lone dissenters in the Oklahoma Legislature, Republican State Senator Harry Coates issued a press conference opposing the bill. Concerned about moral and economic impacts, he called for repealing sections of HB 1804. His motto was "Fix 1804" by repealing employer sanctions.

In February 2008, three months after the bill went into effect, an economic impact study commissioned by the Oklahoma Bankers Association was released assessing the early impact of the new law on productivity and offering an economic forecast if such out-migration continued or if migrants were deterred from entering the state (Economic Impact Group 2008). The economists determined that the out-migration of a significant part of the workforce was posing economic hardship on key sectors of the Oklahoman economy, particularly construction, hotel and hospitality, manufacturing, and services. All told, the study estimated a $1.8 billion reduction in the gross state product if out-migration continued and if future migrants were deterred from entering the state. The study concluded that "the Oklahoman economy is simply not large enough and sufficiently diverse in its industry to make up to accommodate a 3% reduction in the size of its labor force" (Economic Impact Group 2008: 17).

What was surfacing in these developments was a contradictory scenario in which, on the one hand, migrant labor is coveted but, on the other, there is a strong appeal to disaggregate the undocumented component from the workforce pool. The struggle between conserving RtW principles while upholding the ostensible rule of law evidenced inconsistencies marring the immigration debate. Without a federal legalization option on the table and with clear opposition by the pro-1804 camp to provisions of legalization given the widespread perception of "amnesty rewarding border violators," Oklahoma competed against its conflicting agendas. Meanwhile, the migrant community sought safety, guidance, and direction from emerging new actors in the community, including a more vocal role played by Catholic, Evangelical, and other churches; Spanish-language media; and newly constituted ethnic, civil, and immigrant rights groups.[12] Buying into the idea that HB 1804 would translate into job security for them, some rank-and-file union members quietly endorsed the bill. Later, in step with the national AFL-CIO's position, organized labor in the state opposed employer sanctions on the grounds that preoccupation with legal status of workers leads to divisive and distracting tactics preventing them from connecting their mutual interests.[13]

In February 2008, members of the business community, including the U.S. Chamber of Commerce, State Chamber of Commerce, Tulsa Metro Chamber, and other business groups, filed a lawsuit against the employer sanctions provisions of HB 1804 under the argument that the Oklahoma law unfairly shifts the burden of immigration enforcement from government onto the backs of business. In June 2008, a federal district judge blocked enforcement of the employer-related provisions of HB 1804 under the ruling that it preempted federal law, leading to inconsistent regulation between states. The state attorney general appealed. Other lawsuits were also filed against HB 1804 under claims that it fostered discrimination and racial profiling but were struck down.[14] In February 2010, the Tenth U.S. Circuit Court of Appeals ruled against two portions of the law, upholding most of the lower court's preliminary injunction on employer sanctions.

Essentially HB 1804 remains in effect while provisions seeking to monitor employer compliance have been (for the most part) dismissed. The only provision left requires employers to check with the federal computer system, known as E-Verify, to verify eligibility of job seekers in those businesses that contract with government entities for physical performance of services, such as building roads and other infrastructure (Boczkiewicz 2010). Further legal action is likely. The federal courts' order to halt the employer sanctions provisions of HB 1804, which essentially sided with business interests, are not surprising. No state or municipality has been able to pass state or local-level employer sanctions beyond what has been established through the Immigration Reform and Control Act (IRCA) of 1986, which introduced employer sanctions for the first time in the United States. In the case of HB 1804, an attempt at employer sanctions offered high symbolic appeal in an otherwise toothless policy for monitoring employers. Next we turn to an assessment of the efficacy of employer sanctions since the passage of IRCA and to thoughts on the significance this has for labor organizing and worker rights.

Employer Sanctions: An Unenforceable Policy

Prior to IRCA, no federal law prohibited the hiring or employment of undocumented migrants. While immigration raids took place apprehending workers, employers could not be prosecuted for hiring them. In fact, the Texas Proviso, inserted into the Immigration and Nationality Act of 1952 at the behest of the Texas delegation, shielded employers from criminal liability for employing unauthorized workers (Riley 2008: 21). IRCA represented a political settlement after a long reform process that began after World War II, addressing the perennial issue of undocumented labor in the United States (Zolberg 1990). The NAACP and AFL-CIO in the early 1980s favored penalizing employers under the argument that the hiring of undocumented labor drove down wages of U.S. workers even while evidence was lacking (Brownell 2005; Fix 1991: 6). Business groups also opposed the legislation at a time when antiregulatory policies gained wide approval under the Ronald Reagan administration (Fix 1991). Latino civil rights groups called for amnesty and cautioned against discrimination in the workplace. After a long, deliberative process, a compromise addressing the concerns of labor, business, and civil rights groups were met with "special arrangements" to agriculture, including a fast track to legalization for farmworkers under the Special Agricultural Worker (SAW) program, given agriculture's historically high dependence on unauthorized immigrant workers (Martin and Taylor 1991). Together, the compromise consisted of expanding border enforcement, legalization opportunities, and employer sanctions. The employer sanctions component of the law established the first measure to extend federal immigration regulation into the private workplace by prohibiting the employment of unauthorized immigrants (Zolberg 1990: 326). How effective have employer sanctions been since IRCA was enacted in 1986? Have they stemmed the flow of undocumented migration and prevented the hiring of unauthorized workers? Have employer sanctions translated into better wages and job security for U.S. workers?

The poor enforcement of employer sanctions is well documented. Of the millions of employers in the United States, very few are in fact audited each year by federal immigration authorities. While investigations into employer compliance were relatively high in the years immediately following the passage of IRCA, enforcement has dropped precipitously since 1990 (Brownell 2005). The understaffed and underfunded sanctions enforcement budget further explains the lax approach (Hill and Pearce 1990). In fiscal year 2003, 2,200 employers were audited by receiving "warnings." More serious violations result in a "Notice with Intent to Fine" (NIFs), at which point employers may appeal. The shifting priorities of Immigration and Naturalization Services (INS) and now U.S. Immigration and Customs Enforcement (ICE) also help explain declining levels of employer sanctions enforcement. For instance, border enforcement has moved away from workplace investigations toward a Southwest border strategy with the implementation of Operation Gatekeeper, Operation Hold the Line, and other more recent militarized control initiatives on the U.S.-Mexico border. Furthermore, "apprehensions at the border" have now shifted internally, evidenced by the detention and deportation strategies of 287(g) and Secure Communities. Since the 1990s, much of Border Patrol's efforts has focused on alien smuggling and drug trafficking. After September 11, 2001, worksite enforcement took on a national security focus directed at employers on security-sensitive sites such as airports (Operation Tarmac), nuclear power plants (Operation Glowworm), and military bases. These have translated into even fewer funds and commitment to monitoring restaurants, hotels, garment factories, and farms (Brownell 2005). Employer sanctions, then, have been largely ineffective because employers can evade responsibility, they are penalized too little if caught, and the laws are not being effectively enforced.

While the notion of imposing employer sanctions to penalize employers is sold as an appealing strategy, partial and selective workplace enforcement often results in an emboldened and newfound coercive leverage for the employer, equipping them with new coercive powers to fire and deport (Wishnie 2007). One of the unintended consequences of IRCA's policies is that it actually created a new economic incentive for a "bad apple" employer to hire and exploit undocumented workers (National Immigration Law Center 2008). In this way, federal immigration bureaus have deputized employers as immigration enforcers who may threaten employees with deportation but who are often above the law (National Immigration Law Center 2008: 217). Kwong (1997) explains that the legislating of migrants as "illegal" can lead unscrupulous employers to offer jobs to the undocumented in a gesture of "doing them a favor," encouraging abuse and irregularity. This new employer leverage to discipline migrant labor has, in effect, made them a more docile, cheaper, and consequently preferred labor force (De Genova 2002). The high labor force participation rates of migrant workers are an indication of their "preferred" status (Wishnie 2007: 207). The NAACP and other African American civil rights groups, who in the 1980s endorsed employer sanctions, reversed their position by the late 1990s as the rise in discrimination lawsuits rose. In effect, employer sanctions were discriminating against the hiring of domestic workers (Brownell 2005).

Other studies look at the impact of employer sanctions on wages. Burdened by all the new paperwork and risk associated with the hire of the undocumented, employers impose a "tax" on presumably unauthorized workers by extracting a tax in the form of lower wages (Phillips and Massey 1999: 234). That is, employers may transfer the costs and risks associated with hiring "illegals" onto the workers themselves in the form of lower pay. The proliferation of subcontracting industries that emerged to avoid federal regulations also impacts wages. Massey, Durand, and Malone (2002) explain that if a citizen or legal resident alien wishes to get a job in agriculture or construction, they too have to work through a subcontractor and forfeit a portion of their wages in return for the opportunity to work. IRCA thus served to encourage outsourcing and "middlemen" who pocket a portion of the wages, which has become a routine mechanism for hiring in labor markets that employ immigrants (Massey 2007). Thus a perverse consequence of IRCA's employer sanctions has been the lowering of wages and undermining of working conditions not only of undocumented migrants but of legal status holders and U.S. citizens as well.

Other assessments of the role of employer sanctions point to the impact they have on labor organizing. The highly significant Supreme Court ruling in 2002, known as *Hoffman Plastic Compounds, Inc. v. NLRB*, presented a shattering blow to migrant labor rights. Wishnie writes, "[T]here the Court held that an employee who tendered false documents to his employer upon hire, and was later illegally discharged for union organizing, was eligible for neither back pay nor reinstatement" (Wishnie 2007: 212). The message was if the employee was undocumented and had used fraudulent documents toward employment and had been involved in labor organizing, the individual was ineligible for back pay. In other words, reprisals are more heavily shifted onto the backs of employees than employers who may knowingly hire individuals with fraudulent documents, although they may claim otherwise. Bacon (2006) has noted that the highly publicized raids on Swift meat-processing plants throughout the Midwest in 2006 served the purpose of undermining union efforts under way there. Labor leaders have argued that some employers use sanctions as a justification for calling in immigration authorities on their own workforce in retaliation for organizing drives or efforts to assert other workplace rights (Brownell 2005). In this way, a multiple and hierarchical system of legal statuses in the workplace perpetuates inequality and reinscribes class and ethnic racism in the form of legal exclusion and marginalization (Suárez-Navaz 2004: 223).

While initially endorsing the measures in the mid-1980s, organized labor in the United States has reversed its position on IRCA and employer sanctions generally. The AFL-CIO has declared formal and public opposition to sanctions not only due to evidence that the sanctions caused employment discrimination but that they also reflect an internal struggle among unions, with some embracing "traditional protectionist impulses perhaps reflecting a residual nativism" and others that have successfully organized in immigrant-intensive industries where employers use the sanctions provision to retaliate against organizing employees (Wishnie 2007: 208). Today, organized labor has redirected its efforts to focus on building union membership in immigrant-dense industries, developing worker unity beyond legal status, and focusing on the enforcement of labor law. Enacting stronger labor protections to hold employers accountable for labor law violations would remove economic incentives to seek out and exploit undocumented workers (National Immigration Law Center 2008). By standardizing labor protections for all covered employees regardless of immigration status, there may be a diminished incentive to hire undocumented workers, which may translate into better working standards for all employees. Furthermore, mainstream firms would dispense with shadowy labor subcontractors (Wishnie 2007). In this way, labor stands to win because the sanctions law has neither protected U.S. workers nor deterred undocumented immigration.[15]

Deportability in Public Spaces

With the victories won by the U.S. and state chambers of commerce lawsuit, the disciplining of migrant lives has shifted from potential worksite monitoring to a new priority on alien smuggling and the apprehension of unauthorized migrants on highways and public spaces, evidenced by a sharp increase in apprehensions for traffic violations (Jones 2008b). Policing the public sphere results, in part, from the view that the workplace is off-limits. In Oklahoma, what surfaced shortly after HB 1804 went into effect was the news that the Tulsa County Sheriff's Department signed on to the 287(g) program designed by U.S. Immigration and Customs Enforcement (ICE) to assist local law enforcement officers in apprehending "foreign born criminals and immigration violators who pose a threat to national security and public safety."[16] The City of Tulsa issued a memorandum stating that "the Tulsa Police Department shall work with the Tulsa County Sheriff's Office to determine the citizenship status of all individuals arrested and booked. If it is determined that an arrested person's presence in the United States is unlawful during the booking process, the Tulsa Police Department shall promptly report such information to I.C.E." (City of Tulsa archives, June 2007). As of this writing, the Tulsa County Sheriff's Office is the only law enforcement agency in the state to have officers trained to enforce federal immigration laws. Tulsa County Sheriff Stanley Glanz put it this way: "When you have a bunch of illegals in a community, it spawns other types of criminal activity; it helps create an environment where that criminality can exist" (Walker 2008). Other law enforcement heads, including Tulsa's former police chief, Ron Palmer, viewed the Tulsa Police Department's role in immigration enforcement as far more limited. Chief Palmer plainly stated, "Enforcing immigration law is not a high priority. Asking city police to enforce federal immigration laws goes a bit too far. We don't ask them to hand out parking tickets" (Walker 2008).

With still much to be explored about the conflicting roles of local law enforcement and immigration, the atmosphere in the Latino migrant community remains one of deportability (De Genova 2002) with signs of high levels of fear (Urban Institute 2009). Much of the emphasis in the community is centered on "hoping and praying" for legalization through immigration reform.[17] Given the bipartisan political climate of the 2010s and lack of political will on immigration in Washington, DC, petitions for reform are not likely to translate into comprehensive immigration reform with broad measures favoring legalization. Rather than "hoping and praying," a disempowered transnational laboring class would be better served by organizing around its commanding position as workers, even while it appears to be a formidable task in an RtW state. The playing down of legal status and the playing up of labor rights is in order.

Final Thoughts

Blinded by the single-issue preoccupation with stamping out "illegals," Rep. Randy Terrill and his supporters fought back against the chambers of commerce's lawsuit ruling that repealed the employer sanctions provisions of HB 1804. Terrill protested that the ruling came from a "liberal judge . . . exercising judicial activism" and serving corporate interests by continuing "exploitation of cheap, illegal alien slave labor" (Ervin 2008). In another statement, the author of the bill stated, "This is just another in a long series of attempts by the pro-illegal alien lobby and their allies who rely on cheap illegal labor and who try to accomplish through the judicial system what they are unable to do through the Legislature. . . . Their moral dilemma is that they are in the position of supporting the functional equivalent of modern-day slavery" (Gillham 2008; see also Price 2008). In an ironic twist, Terrill and his diehard camp of anti-"illegals" supporters became defenders-of-sorts of migrant laborers who were now perceived as being exploited by profit-hungry corporate interests. He even outed Senator Harry Coates, claiming that as the owner of a roofing company, the senator stood to gain personally from the hiring of undocumented labor. Terrill's mantra of "getting tough on illegals" had become an affront to big business, a tall order in a state that has moved to favor corporate interests and deregulation. If there are lessons to be learned, it is that anti-immigrant populists need to shed the nativist baggage they carry. Working people would be better served by developing transnational labor unity that strengthens labor laws, beyond their restrictive nationalist inclinations, to contest the economic restructuring before both the Mexican and U.S. Heartlands. If Heartland populists could get beyond their xenophobic blinders, perhaps, just perhaps, they might see their interests aligned with those of their across-the-border counterparts.

Notes

1. Former Mexican President Vicente Fox's stop in Tulsa was part of a speaking tour to promote his vision of further economic integration for the NAFTA partnering nations; see his book *Revolution of Hope* (Fox 2007). In his advocacy for making the U.S.-Mexico border more open to the free flow of Mexican workers, Fox aimed to carry out projects, such as microlending programs, to help lift Mexican rural areas out of poverty and encourage more Mexicans to stay home. Ironically, some of these economic-development projects in Mexico have necessitated the importation of workers from states farther south, including from neighboring Guatemala, because locals refuse to work for average Mexican wages (Thompson 2001).

2. In this chapter, I adopt the commonly used term "illegal" instead of other more descriptive terms, such as "undocumented" or "unauthorized," in order to retain the connotations and impact of the term as it is used in the local context and in the legislation itself.

3. There is a long populist tradition of "rural radicalism" in the U.S Heartland. During the farm crisis of the 1980s, when rural America lost more than 700,000 family farms, a nurtured populist sentiment gained favor evidencing feelings of an-

tiauthoritarianism, antielitism, deep suspicion of big business, and contempt for the federal government and big banks. The farm crisis imposed severe economic hardship on farm families, which vigilante-sympathetic groups exploited (Wright 2007: ch. 4). The neonativist brand of populism in Oklahoma between 2006 and 2008 when HB 1804 was being debated and passed found a new political opportunity to express their "outrage" at Latino workers. Such groups include the Outraged Patriots headed by Dan Howard and Immigration Reform for Oklahoma Now (IRON) headed by Carol Helm, both sympathetic and actively involved in Rep. Randy Terrill's campaign to deport "illegals." Coincidently, radical neopopulism also influenced the likes of Timothy McVeigh, who bombed the Alfred P. Murrah Federal Building in Oklahoma City in 1995 as an act of "war against the federal government" (Wright 2007).

4. Taken directly from the author of the bill, Rep. Randy Terrill, in his speech posted on YouTube, http://www.youtube.com/watch?v=Tmq_pQpfs_Y (accessed September 25, 2012).

5. Given mounting opposition, Terrill decided to postpone the "son of HB 1804" until a later date.

6. The predisposition to favor undocumented labor can be understood not as an aberration in capitalist development but as an integral aspect of late-capitalist economies. Sassen (2000) and Cornelius (1998) maintain that although conventionally spun as an incomplete phase of development in the developing world, informal sector work is integral, indeed "structurally embedded" in capitalist development as cheaper labor sources are sought to maximize profits.

7. Many states passed RtW laws in the mid-1940s and early 1950s. Since then, except for the 2001 adoption by Oklahoma, only two other states adopted them: Louisiana in 1976 and Idaho in 1986. Indiana adopted the law in 1957 but repealed it in 1965 (Dinlersoz and Hernandez-Murillo 2002). An RtW law was struck down in Colorado in 2008 (Hogler 2009).

8. Keep in mind that Oklahoma has been labeled the "reddest of the red states" after the 2008 presidential election in which not a single county, of seventy-seven, voted for Barack Obama.

9. A climate of intimidation may also help explain reasons for the migrant exodus. It is worth noting reports of vigilantism by citizens who took on immigration enforcement duties in the wake of HB 1804. Spanish-language media in Oklahoma reported cases of vigilantism in which private citizens "tipped off" local police as they monitored the activity of perceived "illegals"; see William Wynn, "Immigration Bust Under Attack," La Semana del Sur, 27 de abril al 3 de mayo, 2008; William Wynn, "Oologah: A Racist Oasis?" La Semana del Sur, 25 de febrero al 3 de marzo, 2007. Scenes in which Latino migrants are harassed can also be seen in the documentary film Starvation Doctrine directed by Zac Davis and Mike Searcy of Burning Buffalo Films. Also significant has been the rise in hate groups directed at undocumented migrants and their families; see Bill Sherman, "Rise in Hate Groups Noted," Tulsa World, November 8, 2008. The racial fallout of the bill is expressed in the words of a Mexican American business owner: "Some people might harbor dormant racist feelings, but what 1804 has done is brought out that racism. Now, under the pro-

tection of the law, those individuals feel powerful and more likely to harass or say something derogatory to our people and because our people are humble they stay quiet. When I go to Wal-Mart, I look over my shoulder uncomfortably. I feel like I'm being watched. Some people leave rather than stay and feel unwelcomed" (interview by author).

10. Quoted in the *Chicago Tribune,* February 10, 2008 (Witt 2008).

11. Interview by Scott Carter, volume collaborator, with Mr. Buchanan, Altus, Oklahoma, March 2008.

12. For example, the archbishop of the Diocese of Tulsa issued a letter condemning HB 1804. Terrill angrily responded, claiming that the Catholic Church was financially self-serving in its "harboring of illegals" (Jones 2008a). Local Spanish-language media also carefully covered events offering updates and legal counsel. Catholic Charities, the Coalition for the American Dream, COHO, the Hispanic Resource Center of the Tulsa County Public Library System, Community Action Project, Legal Aid, YWCA—Tulsa, Immigration Clinic at the University of Tulsa, and others all expanded services for Latino migrants and their families. Not surprisingly in a "right-to-work" state, there is little organizing along labor/worker rights; instead, much of the activism is centered on helping clients obtain legal status or legal recourse through service-providing entities.

13. Some rank-and-file union members interviewed for this study stated that their work opportunities, particularly in the construction trades, went up immediately following the passage of HB 1804. In this respect, it would appear that the bill translated into better wages and more work opportunity for U.S. workers in the months immediately following the passage of the bill (interview by the author with John Gaines, president of the Northeast Oklahoma Central Labor Council, spring 2008, and an anonymous respondent in a local union). However, much like the lessons learned with IRCA when the legislation was first introduced in 1986, there was a sharp decline in unauthorized entry, but shortly thereafter the numbers of undocumented workers climbed. The employer sanctions policy and rhetoric appear to serve only an immediate impact in turns of deterring unauthorized entry and hire (Fix 1991: xvii–xviii).

14. In October 2007, the National Coalition of Latino Clergy and Christian Leaders challenged the constitutionality of HB 1804. In spring 2008, attorney James C. Thomas also filed a lawsuit against HB 1804 on the grounds that it burdened the Oklahoma taxpayer by unconstitutionally creating a state immigration bureau. Both lawsuits were struck down and now face appeals.

15. Generally business groups and associations remain opposed to employer sanctions on the principle that sanctions are unnecessary regulation of the private workplace and an unfair deputization of the private sector to conduct public law enforcement (Wishnie 2007: 209). At the same time, big business has not aggressively moved to reverse IRCA, suggesting that such measures in fact advance business interests for the reasons explained here.

16. Memorandum of Agreement, July 9, 2007, http://www.ice.gov/doclib/foia/memorandumsofAgreementUnderstanding/tulsacountysheriffsoffice.pdf (accessed September 25, 2012).

17. The idea of "hoping and praying" for legalization is not intended to be a condescending statement but rather results from the observation and disappointment over the virtual absence of labor organizing in immigrant communities in the state.

References

Bacon, David. 2004. *The Children of NAFTA: Labor Wars on the U.S./Mexico Border* Berkeley: University of California Press.

Bacon, David. 2006. "Justice Deported" *The American Prospect,* December 14.

Barlett, Donald, and James B. Steele. 2001. "The Empire of Pigs," *Time,* June 24.

Bazar, Emily. 2008. "Strict Immigration Law Rattles Oklahoma Businesses." *USA Today,* January 10.

Bissett, Jim. 1999. *Agrarian Socialism in America: Marx, Jefferson and Jesus in the Oklahoma Countryside 1904–1920.* Norman: University of Oklahoma Press.

Boczkiewicz, Robert. 2010. "HB1804 Appeal Denied in Part," *Tulsa World,* February 3.

Brownell, Peter. 2005. "The Declining Enforcement of Employer Sanctions." *Migration Information Source,* September.

City of Tulsa. 2007. "Taylor Issues TPD Immigration Policy Clarification." City of Tulsa archives, June.

Clawson, Dan, and Mary Ann Clawson. 1999. "What Has Happened to the U.S. Labor Movement? Union Decline and Renewal." *Annual Review of Sociology* 25: 95–119.

Clay, William L., and Reed Larson. 1998. "Does America Need a National Right-to-Work Law?" *Insight on the News,* August 17.

Cornelius, Wayne. 1998. "The Structural Embeddedness of Demand for Mexican Immigrant Labor: New Evidence from California." In *Crossings: Mexican Immigration in Interdisciplinary Perspective,* ed. Marcelo Suarez-Orozco. Cambridge, Mass.: Harvard University Press.

Cushman Wood, Darren. 2004. *Blue Collar Jesus: How Christianity Supports Worker's Rights.* Santa Ana, Calif.: Seven Locks Press.

Davidson, Osha Gray. 1996. *Broken Heartland: The Rise of America's Rural Ghetto.* Iowa City: University of Iowa Press.

De Genova, Nicolas. 2002. "Migrant 'Illegality' and Deportability in Everyday Life." *Annual Review of Anthropology* 31: 419–47.

Dinlersoz, Emin M., and Ruben Hernandez-Murillo. 2002. "Did 'Right-to-Work' Work for Idaho?" *The Federal Reserve Bank of St. Louis,* May–June.

Dunbar-Ortiz, Roxanne. 1997. *Red Dirt: Growing up Okie.* Norman: University of Oklahoma Press.

Economic Impact Group. 2008. "A Computable General Equilibrium (CGE) Analysis of the Impact of the Oklahoma Taxpayer and Citizen Protection Act of 2007." February 29, 1–34.

Economic Policy Institute. 2001. "Right-to-Work Laws and Economic Development in Oklahoma." Briefing paper.

Ervin, Brian. 2008. "Judge's Orders: Injunction against HB1804 Sparks Debate of Political Playmaking versus a Sound Decision." *Urban Tulsa Weekly,* June 11.

Fix, Michael, ed. 1991. *The Paper Curtain: Employer Sanctions' Implementation, Impact and Reform.* Santa Monica, Calif.: Urban Institute and Rand Corporation.

Fox, Vicente. 2007. *Revolution of Hope: The Life, Faith, and Dreams of a Mexican President.* Viking: New York.

Garrett, Robert. 2008. "Oklahoma's Crackdown on Illegal Immigration Draws Texas Lawmakers' Interest." *Dallas Morning News,* February 13.

Gillham, Omer. 2008. "U.S Chamber Fights 1804." *Tulsa World,* February 2.

Hill, John, and James Pearce. 1990. "The Incidence of Sanctions against Employers of Illegal Aliens." *Journal of Political Economy* 98, no. 1: 28–44.

Hogler, Raymond. 2009. "The 2008 Defeat of Right to Work in Colorado: Is It the End of Section 14(B)?" *Labor Law Journal* 60, no. 1 (Spring).

Jacobs, David, and Marc Dixon. 2006. "The Politics of Labor-Management Relations: Detecting the Conditions That Affect Changes in Right-to-Work Laws." *Social Problems* 53, no. 1 (February): 118–37.

Jones, Todd. 2008a. "Tougher Oklahoma Law Adds Risk to Health-Care Decision." *Columbus Dispatch,* September 9.

Jones, Todd. 2008b. "Tulsa Deputies Say They're Not Picking on Anyone." *Columbus Dispatch,* September 10.

King, Judith L., and Laurel C. Catlett-King. 2007. "Cowboy Campaigning: Patriotism, 'Freedom' and Right-to-Work in Oklahoma." *Labor Studies Journal* 32, no. 1 (March).

Klein, Naomi. 2007. *The Shock Doctrine: The Rise of Disaster Capitalism.* New York: Picador.

Kwong, Peter. 1997. *Forbidden Workers: Illegal Chinese Immigrants and American Labor.* New York: New Press.

Leef, George C. 2005. *Free Choice for Workers: A History of the Right to Work Movement.* Ottawa, Ill.: Jameson Books.

Martin, Philip. 2003. "AgJOBS: New Solution or New Problem?" *International Migration Review* 37, no. 4 (Winter): 1282–91.

Martin, Philip, and Edward Taylor. 1991. "Immigration Reform and Farm Labor Contracting in California." In *The Paper Curtain: Employer Sanctions' Implementation, Impact and Reform,* ed. Michael Fix. Washington, DC: Urban Institute.

Massey, Doug. 2007. "When Less Is More: Border Enforcement and Undocumented Migration." Presentation before the Subcommittee on Immigration, Citizenship, Refugees, Border Security, and International Law Committee on the Judiciary, U.S. House of Representatives, April 20.

Massey, Doug, Jorge Durand, and Nolan Malone. 2002. *Beyond Smoke and Mirrors: Mexican Immigration in an Era of Economic Integration.* New York: Russell Sage Foundation.

Moody, Kim. 1988. *An Injury to All: The Decline of American Unionism.* London: Verso.

National Immigration Law Center. 2008. "State and Local Proposals That Punish Employers for Hiring Undocumented Workers Are Unenforceable, Unnecessary, and Bad Public Policy." January. http://www.nilc.org/employersanctions TPs_2008–01–28.html (accessed September 25, 2012).

Phillips, Julie, and Douglas Massey. 1999. "The New Labor Market: Immigrants and Wages after IRCA." *Demography* 36, no. 2 (May): 233–46.

Postelwait, Jeff. 2008. "Costly Exodus: Hispanic Firms Hurt by HB1804—Related Labor Drain." *Tulsa World*, April 13.

Price, Marie. 2008. "OKC Federal Judge Blocks Immigration Law." *Oklahoma City Journal Record*, June 5.

Reed, Robert W. 2001. "Does Right-to-Work Boost Economic Development?" Labor Studies Series, Oklahoma Council of Public Affairs, February.

Riley, Jason L. 2008. *Let Them In: The Case for Open Borders*. London: Gotham Books.

Sassen, Saskia. 2000. *Cities in a World Economy*, 2nd ed. London: Pine Forge.

Sellars, Nigel Anthony. 1998. *Oil, Wheat and Wobblies: The Industrial Workers of the World in Oklahoma, 1905–1930*. Norman: University of Oklahoma Press.

Stull, Donald, and Michael Broadway. 2004. *Slaughterhouse Blues: The Meat and Poultry Industry in North America*. Belmont, Calif.: Wadsworth.

Stull, Donald D., Michael Broadway, and David Griffith, eds. 1995. *Any Way You Cut It: Meat Processing and Small Town America*. Lawrence: University Press of Kansas.

Suárez-Navaz, Liliana. 2004. *Rebordering the Mediterranean: Boundaries and Citizenship in Southern Europe*. New York: Berghahn Books.

Thompson, Ginger. 2001. "Migrant Exodus Bleeds Mexico's Heartland." *New York Times*, June 17.

Urban Institute. 2009. "Untangling the Oklahoma Taxpayer and Citizen Protection Act: Consequences for Children and Families." Report prepared for the National Council of la Raza.

U.S. Bureau of Labor Statistics. 2010. "Union Membership, 2009," News Release, posted January 22.

Walker, Devona. 2008. "Enforcement Fueling Immigration Exodus." *NewsOK.com*, January 13. http://newsok.com/article/3192112/1200176005 (accessed September 25, 2012).

Wiegand, Shirley A., and Wayne A. Wiegand. 2007. *Books on Trial: Red Scare in the Heartland*. Norman: University of Oklahoma Press.

Wines, William A. 1988. "An Analysis of the 1986 'Right to work' Referendum in Idaho." *Labor Law Journal* (September).

Wishnie, Michael J. 2007. "Prohibiting the Employment of Unauthorized Immigrants: The Experiment Fails." *University of Chicago Legal Forum* 2007: 193–217.

Witt, Howard. 2008. "Where Have the Illegal Immigrants Gone?" *Chicago Tribune*, February 10.

Wright, Stuart A. 2007. *Patriots, Politics, and the Oklahoma City Bombing*. New York: Cambridge University Press.

Zolberg, Aristide. 1990. "Reforming the Back Door: The Immigrant Reform and Control Act of 1986 in Historical Perspective." In *Immigration Reconsidered: History, Sociology and Politics*, ed. Virginia Yans-McLaughlin. New York: Oxford University Press.

PART III

Transnational Identities and New Landscapes of Home

CHAPTER 6

Rooted/Uprooted

Place, Policy, and Salvadoran Transnational Identities in Rural Arkansas

MIRANDA CADY HALLETT

In a globalized world, place and policy continue to matter. While theories of transnationalism emphasize the ways in which migrants' social ties and cultural imaginaries transcend boundaries, this transcendence is structured by the geographies of economic production and state policies. Particular sites of settlement in the United States, often determined by emergent labor markets, also profoundly shape the experiences of particular migrant communities. Rather than an incidental backdrop, place exerts an influence through specific contexts of cultural practice and historical heritage as well as emergent configurations of racial and ethnic identities.

In light of this, the recent trend of Latin American settlement in rural areas of the Heartland requires a reexamination of theories of transnational migration that have primarily been formed with reference to either urban areas or the border region.[1] The particular histories and cultural identities embedded in these rural Middle American landscapes inform the process of Latin Americanization or "tropicalization" of the landscape (Davis 2001). Given the high proportion of migrants lacking full legal status in new destinations, these sites can also shed light on the cultural logics and concrete impacts of deportability and legal marginalization.

Theorization of these new contexts of reception requires an understanding of the particular histories and dynamics of these new locations of settlement and the ways in which those qualities are transformed through the precariously permanent settlement of transnational migrants. I call this settlement "precariously permanent" because the peculiar conditions of these new communities make the process of settlement persistent on the collective scale, yet contingent and vulnerable for many individuals. Even as transnational migrants set down deep roots in these small towns and create enduring communities, many face the imminent threat of being uprooted through deportation.[2]

Yell County, Border Country

Danville, Arkansas, the primary field site for my 2005–2008 ethnographic field research, is a quiet and sleepy town located about halfway between Little Rock and Fort Smith in central western Arkansas. Out of a population of approximately 2,800 people, around half of all Danville residents are first- or second-generation Latin American immigrants; a small population of relocated Laotian refugees lives here as well. Yell County, of which Danville is the county seat, also happens to be an important site in the 1969 Western film *True Grit* starring John Wayne. Danville's main drag features a Sonic Drive-In, a popular Family Dollar store, and the Abundant Life Pentecostal Church. The county is "dry" due to a law prohibiting the sale of alcohol, and conservative evangelical churches as well as the leadership of the local poultry industry have dominated political life for half a century. The physical landscape visibly reflects notions of wholesome, small-town and rural America. Imaginings of the rural southern and western landscape, inscribed and reified in media representation, are repositories of a certain set of value orientations and myths treasured by white Americans, including rugged individualism, personalism and neighborly hospitality, independence and work ethic, and a populist sense of justice. This rural landscape has long been rendered as a space of "heritage" and a site of refuge and preservation for traditional and Judeo-Christian cultural values.

My arrival by car to Danville provided an initial clue regarding the attraction of Arkansas for Latino migrants as well as the relative welcome they have received from locals. For the last five miles of the trip, I drove behind a tractor trailer stacked with wire cages, filled with dirty white-feathered creatures on their way to the "kill plant." Danville is home to two poultry-processing plants, which employ over half the town. The corporate headquarters of Tyson Foods, the largest meat producer in the world, is only a few hours away and serves as the epicenter of the poultry industry in the United States. Since John Tyson began the business in the 1930s, it has grown to be the nation's broiler capital, supplanting earlier geographic centers like the Delmarva Peninsula and parts of North Carolina (Striffler 2005). The triple corporate juggernaut of Tyson, Wal-Mart, and J. B. Hunt brought an unprecedented economic boom to central and northwest Arkansas from the 1980s onward.[3] Even when I left Arkansas in late summer 2008, the region was the last holdout of the Horatio Alger–inspired optimism in the nation. After so many years of relative hardship, Arkansans seemed convinced that in spite of economic ebbs and flows, "progress" had come at last—and wouldn't let up for a long time to come. With this "progress" had come a demand for labor; hundreds of thousands of workers were needed to gut chickens, lift boxes, and clean toilets in Tyson plants and Wal-Mart warehouses throughout the region.

As new migrant groups arrived to various Arkansas communities—including Danville—to fill these jobs in the 1990s and early 2000s, they begin to rework their social and material landscape through a complex process of appropriation and accommodation. Sites that were once seen as a repository of Anglo-American heritage became dynamic border zones, *nuevas fronteras* of cultural encounter. They also became places of economic revitalization. As poultry plants in Yell County were able to maximize their production, boarded-up businesses on the old Main Street were renovated and new small businesses built. This Heartland community, marginalized by the economic restructuring of the mid-twentieth century, found new life through migration and the poultry industry.

As they changed frontier spaces into community places, the lived experience of Salvadoran and other migrants has transformed their identifications with various scales of social entity: local, national, and transnational. In other words, transnational migrants act upon the environment, and the social and material environment also transforms migrant identities. Throughout this process, state definitions of the legitimacy or illegitimacy of migrants serve a mediating role, in particular migrant "illegality" and deportability (De Genova 2002), which make social and legal presence precarious and contingent. This precariousness infuses migrants' process of adaptation to new landscapes of home. Salvadorans in Yell County, Arkansas, acquire vexed identities permeated by the anxiety of legal limbo. Simultaneously establishing emotional and material ties to rural Arkansas, they nonetheless live a "truncated transnationalism" (Miyares et al. 2003) in which current forms of exclusion and an uncertain future motivate their orientation to social worlds in El Salvador as well. From this anxious position, they negotiate their identity vis-à-vis different scales of belonging and affiliation, transforming and reproducing local, national, and transnational projects of place-making and economic production.

Arkatecoluca: Transnational Rural Identities

Gerardo, a Salvadoran man who has been living in Yell County since 2002, once said to me, "*A veces, yo siento desubicado*"—"Sometimes, I feel disoriented." His statement did not surprise me; the social landscape and historical heritage of rural Arkansas seemed light-years away from the small town in El Salvador where he grew up. His disorientation, however, was not as I had expected. He went on to explain that he is from San Vicente, while most of the other Salvadorans who have settled in Yell County that form part of his social world are originally from Zacatecoluca. The Salvadoran community residing in Yell County takes Zacatecoluca as one of its principal social geographies of reference. Many who have lived in Arkansas for years or decades own land and homes in Zacatecoluca, talk frequently with friends and family there, and send items back and forth by way of the *viajeros,* traveling couriers, entrepreneurs lucky enough to have permanent residency who charge a small fee to carry gifts and letters in their luggage for loved ones in the homeland. Although Zacatecoluca and San Vicente are barely half an hour's distance in El Salvador and both are thousands of miles from Yell County, the disorientation Gerardo felt was due to his unfamiliarity with a local social sphere that has become what Peggy Levitt calls a "transnational village" (Levitt 2001).

Zacatecoluca is a word emerging from Nahuat, the native language of Pipil indigenous groups who settled El Salvador's territory before the Spanish conquest. *Zacate* means "grass" or "wild brush," a reference to uncultivated country terrain, and *tecoluca* is a suffix meaning "place of." As I got to know Salvadorans living in Yell County, I came to understand that although Salvadoran geographies remained important in migrants' hearts, minds, and social relations, the "wild brush" landscape of rural Arkansas was also a site of great significance. As one woman said:

> Each place that one lives, one misses, one dreams about it. . . . I miss my country. And some people say, "If you miss your country so much, why don't you leave?" Because one puts down roots here, too, one begins to love this country. And it's not just comfort. Because I have never had the best house, I've never bought the best car. I have always contented myself with only basic needs in order to help my family. It's the place. For example, if you tell me to go to another state, no, I already like Arkansas. I am not going to start over again in another place. I like it here, the quiet, the tranquility; I like it all . . . perhaps because in El Salvador I always lived in the country, too. ("Isabel," February 26, 2008)

Transnational migrants living in Danville, Arkansas, frequently expressed this sense of belonging and rootedness in the rural landscape, as well as feelings of stewardship over land, homesteads, and the Main Street landscape of the small town. In terms of political economy, the expansion of the poultry industry brought Mexicans and Central Americans to Yell County, but this narrative of rural belonging provides an alternate angle on the settlement of these "pioneers" in immigration's new frontier.

The first Salvadoran settlers in Arkansas mostly came from other regions of the United States, such as Houston or Los Angeles, while more recent waves come directly from El Salvador, yet nearly all comment on the pastoral quality of their new home. A young man who had grown up in Los Angeles and Houston felt reconnected to the rural way of life that his Salvadoran parents told him about. He began to hunt, fish, and raise vegetables after resettling in Arkansas, practices that he had heard about but never experienced: "It's true what they say," he said to me, "this really is the Natural State" ("Everardo," October 12, 2006). *Es como un cuento de hadas,*" said one young woman, "It's like a fairy tale, with the mountains and rivers, and all so beautiful" ("Deisy," September 11, 2007). Another young woman told me of her plan to bring her grandmother from El Salvador to settle there, saying, "I couldn't have brought her to Houston, what would she do? But here, there are even some places that remind one of El Salvador" ("Carlita," October 3, 2006).

In particular, the pioneer migrants that first came to central Arkansas in the 1980s and early 1990s feel a sense of rootedness in Yell County. According to oral histories of initial settlement, Latin American migrants to this region first arrived as crew members working for National Forest subcontractors, planting trees in the mountains of central Arkansas. Among the first arrivals were migrants from both El Salvador and Mexico; to this day, tension exists between Salvadoran and Mexican communities in Danville, and elements of this stratification are visible in social life, business patronage, church attendance, and even the way workers cluster in the break room at local poultry plants. Some attributed the tension between Mexicans and Salvadorans in the county to a sense of competition in new destinations:

What happens is that we are the second after the Mexicans—and we also go everywhere, there are Salvadorans wherever you go, in places where you wouldn't think, like here, everywhere! In New York, there are Puerto Ricans and Dominicans, in Florida there are Cubans, but there are Salvadorans everywhere. And here [in Yell County], we even came *before* the Mexicans. The first of us came from Texas, and then some from California, and then we came directly from El Salvador. There have to be pioneers first who come from other parts of the United States to establish the situation, from there they develop the link, the bridge. ("Gerardo," November 10, 2006)

Those who were "pioneers"—a few of whom did come directly from El Salvador—express pride not only regarding their ability to make their way in an unfamiliar world, but also in their active reshaping of the social environment to make things easier for those who came later on. Rubén Aguilar, a man who came to Arkansas directly from El Salvador in 1983 and found work on a small crew in the Ouachita National Forest, describes the way that local stores came to carry tortillas: "We worked for the Forest Service and for Whitehouse [Paper Company]. Planting pines. At that time there were no tortillas in the stores—no tortillas! Only white bread, things like that. There were no tortillas. . . . So then the boss [*patrón*] took a tortilla to the store to show them what it was. From there we made special orders, but they always ran out quickly. So that's how they began to bring Hispanic foods—beans, rice, tortillas, and so on" ("Rubén," August 3, 2007). Magdalena, a Yell County resident, claims that her late brother was the very first Salvadoran to set foot in Yell County in the early 1980s. Having been separated from his group of fellow migrants during the border crossing, he was hiding out in a church in Texas and happened to make friends with a cousin of the brother-in-law of the same forest contractor who later hired Rubén:

> Raúl came [to Texas] for one of his cousins and ended up taking my brother back, too, along with some others, and gave them work there in the mountains. They stayed in tents there and endured cold, heat, swarms of insects . . . they paid them by the seedling, at first 37 cents, later a bit more. When the *señor* saw that they worked well, my brother said to him, look, why don't we go back to Texas to recruit more. And so they did. They put the new [workers] in an old chicken house, without electricity, without heat, nothing. When it was cold they just lit a fire, and the men slept there on the ground like pigs. ("Magdalena," September 28, 2007)

The trees that Magdalena's brother and Rubén planted are now tall, although the harvest cycle for paper plantations is long enough that none have yet been logged. The plantations that these men worked on have now become towering forests filling the rolling hilly landscape between Danville and Hot Springs.

At the time of Rubén's arrival in the 1980s, he and his all-Latino crew were unusual in a labor market dominated by local white youth. However, the successful experiment of his *patrón* in recruiting Hispanic workers from the Texas border area had a domino effect on the industry (his boss was an Arkansas man who happened to have a bilingual Texan brother-in-law). As of 2008, most seasonal work on pine plantations in central Arkansas was done by crews of Mexican and Central American workers, largely undocumented. These crews were supervised by new *patrones*, including three Salvadoran brothers, *los hermanos* Melendez, who came up as laborers in the 1980s but have since achieved permanent residency and begun their own business as contractors in forestry, mostly with the federal Forest Service.

Jonathan Melendez, one of the brothers, came to Arkansas in 1984 at seventeen years of age. "My cousin sent for me," Jonathan said, "and he was pleased because I liked to work." In the early days in that part of Arkansas, he and other Latinos on the crew would avoid Mt. Ida, the closest town to their camp, because they were afraid of the authorities. Yet Jonathan soon found ways to interact with local communities and eventually joined a local Pentecostal church. Although his motivation for the new religious practice was largely his pursuit of a local girl who went to the church, eventually his encounters there became an entry point into local social worlds and a sense of belonging.

Salvadoran migrants emphasize their stewardship of the land and homes through detailed descriptions of their work to maintain and improve properties they have bought or even rental properties. One woman, whom I met in El Salvador after her eventual return, explained to me how she had won the heart of a landlady by refurbishing her trailer: "When we got there it was a big mess, just a big mess. Two *Americanos* had been living there and they had left all this trash. So we made it how it is today, a nice place to live, and she was very happy" ("Lupe," June 2, 2008). Salvadorans also appreciate the farming and gardening traditions in Yell County. One man compared the local production of honey and sorghum sweeteners to the traditional methods of candy making he remembers from his youth in El Salvador. Another young Salvadoran man, who had recently married the daughter of a chicken farmer and gone to live on their farm, said:

> It's very nice; I like gardening. I think Salvadorans come here to Arkansas and find out more about cultivating a garden for the family's consumption. I see that in El Salvador that's almost never done—people grow the *milpa*, yes, corn . . . and beans and rice, but they don't think to plant a few pineapple bushes, or if they have a little piece of ground by their house to put in tomatoes, onion, peppers, everything. I'd like to buy a plot of land around 10–20 acres, enough for a big garden and some animals. ("Gerardo," August 20, 2007)

According to the Yell County Farm Credit Services, there are still very few nonwhites who are full-time farmers, and the three or four Latino or Asian immigrant farmers in the county have all purchased their land since the late 1990s. Though the spaces of exchange are still dominated by older white farmers, Latinos are also frequently present at the River Valley Stock Auction that occurs every Tuesday afternoon, and plots to purchase goats, poultry, cows, hogs, and other livestock are always circulating on the soccer field and in the restaurants and *tiendas* where new Latino residents socialize and share information.

While men establish themselves through the soccer league, ownership of land, and possession of livestock, women experiment with the new cuisines they encounter and participate heavily in church life. In Danville one can dine on Thai sticky rice doused in Mexican hot sauce; soup with *pipián* squash and wild duck brought from the hunt; and a delicious combination of Salvadoran *boudin,* a moist sweet bread, and southern-style banana pudding. Women exalt the benefits of pressure cookers for preparing red beans in a fraction of the time and seek out gas stoves for the purpose of reheating thick Salvadoran-style tortillas over the burner flames, flipping the hot tortillas with bare hands just as you would on a clay *comal.* Women often get together to make large-batch foods such as *tamales* or fried street foods for the purposes of church fund-raisers, either for the rapidly growing Catholic church, Iglesia de San Andres, or for the many evangelical churches that have established Spanish-language missions in the county. The Church of Christ and Jehovah's Witnesses, motivated by strong missions to proselytize, created outreach groups and had established Spanish-speaking "starter churches." Latino churches from California or the Southwest also sent pastors to start new churches, like the evangelical Iglesia Nueva Vida.

Transforming Main Street: Stewardship and Contingent Belonging

Restaurants, *tiendas,* and other businesses owned by new Latina/o residents have transformed the facade of Main Street in Danville. Since the first *tienda,* Morena's Market, started in Danville in the mid-1990s, a number of other businesses have moved into commercial spaces in the downtown. Older storefront presence such as the Abundant Life Pentecostal Church and Horn's Watch and Clock Shop stand adjacent to La Merienda, a Salvadoran cafeteria-style restaurant that also provides the service of wiring money overseas. La Placita a few doors down is a convenience and grocery store, Morena's Pastelería offers specialty cakes, and around the corner is a Mexican restaurant and a place called Vestal's Dairy Bar that has been converted to a lunch stand selling tacos and tortas. Down one of the side streets is an Asian grocery, and in 2007 a Laotian restaurant moved into a vacant site on the edge of town. Walking down Main Street you are as likely to hear Spanish as English.

One small sign on Main Street, advertising the office of a bookkeeper, notary public, and tax preparer, also offers "Immigration Services—*Servicios de Inmigración.*" Patty Sutherland, the owner, moved into this area from southern California, the daughter of Italian immigrants. When she came in the early 1980s, she was considered quite exotic. People asked if she was Asian or Mexican and assumed that she couldn't speak English. "When they found out I was Catholic," she laughs, "I may as well have been a voodoo priestess. They knew my soul needed to be saved." At that time, the signs downtown were accurate—Bob's Hardware was really Bob's Hardware, though the storefront that still bears that sign now houses a *variedades* store, where you can buy flip-flops imported from El Salvador, *quinceañera* dresses, and strings of clay chilies that are made in China.

Sutherland's foray into immigration-application processing happened quite by accident when the bookkeeping business was still owned by her father, known in town as "Mr. G." When a Latino resident, a previous client, walked in one day and asked for help filling out his paperwork, Mr. G. waved toward his daughter and said, "She can help you." From there she began to learn about the complexities of the immigration bureaucracy through experience. Her identification with immigrants via her own heritage and feelings of exclusion from the local social world shaped her attitudes toward her Latina/o neighbors. She describes speaking up as an advocate in a local sphere that has not always been immigrant-friendly, but where feelings of acceptance—even appreciation—have developed over time:

> It's been a rough time for immigrants here in Danville, but times have changed. People still make a lot of comments, but they see the positive side too. When they talk about the newcomers not wanting to become Americans, I say "my family came here from Italy, unless you're Native American your family came from somewhere too so don't be so quick to judge." But you'd be surprised at some of the people that come around—there was a good ol' boy who was practically the only American working at Petit Jean—you would think he'd be the first to be rude and racist, but now after working side by side for years he says "well, they're really good people." People have started to see things differently. (Patty Sutherland, personal communication, August 20, 2007)

Local whites, as a whole, have accepted the permanence of their new neighbors and appreciate what they can while retaining a level of anxiety and resentment about the rapid changes in their social landscape. While nativist attitudes regarding the importance of English-language use in public spaces remain, particularly among older residents, the majority of the white Arkansans interviewed for this study spoke positively about the new and visible signs of cultural and social change around the town. Speaking of his own initial experience with Latino migrants, a retired schoolteacher described some of the ways that communication happens across language barriers:

> Just as soon as they were here, we would get invited to homes, and maybe I'm a little too open-minded . . . we'd go into these homes, mom and dad neither one of them would speak a word of English, but we're communicating. Me and the dad would go out front and he'd lift the hood of the truck, and you know, there's an engine—we got guy talk, it may be in two languages, but he turns on some music and I'm turning up the bass. Good old guy stuff. And Barb's in there in the kitchen with the mother and the little kids just

around, and you can communicate. Of course the kids are our interpreters. ("Robert," February 26, 2008)

Through recognition of shared "Heartland" values and social norms, although sourced in different cultural traditions, connections are built between migrants and the previous residents of rural communities in Middle America. Locally born residents also frequently commented on the relationship between the labor demands in the chicken plants and the presence of the migrant community, while adding an approving remark or two about the work ethic, family values, or Christian commitments of newcomers: "If it weren't for the immigrants, this town would keel over and blow away. We need those chicken plants. Education is great, I love education, but then there's nobody left to work. And that's why all these Hispanics come, is to work. The families are fine; they are good Christian people" ("Rose," March 26, 2007). Some white residents emphasized the apparent intentions of their new neighbors to settle permanently, expressing respect at the sense of stewardship demonstrated by families who are settling:

> What I've noticed is that a lot of the Spanish people are putting down roots here, buying homes and so on. At first just the men would come, live five or six in an apartment, work for a few years, and then all of them would quit at once and evidently they would go back to Mexico, and what they had saved was enough to buy a house, some land. Now, the men still come first, but they check out the place, see what the people are like and the town, then they bring up their wife and the kids, then they tell their friends and cousins about it. You know I've noticed a lot of these guys like farming, they like to have animals and cattle. Lots of them came from the country, so I guess it must seem nice to them here after being in those big cities, more like home, more like a place they would want to settle. ("Stanley," February 12, 2007)

Stanley's remarks express a contingent welcome. He observes migrants' affinity for rural land, implying that this orientation gives new residents a certain legitimacy in their settlement in this place; by appreciating the "heritage" of this Heartland landscape, migrants can belong. These attitudes of contingent inclusion on the part of many whites impact not only casual social relations but meaningful institutional support within local government as well. This is clear to Salvadorans and other Latino migrants; one of my interviewees recounted relations with locals this way: "At first, there were problems with the police, but now they do what they should, no discrimination, they respond to calls. . . . [A] few years ago, the White Revolution came to town,[4] but the whites here rejected them. I think anybody who really didn't like Hispanics left the town. Now it's like a big family that lives in one house; we may argue amongst ourselves, but in the final analysis we are united, *Americanos* and

Hispanos" ("Isabel," May 28, 2007). Isabel was married to a white man who had local roots, although he himself was born in California. His family had been driven west from the Arkansas River valley during the Great Depression and drought of the 1930s. He often told me that he felt a kinship with Isabel from the first because her family, too, had been displaced and forced to travel far for their livelihood. Like migrants from Central America and Mexico, many native-born residents of the central Arkansas River valley have experienced the displacements entailed by economic marginalization and natural disaster, and this too can form a connection.

Even in the context of heightened tensions nationally and statewide, many migrants expressed a sense of contingent security in the local community. After a discussion about recent anti-immigrant laws and enforcement programs in nearby Oklahoma as well as some other counties in northwest Arkansas, one informant said: "Here it's calmer than in other parts of the state—here they have to recognize what we have done for the local economy—and Arkansas more than anywhere else has to recognize that Hispanic labor has helped them to get ahead. Before, it was worse here, less jobs, less money, worse education, and lower levels of social well-being" ("Gerardo," August 20, 2007). In this claim, the profit-making value of transnational migrant labor to regional corporate and state industries is explicitly deployed to assert a right to political recognition. Gerardo points out that the role of Latin American immigrants at the center of economic revitalization has shaped their reception by the community, which can be characterized as a strong but conditional acceptance. Native Arkansan sentiments toward new Yell County residents from Latin America routinely recognize these neighbors as part of Danville and as contributing value, on multiple levels, to the community. Nonetheless, this acceptance was contingent, predicated on perceptions that transnational migrants fulfilled local social norms, as well as serving as the low-wage base of the local economy. These local recognitions, while preventing overt conflict and easing community relations, also did not remove the impact of legal marginality from migrants' lives. The prospect of deportation is, for many Latinos in Yell County, a constant specter haunting both their sense of belonging and the security of this contingent local acceptance.

Yard Sales and Anxious Laughter: The Threat of Being Uprooted

A relatively uneventful excursion with a Salvadoran family from Danville to Hot Springs in summer 2007 reveals both the ties that give migrants a sense of ownership over their community and the ever-present anxiety about having those ties shattered. The double-cab pickup truck was crowded with two elderly sisters, Lucía and Magdalena, Lucía's son Rafa with his partner María, Magdalena's granddaughter Chavelita, and myself with my three-year-old daughter. During the two-hour trip as we drove through the mountains and stopped at yard sales, the family chatted about times in years past they had gone swimming in a particular river or helped cousins move into a small village we passed.

As we drove through the national forest, Lucía turned to me and said with pride, "My brothers planted all these pines." She described to me, as her brothers had described to her, the extremes of weather and hardship they had experienced in their years of living on the mountains in tents or trailers. Lucía's sense of ownership was evident in her voice, and I was the outsider, admiring the labor and hardship that had earned her family their sense of belonging. Magdalena showed me where their younger brother was buried in the Hot Springs cemetery: "We thought about returning his remains to El Salvador, but he had married here, and had a son, and they wanted to be able to visit his grave" ("Magdalena," August 21, 2007).

In the midst of these conversations that revealed a sense of belonging and rootedness, an offhanded and half-joking exchange about deportation demonstrated an underlying anxiety about legal status. The truck was followed briefly by an unmarked white Nissan, and Rafa glanced back at the vehicle several times, nervously. We pulled over at a yard sale and the Nissan kept going. The conversation that followed made light of the fact that four of my five companions were imminently deportable:

RAFA: *Pensé que era la policía.*
LUCIA: *Yo pensé que era la migra!* [Laughing]
MAGDALENA: *Nos van a deportar por sospechosos, demasiado yarding.*
CHAVELITA: *No me pueden deportar a mí, que nací aca.*
LUCIA: *¿Cómo que no? Te van deportar a California.* [All laugh]
MAGDALENA: *Y Ud., Miranda, ¿en dónde nació?*
ME: *En Missouri.*
MAGDALENA: *A pues, ¡la van a deportar a Missouri!* [All laugh][5]

Transforming a consistent source of anxiety into a humorous exchange, my companions mocked the forces of the state for the arbitrary nature of their task. The tension of the real fear they felt in relation to the unmarked car and its potential to uproot them from their lives was dissipated through relieved laughter and a feeling of complicity and escape. Within the dialogue, the suggestion that I would be deported to Missouri spurred the most laughter, revealing the racialization of legal status and recognition of belonging in the United States. Although Chavelita, like me, possesses birthright citizenship, the notion that I could be deportable seemed more absurd since I am Anglo rather than Latino.

This anecdote reveals the way in which a local reality of labor integration, permanent settlement, identification, and growing social acceptance is overlaid by a set of racialized social and legal categories that keep the migrant community disenfranchised and infuse their lives with the contradictions of deportability and contingent belonging. This process of legal exclusion implodes upon migrants' subjectivities, creating an irresolvable tension regarding emotional attachments to places and people and making tenuous any sense of economic security.

In many ways, those who were most integrated into Anglo communities were most keenly aware of this instability and most sensitive to the indignities of their condition. Saúl, a fully bilingual and well-educated man from San Salvador, quit his job as a human resources clerk in one of the poultry plants because he no longer wished to participate in the management practices of the plant. "They only exploit people," he said, "because they think that nobody has papers and nobody has capabilities" ("Saúl," March 25, 2006). He described an incident wherein his boss had suggested they take a trip to southern Texas to recruit more workers. As I learned from others, this plant was notorious for poor treatment of line workers and turnover was extremely high, even compared to the already high industrial average. The company took any opportunity to cut wage costs. One worker claimed that a supervisor yelled at her and called her a thief for refusing to punch out and then return to the disassembly line, telling her that overtime pay was robbery. As Saúl saw it, the most humiliating part of the situation was the dead-end nature of the jobs:

> The work is heavy, yes, and it stresses the body, but the worst part is it's very difficult to get anywhere from those positions. It's repetitive work, you only have to make one movement, just one task, you don't even have to listen and follow directions. So the people don't learn English, don't learn new skills. Educated people, skilled people continue year after year in the same way. People that have degrees in law, or medicine, or business, and there they are, simply because they don't have papers or they don't know English or both. ("Saúl," March 25, 2007)

Rodrigo is a construction worker living with a working-class white woman and her children from a previous marriage. Through her family, he heard occasional slurs against Latinos and listened to the invective on right-wing TV shows and radio spots. More than any other interlocutor, Rodrigo was careful to interrogate my purposes and perspectives before consenting to an interview, although we had known each other a long time. In his interview, Rodrigo said: "There is a lot of insecurity. I feel completely insecure. For example, this weekend a lady came from El Salvador, one of those who travels taking and bringing back small items from El Salvador. But this time in the airport they took everything away from her, every little thing she was bringing. There was a photo of some of my family. I think there was no reason for them to do that. You could say it's not a very big deal, it's a very small thing, but you can tell that it's getting hard" ("Rodrigo," September 24, 2007). The seemingly cruel and arbitrary action of the customs officials, appropriating a token that would maintain Rodrigo's social ties with family back in El Salvador, encapsulates the way in which state policy formations and enforcement practices impose social isolation on transnational migrants. At the same time, the increase in enforcement makes it more difficult for migrants to fully settle and invest in their place of residence.

A few months after our interview, Rodrigo called me at home to vent his frustration. His girlfriend wanted him to help her buy a new house, and when he expressed his hesitancy she got angry and said that he couldn't think about the future, it must be because he was Hispanic and therefore irresponsible. He got angry and stormed out. On the phone he said to me: "How can I invest in a home? How can I invest in a life with her, when they could just take me away at any moment? Her family doesn't like me, but they don't understand. It's not that I want to be irresponsible, but I can't count on anything. I can't live like this. Every day I'm afraid" ("Rodrigo," November 2007). Rodrigo's anxiety is structured by his legal condition, yet those around him interpret his structural dilemma to personal (or a racialized collective) failure. These encounters took place in the context of an emergent national-level backlash against "illegal" immigration that migrants in Yell County were well aware of, though to a certain extent they were shielded from its more vitriolic forms by the notable *tranquilidad* of the county and local whites' contingent welcome. Rodrigo's sense of mounting danger, however, was echoed by other informants in milder terms. Many were conscious that the border area was more dangerous, *que ya no está como antes,* it's not like before. Some were aware of an anti-immigrant law passed in Oklahoma in 2007 as well as an agreement made between the Arkansas State Police and Immigration and Customs Enforcement in April 2008 that permitted some state troopers to enforce immigration law. These signs of nativism made transnational migrants increasingly anxious about the possibility of being suddenly uprooted.

Being the Alien: Refractions of "Illegality"

To comprehend the contradiction between the lived experience of rooted belonging and the legal forms of exclusion, we must further examine the sociolegal production of "illegality" and the ways the proliferation of alarmist discourse around immigration impacts migrants' lives in this particular locale. According to a recent study by the Winthrop-Rockefeller Institute, 51 percent of the foreign-born residents of Arkansas are undocumented, and a sizable number more are semilegalized under deferral of deportation programs or pending residency applications (Capps et al. 2007). In spite of these precarious legal situations, most migrants feel that they are growing roots in their new home communities. When they consider legal status explicitly, it is with confusion and frustration that acquiring a status that fits their growing sense of belonging and responsibility seems unnecessarily difficult. As Magdalena said to me, "I don't understand what the government's problem is with migrants. I don't know what the U.S. has against migrants. Not just [my neighbor], not just me, there are thousands and thousands of people without documents, and what can they do? What is the government's problem?" ("Magdalena," September 16, 2007). The majority of my study participants identify with Danville as their home community, and many more will also claim an identity as "*Arkansano*" (Arkansan) or even "*sureño*" (southerner), distinguishing themselves from friends and relatives living in northern or coastal cities. These immigrants from Central América and Mexico identify with the American Heartland, putting down roots in their new landscape of home. However, the identification becomes more difficult at a larger scale. Migrants often feel excluded from a sense of national belonging and feel that their presence is tolerated rather than embraced. Even those who have naturalized as citizens do not usually self-identify as *Americano,* which is a racialized category applied almost exclusively to whites. They recognize that they are here due to labor demands in the chicken-processing plants, and they have worked out a sometimes uneasy truce with locally born residents, but they as transnational labor migrants continue to be subject to demonization in political rhetoric in the state, region, and nation as a whole.

Anti-immigrant lay discourse—the everyday talk about immigrants heard in mass media outlets, online blogs, and over coffee tables—depends on a racialized nativist imaginary that reduces the complex hierarchies of ambiguous legality to the unambiguous notion of the "illegal" as an illegitimate resident, an intruder. Nativist discourse constructs a dualistic narrative of inside-outside in which the undocumented immigrants—and Latinos as a whole—are framed as problematic intruders. Leo Chávez calls this the "Latino threat narrative" (2008). Often using metaphors of illness or invasion, this narrative suggests that undocumented immigrants, or "illegal aliens" in nativist parlance, are a "plague" on the country. In these ways of framing migrants, a problematic legal status is conflated with cultural difference, which is in turn conflated with criminality or contagion. Undocumented status is criminalized in popular understanding, whereas in legal terms it is merely a civil violation similar to speeding or painting your house a color not permitted by the housing code in your neighborhood. These narratives often conflate Latino identity with Mexican national origin as well. For many Latino residents in Heartland immigrant destinations such as Iowa, Oklahoma, or rural Arkansas, being racially or linguistically marked as Latino is enough to classify them, in the mind of some locals, as "illegal Mexicans," regardless of their true national origin or immigration status. The condition of "illegality" in its social ramifications is not always predicated on documents or formal legal status but on a racialized perception of Otherness that reverberates in discriminatory attitudes. One Arkansas state representative, in an informal conversation following his appearance on a televised panel regarding the implications of immigration for the state, admitted quite freely that his concern was not truly "illegals," asserting that "the real problem is the Hispanics."

Even in Danville where local politicians espoused an immigrant-friendly public rhetoric, "illegality" carried a stigma of criminality. The local state representative from Yell County, Nathan George, considers himself responsible to his immigrant constituency even if they do not vote. He supported a statewide measure to make in-state tuition at the University of Arkansas available to all young people who graduated high school in Arkansas, regardless of immigration status. Nonetheless, he criticized unauthorized entry, saying, "We are a nation of immigrants and we must embrace immigrants—but don't make the first thing you do when you come in the country be breaking the law" (Nathan George, personal communication, February 25, 2008).

In Yell County, the contingent belonging of Latino residents exists in tension with this concept of "illegality." Framed as a personal failure and transgression rather than a structural condition of migrants' lives, "illegal" status appears to delegitimize their presence. Many white citizens in Yell County had a kind of double discourse when it came to issues of immigration: expressions of hospitality and contingent acceptance and, at other moments, participation in nativist statements or conversations. In practice, Yell County natives' contingent acceptance of migrant neighbors includes many undocumented persons but accepts elements of nativist discourse in that to be "illegal" is equated with being unworthy of rights, an illegitimate member of the social world.

Perhaps the most striking impact of "illegality" is on Yell County migrants' working lives. The fear of having their status discovered—and facing the social as well as legal consequences of that stigma—keeps many working residents quiet about poor working conditions. At the poultry plants, injured workers can be and are regularly fired. Supervisors and managers do not hesitate to make direct threats if they sense that workers might resist being overworked, seek to organize, or file a claim against the company. In other words, workers' status as "illegals" serves as a disciplinary mechanism infusing their lives, contributing to labor control in the workplace. While employers may not have perfect knowledge of whose papers are false and whose are genuine, supervisors and even human resources personnel freely admitted that their workforce contained a significant portion of undocumented workers. The widespread perception of this surveillance (the sense that "they know who has papers and who doesn't") served a purpose of intimidation for many, and the aforementioned climate of fear affects even those who have legal status, worsening the working conditions for all. In one case, a woman who suffered severe injuries on the line at one poultry plant was blacklisted as unemployable within the industry due to her legal action against the company to demand back pay and compensation for her injury. After being fired by the company, she hired a local lawyer who she believes was paid off by the owner of the plant to lose her case. Since that time, no one will hire her at any of the poultry plants in the area. Nonetheless, she stands by her feeling that conditions must change in the plants and that it will only happen through struggle: "I decided to fight back because it wasn't right what they were doing; they were punishing me for having reclaimed [my workers' compensation]. Many times this has happened to others, but nobody wants to stand up for their rights because they are afraid. And I tell them we shouldn't be afraid. Why be afraid, I say, if we undocumented have the same rights as any worker" ("Julieta," February 12, 2007). This worker's willingness to sacrifice livelihood for the principle of rights was unusual; most accepted poor treatment at work as a condition of life.

Legal forms of marginalization produce around workers a sphere of exception, a space where those who exploit them can violate various standards for workplace safety, employee treatment, and human rights. Similar to de jure spaces of exception like free-trade zones and company enclaves (Ferguson 2005), the de facto space of exception of individual "illegality" puts workers in a vulnerable position and increases company control. The power relations embedded in deportability are not significantly alleviated by workers' possession of a temporary work permit or visa. Many Salvadorans in Yell County were undocumented; a good number beyond that possessed a work permit under a program called Temporary Protected Status, or TPS. This program offers a collective "deferral of deportation" to around 300,000 Salvadorans in the United States; under the status, migrants are not legal immigrants but cannot currently be deported. Liminal legal statuses such as TPS, alongside consistent demands for migrant labor in specific industries, enable simultaneous labor incorporation and formal exclusion from the polity. This form of differential exclusion has continuities with past racialized forms of labor appropriation, and rather than being transgressive of the social order, the presence of a labor force with second-class noncitizen status contributes to capitalist production systems that require "flexible" labor.[6] This model helps us understand the "inclusive hierarchy" in Yell County that underpins migrants' precarious permanence. Migrants' labor, structured by legal status, reproduces a form of social order that is racially subdivided and fundamentally unequal. Nonetheless, this legal subordination is part of what makes transnational migrant workers so valuable to the companies that hire and communities that receive them. Ironically, migrants' centrality to local economies—the basis of the contingent welcome they receive from the native born—is made possible by their persistent legal exclusion.

Precarious Belonging and Contingent Lives

The quality of "illegality" is not simply an ascribed status that impacts how others treat Latin American immigrants; it is also a definition that pervades migrants' subjectivity. According to Susan Coutin's (2005) study of Salvadoran migrants en route to the United States, clandestinity is an experience that pervades migrants' lives while they are on the journey and makes them feel like changed people. Defined by their legal status as "out of place" and transgressive, migrants begin to feel immoral, even though they don't think they are doing anything wrong. They feel a heaviness, a weight, and a great anxiety about the potential to be discovered. I suggest that this clandestine ethos does not generally end when migrants reach their destination. The same experiences of feeling weighted down and a sense of pervasive angst and fear were described by many of my interviewees. Even as they made inroads into the local social sphere, they felt an internal impact of the stigma of being "illegal" as well as experiencing the disciplining impacts of legal ambiguity.

After a single moment of territorial transgression and transnational mobility, followed by months or years settling into new places and learning to call them home, migrants often feel more constrained and anxious than they were in their home country. This is due not only to the stress of cultural adaptation but also to the problematics of legal exclusion or legal ambiguity. Even Salvadorans eligible for temporary work permits, for example, have difficulty getting permission to travel back and forth to El Salvador. They are immobilized in Arkansas, unable to travel back to see friends and family. They are protected from deportation yet, paradoxically, will immediately be under a deportation order at the end of their "temporary" stay (which has now been extended over ten years). Small legal missteps such as driving violations can also land even legal permanent residents in detention or deportation proceedings. While migrants are often able to participate in the consumer elements of the "American dream," as well as set down roots in the local landscape and establish relationships in the community, these ties are tenuous, haunted by the sense that at any moment they may be deported, uprooted from social networks as well as homes and other material investments. Ironically, although they are often represented as dangerously mobile, transcending nation-state boundaries, or living invisible lives "in the shadows" and out of authority's reach, many migrants feel under surveillance and hypervisible, as well as trapped and spatially enclosed. The contradictions of their liminal legal status complicate what is already a difficult process of incorporation into new social worlds, making new roots and commitments precarious and vulnerable.

Caught in a vexed social position wherein they must disavow the hypervisible image of the immigrant as societal leech, obscure their legal status, and assert belonging in their new landscape of home, Salvadoran migrants work to present themselves as valid neighbors who take care of their homes and contribute to the town's economy and avoid "making trouble." Workers' status serves as a disciplinary mechanism, acting both through external threat and internal shaping of character, contributing to labor control and eventually to company profits, social stability, lower crime rates, and other economic and social benefits accrued by the host society. There are other costs to both migrants and receiving communities, however—costs that I have attempted to make clear in this essay.

Deportability and Neoliberal Landscapes

Debates around immigration in the United States during the first decade of the new millennium have often hinged on characterizations of immigrants as either beneficial or detrimental, either criminals or exemplars of persistence and responsibility. Rarely does the focus of debate shift to "illegality" itself, its historical or bureaucratic origins or the costs this legal system imposes upon the lives of immigrants, the communities that receive them, and the ability of each to adapt and construct a new sense of belonging and community. Responding to Nicholas De Genova's (2002) call to turn the analytical lens onto the underlying cultural logics and purposes of state forms of legal marginalization, this essay discussed the ideology and impact of "illegality" as this social-legal identity is lived by Salvadorans in Yell County.

In the tumultuous process of settlement in rural Arkansas, Salvadoran transnational migrants develop an emergent sense of community and connection vis-à-vis places at various scales: local, national, and transnational. Their creative production of a sense of community and connection to place is often fragmented by precarious or ambiguous legal status that maintains their official disenfranchisement. While Salvadorans and other Latino/a residents of Danville, Arkansas, are fully incorporated as laborers into local systems of production, they continue to be excluded as full rights-bearing subjects. Rather than an accident or transgression, their second-class status is a carefully crafted and legally produced lacuna that facilitates their exploitation by corporations and permits state entities to turn a blind eye to violations of their rights.

While local white residents and the town's leadership recognize the value and legitimacy of migrants' presence overall—thus countering in part the national-level discourse of Latino/a migrants as "intruders"—this hard-won acceptance has come through exploitative incorporation into neoliberal regimes of production. Disoriented by legal marginalization, longing for security for their families and livelihoods, Salvadorans build their sense of connection to place through a discourse of stewardship and rootedness. They assert themselves consistently as valuable members of the local social world, often tolerating a second-class status in exchange for contingent acceptance on the part of locals. The complex (dis)connections to community and place experienced by Salvadoran migrants emerge, not only from concrete experiences migrants encounter at work, with neighbors, and in public spaces, but also in dialectical relationship to processes occurring at the level of the nation-state such as U.S. political discourses and policies around immigration. Disciplined by structures of legal ambiguity, Salvadoran migrants construct contingent lives whose apparent marginality obscures their foundational contributions to social revitalization of the rural Heartland as well as new regimes of economic production in Arkansas.

Notes

1. The data on this trend are well established. Over the last fifteen to twenty years, many Salvadorans and other Latinos/as have settled in the rural, noncoastal areas of the United States that have not experienced this level or type of immigration in centuries. From 1990 to 2000, the growth of the Latino population in the United States was 58 percent, while the regional Latino population growth in the South was 71.2 percent (U.S. census). Central and northwest Arkansas are regions of particularly striking demographic shift for the Salvadoran population specifically. The American city with the highest growth rate of Salvadoran residents during the period from 1990 to 2000, at 61 percent according to the U.S. Census Bureau, was the Fayetteville, Arkansas, metro area (Andrade-Eekhoff 2003: 15). Yell County, Arkansas, where I conducted my fieldwork, has officially the highest per capita Salvadoran population of any rural county in the country and the second highest per capita Salvadoran population of all counties following Los Angeles County (Frago and Reese 2003).

2. Due to this perpetual insecurity experienced by many of my informants, I often use the word *migrant* rather than *immigrant* to emphasize the fragility of their pres-

ence. Conveniently, this is also the best translation for the Spanish word *migrantes*, which most interlocutors used to describe themselves. Juxtaposing the narratives of rootedness and settlement with the terminology of displacement and rupture suggested by the word *migrant* usefully evokes this paradox of rootedness/uprootedness.

3. As Nancy McLean argues, it was in part the regional configuration of cultural values mentioned previously that was instrumental in launching political and economic projects of neoliberal restructuring. This shift in regimes of production was central not only to the careers of notable southern politicians (Arkansas native Bill Clinton, for example) but also helped to launch this globalized and high-growth southern economy.

4. White Revolution is a white supremacist organization based in nearby Russellville, Arkansas.

5. Rafa: I thought it was the police.
Lucia: I thought it was the *migra!* [Laughing]
Magdalena: They'll deport us for being suspicious, too much yard-saling.
Chavelita: They can't deport me, I was born here!
Lucia: Of course they can, they'll deport you to California! [All laugh]
Magdalena: Where were you born, Miranda?
Me: In Missouri.
Magdalena: Well then, they'll deport you to Missouri! [All laugh]

6. The most obvious parallel here is the Bracero Program, which provided temporary work permits for Mexicans to fill demands for menial farm labor from 1942 to 1964 (see Ngai 2005: 128–66). One of my informants also compared temporary status to the system of racialized slavery in the antebellum South.

Sources Cited

Andrade-Eekhoff, Katharine. 2003. *Mitos y realidades: El Impacto economico de la migración en los hogares rurales.* San Salvador: FLACSO.

Bailey, Adrian J., et al. 2002. "(Re)Producing Salvadoran Transnational Geographies." *Annals of the Association of American Geographers* 92, no. 1: 125–44.

Capps, Randy, et al. 2007. *A Profile of Immigrants in Arkansas.* Chapel Hill, N.C.: Winthrop Rockefeller Foundation.

Cash, W. J. 1941. *The Mind of the South.* New York: Random House.

Chávez, Leo R. 2008. *The Latino Threat: Constructing Immigrants, Citizens, and the Nation.* Stanford, Calif.: Stanford University Press.

Coutin, Susan. 2005. "Being en Route." *American Anthropologist* 107, no. 2: 195–206.

Davis, Mike. 2001. *Magical Urbanism.* New York: Verso.

De Genova, Nicholas P. 2002. "Migrant 'Illegality' and Deportability in Everyday Life." *Annual Review of Anthropology* 31: 419–47.

Ferguson, James. 2005. "Seeing Like an Oil Company: Space, Security and Global Capital in Neoliberal Africa." *American Anthropologist* 107, no. 3: 377–82.

Frago, Charlie, and Philip Reese. 2003. "Rural Yell County Draws Many Salvadorans." *Arkansas Democrat Gazette,* July 7, 1A, 5A.

Levitt, Peggy. 2001. *The Transnational Villagers*. Berkeley and Los Angeles: University of California Press.

Loewen, James. 1971. *The Mississippi Chinese: Between Black and White*. Prospect Heights, Ill.: Waveland Press.

Miyares, Ines M., et al. 2003. "The Interrupted Circle: Truncated Transnationalism and the Salvadoran Experience." *Journal of Latin American Geography* 2, no. 1: 74–86.

Ngai, Mae M. 2005. *Impossible Subjects: Illegal Aliens and the Making of Modern America*. Princeton, N.J.: Princeton University Press.

Striffler, Steve. 2005. *Chicken: The Dangerous Transformation of America's Favorite Food*. New Haven, Conn.: Yale University Press.

Wasem, Ruth Ellen, and Karma Ester. 2006. "Temporary Protected Status: Current Immigration Policy and Issues." In *CRS Report for Congress*. Washington, DC: Congressional Research Service.

CHAPTER 7

Contesting Diversity and Community within Postville, Iowa

"Hometown to the World"

JENNIFER F. REYNOLDS

AND CAITLIN DIDIER

Introduction

The most prominent welcome sign to Postville, Iowa, population approximately 2,500, boldly stakes a claim to be "Hometown to the World."[1] This boundary marker is a material trace, indexing a once-held majority position that embraced human diversity within a much-contested human geography of social struggle over who is entitled to live on Main Street. *Main Street* is a metonym standing for the rise of the American middle classes in the period between the American Civil War and World War I.[2] It engenders the promise and fulfillment of the American dream in rural "hometowns" where social class divisions are imagined to be absent.[3] But when author Sinclair Lewis published his popular novel *Main Street* in 1920, his intent was to critique bourgeois, small-town life instantiated in ethnic, gender, and class relationships and social practices. The immigrants whose lives he chronicled largely included Germans, Swedes, and Norwegians, entrepreneurs and farmers whose right to legal citizenship was never questioned, though most Anglo-Saxon characters treated them with distain.[4]

Once again in the early twenty-first century, the American Heartland is now hometown to all sorts of new immigrants. It is an era defined by struggles over how to sustain home place that are additionally configured by ongoing cultural politics of identity and citizenship. The two authors conducted political economic and ethnographic research at different points and periods of time (2000, 2004–2005, 2006, 2007–2008, and 2009). In this chapter, we draw upon this work to consider how the "cultural" identity of rural Iowa, like many other places in the rural Midwest and South, is enveloped within a transnational social field (Glick Schiller 2003) wherein different actors and agencies have struggled over the meanings of citizenship and belonging in contradictory and locally specific ways (De Genova and Ramos-Zayas 2003; Chock 1999; Coutin 2003; Flores 2003). Data include participant observation in the churches, schools, and places of leisure, as well as different residents' homes and open-ended interviews with key cultural brokers in town. Our work builds upon a tradition of critical ethnographic inquiry on transborder meshworks of migration (Escobar 2003; compare Glick Schiller 2003; Stephen 2007). Meat-processing communities constitute important nodes in transborder meshworks (Fink 1998; Grey and Woodrick 2002; Millard and Chapa 2004; Stull, Broadway, and Erikson 1992). Thus it is through this point of entry that we here examine how the interrelated processes of delimiting and regimenting transmigrant and native-born identities are "formed from the interface of material conditions, history, the structure of the political economy, and social practice" (Nagengast and Kearney 1990: 62; compare Brodkin 2000; Kearney and Beserra 2004).

When we arrived at different periods of time within the town's recent history, native and foreign-born residents underscored that debates over collective belonging were ongoing. Iowa natives Veronica Haugen and Ryan Hauss framed these debates in different ways, albeit striking complementary stances.[5]

> **VERONICA:** I think it's just, we're just, we're making history. We're making history in Postville in 2007. And we've got the people that are, are embracing it [i.e., the arrival of newcomer Mexican and Guatemalan residents] and we've got other people that are just not ready, for this change. (Haugen 2007 interview)
> **RYAN:** When I graduated from my high school in a small town near here, my class was the largest in that school system of fifty-five. A generation later, my sons were in classes of twenty to twenty-five. My granddaughter was in a class of five. [**JENNIFER:** Wow, that's pretty dramatic.] So you take three generations you can close a school. . . . So unless you have an industry, in your town, your town is going to be wiped out. So you know people can say what they want. Some people don't like Jewish people, they don't like what they've got at the plant. Well do you want growing pains? Or do you want dying pains? It's just, it's either one or the other, you just don't stay, in the middle. (Hauss 2007 interview)

The dynamics that both interviewees acknowledge began during the mid-1980s when Postville, like many small farming towns, entered an economic crisis. HyGrade, the local meatpacking plant, declared bankruptcy, and banks foreclosed on family farms. The downtown, a Friday-night gathering place, became a barren strip of empty storefronts, and the hospital shut its doors for good. Postville was in danger of becoming a ghost town when, in 1987, an extended family of observant Chabad-Lubavitch Hasidic Jews from Brooklyn, New York, bought the abandoned meatpacking plant. They renovated the facilities and opened Agriprocessors in 1989, a kosher beef- and poultry-processing plant that recruited migrant labor from the ex-Soviet republics, Asia, Israel, and Latin America. Undeniably, the plant stimulated new economic activity within the region and in town; old businesses once again flourished, and new ones were established that catered to different newcomers' consumption patterns.

Postville experienced the same sorts of radical structural and cultural changes that typically happen in rural locales that accept industrial meat- or poultry-processing plants into the neighborhood (Broadway 2000; Stull and Broadway 2004). It was initially ill equipped to shoulder the burden of providing many of the indirect costs (housing, health care, language services, and other human services) that new-breed plants require of their host communities (Hackenberg 1995). The town scrambled to accommodate the large number of native and foreign-born newcomers. Apartment complexes were rapidly constructed, an English as a second language (ESL) program initiated, a soccer league formed, and a bilingual Mass instituted. The chamber of commerce even inaugurated an annual multicultural festival modeled after Taste of Chicago to acknowledge the newcomers' cuisines and popular cultures as well as acquaint long-term residents with a sampling of diversity. The religious and local government support initiated in the first decade after the opening of Agriprocessors was nearly unprecedented, though resident popular support remained divided.[6]

Since that time, however, with the expansion of plant facilities, the vertical integration of the corporation, and its control over the market share in kosher beef, management shifted its stance vis-à-vis its responsibilities to workers and the community. This in turn exacerbated ethnoracial and class divisions between native and newcomer residents and fostered new conflicts. Many town residents who initially supported newcomer workers started to experience "change fatigue" (Stull and Broadway 2004); some grew hostile to plant management and the largely "Hispanic" workforce, even though it had shifted from predominantly itinerant single-male to extended-family networks.

This sentiment was bolstered by national anti-immigrant (i.e., anti-Hispanic) discourses, effecting a change in local government.[7] The campaign slogan called for change, and in 2006 new leadership was elected into office, resulting in the withdrawal of all forms of local government support for "diversity." The successful Taste of Postville that had been held for six years was no more. Most notably during summer 2007, an anti-Hispanic-immigrant rally marched through downtown in response to a fight between two Mexican families that resulted in five men hospitalized, two of whom were arrested. Rumors spread among Guatemalans and Mexicans that some Iowans were fed up and were planning to contact *la migra,* the Immigration and Customs Enforcement (ICE), and be rid of them all. As it turns out, their fears were not entirely baseless.

Situating Agriprocessors within the Political Economic Landscape of Rural Meat- and Poultry-Processing Industries

While neither of us intended to focus on the plant and its operations in our respective research projects, inevitably all roads led back to Agriprocessors. It influenced most rhythms of daily life in this factory town. In fact, in all rural towns where industrial meat-processing plants take up residence, both the native-born and newcomer migrant workforce are located in structurally weaker positions, often not able to exert much pressure on employers to change practices that are destructive to life outside the plant (Hackenberg 1995: 243).

Up until summer 2008, the plant located in Postville was slaughtering cattle and chicken and some lamb and turkey on a seasonal basis.[8] It followed *shechitah,* or ritual rules of slaughter to produce kosher and glatt kosher products. In this section, we examine how Agriprocessors was simultaneously a typical and an exemplary case study of meat- and poultry-processing plants. When the family patriarch, Aaron Rubashkin, decided to expand the reach of his business from a Brooklyn neighborhood butcher shop, he did so by example, following the restructuring and reorganizing strategies of rural industrialized nonkosher meat and poultry oligopolies. The major difference, however, is that the Rubashkin family was able to leverage its reputation for doing charitable works within the Crown Heights Lubavitch Jewish community to gain support within Jewish networks spanning parts of the United States and Israel.[9]

Iowa Beef Packers (later renamed Iowa Beef Processors, or IBP) started the restructuring in 1961, when it opened its first plant in Denison, Iowa.[10] IBP "revolutionized" the meatpacking industry when it relocated plants from urban to rural locales to reduce costs related to urban real estate, transportation of livestock, and labor (Broadway 2000; Fink 1998; Kandel and Parrado 2005; Stull, Broadway, and Erickson 1992). IBP, moreover, restructured meatpacking plants into meat-processing facilities producing value-added products. They relied on a nonunion labor force. Cattle were killed on-site via a deskilled disassembly line, dramatically increasing productivity at the expense of workers' health. The illness and injury rates of workers skyrocketed, rendering industrial meat processing one of the most dangerous of all industries (Stull and Broadway 1995). The meat was then processed and vacuum-packaged, ready for shipment to retail stores and restaurants that now no longer needed to staff their own butchers. In an industry dependent on commodity-priced volume with low profit margins (Bjerklie 1995), other firms in the business adopted similar strategies in order to compete. Firms that could not compete either went bankrupt or were bought out, resulting in a few enormous companies (Broadway 1995).

Poultry plants only began to expand in the 1980s when the American diet started to favor white-meat poultry products. Unlike beef and hog meatpacking firms, poultry firms were rural operations located in southern states with "right-to-work" antiunion legislation.[11] Over time, they became vertically integrated, controlling the production, processing, and distribution of products within the same firm. These firms developed a system of contracts with growers who were placed in charge of factory-size farms that minimized both the length of time and amount of feed needed to raise chickens. While the risk for growers was originally reduced under the contract system, poultry-processing firms, like beef and pork plants, grew oligopolistic with contracts always favoring the firm over the farmer.

The Rubashkin family realized that fresh kosher food was a niche market; the prices of its products were kept artificially high due to the small customer base and to religious prescription. This resulted in meat sitting for longer on the shelf, turning an unappetizing hue of brown (Popper 2008). Access to fresh kosher meat products was also unequal across the country and nonexistent in most places. Many Jewish Americans who wanted to be observant of orthodox tradition simply did not have access to fresh kosher meat in supermarkets. When the Rubashkins bought the first plant in Iowa to scale up their operation, they simultaneously vertically integrated the family business. They experimented with shrink-wrapping and chemical inserts to keep red meat looking fresher longer. All of this gave their business an advantage over other producers and distributors of kosher meat products, especially beef. It became a an extremely lucrative business venture that resulted in Agriprocessors commanding 60 percent market share in kosher beef and an equally impressive 40 percent share business in kosher chicken, reaching 11 million customers with sales nearing $10.5 billion annually (Levine 2008).

News media and magazine reporters that have investigated the rise of the Rubashkin family's prominence within the industry have all acknowledged that their business model was congruent with Chabad-Lubavitch Orthodox faith. Agriprocessors' goal was to afford all American Jews the opportunity to be more observant of traditional dietary restrictions by providing fresh kosher meat at an affordable cost (Dwoskin 2008; Levine 2008; Popper 2008). Critics and competitors, however, have been less charitable in their assessment of Rubashkin business practices. Some have alleged that the Rubashkins leveraged their image as charitable and pious leaders within the community to garner support of Lubavitch rabbis across the country who would encourage congregants not to buy products from competitors on the basis that they were not truly kosher (Dwoskin 2008). A few alleged that the Rubashkins engaged in irregular practices; others went so far as to claim cutthroat business tactics to undercut prices and force them out of business. One ex-business partner interviewed simply stated that they are nice people, except when you get into business with them (Popper 2008). In this regard, the Rubashkin family is like all others involved in meat-processing industries; concern over the bottom line trumps almost everything else.

Transborder Crossings: Geopolitical and Economic Interpenetrations and Interdependencies

Agriprocessors is also identical to other rural industrial plants in the way that it has recruited new immigrants for the most labor-intensive, low-paying jobs. The term *new immigrant* (or *transmigrant*) entered into circulation in the social-scientific literature during the 1990s when anthropologists began with renewed interest to try and make sense of unparalleled levels of migration on a global scale (Foner 2003). Nina Glick Schiller and colleagues Linda Basch and Cristina Blanc-Szanton (1992) termed the phenomena *transnational migration* to demarcate a historically and qualitatively different era defined by the logic of late capitalism and an international division of labor (Harvey 1989). *Globalization,* as it has been termed, is structured by disjunctive transnational flows of capital, media, and labor (Appadurai 1996; Suarez-Orozco 2003), which has led to the creation of deterritorialized borders within the United States and western Europe where the largest proportion, a heterogeneous group of transmigrants, is segmented into subcontracted deskilled, low-wage jobs, some of which compete with outsourced industries overseas. Lynn Stephen (2007) recently underscored how most transmigrants have traversed many boundaries in crossing parts of Central America and Mexico to the United States. These border crossings, moreover, are not just national ones; they encompass crossing ethnic, gender, generational, and socioeconomic class locations. She thus prefers the concept of *transborder* over transnational lives (Stephen 2007: 19–23).

Transborder crossings were first experienced in Postville when American-born Hasidic Jewish families moved from ethnic Brooklyn neighborhoods to rural northeastern Iowa. Management recruited rabbis from Israel to ensure that livestock were properly slaughtered according to *shechitah* procedures. By 2007, Jewish labor made up 10 percent of Agriprocessors' workforce. Also during the first decade that Agriprocessors opened its doors, the majority of plant workers were from ex-Soviet republics, reflecting the owners' East Coast orientation in recruiting from an ethnically segmented labor market. According to two cultural brokers, those who worked extensively with people from Kyrgyzstan, Russia, Ukraine, and the former Yugoslavia, the cost of living and Iowa's reputation of providing a quality public school education is what drew many away from New York City to Postville. Even though the wages were comparatively low, people were still able to save money and send for their family members. They also came from a societal context in which multilingual language acquisition was not treated as problem, and so many were able to tap into prior educational experiences and take advantage of support from the newly formed Diversity Council and ESL programs offered to transmigrants. These workers, however, did not remain. During the later years of the Bill Clinton administration, when undocumented migrants were increasingly criminalized just as naturalization was promoted, many of the workers at the plant took advantage of a national campaign to naturalize citizens and legalize others, though the requirements were very strict. Many workers from ex-Soviet republics went through this process and received sponsorship assistance from plant management. Once the majority had received their papers, they moved away from Postville to find more lucrative, less exploitative employment in surrounding cities in the Midwest and beyond.

Beginning in the late 1990s, the workforce was almost completely replaced, first with primarily newcomers from Mexico, then by Guatemalans. This reflects greater midwestern and southeastern demographic shifts since the 1980s in which increasing numbers of Hispanics have been sought out by meatpacking industries to perform low-wage, deskilled, nonunion jobs (Grey and Woodrick 2002; Griffith 2006; Kandel and Parrado 2005; Stull, Broadway, and Erickson 1992). We outline some of the political economic shifts that have led Mexicans and Guatemalans to Postville. Though more attention is paid to the Guatemala case, as this is the understudied population.

Postville was not the first-stop receiving site for many of the first Mexican newcomers who were drawn from other midwestern cities in search of economic opportunity in a welcoming, peaceful small town where they could put down roots and raise their families. Daisy Hidalgo, a newcomer resident originally from the state of Jalisco, was among the first Mexicans to move to Postville and work at the Iowa Turkey plant, which employed as many as 350 people in its heyday before it burned to the ground in 2003. Since that time, many of the early Mexican families left and were replaced by people who came directly from El Barril, a small agricultural town of about 3,900 inhabitants from the Mexican state of San Luis Potosí.

Farmers from El Barril and other surrounding towns produced maize, beans, dried peppers, and barley for sale in municipal markets. This is typical of the region; 60 percent to 79 percent of the population in San Luis Potosí lives in agrarian villages with less than 15,000 inhabitants. States like San Luis Potosí have been disproportionately impacted by the implementation of economic structural adjustment policies that ended import substitution, subsidies for certain crops, and other protectionist policies. Then in 1994, the North American Free Trade Agreement (NAFTA) erased all nontariff barriers to agricultural trade. The economic impact of these reforms and policies decimated subsistence and small-scale family farms that relied on rain-fed production and favored middle- to large-scale irrigation production (Morales-Moreno 2003; Stephen 2007). Thus, while NAFTA created 5.3 million jobs in the informal and formal sectors,[12] 1.3 million corn and bean small producers were forced to stop farming and seek employment elsewhere (White, Salas, and Gammage 2003). Mexico's economic crisis, compounded by NAFTA, accelerated out-migration to the United States in the 1990s, even from places that historically were not sending regions (Delgado Wise 2006).

In the mid-1990s, there were only a few Guatemalan men living in Postville. The first two to arrive and find employment at Agriprocessors were from different municipalities, Patzún and El Tejar, within the department of Chimaltenango. The majority population in this region is indigenous; many are speakers of different varieties of the Kaqchikel Mayan language and Spanish. These men recruited other men and later families and friends from their social networks encompassing the hamlets surrounding the municipal towns, San Andrés Itzapa and San Miguel Dueñas, in the adjacent department of Sacatepéquez. The majority came from San José Calderas, Chimachoy, and Xeparquiy, though numbers from other towns and regions were increasing as families recruited widely from kin and community networks. In 2008 there were approximately seven hundred Guatemalans residing in Postville.

The Chimaltenango and Sacatepéquez regions of Guatemala suffered political violence in a period spanning the late 1970s to the 1980s during the thirty-six-year-long civil war that ended in 1996. Some of Postville's newcomer residents participated on both sides of the armed conflict, though the majority of Guatemalan newcomers were too young to have been firsthand witnesses to the violence. Most of the newcomers to Postville represent heavily evangelized populations, those who for diverse reasons converted from Catholicism to different Evangelical sects. They are the first generation born into the postwar era that is marked by so-called new violence (organized crime and gang activities coupled with vigilantism) (Benson, Fisher, and Thomas 2008; J. Reynolds 2003). This is the term Guatemalan scholars have coined reflecting forms of civil violence, a sociohistorical precipitate of the decades of state-sponsored violence and structural adjustment policies (Smith 1990).

Beginning in the 1980s, economic-development policies within this region resulted in a reversal in domestic labor migration patterns. Historically, movement was from the central highlands toward coastal plantations. Since the 1990s, the migratory pattern shifted back toward the central highlands. These policies favored the cultivation of nontraditional agricultural exports and transformed the central highlands into export-processing zones with *maquiladoras* (assembly factories) (Goldín and Asturias de Barrios 2001; Fischer and Benson 2005). These forms of economic development have resulted in the semi-proletarianization of the labor force (Goldín 2009). In the late 1990s, the average salary for Guatemalans was three U.S. dollars a day, youth and especially young women found factory wages attractive. Biweekly wages granted them a modicum of independence, and their households depended on them. These households relied on diversified economic strategies for survival, and so young people's ability to earn wages undercut gendered and generational divisions typical of Mayan agrarian households.

As many as eighty-seven Korean-owned maquiladoras picked up shop in the mid-1990s and moved north to Mexico; this is another unintended by-product of NAFTA. During this time, male heads of household and their teenage children considered traveling to the United States. Those who made the move shouldered considerable debt (between $5,000 and $8,000)[13] to ensure safe passage with the assistance of human smugglers through Mexico to the United States. In 2000 the number of Guatemalan residents in Postville was growing as people relied upon their informal community and kinship networks, providing a self-sustaining network of chain migration. By 2003–2004, men were able to send for their wives and families, and the size of the Guatemalan population overtook that of the Mexican newcomer residents.

In traversing these national and cultural borders, Guatemalans and Mexicans have transplanted their own forms of ethnoracial, gendered, and national divisions to northeastern Iowa. There is a long and deep history of geopolitical divisions between the Mexican and Guatemalan states. Guatemalans often complain that Mexicans are too nationalistic and arrogant. Some Mexican newcomers confirmed Guatemalans' prejudiced opinions with clever, albeit pejorative, play on words such as "Guate*malas*" (a play on the Spanish word *mala*, "bad") or "Gautemal*illos*" (little Guatemalans). The second term in particular had racialized overtones as it underscored perceived biological differences related to the shorter stature of indigenous people. In both Guatemala and Mexico, mestizo populations (referred to as *ladino* in

Guatemala) historically have used racial epithets to refer to its diverse in-digenous populations, and so within Mexican and some Guatemalan towns, newcomer residents used these to distinguish themselves in both positive and negative ways. This dynamic continued to play out in Postville, especially on the disassembly lines highlighting the unequal relations between the more experienced, longer-term Mexican residents and newcomer Guatemalans. Some line managers use these epithets to urge Guatemalans to work faster when upper management demanded production to speed up. Other Mexican line workers considered Guatemalans backward and stupid, allowing them-selves to be manipulated and exploited. Reynolds heard Guatemalan women state of their Mexican counterparts, "*Dicen que somos pendejas y muy dejadas*" (They say that we're stupid and too passive). Guatemalans, especially those who acknowledged their indigenous heritage, considered themselves more cultured and industrious. Some would make equally derogatory comments, stating that mestizo Mexicans were lazy and rude. As far as some Guatema-lans were concerned, Mexicans were born troublemakers. A few women, however, started to question these dynamics, noting that Guatemalan line managers were no better. They found ways through informal entrepreneur-ial networks to learn from one another. They devised coping strategies and forged ties to influential people both inside and outside the plant. In these instances, there were opportunities, albeit limited, for transmigrants of color to forge a collective awareness of shared class and gendered experiences. Both were also sensitive to the ways in which the catchall term *Hispanic* could be used by Iowans in its most racialized sense (Didier 2005). When either group would watch the Spanish-language broadcast news stations, they were keenly aware of U.S. anti-immigrant discourses. And when these were felt in Postville, conversational openers often began with phrases like, "*ya no nos quieren aquí*" (they don't want us here anymore).

Labor Struggles and the Politics of Invisibility and Deportability

Agriprocessors' management has been very vocal in its stance with respect to its workforce's right to organize. In an interview with reporter David Levine for the online business magazine *Upstart Business Journal,* Aaron Rubashkin referred to the United Food and Commercial Workers international union (UFCW) as "our enemy." Levine attributed Rubashkin's antipathy for unions and other left-leaning organizations as an outgrowth of his experiences grow-ing up during the early Cold War period of the Soviet Union. This may be the case, but historically U.S.-based meatpacking firms were vehemently opposed to union organizing; the new-breed packers' strategic cost-cutting move to rural areas served to undercut hard-won union victories in urban firms. This union-busting strategy succeeded, and to this day, meat-processing wages in rural locales have not rebounded.

The UFCW has staged a number of campaigns to unionize different businesses within the Agriprocessors family empire. The Rubashkins bitterly fought and lost one of the campaigns to unionize undocumented workers at their Brooklyn-based Sunset Park warehouse and distribution center. Management tried at one point to force several workers to sign union cards with a "sweetheart" union, Local 1718 of the United Production Union, operated by a different sect of Hasidic Jews of the Williamsburg, Brooklyn, neighborhood. The management's tactics failed, and twenty of its workers were allowed to join the UFCW in 2005. When they staged a strike, management promptly fired them for being undocumented. The UFCW petitioned the National Labor Relations Board to intervene and take Agriprocessors to court. Agriprocessors' response was to hire high-powered constitutional attorney Nathan Lewin to petition the U.S. Supreme Court to hear the Rubashkin's complaint and overturn the *Sure-Tan, Inc. v. NLRB* (467 U.S. 883, 1984) Supreme Court decision that upheld the National Labor Relations Act wherein "employees" could be interpreted as "any employees," including undocumented workers, who have the right to organize. In November 2008, the Supreme Court refused to hear the case, effectively siding with labor on this issue.

In Postville, management strategies were more successful in undermining UFCW attempts to organize the majority Guatemalan and Mexican workforce. When Reynolds first visited Guatemalans living in Postville in 2000, there was no sign of union activity. At that time, the Guatemalan workforce was still relatively small, but it was growing. The plant provided accommodations for them in a house adjacent to its property. Between twenty and twenty-five single men co-resided there, sleeping in shifts following their work schedules. The shifts were long, approximately ten to twelve hours, Monday through Friday. Several men reported that Saturday was their day off in observance of the Sabbath. Agriprocessors expected employees to work almost a double shift on Sundays, eighteen-plus hours to make up for lost hours from Saturday. Plant management also had very little fear of scrutiny from outsiders at that time, too. One of the Guatemalan shift managers insisted on giving Reynolds a tour of the facilities to get a better sense of what they were like.

When Reynolds returned to Postville in 2006 to learn what changes had occurred and find out what Guatemalans felt were the current issues that the town and the plant faced, the social climate had completely changed. Guatemalans reported that important changes had happened, the shifts were now shorter, and workers could now claim paid vacation time. The plant had also expanded its operations, more than doubling its size to a workforce that was well over seven hundred workers. The management of Agriprocessors added extra levels of security; for example, no one could now come inside without a proper identification card. There were round-the-clock shifts, and management demands to speed up production were relentless. It was also clear that Agriprocessors was concerned about the presence of union organizers from the UFCW, who had begun an organizing drive to educate workers about what unions are, how they operate, and workers' rights to unionize.[14] Organizers suspected that plant management was engaged in its own "misinformation" campaign to block their efforts, spreading rumors that they were ICE agents instead of union representatives. Reynolds witnessed one way how this happened; residents received warning calls from family and friends working at the plant. They were allowed to take a break from the line to warn their families that an announcement about the presence of ICE officers had been broadcast over the intercom in the plant facilities; everyone was advised to remain inside and not answer a knock on the door.

Concern over the impact of union organizing was even apparent in how plant management interacted with other institutions and organizations in the community that had nothing to do with how the plant operated or treated its workforce. In a 2006 conversation about how well the elementary school was adapting to the rapid influx of newcomer Spanish-speaking children, an employee volunteered that the school had run into some difficulties securing Agriprocessors' sponsorship for a multiethnic children's soccer team. Management had agreed to do so but then reneged on the promise when it learned that the children wanted the name of their team to be La Union. The Spanish word sounded too much like the false cognate in English, referring to a labor union. Far from being a subversive move to challenge the plant's antiunion stance, the name was chosen to underscore the diverse ethnic composition and cooperation, the unity forged among the players.[15]

In 2007 it was still clear that plant management fears of unionizing had not been tempered. They most likely had intensified even though the UFCW organizers were no longer actively engaged in an organizing drive.[16] One Guatemalan newcomer was of the opinion that the union's efforts failed largely in response to rumors circulating that management was prepared to close shop in Postville and move elsewhere. These rumors were coupled with the falsely cultivated belief that the Rubashkins' lobbying power at the state and federal levels of government was what kept them safe from ICE raids. However, by May of that same year, more than one hundred workers in the poultry division spontaneously walked out of the plant in response to an executive order. Their line supervisor told them that all would have to change their names and social security numbers if they were to continue working at the plant. This change in policy effectively erased *all* employees' accrued vacation time and lowered their wages back to the starting wage of $6.25 per hour.

According to some of the poultry-line workers interviewed, this management mandate was precipitated by the union's ongoing strategy to have Mexicans and Guatemalans obtain Individual Taxpayer Identification Numbers (ITIN) and properly fill out their W-2 forms to ensure that the appropriate amount of taxes were being withheld from paychecks. They surmised that this would pave the way for a smoother legalization process in the event that an immigration-reform bill was enacted. Some workers suspected that though management had been withholding social security and state and federal tax monies, they did not believe that these were actually being reported. When some workers openly declared their earnings and filed withholdings, discrepancies were revealed to the Internal Revenue Service. This is what allegedly precipitated management's decision to "fire" everyone and rehire them only after the workers obtained different documents.

Management reacted quickly and promised that those who immediately returned to work would not be impacted by the policy; those who did not, would. Everyone went back to work, though all the workers were concerned about potential repercussions. They turned to one of their most trusted cultural brokers in town, a newcomer native-born Iowan, for advice. He facilitated a meeting at which workers could consult with legal representation; however, instead of disseminating information about workers' rights, the lawyers educated the Guatemalans and Mexicans about what to do in the event that the plant was raided. One of the Guatemalan cultural brokers, Jerónimo Santa Ana, who was very critical of plant management, stated that this form of assistance served to scare workers by reminding them of their vulnerable status as deportable, disposable people. He likened it to colonial patron-client relations that kept both rural *ladinos* and indigenous Guatemalans in a perpetual state of slavery. "We still have an umbilical cord of slavery; there [in Guatemala] we wear it on our backs, and when we come here to the United States, it's the same bullshit" (Santa Ana 2007 interview). Most of our collective conversations with undocumented transmigrants from Mexico and Guatemala underscored the untenable position of having to remain invisible in plain sight while at the same time experiencing all types of surveillance, inside and out of the plant (compare Stephen 2007 on a similar dynamic among indigenous farmworkers in Oregon). Daisy Hidalgo vividly expressed how relieved she felt once she was allowed to become a naturalized citizen. Before that she said, "Sometimes, I felt like less of a person. Words fail to describe just how terrible I felt for the simple fact of not having papers" (Hidalgo 2007 interview).

Small-Town Life, Small-Town Strife

In this section of the chapter, we briefly explore the cultural politics of identity in some of these dense, multiplex networks that entangled and divided *all* of the town residents. This will not be an exhaustive discussion as space is limited; we only hope to give a sense of how ethnicizing and racializing discourses circulated and operated to constrain and enable newcomer migrants and those who sought to provide assistance to them. We pay attention to the ways in which residents were able to individually and collectively overcome, but more often succumb, to the divisiveness of identity politics.

Rural people, including both authors, who grew up in the U.S. Heartland acknowledge that local politics of place are simultaneously class struggles about who belongs on Main Street. Rural sociologists underscore that rural towns' and residents' relations are not bound territorially but encompass a social field wherein differently positioned actors and agencies continuously shape and reshape the local social order (Wilkinson1991). While *social class* is not the term people use, it is nevertheless acknowledged in the social networks that one belongs to as well as enacted in practices of social distinction observable in town members' residential and consumption patterns (Bourdieu 1984). Before the arrival of the Rubashkin family, community internal forms of local identification were shaped by kinship, occupation, and place of worship (Lutheran, Catholic, Episcopalian). Ethnicity was marked insofar as residents embraced different northern European heritages. The ascribed racial identity, however, was de facto unmarked, white. The local public school was the one place that brought everyone together; hence, school events were venues for families' displays of social-class distinction in explicit ways. In Iowa, it is generally observed that only those who attended the local public school can legitimately claim the hometown identity (D. Reynolds 1999).

When the Rubashkin family established Agriprocessors and a synagogue and provided private religious schooling for Hasidic children, it became apparent how isolating participation in different local social networks was. Native Postvillians, however, did not see it that way; many criticized the Hasidic Jews for separating themselves from the rest of the population. Racialized discourse manifested itself in negative evaluations of how these newcomers from the city snubbed local politeness norms (Bloom 2000; Tundel 2001). An Iowan cultural broker, Ryan Hauss, recounted, "I know for awhile that the people in this town said, 'We have a population in this town, the Jewish people, they are the most unfriendly people you would ever see walk on the face of the earth. . . . We wave and they never wave back'" (Hauss 2007 interview). Popular media accounts for the most part deflected the cross-class, racialized dimensions of this discourse by highlighting naturalized stereotypes of city people versus country people. Didier, nevertheless, observed how many articulations of racialized discourse were directed at the plant owner's accumulation of real estate in town. To the dismay of native Postvillians, the Rubashkin family alone owned and managed, through Nevel Properties and other company names, approximately one-third of all real estate in town, housing much of the newcomer migrant workforce. The reason why plant management was able to acquire so much of the real estate was due to the increasing "white flight" from town. According to Santa Ana, many families with school-age children had moved to other locales in the region where the public school enrollments of Hispanic children and youth were not so high.

While plant management was accommodating of its transmigrant workforce, many of Postville's long-term residents felt ambivalent about their arrival, some more so than others. Daisy Hidalgo recalls feeling so isolated that she would rejoice at the opportunity to get out and wash clothes at the town Laundromat. This isolation ended only when a retired teacher reached out to her and offered to tutor her in English (Hidalgo 2007 interview). A majority of native Postvillians, however, simply went about their daily lives without making meaningful contact. They did not really have many opportunities to do so, as local practices indeed were self-segregating. Racial prejudices also played a role as a few were outright vocal about rejecting transmigrant Mexicans: they sought to contain them within a trailer park by refusing to rent apartments or homes to them (Hidalgo 2007 interview; compare Tundel 2001). Affordable housing and care for private property, not surprising, became one of the enduring issues that polarized residents. There were some individual residents, organizations, and civic institutions of Postville, however, in a better position to reach out to and provide different forms of assistance to foreign-born newcomers. Here we will focus on a subset of these organizations and actors, namely the Catholic Church, the school, and a fragile coalition of cultural brokers.

St. Bridget's Catholic Church was one of the few places of worship that attempted to bring together people of different nationalities and ethnoracial identities. The Lutheran and Episcopalian churches have made spaces available for Guatemalan Evangelical sects to meet on a weekly basis, but native Postvillians and Guatemalans worshipped apart. St. Bridget's was the first to institute a bilingual Mass, though it occurs only once a month.[17] The rectory building also houses a Hispanic Ministry, a center that reaches out to both Mexican and Guatemalan parishioners.

Not all of the Iowan parishioners were happy when the church embraced Hispanic newcomers, though many attended the bilingual services and participated in holy days celebrated in Mexico, like the Día de Nuestra Señora de Guadalupe, on December 12. At least two of the cultural brokers who had experienced the possibility of community empowerment professed in the Catholic liberation theology during Guatemala's civil war felt that the church should be doing even more. One said, "Human mobility is a right, of a kind. *La mobilidad humana es un derecho, no es un crimen* (human mobility is a right, not a crime). Catholic Church doctrine says that" (Haugen 2007 interview). Mexican cultural brokers were not so critical, reflecting their own community's less radical experience of practicing their faith. One woman stated, "The church is not that active [in Postville], but it's always there. It's there for you to go to it. The Catholic Church is not going to seek you out, nor pressure you to join" (Hidalgo 2007 interview). Almost everyone interviewed referenced how the church had been instrumental in providing assistance when the Iowa Turkey plant burned.

Administrators and staff at the public elementary school mobilized early on to welcome newcomers' children. In fact, the school was able to garner funding to hire more teachers and expand the facilities to support the increased enrollments. The elementary school in particular had done much to integrate Hispanic newcomers into the community. When Reynolds visited the school in 2007, it sported signage in English and Spanish advertising its embrace of diversity. For example, inside the front door was a sign in Spanish stating all people's rights to a continuing education, emphasizing the binational agreement between the United States and Mexico. There were also a number of glossy posters from the University of Northern Iowa's New Iowan series that showcase Iowa's history of receiving immigrants from all backgrounds. There was a collage of images of families of different nationalities and ethnicities from different time periods. As in most U.S. elementary schools, children's schoolwork and art are prominently displayed outside classrooms. The school encouraged children to draw upon their families' diverse heritages in social studies curricula and in art. The elementary school also offered instruction in Spanish and American Sign Language. The school was moving toward adopting a dual immersion program with the ambition of making all students bilingual and biliterate. Observations made by both Reynolds and Didier in the middle and high schools revealed that these educational spaces were less inclusive.

There are a number of native-born Iowans and transmigrants who individually shouldered the day-to-day responsibilities of paying for the so-called indirect costs, working the civic-service posts in schools, health clinics, and other community-based organizations that enable the transmigrant workforce to live in town and for the plant to operate effectively.[18] Most of the native-born cultural brokers are not originally from Postville. They came to live here, some by accident and some by design, but all due to their personal experiences and translocal social networks that have enabled them to move betwixt and between the native Iowan populations and the different transmigrant communities. The foreign-born cultural brokers came to Postville in the mid-1990s and for personal reasons chose to stay. Many were in the United States long enough to take advantage of the last legislative immigration reform during the Clinton administration and become naturalized citizens.

Veronica Haugen was a newcomer to Postville, though she grew up in eastern Iowa. She had many important insights into local dynamics that we independently confirmed in our observations and other interviews. One pattern that Veronica was quick to point out was that the majority of cultural brokers in town were women, revealing a gender bias in the types of service work that provide human services for families and children. These jobs also tended to be the most "flexible" insofar as they were posts that native and foreign-born women pieced together for themselves. They networked with local businesses and organizations, often purely out of personal necessity. Much of this employment was not sustainable, as the funding sources were soft-money, community-development grants obtained through both governmental and nongovernmental organizations like Vision Iowa or Helping Services of Northeast Iowa. In reflecting upon their experiences working as cultural brokers, these women often lamented that they could not do more; their occupational and gender roles as mothers and primary breadwinners constrained what they could accomplish.

The male cultural brokers, however, both foreign and native born, did not face these same constraints. Men like Ryan Hauss, Raymond Hueber, and Jerónimo Santa Ana were of means in that they owned property or ran businesses. In addition to actual capital, they commanded cultural and social capital, which empowered them to help transmigrants find more affordable housing and alternative employment in the event that they left the plant. Hauss and Hueber were also grandfathers and were at a stage in life when they were no longer primarily responsible for the well-being of their immediate families. The men also had one other major gendered advantage over all the women: they all were able to deal directly, although not equally, with plant management at different times and in different capacities.

Several events brought cultural brokers and secular and religious organizations together. These events also provided opportunities for other members of the town to interact with newcomers in ways that they normally would not have done. These included major events like the Taste of Postville festival and when Iowa Turkey was destroyed in the fire. Other more episodic and racially charged encounters include police roadblocks stationed to check for proof of car registration, insurance, and driver's licenses, as well as work-related crises, the most notable one being when workers suffered extortion in the plant by the hands of one of Agriprocessors' management team.[19] In fact, several cultural brokers attempted to intervene in instances of blatant corruption and exploitation at the plant. Their efforts included directly contacting the CEO, Sholom Rubashkin, to notify him of what was going on. Their appeals fell on deaf ears. Others took more dramatic actions, such as contacting the Equal Employment Opportunity Commission, the Federal Bureau of Investigation, and even Immigration and Customs Enforcement to report the abuses. As of 2007, most were under the impression that their appeals made a minimal impact.[20] Many were experiencing burnout; they feared that there would never be any stability as the newcomer population continued to turn over. Some of the native-born cultural brokers who were not from Postville had already left or were making plans to do so. Meanwhile, others hoped for the day when Mexican and Guatemalan migrants themselves would organize and participate more actively in public forums giving voice to their needs. Finally, Mexican and Guatemalan cultural brokers in fact *were* doing what they could to serve and represent their people, but not always in ways that were recognizable to Iowans. And then there was the raid, when everything really fell apart.

Postville's Politics of Place Make National Headlines

On May 12, 2008, ICE raided Agriprocessors, adding to the town's fame. Postville became the first of a series of spectacular single work-site raids aimed at efficiently apprehending and prosecuting migrant workers for federal crimes under the George W. Bush administration's initiative to enforce post-September 11, 2001, legal provisions.[21] At that time, Agriprocessors employed about 968 people; the raid captured 40 percent of its workforce. Most were immediately charged and convicted for committing acts of aggravated identity theft and the misuse of social security numbers. About fifty-six of those arrested, the majority women with dependents, were shackled with GPS ankle bracelets. The federal government also arrested Sholom Rubashkin, the person responsible for all plant operations in Postville. At that time, prosecuting attorneys alleged he committed a number of crimes, from harboring undocumented immigrants for financial gain, aiding and abetting document fraud, aiding and abetting aggravated identity theft, child labor violations, bank fraud, mail and wire fraud, money laundering, and nonpayment for livestock.[22]

The raid shocked all of the town residents, ripped transmigrant families apart, and caused a cascading economic impact across the region. State officials never recognized Postville to be a disaster zone, as it was a human-generated one. Thus the town did not qualify for assistance from the Federal Emergency Management Agency.[23] Moreover, it exacerbated and accelerated the constant experience of change that opponents of "diversity" had hoped would end when the plant was raided. With the majority of Guatemalans and Mexicans gone, the plant turned to various sources to replace its workforce: Somali refugees who wanted to relocate from Minnesota, itinerant men from Texas and other southwestern states, and even people with temporary work visas from the Republic of Palau, a Pacific island nation. Maryn Olsen, the response coordinator and director of the Resource Center noted that some Postvillians, opponents to Hispanic newcomers and their families, started to lament their coerced departure (Olsen 2009 interview).

St. Bridget's was the first place that all Mexicans and Guatemalans, regardless of their faith, turned to for refuge when ICE raided the plant. This small parish raised approximately $1 million to provide food, shelter, clothing, and legal services for detained women and their families. They held vigils and rallies demanding comprehensive, nonpunitive immigration reform and brought Guatemalan Nobel Laureate Rigoberta Menchú to address the detainees and publicly decry the situation in Postville. Much of this hard work has paid off; as of August 2009, the pro bono work of Des Moines attorney Sonia Parras, working in conjunction with St. Bridget's Hispanic Ministry, secured U-visas for many of the women.[24] These women are able to work legally in the United States for up to four years.

Yet divisions within the Catholic Church are as apparent as ever. Migrant families not caught in the raid were nevertheless impacted by it; furthermore, they were unable to tap into any donations raised by the church. Some left town, but others who were extended family to the women *de bracelete* (those with GPS ankle bracelets) remained behind to provide emotional support. This increased tensions within groups of migrants from the same sending communities. To make matters worse, some parishioners in the months after the raid openly recirculated conservative neoliberal discourses that blame immigrants for the situation in which they find themselves.

STEPHANIE: The town is really upset with the Catholic Church because even some of its congregation doesn't want to support the work 'cause they feel all their *money* now is being drained going to support illegals. Some of them don't look at it from a compassionate way they look at it—they're illegal. That's as far as they'll go [as in, reflect on the situation], there's a brick wall there, get rid of 'em, send them home, they're illegal, so no money should be going to illegals. They don't look at it as a Christian. . . . So

> there's quite a few people upset with the Catholic Church, but
> they're [the church] still working, they're working very hard to
> reform the government as to how ICE handled this and every-
> thing. (Schumacher 2008 interview)

The raid ruptured the uneasy status quo, which consequently enabled a
public dialogue that crosses many boundaries within Postville, the United
States, and beyond. It inadvertently brought other northeastern Iowans together, like disaster response coordinator Maryn Olsen, to forge alliances
with regional organizations, local stakeholders, and cultural brokers, like
Stephanie Schumacher cited previously. The coalition sought ways to talk
critically about the social trauma differentially experienced by all town residents without falling into the trap of polarized debates that seek to spread,
and not shoulder, any of the blame. Moreover, members realized that soft
money and other well-intentioned, unorganized sympathizers and volunteers
could not fill the gaping hole ripped in the local social fabric. It is women
like these who became active in the Interfaith Coalition for Humane Immigration reform. These were examples of globalization from below, emergent
social spaces open to the politics of possibility.

Mexican and Guatemalan laborers also did not passively accept the outcome of the raid. Activists who once despaired over how difficult it was to
organize migrant workers to stand up for their rights were probably struck
by how many of the Guatemalan women were finding a political voice that
has the potential to challenge the laws that imprison them and demand a
different type of assistance that does not perpetuate servitude. There was an
explosion of creative activities through which men and women articulated a
politicized consciousness and gave public testimony. Two women from San
Antonio Aguas Calientes formed a weaving group in Postville to provide
migrant women left behind an alternative means of social and economic
support. They taught women from Calderas to weave simple handicrafts,
and they began to sell their wares at the farmers' market in Decorah. They
forged alliances with members of diverse regional organizations, speaking at
churches and colleges, to teach Iowans about their experiences. Dr. Jennifer
Cooley, a faculty member in the Spanish Department at the University of
Northern Iowa, worked in collaboration with this group to produce a play
titled *Nuevo Amanecer: Weaving a New Beginning?*

The nearby college town of Decorah, Iowa, also became home to nine men
who served federal sentences of five months and were retained to serve as
material witnesses for the prosecution against the Rubashkins. The Decorah
Areas Faith Coalition created Project Jubilee, a fund drive to raise a pool of
money. Funds were divvied up as no-interest loans that the men applied for

to help pay off the debt incurred while crossing the many borders to reach Postville. The money, once repaid, was then to be administered by Share Guatemala, a nonprofit organization located in San Lucas Sacatepéquez, Guatemala, to support these men's microenterprises after deportation. Like the women of *Nuevo Amanecer,* seven of the nine men devoted part of their time to consciousness-raising activities. Six Guatemalans and one Mexican formed the theater group Teatro Indocumentado (Undocumented Theater). In their play *La Historia de Nuestras Vidas* (The Story of Our Lives), they spoke in their own voices directly to other midwesterners at churches and university and college campuses about experiences in Guatemala and the United States.

At a national level, the scandalous treatment of migrant labor provoked debate among Jewish Americans. In April 2007, the Rabbinical Assembly in conjunction with the United Synagogue of Conservative Judaism formed the Hekhsher Tzedek commission with the aim to strengthen the connection between halacha and social justice. In May 2008 following the allegations of worker abuse at Agriprocessors, the rabbinical assembly advised members of the Jewish community to reevaluate whether it was ethical to consume meat from the Agriprocessors plant. The Hekhsher Tzedek commission established Magen Tzedek, a kosher certification process to ensure that kosher food products conform to Jewish ethical values and ideals of social justice. The establishment of Magen Tzedek was a step toward bringing awareness to the problem of the exploitation of workers endemic to the meatpacking industry and specifically within Agriprocessors. The work of the Rabbinical Assembly, the United Synagogue of Conservative Judaism, and Magen Tzedek all have contributed to ongoing public debates about the meaning of kosher and how it relates to wider concerns, including labor conditions and environmental justice around the world.

Finally, the nonprofit transborder humanitarian organization Guatemalan Human Rights Commission (GHRC) reinvented itself. What was once an organization primarily concerned with denouncing state-sponsored violence expanded its mission to include the documentation of human rights violations that occur within the interstices of transborder lives. So, in addition to continuing support of political asylum cases and documenting violence within Guatemala, GHRC is now a part of the STOP-CAFTA coalition, which lobbies against neoliberal trade agreements that contribute to the south–north migration pattern. Specific to the Postville case, GHRC helped women back in Guatemala locate where their husbands were serving prison sentences in the United States and explored the possibility of initiating a lawsuit on behalf of deportees from the municipality of San Miguel Dueñas.

For these reasons and many others, Postville will continue to serve as a fascinating case study for the politics of possibility rather than just the politics of identity. Residents, in forging new sorts of local and translocal alliances, continue to struggle and imagine more inclusive, holistic solutions that respect human rights, create just and equitable transnational spaces, and respond to the forces that connect the industrialized agrarian economies and their decimated rural places in both the global North and South.

Notes

1. The 1990 U.S. census reported that Postville was home to 1,472 residents. By 2007, there were an estimated 2,320 residents. When Reynolds spoke with different residents in summer 2007, they presumed 2,500 to be a better figure, though they acknowledged that it was hard to know, given that the plant was expanding and the workforce always turning over. The 2000 demographic profile of the town reveals that at that time, approximately 33 percent of town residents were foreign-born. Additionally, 38.8 percent of the population over the age of five reported speaking a language other than English at home.

2. This is the significance that Sen. Barack Obama invoked in his stump speeches in his successful 2008 campaign for the U.S. presidency. He called for a change in governmental economic and regulatory policies that were crippling Main Street in favor of Wall Street finance capitalists and multinational corporations that had been living high on the hog since the 1980s.

3. This is the ideological legacy of the early-twentieth-century Country Life movement and concomitant rural educational reforms that strove to forge rural people's collective, classless identification with new "country towns," ideally containing no more than eight hundred residents (D. Reynolds 1999).

4. Lewis articulates his critique of Main Street through the main character, Carol Kennicott. She is a newcomer and bride to the town doctor with ambitions to become a town reformer. Lewis even has Carol's character adopt a patronizing attitude toward immigrants, though her views are cast through a cultural essentialist lens. For example, in one passage Carol bemoans the impact that Main Street (aka "the Village Virus") makes on foreigners. Lewis writes from her perspective, though in the third person: "But she saw these Scandinavian women zealously exchanging their spiced puddings and red jackets for fried pork chops and congealed white blouses, trading the ancient Christmas hymns of the fjords for 'She's My Jazzland Cutie,' being Americanized into uniformity, and in less than a generation losing in the grayness whatever pleasant new customs they might have added to the life of the town. Their sons finished the process. In ready-made clothes and ready-made high school phrases they sank into propriety, and the sound American customs had absorbed without one trace of pollution another alien invasion" (Lewis 1920: 225–26).

5. Participants in our studies either chose their own pseudonyms or were assigned one. Real names, however, will be used when referring to highly public personae, especially those elected to public office or who own and managed Agriprocessors.

6. In early 2000, two mass-mediated representations of Postville and its "clash of

cultures" appeared in print and on film. University of Iowa Professor Stephen Bloom published a journalistic account in his book *Postville: A Clash of Cultures in Heartland America*. Bloom's monograph provides a stereotypical depiction of rural life from an outside, big-city perspective. His account, however, is sympathetic in its treatment of how native residents of German descent responded to the economic and cultural changes that were occurring when the two youngest sons of Aaron Rubashkin, Sholom and Tzvi (Heshy), moved to town with their families and opened Agriprocessors. Bloom in fact appears quite critical of how plant upper management dealt with labor and community relations. Nikki Tundel similarly wrote and directed a documentary film, *Postville: When Cultures Collide*. It was broadcast on PBS channels and showcased Postville as a work in progress. Stephen Bloom and University of Northern Iowa professor of applied anthropology Mark Grey were both featured in expert-interview segments discussing social divisions in town. In the early stages of production, the film focused solely on the relationship between Iowans and Hasidic Jews. Grey disclosed in a separate publication that he had to urge the director to also attend to the population of resident migrant Mexicans who at that time mostly worked at the smaller plant in town, Iowa Turkey Processors (Grey, Devlin, and Goldsmith 2009). The documentary minimizes attention to political economic divisions within the town. In the end, the film promotes a type of "multiculturalism" that is in opposition to an ideology of melting-pot assimilation, where residents must learn to co-reside and tolerate one another's differences in spite of socioeconomic inequalities.

7. One of the city council members wrote a thinly veiled letter of critique that was published in the local newspaper, the *Postville Herald*. The following excerpt of that letter was republished in the *Cedar Rapids Gazette* in an article written by Roxana Hegemen on August 26, 2007, as evidence of the more strident voice engendering a racialized antinewcomer sentiment. One statement was directed toward the Hassidic population: "One group wants to isolate itself . . . and wanting a different day for the Sabbath," while the other homogenizes the "Hispanic," newcomer population as one that "sends money back to foreign countries and brings a lack of respect for our laws and culture which contributes to unwed mothers, trash in the streets, unpaid bills, drugs, forgery, and other crimes."

8. At that time, the Rubashkin family also owned two additional slaughterhouses and two warehouses. The plants were located in Gordon, Nebraska (managed by son Sholom Rubashkin), and an undisclosed location in South America. The warehouses were located in Brooklyn (managed by son, Yossi Rubashkin) and Miami (managed by daughter Gittel Goldman).

9. In order to provide background on the Rubashkin business model, we had to draw heavily on secondary sources provided in journalistic interviews published in online media sources. *The Village Voice* (local regional), *Upstart Business Journal* (business magazine), and the highly respected online Jewish newspaper *Jewish Daily Forward* all ran investigative stories on the impact that the Rubashkin family had on Postville. All articles were written approximately six months after the raid took place in 2008, and all reporters sought to provide as balanced a portrait of the family as possible amid a firestorm of negative press. Rubashkin family members were

interviewed along with a number of people who have interacted with the Rubashkins over years; these people have experienced firsthand the impact of their generosity, their way of doing business, their antipathy for union organizing, and their myriad relationships with different town residents in Postville. We did not draw from news media publications written by and for strictly Hasidic audiences. As Ayala Fader's (2009) ethnographic account of growing up Hasidic in the boroughs of New York attests to, much publicly circulating discourse within New York Hasidic communities relies on hyperbole to differentiate between insider and outsider perspectives and does not pretend to provide an unbiased point of view.

10. See *Denison, Iowa: Search for the Soul of America through the Secrets of a Midwest Town* (2005) by Dale Maharidge for a journalistic account of local politics in this meatpacking town.

11. The state of Iowa has had right-to-work legal provisions since 1947.

12. Of these jobs, 36 percent were in the informal sector, where there are no benefits, no vacation time or overtime pay, and few to no contract protections. The remainder of these jobs were in the manufacturing industries; maquiladoras have increased women's economic autonomy, which has done so at a significant cost as they are low-paying, insecure jobs where the working conditions may be highly exploitative.

13. The director of Guatemala's Commission on Human Rights in the United States, Amanda Martin, reports that some of these loans have interest rates as high as 12 percent (personal communication with the author, October 2008).

14. In Nathaniel Popper's article "How the Rubashkins Changed the Way Jews Eat in America," he writes that union organizing began back in 2004. Reynolds was told by an organizer that activities began sometime in 2005. Regardless of the actual year, by the time of her 2006 summer visit, it was apparent that representatives of the union had been visiting Postville on a regular basis.

15. Had they wanted to do what the plant representative envisioned, they would have chosen *sindicato* (union) for the team name. Reynolds did note, however, that by 2007 Spanish speakers were no longer using the term *sindicato* to refer to organized labor. The English term was fully incorporated as *the* local term to denote the UFCW union.

16. The UFCW representative would not disclose detailed information about the union's strategies. Based on Reynolds's observations around town and conversations with other Guatemalan migrants about union activities, it was clear that the union was doing all that it could to document cases of labor violations and poor working conditions, including instances of child-labor violations, work-related injuries caused by not following safety protocols, and sexual harassment. The representative did, however, state that the union in the meantime was partnering with other kinds of organizations to build a coalition that could more effectively pressure Agriprocessors to change its policies and practices.

17. In recent years, another place of worship was built on the outskirts of town and sought to bring born-again Christians together. Some sermons were also conducted in Spanish.

18. We are not including publicly elected officials in this sample because we are concerned here with the informal ties that outsider residents were able to forge. Public officials also made a difference, although not usually in the capacity as cultural broker. John Hyman, the mayor during most of the 1990s and early 2000s, probably did the most to negotiate turbulent political waters. A few of the cultural brokers acknowledged that he was the most "progressive" mayor that Postville has ever seen in recent years. After fourteen years in office, however, residents voted in new leadership. Stephanie Schumacher, one of the long-term newcomer cultural brokers, was of the opinion that this shift in public support was due to the accumulation of years of decisions that different people disapproved of; this combined with change fatigue helped cinch the 2006 victory for Mayor Penrod and supporters who ran on a platform of "change," which she interpreted as a code word for a withdrawal of support for "diversity."

19. The two men allegedly responsible fled town at the time of the raid. The FBI issued warrants to arrest them based on the following charges: one count of conspiracy to harbor undocumented aliens for profit, twenty-four counts of aiding and abetting the harboring of undocumented aliens for profit, one count of conspiracy to commit document fraud, and one count of aiding and abetting document fraud. One man was arrested on March 31, 2011, in Israel. Extradition proceedings were held in May 2011, and it was decided that he was to be extradited to the United States. The detained man, however, fought the extradition and made an appeal to the Israeli Supreme Court. To date, a decision has yet to be rendered.

20. The U.S. Department of Labor was in the middle of an investigation at that time, but no one interviewed was aware of it.

21. ICE had been raiding other meat-processing plants across the nation before May 12, 2008. For example, the Swift plant in Marshalltown along with other Swift plants in Nebraska and elsewhere were raided on December 12, 2006. Mexican and Guatemalan residents often recounted the Spanish-language news reportage of children left unattended, a consequence of ICE procedures at that time that favored efficiency of apprehension and deportation at the expense of verifying dependents' well-being.

22. Preparation for three court cases ensued: one related to the charges related to bank frauds, a second related to aiding and abetting aggravated identity theft, and the third for child labor violations. He was convicted at the first trial, the second charge was dropped, and at the third he was acquitted of all charges.

23. The town did successfully secure a grant for $698,000 from the Iowa State Department of Economic Development. The Postville Immanent Threat project helped provide soft monies to establish a Postville Resource Center to administer funds to U.S. citizens whose livelihoods were also indirectly tied to the plant. The center had funds to cover three-months' rent, basic bills, and transportation out of town for those who wanted to make a permanent move. The center closed on September 30, 2009.

24. The U-visa is a nonimmigrant visa awarded to a person who is victim to some sort of criminal activity. Historically, most U-visas have been awarded to women and their children who have suffered domestic abuse and/or rape.

References

Appadurai, Arjun. 1996. *Modernity at Large: Cultural Dimensions of Globalization.* Minneapolis: University of Minnesota Press.

Benson, Peter, with Edward F. Fischer and Kedron Thomas. 2008. "Resocializing Suffering: Neoliberalism, Accusation, and the Sociopolitical Context of Guatemala's New Violence." *Latin American Perspectives* 35, no. 5: 38–58.

Bjerklie, Steve. 1995. "On the Horns of a Dilemma: The U.S. Meat and Poultry Industry." In *Any Way You Cut It: Meat Processing and Small-Town America,* ed. Donald D. Stull, Michael J. Broadway, and David C. Griffith, 41–60. Lawrence: University Press of Kansas.

Bloom, Stephen G. 2000. *Postville: A Clash of Cultures in Heartland America.* New York: Harcourt.

Bourdieu, Pierre. 1984. *Distinction: A Social Critique of the Judgment of Taste.* Cambridge, Mass.: Harvard University Press.

Broadway, Michael J. 1995. "From City to Countryside: Recent Changes in the Structure and Location of the Meat- and Fish-Processing Industries." In *Any Way You Cut It: Meat Processing and Small-Town America,* ed. Donald D. Stull, Michael J. Broadway, and David C. Griffith, 17–40. Lawrence: University Press of Kansas.

Broadway, Michael J. 2000. "Planning for Change in Small Towns or Trying to Avoid the Slaughterhouse Blues." *Journal of Rural Studies* 16, no. 1: 37–46.

Brodkin, Karen. 2000. "Global Capitalism: What's Race Got to Do with It?" *American Ethnologist* 27, no. 2: 237–56.

Chock, Phyllis Pease. 1999. "A Very Bright Line: Kinship and Nationality in U.S. Congressional Hearings on Immigration." *PoLAR: Political and Legal Anthropology Review* 22, no. 2: 42–52.

Coutin, Susan Bibler. 2003. "Cultural Logics of Belonging and Movement: Transnationalism, Naturalization, and U.S. Immigration Politics." *American Ethnologist* 30, no. 4: 508–26.

De Genova, Nicholas, and Ana Y. Ramos-Zayas. 2003. "Latino Rehearsals: Racialization and the Politics of Citizenship between Mexicans and Puerto Ricans in Chicago." *Journal of Latin American Anthropology* 8, no. 2: 18–57.

Delgado Wise, Raúl. 2006. "Migration and Imperialism: The Mexican Workforce in the Context of NAFTA." *Latin American Perspectives* 33, no. 2: 33–45.

Didier, Caitlin. 2005. "'¿Eres Latina? No. Soy La Tona': Cultural Encounters and the Dynamics of Identity in Postville, Iowa." Paper presented at the 82nd Annual Meeting of the Central States, Oxford, Ohio, March 10–12, 2005.

Dwoskin, Elizabeth. 2008. "The Fall of the House of Rubashkin." *Village Voice,* December 3. http://www.villagevoice.com/2008-12-03/news/the-fall-of-the-house-of-rubashkin/ (accessed September 27, 2012).

Escobar, Arturo. 2003. "Actors, Networks, and New Knowledge Producers: Social Movements and the Paradigmatic Transition in the Sciences." In *Conhecimento Prudente para Uma Vida Decente,* ed. Boaventura de Sousa Santos, 605–30. Porto, Portugal: Afrontamento.

Fader, Ayala. 2009. *Mitzvah Girls: Bringing Up the Next Generation of Hasidic Jews in Brooklyn*. Princeton, N.J.: Princeton University Press.

Fink, Deborah. 1998. *Cutting into the Meatpacking Line: Workers and Change in the Rural Midwest*. Chapel Hill: University of North Carolina Press.

Fischer, Edward F., and Peter Benson. 2005. "Something Better: Hegemony, Development, and Desire in Guatemalan Export Agriculture." *Social Analysis* 41, no. 1: 3–20.

Flores, William V. 2003. "New Citizens, New Rights: Undocumented Immigrants and Latino Cultural Citizenship." *Latin American Perspectives* 30, no. 2: 87–100.

Foner, Nancy. 2003. "Introduction: Anthropology and Contemporary Immigration to the United States—Where We Have Been and Where We Are Going." In *American Arrivals: Anthropology Engages the New Immigration*, ed. Nancy Foner, 3–44. Santa Fe, N.M.: School of American Research.

Glick Schiller, Nina. 2003. "The Centrality of Ethnography in the Study of Transnational Migration: Seeing the Wetlands Instead of the Swamp." In *American Arrivals: Anthropology Engages the New Immigration*, ed. Nancy Foner, 99–128. Santa Fe, N.M.: School of American Research.

Glick Schiller, Nina, with Linda Basch and Cristina Blanc-Szanton (eds.). 1992. *Toward a Transnational Perspective on Migration: Race, Class, Ethnicity, and Nationalism Reconsidered*. New York: New York Academy of Sciences.

Goldín, Liliana R. 2001. "Maquila Age Maya: Changing Households and Communities of the Central Highlands of Guatemala." *Journal of Latin American Anthropology* 6, no. 1: 30–57.

Goldín, Liliana R. 2009. *Global Maya: Work and Ideology in Rural Guatemala*. Tucson: University of Arizona Press.

Goldín, Liliana R., and Linda Asturias de Barrios. 2001. "Perceptions of the Economy in the Context of Non-traditional Agricultural Exports in the Central Highlands of Guatemala." *Culture and Agriculture* 23, no. 1: 19–31.

Grey, Mark. 1995. "Pork, Poultry, and Newcomers in Storm Lake, Iowa." In *Any Way You Cut It: Meat Processing and Small-Town America*, ed. Donald D. Stull, Michael J. Broadway, and David C. Griffith, 109–27. Lawrence: University Press of Kansas.

Grey, Mark, with Michele Devlin and Aaron Goldsmith. 2009. *Postville, U.S.A.: Surviving Diversity in Small-Town America*. Boston: GemmaMedia.

Grey, Mark, and Anne Woodrick. 2002. "Unofficial Sister Cities: Meatpacking Labor Migration between Villachuato, Mexico, and Marshalltown, Iowa." *Human Organization* 61: 364–76.

Griffith, David C. 2006. "Food Processing." In *Immigration in America Today: An Encyclopedia*, ed. James Loucky, Jeanne Armstrong, and Larry J. Estrada, 126–29. Westport, Conn.: Greenwood.

Hackenberg, Robert A. 1995. "Conclusion: Joe Hill Died for Your Sins. Empowering Minority Workers in the New Industrial Labor Force." In *Any Way You Cut It: Meat Processing and Small-Town America*, ed. Donald D. Stull, Michael J. Broadway, and David C. Griffith, 231–64. Lawrence: University Press of Kansas.

Harvey, David. 1989. *The Condition of Postmodernity: An Enquiry into the Origins of Cultural Change.* Cambridge, Mass.: Blackwell.

Kandel, William, and Emilio A. Parrado. 2005. "Restructuring of the US Meat Processing Industry and New Hispanic Migrant Destinations." *Population and Development Review* 31, no. 3: 447–71.

Kearney, Michael, and Bernadete Beserra. 2004. "Migration and Identities—A Class-Based Approach." *Latin American Perspectives* 31, no. 5: 3–14.

Levine, David. 2008. "A Beef with the Rabbis." *Upstart Business Journal,* October 15. http://upstart.bizjournals.com/news-markets/national-news/portfolio/2008/10/15/Kosher-Meat-Business-Scrutinized.html (accessed September 27, 2012).

Lewis, Sinclair. 1920. *Main Street.* Harcourt, Brace

Maharidge, Dale. 2005. *Denison, Iowa: Search for the Soul of America through the Secrets of a Midwestern Town.* New York: Free Press.

Millard, Ann V., and Jorge Chapa. 2004. *Apple Pie and Enchiladas.* Austin: University of Texas Press.

Morales, Isidro. 1999. "NAFTA: The Institutionalisation of Economic Openness and the Configuration of the Mexican Geo-Economic Spaces." *Third World Quarterly* 20, no. 5: 971–93.

Morales-Moreno, Isidro. 2003. "Mexico's Agricultural Trade Policies: International Commitments and Domestic Pressure. Managing the Challenges of WTO Participation: Case Study 28." *World Trade Organization.* http://www.wto.org/english/res_e/booksp_e/casestudies_e/case28_e.htm (accessed March 9, 2008).

Nagengast, Carole, and Michael Kearney. 1990. "Mixtec Ethnicity: Social Identity, Political Consciousness, and Political Activism." *Latin American Research Review* 25: 61–91.

Popper, Nathaniel. 2008. "How the Rubashkins Changed the Way Jews Eat in America." *The Jewish Daily Forward,* December 11. http://forward.com/articles/14716/how-the-rubashkins-changed-the-way-jews-eat-in-ame-/ (accessed September 27, 2012).

Reynolds, David R. 1999. *There Goes the Neighborhood: Rural School Consolidation at the Grass Roots in Early Twentieth-Century Iowa.* Iowa City: University of Iowa Press.

Reynolds, Jennifer F. 2003. "Discourses of Persecution and Maya Youths' Practices of the Imagination in the Post-Peace Accords Era of Guatemala." Paper presented at the 102nd Annual Meeting of the American Anthropological Association, Chicago, November 19–23.

Smith, Carol A. 1990. "The Militarization of Civil Society in Guatemala: Economic Reorganization as a Continuation of the War." *Latin American Perspectives* 17, no. 4: 8–41.

Stephen, Lynn. 2007. *Transborder Lives: Indigenous Oaxacans in Mexico, California, and Oregon.* Durham, N.C.: Duke University Press.

Stull, Donald D., and Michael J. Broadway. 1995. "Killing Them Softly: Work in Meatpacking Plants and What It Does to Workers." In *Any Way You Cut It: Meat*

Processing and Small-Town America, ed. Donald D. Stull, Michael J. Broadway, and David C. Griffith, 61–84. Lawrence: University Press of Kansas.

Stull, Donald D., and Michael J. Broadway. 2004. *Slaughterhouse Blues: The Meat and Poultry Industry in North America.* Belmont, Calif.: Wadsworth.

Stull, Donald D., Michael J. Broadway, and Ken C. Erickson. 1992. "The Price of a Good Steak: Beef Packing and Its Consequences for Garden City, Kansas." In *Structuring Diversity: Ethnographic Perspectives on the New Immigration,* ed. Louise Lamphere, 35–64. Chicago: University of Chicago Press.

Stull, Donald D., with Michael J. Broadway and David C. Griffith (eds.). 1995. *Any Way You Cut It: Meat Processing and Small-Town America.* Lawrence: University Press of Kansas.

Suarez-Orozco, Marcelo M. 2003. "Right Moves? Immigration, Globalization, Utopia, and Dystopia." In *New Arrivals: Anthropology Engages the New Immigration,* ed. Nancy Foner, 45–74. Santa Fe: School of American Research.

Tundel, Nikki (director/producer). 2001. *Postville: When Cultures Collide.* 60 mins. PBS.

White, Marceline, with Carlos Salas and Sarah Gammage. 2003. *Trade Impact Review: Mexico Case Study. NAFTA and the FTAA: A Gender Analysis of Employment and Poverty Impacts in Agriculture.* Washington, DC: Women's Edge Coalition.

Wilkinson, Kenneth P. 1991. *The Community in Rural America.* Westport, Conn.: Greenwood.

PART IV

Media and Reimagined Sites of Accommodation and Contestation

CHAPTER 8

Humanizing Latino Newcomers in the "No Coast" Region

EDMUND T. HAMANN
AND JENELLE REEVES

HYRUM, UT—When they left for school Tuesday, they had a mom at home. Now, they don't.

The three Paulino girls are waiting for a call from their mom, who was picked up by Immigration and Customs Enforcement (ICE) agents when she was working at a meat-cutting plant here. Seven-year-old Kathya can't sleep without her. Eleven-year-old Jacqueline is wearing Mom's brown Old Navy sweatshirt until she comes home. And 9-year-old Brenda is keeping Mom's rosary close to her heart.

"Nothing has ever made us feel this sad," Jacqueline said, her eyes puffy from crying.

The girls were among the 300 people—husbands, wives, sisters, brothers and children—who attended a meeting Wednesday at Iglesia de Dios Ebenezer in hope of getting answers from community leaders about the whereabouts of their loved ones who were picked up in the ICE raid at the Swift & Co. meat-processing plant Tuesday. (Sanchez and Burr 2006)

Heartland Sensibilities and the
ICE Raids of 2006 and 2008

Where we live, in Lincoln, Nebraska, home to the National Roller Skating Hall of Fame, there is a popular all-women's roller derby team called the No Coast Derby Girls. This is neither a chapter about roller-skating, nor roller derby, nor the boundary between amateur and professional athletics, but we start with the reference to our local team to highlight a regional sensibility that earns the label "No Coast." Where we live, a city of 250,000, and across the region in both cities that are bigger and towns that are smaller, there is an unassuming sensibility that sometimes is implied in references to our region, whether the actual label is Midwest, Great Plains, Heartland, Fly-over Country, Middle America, or our preferred No Coast. This sensibility, which, in synch with other chapters in this book, we will subsequently call "Heartland," is perhaps a remnant of the populist sensibilities of William Jennings Bryan or the Progressive Era, illustrated by the laconic steadiness of the twentieth century's two Heartland presidents (Harry Truman of Missouri and Dwight D. Eisenhower of Kansas) and captured in writings as diverse as those of Willa Cather, Mari Sandoz, M. J. Andersen, and Laura Ingalls Wilder. It argues against both pretense and judging others and celebrates "just plain folks" and common decency. It is this often sympathetic sensibility that is evident in the local mainstream newspaper accounts of Latinos in the immediate aftermath of the Immigration and Customs Enforcement (ICE) raids on six Heartland meatpacking facilities in December 2006 and a seventh in May 2008. Moreover, it is a description of this sensibility, in complex combination with other lenses and stances, that forms the body of this chapter. In a volume devoted to considering how Latin American migrations are reshaping senses of community in the Heartland, it seems important to see how an opinion-shaping local establishment, in this case the local print media, makes sense of the newcomers.

Regional texts generated in situ by mainstream Heartland print media (such as the *Des Moines Register* and *Greeley Tribune*) in response to the raids tell us about the Heartland's contemporary negotiation of a new Latino presence. Perhaps they also tell us why then-presidential-candidate Barack Obama referenced the raids during a 2008 campaign speech to the National Council of La Raza's (NCLR's) annual meeting. To an immediate NCLR audience, but no doubt with an eye to electorates well beyond the California convention hall where he was speaking, then-Senator Obama suggested: "The system isn't working . . . when communities are terrorized by ICE immigration raids—when nursing mothers are torn from their babies, when children come home from school to find their parents missing, when people are detained without access to legal council" (Navarette 2008: 5B). In the 2008 election, Obama carried the Heartland states of Iowa, Ohio, Indiana, and Colorado, all states lost by Democratic candidate John Kerry in 2004. (Obama also carried Minnesota, Wisconsin, Illinois, and Michigan, where Kerry had also won; and Pennsylvania and North Carolina, which may not be considered traditional Heartland states but are the focus of other chapters in this book.)

In referencing the raids, Obama presumably had a straightforward intention to connect to ideas and sentiments that were more broadly extant at least in certain parts of the country and that guide and shape how we think and act and vote. He calculated that invoking parents' separation from children, children's terror, and children leaving school uncertain of whether adults in their life would be home to greet them would lead most listeners to feel sympathy for the disrupted and to feel solidarity with Obama in his criticism. Candidate Obama could have referenced other story lines and details related to the raids. It is telling that he did not.

Still, our interest is less in national politics than in understanding a region, although it is surely salient that these regional experiences were invoked in national arguments. Instead it is our goal to look at how community, migration, newcomers, workplace, school, and children were all being understood regionally in mainstream print media. These media surely include a range of opinions and particular understandings, but it is our claim that certain understandings dominated and these, in turn, formed regional patterns that can be depicted if we study these media.

Print Media as a Source of Scripts

In earlier work focusing on the established community's (Anglo) response to Latino newcomers in a small Georgia city (Hamann 2002, 2003, 2011), we invoked Marcelo Suárez-Orozco's (1998) intertwined concepts of pro-immigration and anti-immigration scripts to not only clarify two dominant strains in local response to Latino newcomers but also to consider how these superficially substantially different scripts nonetheless precluded ready consideration of other ways of making sense of newcomers. In the current cases, however, we identify the emergence of some third scripts or, more accurately, of the application of long-standing Heartland scripts to this new population (although not purely in a colonizing fashion, as will also be clarified).

The core premise of scripts is that there are foundational story lines—like "rooting for the underdog" or "hero as a rebel victim"—that can be and are retold in myriad ways but that resonate because of a simple and familiar core message. Moreover, scripts, because of their familiarity and ubiquity, steer us away from more nuanced or less expected interpretations.

Suárez-Orozco's (1998) pro-immigration script casts immigrants as familial, hardworking, religious, loyal, and willing to take jobs that others will not. It derives much of its appeal from its nostalgic reiteration of the important assimilationist story line that America is a land of opportunity—a land where hard work, even in trying circumstances, can lead to success—and, thus, that America is essentially fair. In a time of anxiety and dislocation, such a familiar script is comforting. Immigration validates and rejuvenates America, but per the script's understanding, it only imagines America within preexisting terms of what it means to be a good American.

In contrast, Suárez-Orozco's (1998) "anti-immigration script" views the same demographic change as threat. In this script, immigrants are illegal aliens, welfare cheats, criminals, and job stealers. Notably, the contradiction between alleged government dependency and stealing jobs is unexplored. As will be a little further explored momentarily, the anti-immigration script closely matched the virulently anti-immigrant content of some of the reader comments to mainstream media coverage of the ICE raids but very few of the stories with newspaper bylines.

Our goal was to capture and consider dominant local understandings, to see how Latino newcomers were constructed in those stories with newspaper bylines. Reviewing only print media (and some reactions to those media) provided a useful filter for our data collection. Our goal was not to capture a cross-section of local responses but instead to capture in depth the thinking of a traditional influence on public-sphere thinking. So we examined seventy-four articles that "made it to print." Consideration of that coverage, which included the time span during which there was a change in ICE strategy related to children that may have been directly linked to criticism from the first six raids, allowed consideration of the scripts that were invoked (wittingly or not) by the reporters and editors who prepared the examined copy. Examining the copy also offered some measure of what readers would find most interesting, salient, and/or evocative. We use this archive to illuminate the grounds that leading local public-sphere voices invoked related to newcomers, work, racial/ethnic/national identity, school, and children as the raids were made sense of.[1]

Reviewed sources include:

- Associated Press (carried in local newspapers and on their Web sites)
- *Dallas Morning News*
- *Des Moines Register*
- *Grand Island* (Nebraska) *Independent*
- *Greeley* (Colorado) *Tribune*
- *Lincoln* (Nebraska) *Journal-Star*
- *Logan* (Utah) *Herald Journal*
- *Marshalltown* (Iowa) *Times-Republican*
- *New York Times*
- *Salt Lake Tribune*
- *Sioux City* (Iowa) *Journal*
- *St. Paul* (Minnesota) *Pioneer Press*
- *Worthington* (Minnesota) *Daily Globe*

Because of their proximity to the sites of the raids, most of these media sources were monitored daily from the date of the first raids, December 12,

2006, through December 31 of that year, and, using a cut-and-paste function, an archive of local coverage was created. Later we monitored the May 2008 raid in Postville, Iowa, in the *Des Moines Register* and the *New York Times*. That monitoring was more intermittent, but because of both newspapers' inclusion of "related links," we are confident that our monitoring captured most of both papers' coverage. While the *New York Times* in most ways is not a daily local newspaper of record for the Heartland, because the raided Postville, Iowa, kosher meat-processing company was owned by New Yorkers, with that source, too, there was a local interest tie-in. Mainly, however, our inclusion of the *Times* allows the chance to show that a national media outlet known and critiqued (in certain circles) for its "liberal" tendencies offered coverage that was not substantially out of synch with the other more local or regional voices.

For only some of the articles did the newspapers' Web sites allow reader comments, and, when they did, only sometimes did we monitor such commentary. However, we did read enough of the commentaries to note that they were often outlets for a few heated and shrill local voices that were very much in dissent with the tone of coverage of the local paper. Similar to shrill letters to the editor that we chronicled in Georgia (Hamann 2002, 2003), "Jeffrey J.," for example, posted on the *Worthington* (Minnesota) *Daily Globe* Web site on December 15, 2006, "A wet back is a wet back, send them all back!" Yet even the commentary section was not always vitriolic; Sherry S. posted also to the *Worthington Daily Globe* on December 14, 2006:

> I see a lot of judging going on here and while everyone is entitled to their opinions, I still wonder how many of you are perfect. About the kids leaving the Worthington School District because of the population of Hispanics, I find that funny. My kids (who are caucasian) went to Worthington Schools for a few years and the only problems they encountered were from other caucasian students bullying and always wanting to fight. I wouldn't want my identity stolen and used by someone else and if anyone commits a crime there are consequences for everyone. Unless we are on the jury, who are we to judge? That's life. There is good and bad everywhere no matter what color anyone is or where they come from. Americans visit Mexico and some see the bad there, some don't. Just like here in America. Some is born and raised in the Bronx, it's hard to get out. Good and bad in Mexico and America. Say what you will, do what you want, our home and hearts are open to children and their family who are scared and have no place to go now. I called everyone I know to call to let everyone know we are willing to help out and we have not been called back yet, leaving me to believe that Worthington still has a great number of good people willing to come together when members of the community need it no matter where they came from.

Whether sympathetic or aggrieved, immediate postings by readers in the heat of the raids and their aftermath were not our focus. Rather we wanted to examine the framing roles newspapers played in determining what words were used to talk about the ICE raids and those affected, in providing a venue for public meaning making related to those raids, in delineating which interpretations were mainstream and which were not seen in such a light, and in reiterating their own authority as mainstream "sensible" news sources. Ironically, that mainstream media played such roles was sometimes referenced in dissenting (and angry) reader commentaries, like this passage also posted to the *Worthington Daily Globe* by Jennifer O.:

> Why do you continue to use children to garner sympathy for people who take advantage of what this country has to offer when most of them have no intention or desire to become loyal citizens of this great country? The media is just as guilty, if not more so, for spreading and enflaming outright lies to a compassionate and gullible public. If it weren't for your duplicity, these immigrants would never have arrogantly believed that they were welcomed with open arms in spite of their illegal status. Their comfort in breaking the law came in large part from the liberal media. Where do you think they learned how effective it is to use the plight of children to get what they want? You should be ashamed.

Jennifer O. felt compelled to reference the mainstream media's emphasis on children in its accounts of the raids, even if her goal was to try to change the terms of the debate. Local media had set the stage regarding what mattered and what was under discussion; Jennifer O., Jeffrey J., and others like them could only react.

If we look again at the turns of phrase from Obama's speech noted in the introduction, he used terms like *nursing mother, children, school,* and *parent,"* but (at least here) he refrained from the term *illegal.* Obama's word choices were no doubt purposeful, positioning him to be seen as an advocate of nursing mothers, children, schools, and parents, and inviting his audience to join him in concurring with this framing of the Heartland raid victims he was alluding to. As U.S. Senator John D. Rockefeller recently noted (cited in Rosen 2009: 269), "There are very few symbols as powerful as kids."

In invoking children (and the other terms), it is unlikely that Obama thought he was introducing something new to his immediate audience. Rather he was invoking themes and knowledge that his audience had brought with them to his speech. In saying "nursing mothers" to a largely Latino audience, his goal would have been for audience members to think of particular, likely Latina, nursing mothers they knew (or other mothers or potentially nursing mothers), mothers who may well have been quite similar to those caught up in the raids. Yet Obama would also have thought of the much larger audience beyond the NCLR conference setting that may not be Latino and that would hear a much smaller snippet of his remarks. To that audience, too, presumably the idea of separating a nursing mother and baby would both resonate and be understood as wrong. After inviting these connections to his words and his audience's memory and senses of selfhood, it would then be Obama's calculation that an allusion to how such people were wronged through the course of ICE enforcement should generate agreement about both his interpretation and his invitation for them to join him in producing/supporting different outcomes.

While acknowledging that humans are not perfectly rational creatures, it does seem to be the case that we make sense of the world and derive from that sense making both an understanding of what the nature of the world is, how we should act, and our place in it. Further informing these is our sense of self or identity. Each of these is socially mediated. Human interaction is replete with intertwined ideas and actions that embed varying versions of what is and what should be. Suárez-Orozco's (1998) proimmigration and anti-immigration scripts are part of that. Written text that functions as a kind of in situ community record is a particularly appropriate site (1) to look for scripts and (2) to characterize the social cognition in play in those communities as, in this case, demographic transition and community identity are negotiated.

Newspaper Coverage and the ICE Raids, December 2006

On December 12, 2006, concurrent ICE raids were conducted in six Swift meatpacking plants across the Great Plains and into the Rocky Mountain region, including Worthington, Minnesota; Marshalltown, Iowa; Grand Island, Nebraska; Greeley, Colorado; Hyrum, Utah; and Cactus, Texas. The raids took place during the day, mostly in the morning hours, while the school-age children of many detained in the raids were attending their elementary and secondary schools, on an otherwise typical Tuesday. Media reports of the events focused not only on the alleged crimes of the detainees (such as identity theft) but also on the chaos and upheaval experienced by detainees' children, their schools, and others collaterally impacted by the raids in each of the six communities.

Broadly, newspaper accounts referenced two story lines that did not easily fit the proimmigration or anti-immigration scripts (Suárez-Orozco 1998): first, a narrative of children as innocent victims applied to detainees' children, with an accompanying narrative of schools as sites of refuge and teachers and administrators as step-in family for children, and, second, a narrative of raids as a violent act visited upon communities in which the fabric of community life was rent with even legal residents erroneously detained and all community children terrorized. Not only were each of these story lines evident in the local newspaper accounts from each site, the models informed and supported each other. Children's innocence was highlighted and strengthened by the story line of ICE's aggression and unnecessary brutality. Schools became sites of refuge while communities came apart at the seams. An account in the *Times-Republican* three days after the raid in Marshalltown, Iowa, was typical:

> The Marshalltown school possibly most affected by the Immigration and Customs Enforcement raid on Swift & Company Tuesday was Woodbury Elementary. Just blocks from the Swift plant, and with a vast majority of its students being Hispanic, Woodbury students and staff are just now starting to recover from Tuesday morning's shock. Woodbury Principal Dr. Tom Renze was at the front of it all, and he said although it will be weeks before the school can adequately assess how many students will or will not be coming back, the school is doing its best to recover as a family. "People around here were stunned. We had teachers in tears here and there throughout the day," he said. "The mood was very somber; one teacher said what was so upsetting was she didn't have a chance to say goodbye." . . . He said the teachers and staff were likely the most affected. "They took it very hard, and very personally," Renze said. "The students could see that the teachers were sad, but our teachers and staff did a good job of answering questions the students had." (Pierquet 2006)

It might be hard to claim children as innocents as a Heartland story line (as presumably its appeal is not just regional), but it was a story line that resonated in this region. Moreover, it permeated the media coverage of the ICE raids in December 2006. In some cases, school-age children of detainees returned home to empty houses or homes with one less parent or guardian. In the cases where schools were notified of the raids, other detainees' children were kept at school until friends or relatives could be identified. (Per a 1982 U.S. Supreme Court case, *Plyler v. Doe*, schools are prohibited from asking about children's or parents' documentation status, but one consequence of this ruling in this instance was that schools generally lacked information regarding what parents/guardians would be available in the case of an ICE raid.) In either case, the tragedy of children separated from parents and guardians became a primary and persistent story line. A December 14, 2006, article in the *Worthington Daily Globe* read:

> Jesús Alcantar, a Swift employee and union representative, said through an interpreter that he had found four children knocking on doors looking for

their mother. "I took them by the hand and started knocking on doors, looking for family members who would take them in," he said. "I saw a little
girl on the street. I saw someone take her, but I don't know who that was."
Alcantar said if anyone knows of children still misplaced to take them to
churches, so they can be placed or "paired up" with their families. There
were no concrete numbers about how many children were displaced, but De
Leon said one child is too many. (Wettschreck 2006)

Although, by one way of reading, this is just a factual account of what
came to pass, a search of word choices in even this snippet of the larger article can be revealing. For one, even ignoring the happenstance of the first
quoted source having the name Jesús (produced in the article without an
accent), it is intriguing to see that the first source is identified by his full
name, a reminder of his personhood, that, in turn, inflects how the next
passages are to be read. These next turns of phrase include "I took them
by the hand," "looking for family," and "little girl on the street," with each
raising the specter of vulnerability and innocence. The article then notes the
role of churches as institutional settings for family reunification. The framing here is decidedly not one of rule breaking, violations, and punishment
(although that would be an alternate way of conveying the same story).
Yet this framing also lacks the narrowness of the pro-immigration script
(Suárez-Orozco 1998). It does not depend on evoking nostalgic themes of
being more hardworking or virtuous than the more established population.
Its claims depend mainly on affirming personhood.

In Logan, Utah, the *Herald Journal* reported community members' worries,
in nearby Hyrum, over children's emotional welfare. "Another parent, Judith
Quan, said her main concern was for the children: 'These poor children. I
can't imagine what they're going through. People are very afraid'"(Geraci
2006). This story line echoed in Grand Island, Nebraska: "'I know this is the
law, but it is very hard when they take the fathers and leave the kids alone
at home,' Alvaro Paiz of Grand Island, president of the Hispanic Chamber
of Commerce said. 'I think they can find better ways to make this process
happen'" (Pore 2006).

The *Dallas Morning News* reported more than four hundred children were
left parentless in the Cactus, Texas, raid, noting that the situation was made
all the more poignant by the approaching holiday season. In an article a few
days after the first flurry of raid coverage, the *Greeley Tribune* reported the
story of detainees' children facing the holidays without one or both parents:

Holding a small rectangular box wrapped in white Christmas paper, 6-year-
old Esperanza Zarate of Greeley stood debating what it could be. "I was a
good girl this year," she said, smiling. "I asked Santa Claus for a pony for

Christmas. A big one." She was among nearly 1,500 families who attended the ninth annual Migrant Christmas Fiesta at Northridge High School on Saturday. Her father, Candido Zarate, was taken in the raid Dec. 12 at Swift & Co. meat packing plant in Greeley. Her mother, Sara Zarate, said she's been trying to keep her five children busy but still they are beginning to ask where their dad is. "I know my 8-year-old is trying to be strong," Zarate said. "I don't think it's hit them yet. They just keep seeing me cry." (Delgado 2006)

In this instance, the invoked story line of children as innocent victims of this larger enforcement action was amplified by references to Santa Claus (positioning readers to think of their own childhood Christmas experiences and/or their experiences perpetuating the Santa Claus story to their children or others). Readers here were also asked to consider a mother's struggle (in the face of the ambiguity of what happens after her husband's detention) to share or not share painful news with her children.

The December 12 raids took place on a Tuesday when detainees' school-age children were at school. Children attending classes were unaware of the detention of their parents, and in some instances it appears schools were unaware, too. There was more emphasis, however, on schools' improvised and extended role of providing safe harbor to children as efforts were made to identify with whom children could go home. Newspaper accounts highlighted the role of "schools as sites of refuge" and "educators as stand-in parents." The *Herald Journal* in Logan, Utah (near Hyrum), reported: "In the midst of legal jargon and arrest statistics, the children of adults detained in Tuesday's E. A. Miller raid are the innocent victims, and the puzzle piece that makes this situation human, local educators are saying. School officials have been working overtime in the aftermath of the multi-state police action to comfort students affected both indirectly and directly by the raid at E. A. Miller, officially known as Swift" (Wheeler 2006). The newspaper account emphasized that the plight of the affected children, portrayed as the "innocent victims," literally made "this situation human." In this way, the human tragedy of the raids and the compassionate but onerous extra work of schools, rather than other themes such as the lack of documentation of workers or the detainees' "theft" of identity papers, foregrounds community discussion of the situation. The presence of children moves us away from the proimmigration or anti-immigration scripts.

Some schools at the raid sites, like those in the Cache County School District that includes the town of Hyrum, Utah, received same-day notification of the raids and scrambled to make plans to hold detainees' children after school hours, a plan that was complicated by the fact that schools were not told whose parents or guardians were actually detained. Schools became de facto sites of refuge, and media noted the stand-in parental role teachers and administrators played in protecting and calming affected children:

> Just a few miles up the road from E. A. Miller, Mountain Crest High School administrators spent part of their day addressing the concerns of the roughly 100 Hispanic students who attend. And at South Cache 8–9 Center, about 30 students with Spanish surnames were called to the front office over the public address system.
>
> Mountain Crest Assistant Principal Sheri Hansen said officials are steeling themselves for the possibility of having students with one or both parents in federal custody.
>
> "We have ownership of these kids, and we love them," Hansen said. "The fact that they're devastated kills me. I hate it."
>
> She said the school's guidance counselors and ESL teachers were made available to students who might have questions about the incident, and Murillo met with some of them at a gathering on Tuesday.
>
> "A lot of the kids were really worried sick and crying," he said. "One of the problems is they see this raid as a nightmare they always knew about, and now it's coming down on their parents and aunts and uncles."
>
> Milt Liechty, deputy superintendent of the Cache County School District, said the schools will continue to be a safe haven for all students enrolled in them.
>
> "The bottom line is we're going to absolutely help these kids as much as we can," Hansen said. (Benson, 2006)

This account identifies educators as loving their students and uses that claim (articulated by Assistant Principal Hansen) to emphasize the tragedy of the raids and the humanity of the Latino newcomer children. In a sense, the article admits that "you may not know these kids, but you know me (or people in my role), and because I know and love these kids and feel their devastation, so should you."

Similar reports were given of schools and school officials in Cactus, Texas, and Worthington, Minnesota:

> Some of the most dramatic scenes during Tuesday's raid occurred at Cactus Elementary School. Officials kept students inside until parents, relatives, or close adult friends came to pick them up.
>
> Superintendent Larry Appel said he expected all the students to be retrieved by relatives by nightfall. (Trejo and Morales 2006)

· · ·

> "I've never seen anything like it, the sadness, the emptiness, the fear," a schoolteacher [from Worthington, Minnesota], Barbara Kremer, said. Ms.

Kremer said she had provided shelter in her house since the raid for 24 immigrants who were afraid to return to their homes. (Preston 2006)

In both of these examples, we see invocations of schools as a site of safety and shelter, with that understanding, in Ms. Kramer's case, casting her as a source of shelter even away from the school setting. Within this kind of framing, it is not unexpected that a superintendent is quoted assuring community members that students were being looked after, nor that a teacher takes personal action to care for students. These invocations help advance the larger point. While the idea of schools as safe places is not new (rare dramatic examples of high school shootings being an exception to this understanding and horrifying in part because they violate expectations), this extension of school to be a safe site in the face of a raid could concurrently fit readers' expectations (of schools as safe places) but also support outrage against the raids (schools should not be asked to carry this burden, too). As important, this framing points out that prominent local institutions—schools—function as sites where Latino newcomers are to be safe and welcome.

If we accept the idea that print media coverage of ICE raids was reflective of particular regional understandings (understandings of what should and should not occur/be tolerated vis-à-vis the presence of newcomers), then these invocations in the media of other story lines, of protesting innocents being hurt and valued institutions (schools) being asked to carry an unfair burden, challenges both the particular strategy of workplace raids and the larger logic that permits/encourages them. In this sense, these local accounts challenge the righteousness and appropriateness of the ICE actions, which, in turn, interfered with and/or perhaps compelled adaptation of the raid strategy in future enforcement actions.

Sympathy for detainees' children and admiration for schools that stepped in as sites of refuge accompanied anger at immigration officials who planned and executed the raids with little thought of consequences to children and community. Two days after the raids, the *Worthington Daily Globe* included this reportage:

"I'm ashamed to live in a country where this kind of thing happens," Ricker said, "where laws are enforced with a club instead of with intelligence and forethought."

Ricker added that he couldn't believe ICE, with all its years of experience, couldn't take more steps to ensure children were not sent to empty homes. De Leon also commented about ICE not taking steps to make the schools aware of what was happening. (Wettschreck 2006)

Further anger was directed at ICE for detaining even those legal residents who simply did not have their identification cards with them at the time of the raid. In what was likely a case of racial profiling, all suspected of being undocumented were detained and transferred to detention facilities, sometimes out of state. Some seventy-five legal residents detained in the Greeley, Colorado, Swift raid were taken into federal custody and transferred to Texas before their status could be verified (*Greeley Tribune* 2006a). Dan Hoppes, president of the United Food and Commercial Workers Union Local 22 in Grand Island, Nebraska, was among those pointing up ICE's ineptitude: "It's my opinion, and the opinion of the international union, if there's criminal action, we don't condone criminals or any kind of illegal activity, but, by the same token, they could have come into these plants with warrants and arrested these people who are in violation without completely disrupting the whole community and the Hispanic population and whoever may be an immigrant" (Overstreet 2006). Here again we see accounts that challenge the justification of the government action. In both the Colorado and Nebraska cases just noted, those challenges were grounded by an understanding that offers little sympathy for disrupting the innocent (although it tolerates characterizing those who were legally detained as "criminal"). The raid was even less tenable if seventy-five legal workers were unwittingly caught in its sweep.

The raid (and the strategy of raids) was less OK if cherished understandings, like the importance of community, were interrupted in its implementation. These challenges could not undo history, but they appear to have affected ICE's strategy for the Postville raid in 2008, and they have a second relevance in the ways they reiterated or amplified existing latent understandings related to community and place. Greeley should not be a place where the innocent are detained. Nor should Grand Island be a place where the whole community could be profoundly disrupted.

In the aftermath of the raids, reports detailed the community disruption of children separated from parents, Hispanic community members living in fear, and a ripping of the fabric of community life in general. The *Dallas Morning News* coverage of the raid in Cactus reported: "I feel sadness for my people," he said. "We're very emotional here today. . . . The town is in emotional upheaval. . . . I don't know what we can do, and I don't know what I can tell them. Nothing like this has happened to us before" (Trejo and Morales 2006). Yet the story continued with a personalized, determined account of one patriarch who stepped in to care for children of detained family members:

> Mr. Escarcega said his family would continue as best they could, even though residents feared that immigration agents would soon be going door-to-door. As dusk fell and temperatures dropped into the 30s, other residents of Cactus waited anxiously behind closed doors or visited homes of relatives and

friends. They struggled to make sense of what had happened. (Trejo and Morales 2006)

In response to the similar dilemma in their town, the editorial board of the *Greeley Tribune* invoked respected community institutional entities, like businesses, churches, and schools, and was intentionally ecumenical in its inclusive reference of proximate celebratory rituals as it rearticulated a vision of community that the raid had disrupted:

> We call on residents, city officials, businesses, churches, organizations, schools and community leaders to help keep the raid at Swift from further dividing us. Instead, let's use this as an opportunity to join together. What better way to experience such bonding than through helping others—especially during this intense holiday season: The Jewish holiday Hanukkah began Friday night, Christmas is in eight days and Kwanzaa begins in nine days. Greeley has a giving, loving soul. (*Greeley Tribune* 2006b)

In some sense, a dominant theme in the raid-protesting articles was about the inappropriateness or tragedy of those collaterally affected by the raids. Throughout the reporting on the December 2006 ICE raids, there was little said about alleged crimes of those detained; as common were accounts that gave voice to family and relatives who portrayed the detained employees as "a good dad" (Benson 2006) and people "just here to work" (Trejo and Morales 2006). The only serious challenge to the detentions was in regard to those who were wrongly detained. Moreover, very little attention was given to Swift (although worries that Swift would not be punished was a theme in reader responses in the *Worthington Daily Globe*). What was and was not controversial seemed to matter for how ICE planned and implemented the later, May 2008, raid in Postville, Iowa. In the latter raid, there would be a marked shift in ICE strategy, but less of a change in media portrayals of employers, detainees, and detainees' families.

Shifts in Raid and Detention Tactics: Postville, 2008

Perhaps in response to the negative public portrayals the agency received, ICE changed its capture and detention tactics when it raided the Agriprocessors meatpacking plant in Postville, Iowa, on May 12, 2008. In that raid, ICE made a much more concerted effort to verify whether those being detained had children in school or day care. And there were no accounts that time of children stranded at school or of teachers becoming providers of shelter. Instead, in the Postville raid, one detained parent (usually the mother) was banded with an ankle bracelet and released to house arrest to care for her children. This strategy avoided the separation of mothers and children, avoided the hazard of children being stranded at schools with it being unclear if there were adults at home to go home to, and at least superficially appeared to have solved some of the collateral hazards that had lessened local support for the earlier Swift raids. Yet local print media (in this case mainly the *Des Moines Register*) did not portray this raid more favorably and, if anything, seemed as willing to humanize the Latino newcomers caught in it directly or collaterally.

Maybe because it was easiest to invoke familiar story lines, coverage did portray detainees' children as innocents and victims in the May 2008 Postville raid. This time, however, the model shifted to include mothers as victims, too. In Postville, mothers who had been released to a kind of house arrest (monitored by electronic ankle bracelets) were available for reporters to access as they continued coverage of the story. In this new coverage, while the unauthorized nature of the mothers' predetention employment remained a salient fact, the more overwhelming fact in the way they were portrayed in print media accounts was their status as mothers. After all, it was this status that helped explain their continued temporary presence in the community (although they also were kept in the community to be witnesses for prospective prosecution of Agriprocessors management). Thus, although these mothers may have been "guilty" of working without documentation, their treatment at the hands of ICE was storied sympathetically, even tragically. The story of Irma Hernándes, as told in the *Des Moines Register* a few weeks after the raid, provides an example.

> When Irma Hernándes lies to her children, she does it modestly. She tells them things will be fine, that school will be easy, that they'll make new friends.
>
> When Hernándes and her children return to Guatemala—and they almost surely will—they will be going back to a country Hernándes left four years ago for a better life in the United States. She came here illegally, as did at least 388 other workers at the Agriprocessors Inc. meatpacking plant. She was caught in the poultry section with her husband in a raid on May 12.
>
> He was detained, processed and sentenced to five months in jail. She was released on humanitarian grounds—she had to care for her children, ages 9 and 11. . . .
>
> Now, she wears a tracking bracelet on her ankle, one of 42 women and three men who were released and still await their fate. . . .
>
> She lives in a modern A-frame in Postville that costs $700 month. She doesn't have much money. What little she and her husband saved went to immediate costs after the raid. That ran out quickly, and now she's reliant on the local Catholic church to pay for her rent and utilities. (Duara 2008)

In this account, Hernándes is first described as a modest and protective mother; then America (and by extension Postville) is characterized as a place for "a better life"; then the Catholic church is named as assisting her in her moment of need (conveying a Christian service connotation to how she should be understood).

Hernándes and other mothers like her became known in town and in the media as the *mujeres de braceletes,* women freed (sort of) to care for their children but left without an income in the United States and without the clearance at that point to return to Guatemala, the home country of many Postville detainees, to seek employment there, either. As noted in another *Des Moines Register* account that came later than the one just quoted: "Now, about 20 to 25 women remain tethered to the bracelets' black electronic monitoring devices that dig into the skin of their right ankles, leaving dark bruises and painful cuts. Some women try without success to protect their flesh with makeshift bandages fashioned from bandanas and short socks" (Rhor 2008). As the characterization of children as innocents enlarged to include their mothers, the portrayal of detained employees grew more sympathetic, as the salience of their "illegal work" faded in relation to their framing as mothers, as adults stuck in a legal limbo, and literally as victims physically pained by the monitoring devices.

Three hundred eighty-nine people were detained in the Postville raid. As with the previous raids, community disruption was widely reported, "'A lot of good workers were taken away, a lot of good families are gone,' said Kim Deering, 48, a lifelong Postville resident. . . . '[T]he community is drained . . . we are grieving, sad, apprehensive'" (Rhor 2008).

Although Jennifer Reynolds and Caitlin Didier (chapter 7 of this volume) found through their ethnographic studies that the orientations of non-Latino longtime Postville residents to Latinos were varied and were far from uniformly accepting, in the media accounts there was a noticeable sympathy. The culture models invoked were emblematic of community mores, mores that more ardently portrayed detainees as "good workers," welcome community members, and even victims of an exploitative employer, a story line that had rarely emerged in the previous Swift coverage. With the Agriprocessors raid, newspaper accounts reported tales of employee abuse. "In one case, a supervisor [had] covered the eyes of an employee with duct tape and struck him with a meat hook . . . [a]nother plant worker told federal officials that undocumented workers were paid $5 an hour for their first few months before receiving a pay increase to $6 per hour. The minimum wage in Iowa is $7.25" (Duara, Schulte, and Petroski, 2008).

Agriprocessors, a kosher meatpacker, received much criticism for its management of the plant in Postville, including a scolding from Iowa's governor, who reminded the company in a guest column in the *Des Moines Register* that they must, "operate responsibly" (Culver 2008). The governor, Chet Culver, further noted, "The sad events surrounding the federal Postville raid, resulting in multiple federal criminal-law convictions of line workers and low-level supervisors—and, notably not yet of the company's owners—are strong evidence of a company that has chosen to take advantage of a failed federal immigration system" (Culver 2008).

Perhaps the most illustrative example of the new cultural model of employees as victims was the *Des Moines Register*'s continued coverage of Postville detainees who were "serving" their detention in federal prison (from which they could be retrieved as witnesses) before their eventual deportation to Guatemala. Even after detainees had returned to Guatemala, the *Register* sent a reporter to cover some detainees' return to their native land, including Vincent Sanail Lopez who, upon return to Guatemala after months of detention and no income, faced losing his family's ancestral land. Of course, to Iowans who remembered the farm crisis of the 1980s and '90s, a loss of land would be a particularly potent cultural model to invoke:

> Sanail put the property up for collateral for a loan that covered the travel costs for him and his 30-year-old son, Benjamin. They still owe about $4,000 on the loan, and if they can't repay it, they could lose the land. . . .
>
> Before he was arrested, Sanail sent home about three-quarters of his earnings from Postville. The family used the money to buy concrete blocks, mortar, and steel reinforcing rods. Now, the rusting rods stick out from the top of the walls, which are about 5 feet tall. Sanail had planned to move back after the project was done, and live out his days in a decent house. Now, the unfinished project is a constant reminder of dashed hopes. (Leys 2008)

As in the coverage of the Swift raids, mainstream regional print media coverage of the Postville raids invoked human tragedy, innocence, vulnerable children, and other sympathetic story lines. Although, as in 2006, angry anti-immigrant voices could be found in online responses to local coverage, those were not the mainstream-approved interpretations as manifest in the newspapers.

Conclusion

Related to the Swift raids in 2006, we flagged two discourses that reference but transcend the dualism of Suárez-Orozco's (1998) pro-immigration and anti-immigration scripts: the first decried the horror visited on children and families related to separating parents and innocent children and bemoaned schools needing to step in as sites of safety and custodianship; the second lamented the cleaving of alleged community cohesion caused by the raids. Both of these discourses asserted the same mainstream understandings as candidate Obama invoked in his later speech, and both gave little attention to more marginal and angry local voices (like some of the readers who posted to the *Worthington Daily Globe* Web site) who rejected the mainstream interpretation. The parameters for mainstream consideration of both raids and newcomers were delimited.

In the first series of raids, when parents were detained, schools faced the challenges of what to do with those parents' children and how to negotiate many children's new fear that somebody could come and take their parents while the children were at school. Print media protested at least the collateral damage of the raids and, in so doing, not only perhaps provoked ICE to change its strategy for the later Postville raid but also offered several important local articulations about what local reality and activity should and should not entail. Media voices projected a familial, coherent, and communitarian, albeit no longer homogenous, sensibility about what No Coast towns and cities were and should be.

Since then, for example with the ICE raids in Postville, Iowa, in May 2008, there was a small but important change in the rhetoric about children and schooling (as a portion of the discourse related to ICE enforcement) and a misleading larger change in the practice of ICE. In the newer raid, parents, or at least mothers, apprehended in ICE raids were treated differently; they were not immediately deported or even transported away from the community where they lived (and were arrested). Rather, the new practice, rationalized as a way to avoid separating children from their mothers and leaving children without a caretaker, was to place mothers in at-home detention. In turn, at least temporarily, children of detained parents could stay in local schools.

We suspect this newer ICE practice stemmed directly from the ways the first raids had been portrayed. We also note that this new strategy, if less swiftly and thoroughly traumatic, nonetheless perpetuated the actual vulnerability of the children, although their safety was cited as a reason for the policy change. The policy change reduced the dilemma of schools serving as sites of refuge. However, keeping parent and child together when parents were blocked from any kind of viable livelihood (as the *mujeres de braceletes* were) was hardly an improvement in that child's or parent's circumstance. In other words, attending to the understanding that lamented schools needing to be sites of refuge and the continuing cultural model of children as innocent and vulnerable led to a reimagining of the appropriate "how-tos" of ICE enforcement. While this "kinder, gentler" enforcement was ultimately not much more helpful to the newcomers (they still had to leave in the end after savings were depleted and months were spent in federal or house-bound detention), it was consistent with regional sensibilities of avoiding drama and trauma. Moreover, it maintained a stance that humanized the Latino newcomers. In addition to being laborers, media depictions insisted that they were mothers, Christians, and students.

Related to the Postville raid, Iowa and national media (notably the *New York Times*) maintained outraged stances toward allegations of employee abuse. Then the continuing presence of the home-detained women, which made their status as mothers as a regularly invoked cultural model, meant continued contestation of the consequences of the raids and of the framing of immigrants, established residents, teachers, parents, children, and detainees.

Heartland meatpacking communities were not, per mainstream media voices, acquiescent to the appropriateness and consequences of the raids. Indeed, in a region that is better known for its conservatism, it is striking that the local print media portrayals stood apart from the ostensibly national conservative story lines that supposedly rationalize the strategy of raids, detentions, and deportations. Everyday sensibilities for keeping parents with children, for assuring that kids had parents to go home from school to, for not adding to the obligations of schools, for receiving a fair wage for hard work, and the like, tell a different story of this region and of the ways newcomers' place and membership are understood there. Mainstream media voices are not the only voices, but they are powerful ones, and, in moving beyond just the pro-immigration and anti-immigration scripts, they reasserted claims of community cohesion, decency of neighbor to neighbor, and the inappropriateness of children being subject to the collateral damage that are inevitable by-products of ICE enforcement actions. While these mainstream voices may neither have stopped raids nor made children less vulnerable, they are compelling for at least two reasons: they suggest a Heartland resistance to dehumanizing and thereby pejorative characterizations (Murillo 2002) of Latino newcomers, and they point to at least some of the constituent pieces, the already extant conceptualizations, that could be invoked in a long-term and broader effort to include Latino newcomers as welcome members of larger communities.

Notes

1. For a much more extensive discussion of the concept of media and the public sphere, we refer readers to an article about the ICE raids that we published in *Anthropology and Education Quarterly* (Hamann and Reeves 2012).

References

Benson, Adam. 2006. "Families Stunned by Sweep." *Logan* (Utah) *Herald Journal,* December 13.

Culver, Chet. 2008. Guest column: "Governor—Agriprocessors Must Operate Responsibly." *Des Moines Register,* August 24.

Delgado, Vanessa. 2006. "After ICE Raid, Families Celebrating Christmas But Still Searching for Family Members." *Greeley Tribune,* December 17. http://www.greeleytrib .com/article/20061217/NEWS/112160109 (accessed September 28, 2012).

Duara, Nigel. 2008. "Mother, Two Kids Contemplate Eventual Return to Guatemala." *Des Moines Register,* July 31.

Duara, Nigel, Grant Schulte, and William Petroski. 2008. "ID Fraud Claims Bring State's Largest Raid." *Des Moines Register,* May 13.

Geraci, Charles. 2006. "Police Assisting Hispanic Community." *Logan* (Utah) *Herald Journal,* December 19.

Greeley Tribune. 2006a. "Greeley Detainees Being Transported Back to Colorado." December 17.

Greeley Tribune. 2006b. Editorial: "It's Not Just About Illegal Immigrants." December 17. http://www.greeleytrib.com/article/20061217/TRIBEDIT/112170096 (accessed September 28, 2012).

Hamann, Edmund T. 2002. "¿Un Paso Adelante? The Politics of Bilingual Education, Latino Student Accommodation, and School District Management in Southern Appalachia." In *Education in the New Latino Diaspora: Policy and the Politics of Identity,* ed. Stanton Wortham, Enrique G. Murillo, and Edmund T. Hamann, 67–97. Westport, Conn.: Ablex. http://digitalcommons.unl .edu/teachlearnfacpub/70/ (accessed September 28, 2012).

Hamann, Edmund T. 2003. *The Educational Welcome of Latinos in the New South.* Westport, Conn.: Praeger.

Hamann, Edmund T. 2011. "The Anglo Politics of Latino Education: The Role of Immigration Scripts." In *The Politics of Latino Education,* ed. David L. Leal and Kenneth J. Meier, 103–21. New York: Teachers College Press.

Hamann, Edmund T., and Jenelle Reeves. 2012. "ICE Raids, Children, Media and Making Sense of Latino Newcomers in Flyover Country." *Anthropology and Education Quarterly* 43, no. 1: 24–40.

Leys, Tony. 2008. "Guatemala: Hope at Any Cost." *Des Moines Register,* November 29.

Murillo, Enrique G. 2002. "How Does It Feel to Be a *Problem*? 'Disciplining' the Transnational Subject in the New South." In *Education in the New Latino Diaspora: Policy and the Politics of Identity,* ed. Stanton Wortham, Enrique G. Murillo, and Edmund T. Hamann, 215–40. Westport, Conn.: Ablex.

Navarette, Ruben. 2008. "Those Against Immigration Raids Railing Against Wrong Issue." *Lincoln Journal-Star,* July 31, 5B.

Overstreet, Tracy. 2006. "Union: Civil Rights Violations Occurred with Swift Raid." *Grand Island* (Nebraska) *Independent,* December 20.

Pierquet, Greg. 2006. "Woodbury Principal Says School Recovering." *Marshalltown* (Iowa) *Times-Republic,* December 15.

Pore, Robert. 2006. "A Community's Pain: Hundreds Attend Vigil for those Affected by Last Week's Immigration Raid." *Grand Island* (Nebraska) *Independent,* December 18.

Preston, Julia. 2006. "Immigrants' Families Figuring Out What to Do After Federal Raids." *New York Times,* December 16.

Rohr, Monica. 2008. "A Small Town Struggles after Immigration Raid." *Associated Press Online*, August 17. http://apnews.myway.com/article/20080816/D92JGJ8G2 .html (accessed August 20, 2008).

Rosen, Lisa. 2009. "Rhetoric and Symbolic Action in the Policy Process." In *Handbook of Education Policy Research*, ed. Gary Sykes, Barbara Schneider, and David N. Plank, 267–85. New York: Routledge.

Sanchez, Jennifer W., and Thomas Burr. 2006. "The Day After the Raid: Relatives Angry, Worried Over Fate of Detained Workers." *Salt Lake Tribune*, December 14.

Solis, Dianne, and David McLemore. 2006. "Federal Raid Casts Pall Over Cactus." *Dallas Morning News*, December 13.

Suárez-Orozco, Marcelo M. 1998. "State Terrors: Immigrants and Refugees in the Post-National Space." In *Ethnic Identity and Power: Cultural Contexts of Political Action in School and Society*, ed. Yali Zou and Enrique T. Trueba, 283–319. Albany: State University of New York Press.

Trejo, Frank, and Isabel Morales. 2006. "Raid, Fear Tear Apart Families: Many Uncertain about Future, and Children's Plight Is Foremost Worry." *Dallas Morning News*, December 13.

Wettschreck, Justine. 2006. "Union Decries Action." *Worthington Daily Globe*, December 14.

Wheeler, Emilie H. 2006. "Educators Focused on Well-Being of Children." *Logan* (Utah) *Herald Journal*, December 14.

Worthington Daily Globe. 2006. "What are Your Thoughts on the U.S. Immigration and Customs Enforcement (ICE) Raid at Swift?" Online open forum. http://www .dglobe.com/talk/index.cfm?id=28&talk_page=12 (accessed December 21, 2006).

CHAPTER 9

Immigrant Integration and the Changing Public Discourse

The Case of Emporia, Kansas

LÁSZLÓ J. KULCSÁR

AND ALBERT IAROI

Introduction

> Now that the problem with the Somalis has been resolved, Emporia can now focus on the real problems at hand. Dogs riding in the back of trucks, the Mexicans, and continue to save the fairgrounds.

The above comment, posted on a local blog in Emporia, Kansas, sums up a fascinating story of immigrant integration and acceptance in the American Heartland. In January 2008, Tyson Foods, Inc., the largest employer in town, announced that it would discontinue the slaughter operations in Emporia and eliminate 1,500 of the 2,400 jobs in its meatpacking plant. In its press release, Tyson pointed out that the cuts were a response to an increasingly challenging beef market and the less optimal location of the Emporia plant in eastern Kansas, relatively far from the feedlots. This decision created significant challenges to the city of Emporia but also triggered reactions of approval from constituents who had been upset by the fact that the plant was operated by immigrant laborers, mostly Latinos and Somalis.

The story of immigrant integration in Emporia is similar to many places in the Midwest where the Latino population has suddenly increased. At the same time, however, it is peculiar because for a short period of time, the issues of Latino integration were overshadowed by the arrival and later departure of Somali refugees. This study examines the challenges of the Latino integration in the context of the arrival of the Somali refugee workers, which reshaped the community perception of local Latinos and altered the general public discourse on immigrant workers. We focus on how community members perceived the social and economic impacts of the influx of the Latino migrant workers and Somali refugees, as well as the individual and institutionalized efforts addressing the same question. Therefore, this is not simply a story of immigrant integration but also a discussion on the roles of various governmental actors and the local impact of the refugee resettlement program.

Foreign in-migration resulted in a dramatic change in population composition in several Kansas communities. Most of this immigration is Hispanic, corresponding with a larger structural redistribution trend of the Hispanic population across the Heartland, which is characterized by both the unprecedented Hispanic population boom outside urban areas and a regional change of Hispanics who no longer live only in the traditional southwestern states (Kandel and Parrado 2005). In Kansas, this trend manifested mostly in counties with established meat-processing industry, experiencing a dramatic influx of foreign migrant workers (Fink 1998). There seemed to be a concern about newcomers since the early 1990s, culminating in a recently published edited volume from the National Research Council (Tienda and Mitchell 2006); however, relatively little is known about the local particularities of the establishment of their social networks in Kansas and their integration challenges in rural communities (Broadway and Stull's 2006 account of Garden City being a good exception).

The proportion of Hispanic population of Kansas has traditionally been lower than the U.S. average. In 1980, it was only 2.7 percent, less than half of the national average (6.4 percent). By 2000, it increased to 7 percent, although this number was still only a bit more than half of what the U.S. average was at that time (12.5 percent). In 2010, the proportion of Latinos was 10.5 percent, about 6 percent lower than the national average. These numbers, however, mask significant spatial unevenness. Southwestern Kansas already had three times as many Hispanics as the state average in 1980 due to the booming meatpacking industry in Garden City, Liberal, and Dodge City. In these localities, the proportion of Hispanics exceeded the national average as well. By 2000, the share of the Hispanic population was beyond 40 percent in those three cities and was estimated to have increased over 50 percent by 2008. Such concentration of Latinos in micropolitan places in Kansas is a unique phenomenon.

Emporia is also a micropolitan place in east-central Kansas with about 27,000 people, which is approximately 75 percent of the population of Lyon County. The percentage of Hispanic population is higher than the Kansas average but not as large as in the southwestern corner of the state. In 2000, 21.5 percent of the population was Latino, and it had increased only little by 2008. The Latino presence, however, has helped Emporia to grow slowly, mostly due to in-migration. Consequently, as migration is an age-specific process, Emporia is much younger than the state or national average (figure 9.1). The population age sixty-five and older is around 10 percent, while the same indicator for nonmetropolitan Kansas is almost twice as much. On the other hand, immigration has other impacts on local socioeconomic conditions as well. Lyon County used to have a higher rate of some college completion than that of nonmetropolitan Kansas or the United States due to the presence of Emporia State University. This advantage gradually lessened until almost disappearing in 2000, parallel with the increase of low-skilled immigrant population. Manufacturing accounts for most of the employment in Emporia; its share is close to 25 percent of all employment. This manufacturing is almost exclusively food processing and packing, dominated by Tyson Foods.

As a summary, Emporia is representative of micropolitan Kansas, but not necessarily rural Kansas in general. Rural Kansas is still very much agricultural, with a predominantly white population. On the other hand, Emporia is not like the southwestern Kansas meatpacking triangle, either. This is

Figure 9.1. Age-specific net migration rates 1990–2003.

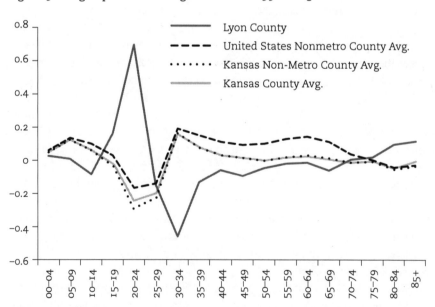

Note: Nonmetropolitan status is determined by the 1990 Beale codes.

important because integration experiences are strongly influenced by the actual impact of immigrant populations. In southwestern Kansas, locals cannot ignore migrant workers as they are a quasi majority. In Emporia, Latinos are numerous enough to be a factor in local community development considerations but are still only about a quarter of the population. Hence, the local public can still perceive them as an actual minority, which can alter the discourse on their integration.

Data and Methods

We employed a mixed-method approach of community demographic profile, in-depth interviews, as well as media-content analysis of the local newspaper and the blog entries hosted by the newspaper's online edition. We conducted in-depth interviews with key informants, such as community decision makers, local business owners, representatives of the local media, bloggers, charities, and leaders of a concerned citizens' group. The interviews provided important insights on how different actors and community members perceive having a large corporation in their community that employs a large number of Latino migrant workers and Somali refugees, as well as the social, economic, and cultural costs and benefits. Individual interviews were digitally recorded, transcribed, and analyzed.

Besides the interviews, we applied media-content analysis[1] on the local newspaper, the *Emporia Gazette*.[2] We searched all articles of the *Gazette* between June 2007 and December 2008 containing various search terms such as *Tyson, migrant, refugee, Latino,* and *Somali,* using News Bank, an online database that provides access to current and archived content from more than 2,000 newspapers, newswires, transcripts, business journals, periodicals, and government documents. We focused on the plain content of the articles but also identified the tone of the writings. For example, we categorized information about different community members' feelings on social and economic issues associated with the meatpacking plant, the attitudes toward the local government and institutions, and the influx of Latino migrant workers and Somali refugees as being positive or negative, based on whether those feelings painted the social and economic impacts as being positive or negative. A total of forty-seven articles were drawn from the *Gazette*. First we identified the dominant themes regarding the Latino migrant workers and the Somali refugees as well as the meatpacking plant's social and economic effects on the community. Then we sorted the articles into several different categories dealing with the integration of Latinos and the presence of Somalis in the community and their respective acceptance by the community.

To encourage an open exchange of information and ideas, the *Gazette* hosts and maintains a blog space where people from a variety of points of view can discuss community-related or wider issues. Anonymity is guaranteed, but each user is solely responsible for what is posted or contributed to this site. In his study on strategies for using blogs in social research, Hookway (2008) notes that blogs became a significant feature of online culture, and he argues that the blogosphere can provide a legitimate additional data source for researchers.

Blog analysis has both certain benefits and shortfalls. Data collection is simple; text can immediately be created, skipping recording and transcription. As noted, "the anonymity of the online context also means that bloggers may be relatively unselfconscious about what they write since they remain hidden from view. Like the majority of online research strategies, they also enable access to populations otherwise geographically or socially removed from the researcher" (Hookway 2008: 93). At the same time, bloggers are not a representative sample of the population. To begin with, computer literacy and access to the Internet are partly functions of education, income, and status. Also, blog entries tend to reflect the opinion of those who have more polarized perspectives and thus are more likely to express those. In fact, it is common that blog entries are driven by a few very active bloggers who dominate the online discourse. This is an obvious limitation of blog entries that are analyzed as the voice of the public, and in this study we do not claim this either.

Data collection from blogs is also very time-consuming and still can be relatively ineffective even with carefully established search parameters and guidelines. The blogosphere hosted by the *Gazette* exploded three times during the studied time frame, each occasion resulting in several hundred entries. The first increase in individual contributions to the forum was triggered by the announcement of plans to transform Emporia into a refugee resettlement destination (*Emporia Gazette,* November 3, 2007). The second big swell of blog entries came after the town-hall meeting organized to elucidate misunderstandings related to the social and cultural aspects of the influx of Somali refugees and their employment at Tyson Fresh Meats (*Emporia Gazette,* November 29, 2007). The announcement of the meatpacking plant restructuring and the imminent perspective of losing 1,500 jobs created an uproar in Emporia, and the bittersweet attitude toward the news was reflected through the over 1,200 blog entries, too (*Emporia Gazette,* January 25, 2008).

Immigrants in Emporia

Emporia had a sizable Hispanic, mostly Mexican, population for a long time because the town was a major westbound railroad hub. The first large influx of Mexicans in Emporia occurred in the early 1900s due to the depressed economy in Mexico and the available jobs in Kansas at the Atchison, Topeka & Santa Fe Railway. The Mexican workers—who tended to be rural, uneducated, and unskilled men hired for hard manual labor—lived in camps in the southern part of Emporia right by the railroad tracks. These railroad-worker communities functioned as supportive networks for arriving relatives and friends until they could save enough money to live on their own. In the beginning, the Latino community remained separated from mainstream society because of discrimination as well as their own desire to preserve their own culture. However, these Latinos slowly blended into the community and have been referred by the locals as "old-guard Latinos," accepted and respected in town.

A recent wave of Latinos came to Emporia in the mid-1990s, when migrant workers were lured by the jobs offered at Iowa Beef Processors' slaughter and meatpacking plant. The "new Latinos," however, were quite different from the "old guard," even though all of them tended to be perceived as "Mexicans" by many in the community. Old-timer Latinos in Emporia are rural Mexicans from Michoacán and Durango (Aguilar 2008), while new Latinos are more diverse in terms of their origin. At the same time, while most of them are still from Mexico, many have come from El Salvador, Ecuador, and Guatemala, too. Spatial division is also visible, as many newcomers live in the west end of the town, near the Tyson plant, while the long-term Latino residents are more scattered, based on the social status of their families.

The town and the community hardly had enough time to address the integration issues of the newcomer Latinos when these challenges were trumped by the arrival of the Somali workforce. The Somalis came as refugees, fleeing war-weary Somalia in the 1990s and spending years in Kenya's refugee camps. Their arrival and resettlement were administered under the Refugee Resettlement Program for Africa.

The legal basis of the refugee admissions program in the United States is the Refugee Act of 1980. The refugee program emphasizes the goal that refugees become economically self-sufficient as quickly as possible, and those resettled in the United States are generally perceived as contributing positively to the diversity and enrichment of the country. Refugees get employment authorization upon admission, and after one year they are eligible to apply for adjustment of status to permanent resident and eventually for American citizenship. The three main agencies involved in the U.S. Refugee Program are the United States Citizenship and Immigration Services (Department of Homeland Security, or DHS), the Bureau of Population, Refugees and Migration (Department of State), and the Administration of Children and Families, Office of Refugee Resettlement (Department of Health and Human Services, or DHHS).

Emporia has never been a direct resettlement site in the sense of bigger cities that receive large groups of refugees as primary resettlement locations. The local Tyson plant offered transfers to some of the workers laid off in February 2006 at a Tyson Fresh Meats plant in Norfolk, Nebraska. The *Emporia Gazette* estimated the number of Somalis employed by Tyson to grow to 400 by the end of 2006. The assumption that these employees had families with them put the total refugee population between 750 to 1,000 (*Emporia Gazette,* November 3, 2007). The actual resettlement of the Somali refugees in Emporia was organized by the Catholic Community Services (CCS, a branch of Catholic Community Charities in Kansas City, Kansas), which received a $104,495 grant through the Kansas Department of Social and Rehabilitation Services from the DHHS. Employing refugees has an obvious advantage from the employer's perspective: refugees are legally present in the United States and have all the necessary papers and permits. There is no direct evidence that Tyson preferred hiring Somali refugees at its plant in Emporia as an effect of increased workplace raids and stepped-up U.S. Immigration and Customs Enforcement practices around 2006, although this may have been one of the considerations behind the decision.

Concerned citizens of Emporia formed the Emporia Refugee Resettlement Alliance (ERRA) "to deal with issues that have arisen from the arrival of Somali refugees" (*Emporia Gazette,* November 11, 2006). The group brought together representatives from a variety of agencies and governmental units for "educating Lyon Countians to the cultural and religious traditions of the Somalis and educating Somalis to the cultural and religious traditions of Americans in general, and Lyon County in particular" (*Emporia Gazette,* November 3, 2007).[3] The two organizations (CCS and ERRA) collaborated and helped Somalis apply for benefits, retrieve missing documents, find opportunities for continuing education, and arrange affidavits of relationships to bring relatives to America and provided counseling assistance and other day-to-day help the refugees required. The Somali refugees themselves were organized and led by the elders of their community, and they had a liaison that facilitated the negotiations with Tyson and the city and state government, as well as different organizations.

Tyson and the Immigrant Workers

Tyson Foods, Inc. is the world's largest meat processor and marketer and the second-largest food-production company in the Fortune 500. The company has more than 100,000 employees at over 300 facilities and offices around the world. Tyson Fresh Meats is a subsidiary of Tyson Foods, Inc. and maintains seventeen production sites throughout North America and employs nearly

41,000 people. Emporia became part of the Tyson Fresh Meats, Inc. opera-tion in 2001, when Tyson Foods purchased Iowa Beef Processors (IBP), the previous owner. IBP had produced meat in the Emporia plant since 1969.

In his analysis of the development of the meatpacking industry in the Midwest, Wilson Warren (2007) notes that as a result of industrial changes from the 1960s through 2000, most of the meatpacking locations shifted to the Midwest. In Kansas, Dodge City, Garden City, Emporia, and Liberal had the most significant beef-slaughtering facilities. According to some of our interviewees and from what we can deduct from the blog entries, although they were not the typical "American Dream" jobs, employment at the meat-packing plant paid fairly well in the 1980s.[4]

> [M]ale and female young people from Emporia and many surrounding com-munities worked at IBP and many were enrolled at Emporia State University and were afforded flexible work hours in certain jobs to attend their classes. Some worked afternoons and nights on full shifts and went to college during the day. It was hard but it afforded them the education to go on to wonderful careers. (Blog entry)

However, these conditions eventually ended.[5] The influx of immigrant workers to the meatpacking industry has been documented by others (Broad-way and Stull 2006; Warren 2007), and it was pointed out that a number of factors have contributed to this change. The 1986 Immigration Reform and Control Act modified the migration strategies and the operation of migration networks (Massey, Durand, and Malone 2002), leading to migra-tion to previously neglected destinations such as the Midwest states. Others pointed out the internal redistribution of Hispanic workers, suggesting that these people were not new immigrants but new domestic migrants who left metropolitan areas for new rural destinations (Hernández-León and Zúñiga 2000). Some scholars argue that the corporate recruitment strategies had a large impact in developing these new migration streams (Krissman 2000). This was parallel with the move of these firms from urban to rural locations, away from powerful unions (Compa 2005). This latter consideration was in line with the changing face of the labor force, as immigrant workers are easier to control and less likely to form unions.

As stipulated in the Team Member Bill of Rights, Tyson workers "have the right to choose whether they want to join together for collective bargaining purposes." However, efforts to unionize the Emporia plant have failed. After a thirty-seven-year hiatus—the last union election took place in April 1971, when representation by the union was voted down by a majority of workers at the plant—in November 2008, Tyson Fresh Meats employees in Emporia had the opportunity to vote for representation. The more than eight hundred hourly production and maintenance workers who participated in the process rejected representation by the United Food and Commercial Workers union. This outcome was not seen as a defeat for workers in the community. A few days after the vote, the editor and publisher of the *Gazette* called the failed attempt in Emporia "the vote for survival" and "the right thing by voting not to unionize the Emporia plant" in hard economic times (*Emporia Gazette,* November 12, 2008). Unionized labor would have meant higher costs for the employer, hurting competitiveness, so it is not surprising that the local community perceived this outcome to be for the greater good.

Immigrant Integration: Local Perceptions

Immigrant integration occurs in multiple spheres. A variety of actors (organizations, social networks, individuals, government bodies, etc.) can facilitate, promote, or hinder the integration experience of an immigrant or an immigrant group. In our particular case, the local actors include a crucial one: the meatpacking plant. However, integration in the plant is very different from integration in the community. The plant needs workers while the community needs citizens. Thus both the expectations from and support to the immigrant workers are different. Conflict may arise when the costs and benefits of immigrant integration as workers and citizens are uneven. Food-processing plants are often criticized for externalizing the costs of immigrant workers, keeping the cheap labor but passing the cost of their social integration to the community. This is especially important when the plant is the major employer in town.

Regarding the integration of Hispanics in Emporia, the first difference is the one between the "old guard" who are well embedded in the community and the newcomers. The general public seems to simplify the matter, perceiving the length of time being the most important factor. In other words, the long-term resident Latinos are seen as more Americanized and acculturated, even to the extent that they have little in common with the newcomers. As we were told, the newcomers usually do socialize with one another and seldom have any activities with the old-time residents.[6] Since the migrant flow from Mexico to Emporia was not continuous but had two very different waves generations apart, there is little original connection between the two migrant groups. So while in theory the presence of an established Latino community may help the integration of the newcomers, in Emporia it was not necessarily the case. We were told that the community had an established collaborative relationship with Hispanics in general, and this was applied to the newcomers as well, until "they started being who they were, and then there were problems." The local community sees and perceives the two groups very differently, as another interviewee put it:[7]

Well, there is a big difference between the old family Hispanics, and the first generation Hispanics. The old family Hispanics have been here hundred plus years, and blended into the community. There is not a lot of racial prejudice against the old Hispanics—they don't like the first generation Hispanics that has brought with it gangs, it has brought a lot of dope which is not good in the Hispanic community. The old Hispanics don't believe they have family values, Christian values—basically they are thieves.

It is not entirely clear to what extent this negative opinion is shared by the "old-guard" Latinos, but at least some of them feel little resemblance to the newcomers. It is not unlikely that this tension partly comes from the fear of the old-timers that if the newcomers bring certain problems (a typical result of a sudden population influx), the majority white population might associate these problems with all Latinos. On the other hand, many of the newcomers feel that the long-term resident Latinos are "not Mexican enough" because their norms and way of life are much too influenced by the Anglo community. In any case, the local opinion about the "old guard" is still largely positive, as they have been "model citizens" and "they work hard and they pay their taxes and they keep their properties up."

The complaints regarding Latinos were directed toward the newcomers, and the most common topics were their housing solutions (many families living in the same house), not keeping up their houses and yards (especially that they tend to park their cars on their lawns), contribution to increased crime in the community, and that they "have music blasted and do a lot of drinking."

In addition, there is the difference between the Mexicans and the Central American immigrants. Mexican networks are larger and stronger and can help offset the initial social costs of immigration. We heard of tensions between Mexicans and immigrants from other countries, especially El Salvador and Guatemala, rooted in the peculiar fact that those two countries have a large immigrant workforce in Mexico. Thus some of the tension actually originated in Mexico and was transplanted in the United States. Guatemalans are especially vulnerable if they are of indigenous Mayan descent who often do not speak good Spanish, which is a key to be employed in the Tyson plant. While most social clubs are organized by Mexicans and other Latin Americans seldom interact with them, this does not mean that the Latino community is ultimately divided. A good example for a collaborative action was the local rally in April 2006.[8]

Even if there were problems with the newcomers and the influx of Latino migrant workers did not go unnoticed, their presence has never generated as much criticism as the refugees' did. In retrospect, the presence of the Latinos was not unacceptable despite the suspicions about undocumented workers in the plant. Once the Somali refugees arrived, the local community suddenly realized that the cultural differences between whites and Hispanics are not even that big. Compared to the Hispanics, the Somalis were indeed different, in physical appearance, culture, religion, and everyday routines, differences that were big enough to generate substantial opposition in the community.

> I think that the Hispanic group was much more easier to except and to adapt to because they were from the country that is our neighbor to the South, so there is more understanding of those cultural values and believes and traditions and from the language to the food and everything; to where the Somalis were totally, totally something different and I think that the fear factor played in a lot and the lack of knowledge—not knowing how to approach, how to communicate—it's just too . . . it was different, very different.

It was quite obvious from the beginning that the integration of the Somalis would be very difficult. As somebody put it plainly: "These people coming from a third-world country do not fit in well in the Midwest." Being foreign, black, and Muslim certainly made life quite difficult in the Heartland. "Honestly, I'm not sure I would have the courage to go out every day if I were in their shoes," said a blog entry.

To test the local perception about the characteristics of a "good immigrant," we asked our key informants to describe the successful immigrant worker integration in Emporia. The most common answer our key informants had was the need to learn the language, adopt the culture, and obey the local laws and customs, not surprisingly reflecting the common complaints about immigrants. Hispanics certainly had advantages in this respect, as Emporia had an established Hispanic community with formal and informal resources for newcomer Latinos. Also, as one of our interviewees noted, the community was more ready for new Hispanics then for the Somalis.

The cultural differences the Somalis had to face seemed too big to handle. For example, Somalis were almost always in large groups, the safe way to behave in Somalia, but it was viewed as intimidating in Emporia. Law enforcement had difficulties with such behavior. Later the community learned that in Somalia, group action was the main way to prevent police brutality, kidnapping, and other dangers of a lawless country. Apparently Somalis were not adequately prepared for the fact that law enforcement in the United States is different. And while it was not easy to learn the American norms and methods of social interaction, it was even harder to figure out how many of the traditional Somali customs and values can be kept in everyday life. The public perception is that this effort was unsuccessful, although some respondents suggested that this should have been a mutual effort:

Understanding mainstream and how things function, how the law functions, how to respect those laws because a lot of the problems we run into is that they are still rooted in their traditional values and beliefs, and they want to implement the same values here and it just doesn't work.

Oh, I'm not sure the migrant workers need to be better. We need to be better, I think, we need to integrate ourselves into them, we need to help them to understand our customs so that they are not constantly in trouble with the law because they don't understand what the law is.

There were complaints in the community about the Somalis' poor driving skills, their inadequate hygiene practices, their customary gatherings, as well as their lack of respect toward women. They "sit outside [the local Somali restaurant] and smoke their cigarette and smoking their dope and nobody, you know, cared," said one of our respondents. Race, perceived as the color of the skin, has also been an issue, especially since Emporia does not have a significant African American population, so the community had less exposure to "blacks." However, one of the main differences between the Latinos and Somalis in terms of them being accepted by the community stemmed from their religious beliefs, and Catholic Latinos could blend in easier in Emporia than could Muslim Somalis.

This difference between the two minority groups made it impossible for them to cooperate and to share resources and information. Their respective cultures seemed to be far apart, and when asked about mixed relationships between the two groups, one respondent reacted, "I don't know that a Muslim would date a Catholic . . . it could happen but maybe not black Muslim and a Hispanic Catholic."

It is actually perceived that there were tensions between the two groups. The tension was related to religion, as Muslim Somalis requested special accommodation from Tyson for their religious practices. Most of the Latino employees at Tyson felt that the plant management gave too many concessions to the Somali workers by giving them a prayer room and five prayer breaks per day and for operating special shuttle vans for them. The news about tensions between the Latinos and Somalis spread mainly on the blog, but also was reflected in the in-depth interviews with key informants. However, this conflict has never spilled outside the plant site. Both the Latinos and the Somalis lived in close-knit communities on the opposite ends of the town, therefore there was very little interaction between them when not at work.[9]

The lack of open conflict did not prevent many in the community from drawing a comparison between the two groups, indirectly improving the perceptions about the Latinos, even the newcomers. It is interesting that the positive picture was related to work ethic rather than the previously objected stereotypes of their behavior outside the plant. This shift in focus helped the Hispanic community to be seen as hardworking people who ask for no special treatment.

> The Latinos are hard workers. That's why they take the jobs nobody else wants, and all they want is to provide for their families. With that said, many of these workers thought the Somalis were receiving special treatment, because they were getting paid the same and a Latino was pulling double the load than a refugee was, a Somali refugee. So that had lots of folks upset because they thought that that was unfair.

It is obvious from the already discussed information that public discourse on immigrant integration changed after the arrival of the Somalis. As it was noted by one of our respondents, the heat was taken off of the "Mexicans." Our key-informant community leaders were aware of this:

> [B]efore the Somali refugees came here, the Latinos were more the target of being viewed negatively or, you know, "they are here, they have to learn English," "this is America"; and then when the Somali refugees came in, that was lifted somewhat and focused on the Somalis.
>
> I think in all honesty, that the community for the most part did not think too highly of the Hispanic immigrants that came in—although they are generating money for the local economy—it was not necessarily a welcomed thing; but when the Somali refugees came in, that was worse. They took the hate they felt for the Latino community and put it on the Somali refugees.

Immigrant Perception in the Local Media

Public discourse on immigrant integration largely took place around the *Emporia Gazette*. The paper presented both sides of the conflict, especially around the Somali workforce. In the analyzed time period, there were six articles about different Latino social and cultural activities and fifteen articles written to inform the readers about the ordeals Somalis had to endure until they arrived to the United States as refugees, their culture, and traditions. There were also four articles describing the activities of different officials, institutions, organizations, and churches held to help accommodate the refugees in the community. Several letters to the editor also reflected the public opinion regarding the situation of Somalis in town: two of them voicing the authors' uneasiness of seeing the sudden influx of people so different from what they had been used to, as well as fear for potential changes in the way of life in Emporia; two of the letters embracing the cultural diversity brought by the refugees; and one coming from a Somali student studying at Emporia University thanking the community for their support.

The *Gazette* was able to present both sides of the conflict, and the articles related to this issue were fair and balanced. Shortly after Tyson's announcement of the plant restructuring, the *Gazette* ran eleven articles on the subject and tried to mobilize the whole community to help all those who lost their jobs and their families, as well as to inform the public about the developments in the Latino community and the Somali refugees: the willingness of the former to commute to different towns for work but keep their families in Emporia, and the decision of the latter community to leave and take the jobs offered by Tyson elsewhere.

The *Gazette* moderator's intervention on the blog was very sparse and professional. Due to the nature of the medium, blog entries were usually short, heated, and ignited rapid responses. Unlike the *Gazette*'s reporting on immigrants in general, the blog focused almost exclusively on the Somalis and had a number of surges in terms of entries, all related to particular events in the community.

On January 18, 2007, the *Gazette* published the findings of the coroner's report showing that an active case of tuberculosis was a factor in the death of a Somali worker two weeks earlier at the Emporia plant. The article unleashed a tide of eighty-seven blog entries. Although some of the comments were directed against the refugees and illegal workers, the large majority complained that the tuberculosis case went undetected by the gatekeepers: the Immigration and Naturalization Service, Homeland Security, the Centers for Disease Control and Prevention, as well as Tyson and the local health department. This case made a permanent mark on the Somali community in Emporia, fueling fears and negative stereotypes.

When in November that year the news broke that "Emporia may become a major settling point for refugees within the next several years, and a diverse committee of local, state and private leaders" were working to prepare for the next step (*Emporia Gazette,* November 3, 2007), the blog hosted by the newspaper burst again. There were 659 comments posted in the ten days following the publication of the news, and because of the length of the thread, the newspaper editors had to open a separate forum for further comments on this story. About 85 percent of these comments vehemently opposed any new refugee resettlement in Emporia, but there were close to one hundred entries that tried to appease the negative (sometimes outright racist and xenophobic) tone of these comments by appealing to Christian values and the benefits of cultural diversity. Most of the chagrin was vented against the federal Office of Refugee Resettlement, Catholic Charities, and city leaders; however, the *Gazette* also got its share of blame for not informing the public about the influx of refugees. The biggest fear among those who were revolted by the possibility of Emporia becoming a refugee center was the loss of their way of life.

The publication of these stories energized those bloggers who voiced their unhappiness, and they prepared a small meeting (about thirty-five people attended it) on November 8, 2007, that lead to the big public meeting organized by the city (*Emporia Gazette*, November 29, 2007), which drew a large crowd made up of area residents and a handful of Somali refugees. Anger, pleas for understanding, and references to Christianity surfaced during the meeting, which tried to provide answers to questions about refugees who had moved in the community during the past two years. The very heated debate of the forum hall seeped through the walls and quickly found its way back to the blogosphere, where about 1,024 entries reflected the attitude of some community members toward migrant workers and refugees in their community. The sentiments ran very high, although with this second surge we noticed that the rate of those comments trying to pacify the general mood was higher than before. About one-fifth of the 1,024 entries related to the public meeting tried to appeal to Christian love (aided by the fact that Christmas was approaching) and the need for multiculturalism in town or tried to deconstruct negative myths surrounding the traditions and behavior of Somali refugees.

Several recurring themes can be identified in the blog discourse. One classic fear was that the Somalis would change life in Emporia, both the way of life and the quality of life. Robert Park's classic theory on the race relations cycle (Park 1950) argues that competition comes before accommodation, because of the socioeconomic composition of Emporia, where blue-collar manufacturing jobs provide employment for the majority of the population. In certain cases, the concern about the quality of life can be a proxy for racism, and this was visible in the blog entries as well:

> With regard to the comments that more or less call anyone not overjoyed with this influx of foreigners a racist, some of us are just concerned we are about to see a way of life vanish and be replaced by a lot of things we aren't comfortable with. (Blog entry)
>
> I don't think these posters should be ashamed of themselves. I see them speaking out of anger, out of fear, out of concern. . . . But through my eyes, I do not see racism, I do not see selfishness. I see good old fashioned fear; they are scared that the quality of life they have the right to have is being taken from them; that no one else cares. (Blog entry)

Connected to the issue of way of life in Emporia was the fear that the city would become a permanent refugee resettlement place. This fear eventually triggered collective action and led to the aforementioned town-hall meeting. The common ways to address this issue on the blog were similar to the usual sentiments of many anti-immigrant groups, partly quasi economic, partly simply xenophobic.

What a nightmare, we cannot even support the people who live and work in Emporia as it is but we allow our tax dollars to cater to every need the Somalis. Emporia has become the joke of Kansas it's no wonder companies don't want to build here and this is only making things worse. (Blog entry)

On the other side of the debate were the pacifiers, as not everybody who expressed their opinion on the blog shared the animosity toward the Latino migrant workers and the Somali refugees. Given that the leading local agency for refugee resettlement was Catholic Charities and that religion is an important factor shaping opinions in the region, no wonder there were many references to Christian values ("Don't forget that God made all of us—white, black, brown or whatever color," posted one blogger) as well as remarks about demographic decline without the immigrants, the experience of immigrant forefathers, and diversity:

You people should be ashamed of yourselves. You just prove to me what I have thought about Emporia for many years. Emporia is old-fashioned and racist. Everyone deserves an equal opportunity in life, not everyone has grown up spoiled and hand fed like us here in the United Stated, but very few of us seem to see it that way. We are just selfish and look at it as people trying to take what is ours and not trying to spread the wealth. This is an opportunity to expose ourselves to different cultures and races, we should be using this as a learning experience. (Blog entry)

Eventually the discourse became more general and bloggers started to discuss the issue of immigrant integration in town. Language and customs were the most common topics to complain about. Although many community members blame the migrant workers or the refugees for their slow or ineffective integration, others argued that assimilation (or, rather, integration) should not mean leaving all native traits behind. Public opinion perceived Somalis as being illegal workers, a "drain on public assistance programs," even though they had the right to work in the United States, and being a drag on local health services, even though all who were employed at Tyson had health insurance.

The immigrants here, legal and illegal, have no interest in assimilating into our society or adopting our customs or language. Instead, they isolate and divide themselves by dressing differently, acting differently, speaking differently, and then act offended when we treat them differently! . . . Reaching out is a two-way street and I don't see many extended arms from the Somali or Latin communities in Emporia. (Blog entry)

Finally, blog entries also addressed the lack of information about the refugees and complaints about the way they were brought to Emporia. The general opinion was that the community had not been informed about this step, but the responsibility for this was divided between Tyson, the city, and the organizations that worked on the resettlement. The lack of information then was extended to the group itself, and several bloggers acknowledged that the community knew little about the Somalis.

The case of the Somalis highlighted the role of various institutions and groups that mediate the process of immigrant integration. The next section of this study examines how the city of Emporia, Tyson, and other actors shaped the discourse and the integration experience of Latinos and Somalis alike.

Integration and the Local Actors

The main actors facilitating the integration of Latino migrant workers and the Somali refugees in the community as well as their acceptance are the City of Emporia, Tyson Foods, and the various local charities and churches. We will use the case of the Somali refugees to highlight some of the controversies around immigrant integration and refugee resettlement.

The conflict between the community and the newly arrived Somali refugees stemmed from the lack of communication between the Tyson representatives, resettlement organizations, and city officials and local people. Moving a culturally and religiously different large group to this rural town was a business decision, and neither the community nor the refugees were prepared enough for the social consequences.

Interestingly, it was not entirely clear which organization was the driving force behind the Somali resettlement. Catholic Community Charities, the Kansas City–based group was the main coordinator of this segment of the refugee program in the state. However, the public in Emporia was generally uninformed about their role and they seldom made it to the discourse. In the public eye, the main responsible party was Tyson itself. "Tyson dropped them [the Somalis] in here without any preparation, whatsoever," said one of our key informants.

Although Tyson was the biggest employer in the community, many people were ambivalent regarding its presence and hiring practices. On the one hand, most people were aware that even though it provided mostly low-skill and low-paying jobs, it substantially contributed to the economic base of Emporia. On the other hand, it attracted migrant workers, and this did bother many in the community. One of our key informants noted: "They wanted Tyson gone. There was a segment of the population that said if this is what Tyson is doing to us, we want to get rid of Tyson." The animosity toward the meatpacking plant grew exponentially with the arrival of the Somali refugees and culminated with the announcement of the plant restructuring. Tyson was accused of taking advantage of the refugees and externalizing the costs of the immigrant workers by indirectly benefiting from the fact that the city had to cover some of the integration costs while they got the cheap immigrant labor. Thus, for some, it was not even the immigrant integration but the business practice in general that they opposed.

> "Using alleged illegal immigrants and refugees to inflate the supply of low skilled labor to enhance corporate profit margins and maintain a current wage structure is ethically repugnant." (Blog entry)

It seems that Tyson was more involved in accommodating and helping their Somali refugee employees to integrate in the community than they had been with their Latino workforce. However, the installation of a Muslim prayer room at the meatpacking plant and the five allotted prayer breaks per day for the Somali employees attracted harsh criticism from the public and became a source of constant conflict between the Latinos and Somalis at the job site.

> The Somalians' transfer to Emporia was woefully mishandled from the start. . . . Instead of working with churches, charitable, volunteer and civic groups to integrate the Somalians into the community (a practice which has been successfully employed in other cities in which smaller populations of Somalians have been resettled), Tyson and others handled the material needs of the Somalians (signing up for government assistance, setting up medical appointments, arranging housing), but did nothing to facilitate their social integration into the community. . . . [T]he unique needs of the sizeable Somali population placed a significant burden on Emporia's already overstretched infrastructure, a burden neither Tyson nor any other social agency made an effort to share. (Blog entry)

It became clear quite soon after the first Somali workers arrived that the city would have to address their presence. Although the local government seemingly did not know about the sudden influx of refugees in advance, the community leaders and all the institutions coordinated by the city tried to do their best to accommodate the Somalis as well as to inform and soothe the public about the developments. Despite all these efforts, the general belief reflected through the newspaper articles, blogs, and interviews was that the city was not prepared in any way for this demographic swell:

> The city wasn't prepared because they didn't know what to prepare for, and number two, I don't think they were aware in time that this was going to happen and they would really need to take an active role. . . . A large city like Kansas City can accommodate 800 people from a different country, but not Emporia.

The city of Emporia was not the only mediator in immigrant integration. Various charities and local churches worked hard to help mitigate some of the social costs of integration. The Salvation Army handled most of the community's immediate needs and worked with the United Way and Friends in Faith to hold food drives and fund-raising events.[10] When asked about the reaction of the Latino and the Somali communities to the help offered by the local charities, one of our key informants noted that while the Hispanics were used to their presence, Somalis did not show up asking for assistance.

Local churches also played a very important role in bringing the locals and the Latinos as well as the locals and the Somalis together through different social activities, English classes, and shared dinners. The Catholic Church was historically quite successful in integrating Latinos in the community (for a more detailed account, see Call 2005), although the long-term Latino community members and the newcomers were divided, usually going to separate Catholic churches.

Some of the local churches tried to attract Somalis and organized different activities to create opportunities for local people and the refugees to get to know each other's culture and traditions; however, these initiatives were short-lived and largely unsuccessful. So while Mexican immigrants could use the Catholic Church as an additional help for their integration process, there was no equivalent support for the Muslim Somalis in Emporia. Now we can only speculate if more time would have helped the Somalis in this respect, as on January 25, 2008, Tyson made an announcement that they would restructure their operations in Emporia.

Departure of the Somalis: The Plant Restructuring

Tyson's decision to restructure its operations at the meatpacking plant in Emporia affected virtually everybody in town. The sudden loss of 1,500 jobs projected dark clouds on the horizon for many families and for the community as a whole. Tyson offered help for those who wanted to relocate to its other plants, and all the Somali refugee workers left town in about four weeks.[11] However, most of the Latino workers had families and houses in Emporia, and they chose to either find other local jobs or commute to different towns but keep their families in Emporia.

Again, public discourse seemed to be divided based on whether it was about the Latinos or the Somalis. The Latinos came out as good, hardworking people. "We lost an awful lot of good Hispanic people because of the Tyson layoffs," said one of our informants. It seems that there was more compassion toward Latino migrant workers in the hard times after Tyson's announcement, a fact that suggests that they were better integrated and accepted in the large community.

A lot of the people who are in the process of losing their jobs will be our Hispanic families. These are hard working families, often times both the mom and dad working to provide for their children. They can't just stop and go to college. Unfortunately, a lot of them haven't had the opportunities we have had to get a complete and uninterrupted education in their lifetime. I feel very sad for them knowing that they will probably have to leave Emporia. (Blog entry)

At the same time, the issue of the perceived special treatment of the Somalis by Tyson came up again. Some felt that even after 1,500 workers lost their jobs, the company helped the Somalis more than the others.

See now that is what irritates a lot of people! All the special treatment the Somalis get. They are not the only people that are relocating because of the Tyson layoffs. Ever since they came to town it has been all about them and what we can do for them. Meanwhile everyone else that lives in this town is pushed to the sidelines and get jack when they have the same problems as the Somalis. This community should not revolve around the Somalis. They can be a part of this community and get the same treatment as everyone else in the community. (Blog entry)

This was the third time that the blogosphere lit up. There were 267 blog entries in the two weeks following the news about the restructuring, and we found that, although there were many who felt excited that Tyson's decision drove out many Latino migrant workers and all the Somali refugees from Emporia, the rate of those who voiced sympathy for those who had to leave increased substantially. More than a hundred entries expressed sorrow for the possible loss of the community's cultural diversity, or remorse that Emporia as a community did not do enough to accommodate and integrate the refugees, or just made fun of those who did not recognize the value of the other groups and wanted them out of town.

The Tyson restructuring closed an intensive period of debate on immigrant integration. During the time when Tyson employed Somalis in the Emporia plant, public discourse on their impact on the community was heated. Since the Somalis' departure, the question remains whether their presence made a long-term impact on how the community sees immigrant workers.

Conclusion

Immigrant integration in the community is facilitated by the knowledge of "the others," including language, culture, traditions, and norms. The existence of an earlier settlement of Mexicans in Emporia, the community-wide acceptance and taste for their food, and their strong Christian (Catholic) background favored newer waves of Latino migrant workers in blending into the community. At the same time, local institutions (schools, city offices, banks) were reasonably prepared to operate in bilingual mode. Thus the Latino integration in Emporia had been helped by many of these factors, and despite the occasional complaints and tensions between old-timers and newcomers, Mexicans and other Latinos, and Hispanics and Anglos, they were more or less able to become an integral part of the community.

With the arrival of the Somalis, the discourse about immigrant integration fundamentally changed. Incomplete information about them and the circumstances of their arrival fueled irrational fears and stereotypes, while their physical appearance, cultural norms, and religion significantly hindered their integration. They did not have as much help as the Latinos in terms of social networks and resources. Consequently, their integration was extremely difficult and eventually unsuccessful. Their impact was temporary, partly because they stayed only for a short time, and partly because they lived in a close-knit community, a miniature ethnic enclave. A community that isolates itself from others makes a very low and slow contribution to the cultural diversity or its impact is not perceptible or appreciated by the majority.

The Somalis had all the institutional help behind them. They were legal immigrants with appropriate papers and work permits. Their presence in the United States was not driven by economic supply and demand (except their local redistribution), rather by societal moral considerations and support for refugee resettlement. Despite these advantages, their integration was derailed by their racial and religious differences not only from the mainstream community but from the dominant minority as well.

It was very interesting to see how the community made a distinction between the two groups in the context of the immigration-policy debate. Some of the new Latinos were probably undocumented workers, while all Somalis had legal papers. Latinos were part of a labor flow many opposed, while Somalis were part of a refugee policy most people approved. Somali workers had health insurance through Tyson, while many Latinos in town did not have that. If not for that one tuberculosis case, this issue probably would not have even emerged. So in many ways, Somalis should have been the accepted, legal foreign workers, while the Latinos would have met resistance due to their perceived undocumented status. Yet the discourse had been very different regarding the two groups. Although both groups were perceived by many as "intruders" who took jobs from the locals and drove wages down, the conflict never became physical. The perception of immigrants taking jobs from locals was a general and often nativist statement.

However, someone who was perhaps an active ERRA member, on November 9, 2007, posted on the *Emporia Gazette*'s forum: "I was told on Wednesday, by a Tyson representative, that they currently have about 200 job openings at the Emporia plant. That doesn't mean 200 refugees are coming here, it just means Tyson needs more workers and they don't get enough applications from the people who already live in or near Emporia, to fill those jobs."

The blog hosted by the local newspaper became the galvanizing forum for the strongest anti-immigration advocates in the community. The discourse in the *Emporia Gazette* as well as on its blogs revealed a complex picture in which emotions and tensions ran high. As a side effect, this discourse facilitated a change in the perception of the Hispanic population.

The question now is whether the public sentiment and discourse about immigrant workers and integration will go back to what it was before the Somalis came, or has the community's perception on the issue changed given all the conflict around the Somalis. The pessimistic scenario is that there will be more tension related to the Latino community as once again they will be the most visible, dominant minority in town. The more optimistic scenario is that the tension will be mitigated, even if it will not go away entirely. There are a number of reasons why this might be the case. First, with the plant restructuring, many Latinos left Emporia, and this out-migration was probably selective for the newcomer Latinos who drew most of the heat earlier. Second, it is possible that the changing perception of Latinos will be permanent, taking away some of the earlier critiques of immigrant laborers. Finally, the community may have moved to a more integrative stand after this high-profile experience about immigrant laborers in a relatively short time period.

The lessons learned from this case can help refugee resettlement agencies as well local governments and stakeholders to better address such influxes of immigrant populations. These are not purely business decisions, and the local government should work with the prospective employer(s) and the state and federal agencies to address the challenges of relocation. Integration as a worker is not identical to integration as a community citizen. Characteristics of the local community can make a huge difference in immigrant integration, and if the local population feels it has been left out of the discussion, the integration of immigrants will be extremely difficult. In any case, immigrant integration in Emporia is an ongoing process, and not everybody is optimistic that the situation permanently improved after the Somalis left.

"Just wonder what all these poor Klansmen are gonna do on their Saturday nights now that there's no one to whine about. Guess they'll have to find another group to hate" (Blog entry).

244 · LÁSZLÓ J. KULCSÁR AND ALBERT IAROI

Notes

1. Content analysis is a highly flexible research method that has been widely used in social sciences. According to Goffman (1974), the methodology has been developed for systematic analysis of the characteristics of messages in support of identification and categorization of texts relative to the core questions of communication theory. The emphasis is on discovery and description, including search for contexts, underlying meanings, patterns, and processes, rather than mere quantity or numerical relationships between two or more variables (Altheide 1995).

2. The *Emporia Gazette* is a daily newspaper covering local news, sports, business, jobs, and community events. It rose to national attention after William Allen White—who later won the Pulitzer Prize—bought the newspaper in 1895, and it is still an example of a small-town newspaper that transcended local importance. The newspaper is published six days a week by the White family and has a circulation of almost 7,000 copies.

3. These agencies and governmental units included the Flint Hills Health Center, Kansas Department of Social and Rehabilitation Services, Flint Hills Technical College Adult Education Center, Tyson Fresh Meats, the City of Emporia, the Emporia school district, the Emporia Area Chamber of Commerce and Convention and Visitors Bureau, the United Way, and Newman Regional Health.

4. The average wage of animal slaughterers and processors remained comparatively strong from the 1960s through the early 1980s. The average wage earned by a meatpacking employee during the 1960s and '70s was 14 percent to 18 percent higher than their counterpart in the larger U.S. manufacturing sector. The peak average hourly wage of a meatpacking employee during this period was nearly $20 an hour when adjusted for inflation (Public Broadcasting Service 2006).

5. According to Stanley (1992) average hourly wages in the meatpacking industry between 1969 and 1981 were 13 percent to 17 percent higher than those in manufacturing; however, they decreased from 97 percent in 1983 to 82 percent by 1989.

6. "Latinos have cultural or societal groups within the churches they attend. I have not heard of the newer immigrants having an organization outside the church. However, the offsprings of the original immigrants who arrived due to the railroad do have an organization. They are the Hispanics of Today and Tomorrow also known as HOTT. There are also organizations at Emporia State University and Emporia High School. The university has HALO which I believe stands for Hispanic American Leadership Organization. The high school has Latinos Unidos," said one of our key informants.

7. All quotes are from our key informants unless noted otherwise.

8. This rally was organized to show opposition to HR 4437, a congressional bill that would have made illegal immigration a felony. The rally was part of the national Day Without Immigrants protest.

9. The conflict over religious practices between Latinos and Muslims, mostly Somalis, is not a unique case. In the past few years, a number of meatpacking plants had similar conflicts. See, for example, Phred Dvorak's article "Religious-Bias Filings Up" in the *Wall Street Journal* on October 16, 2008.

10. It must be noted that most people think Tyson was quite generous with donating food to the community as well as funding its employees' United Way commitment. Tyson had donated meats specifically for its former workers, in addition to the meats that it normally donated to the Salvation Army.

11. The large majority of the Somalis went back to Norfolk, Nebraska, where they originally came from, but some found employment at Tyson plants in Dodge City, Kansas. More than 150,000 Somalis now live in the United States, most in larger cities like Minneapolis, Nashville, Boston, Seattle, and Columbus, Ohio, but they are also sinking roots in midwestern cities like Dodge City, Kansas; Grand Island, Norfolk, and South Sioux City, Nebraska; and Fort Morgan and Greely, Colorado, all towns with slaughterhouses that depend on assembly-line labor.

References

Aguilar, Daniel. 2008. "Adaptation as a Process of Acquisition of Cultural Capital: The Case of Mexican Immigrants in Meatpacking Areas in Kansas." *Journal of Latino-Latin American Studies* 3, no. 2: 1–25.

Altheide, David. 1995. *Qualitative Media Analysis*. Thousand Oaks, Calif.: Sage.

Broadway, Michael, and Donald Stull. 2006. "Meat Processing and Garden City, KS: Boom and Bust." *Journal of Rural Studies* 22: 55–66.

Call, Ray. 2005. *Emporia's Ascent: How the Town Grew and Life Changed from 1950 to 2000*. Emporia, Kan.: Self-published.

Compa, Lance. 2005. "Blood, Sweat, and Fear: Workers' Rights in U.S. Meat and Poultry Plants." *Human Rights Watch, January 25*. http://www.hrw.org/en/reports/2005/01/24/blood-sweat-and-fear (September 29, 2012).

Fink, D. 1998. *Cutting into the Meatpacking Line: Workers and Change in the Rural Midwest*. Chapel Hill, N.C.: University of North Carolina Press.

Goffman, Erving. 1974. *Frame Analysis: An Essay on the Organization of Experience*. London: Harper and Row.

Hernández-León, R., and V. Zúñiga. 2000. "'Making Carpet by the Mile': The Emergence of a Mexican Immigrant Community in an Industrial Region of the U.S. Historic South." *Social Science Quarterly* 81: 49–66.

Hookway, Nicholas. 2008. "'Entering the Blogosphere': Some Strategies for Using Blogs in Social Research." *Qualitative Research* 8, no. 1: 91–113.

Kandel, William, and Emilio Parrado. 2005. "Restructuring of the US Meat Processing Industry and New Hispanic Migrant Destinations." *Population and Development Review* 31: 447–71.

Krissman, F. 2000. "Immigrant Labor Recruitment: U.S. Agribusiness and Undocumented Migration from Mexico." In *Immigration Research for a New Century*, ed. N. Foner, R. Rumbaut, and S. Gold. New York: Russell Sage.

Massey, D. S., J. Durand, and N. Malone. 2002. *Beyond Smoke and Mirrors: Mexican Immigration in an Era of Economic Integration*. New York: Russell Sage.

Park, Robert. 1950. *Race and Culture*. Glencoe, Ill.: Free Press.

Public Broadcasting Service. 2006. "Meatpacking in the U.S.: Still a 'Jungle' Out

There?" PBS, week of December 15. http://www.pbs.org/now/shows/250/meat
-packing.html (September 29, 2012).

Stanley, Kathleen. 1992. "Immigrant and Refugee Workers in the Midwest Meatpacking Industry: Industrial Restructuring and the Transformation of Rural Labor
Markets." *Policy Studies Review* 11, no. 2: 106–17.

Tienda, Marta, and Faith Mitchell. 2006. *Multiple Origins, Uncertain Destinies: Hispanics and the American Future.* Washington, DC: National Academies Press.

Warren, Wilson J. 2007. *Tied to the Great Packing Machine: The Midwest and Meatpacking.* Iowa City: University of Iowa Press.

PART V

Religion and
Migrant Communities

CHAPTER 10

"They Cling to Guns or Religion"

Pennsylvania Towns Put Faith in Anti-immigrant Ordinances"

JANE JUFFER

When images of Barack Obama bowling in Altoona, Pennsylvania, appeared on national television in April 2008, it was clear that he was not exactly in his element. Perhaps it wasn't, however, the fact that he is a terrible bowler. Perhaps it was his discomfiture with local politics, a possibility seemingly confirmed a few days later when, in San Francisco, he made the comment for which Hillary Clinton and John McCain would level charges of elitism. Noting that small towns in Pennsylvania and the Midwest have lost jobs and been ignored by both the Bill Clinton and George W. Bush administrations, he said, "And it's not surprising that they get bitter, they cling to guns or religion or antipathy to people who aren't like them or anti-immigrant sentiment or antitrade sentiment as a way to explain their frustrations."[1]

Clearly, Obama had spent enough time in Altoona and elsewhere in small-town Pennsylvania to discern the lay of the land. Altoona is one of the many towns, counties, and states across the country that have either passed or proposed anti-immigrant ordinances imposing fines on employers who hire and landlords who rent to undocumented people.[2] While some of these towns do have significant immigrant populations, Altoona does not: only one-half of 1 percent of its 50,000 residents were born outside the United States. The city council even admitted that the point of its ordinance was to serve as a "preemptive strike" against immigration. Yet the town is one of those decimated by deindustrialization, and immigrants serve as a convenient scapegoat for economic woes, as they do across the state in Hazleton, Pennsylvania, where there is a larger immigrant population and which in summer 2006 passed the harshest anti-immigrant ordinance on record at that point in the United States.[3]

In both Altoona and Hazleton, debates over the laws served as platforms for politicians to make arguments about "family values" in small-town America; in that sense, the "Heartland" represents a set of values that must be protected from those perceived outsiders who are seen to threaten a way of life. However, while the local is valorized in these debates, the specifics of each location do not likely matter to the national anti-immigration groups such as the Federation for American Immigration Reform (FAIR), which underwrites many of these local ordinances, including Altoona's. Nor does the local really matter to national figures such as then CNN newsman Lou Dobbs, even though in spring 2007, he held a town forum in Hazleton to discuss how small towns are "being decimated" by immigration and to hail then Mayor Lou Barletta as a defender of "small-town values." FAIR and Dobbs are more invested in advancing a national position than in taking up the particular economic and political problems of small towns.

While on the surface these events seem like secular occasions, Obama was also right to link religion to politics, for what is forming in the United States is an unholy alliance of politicians, white supremacists, the Christian right, and anti-immigrant activists whose platform rests on delineating the "Outsider" from the "citizen." The Southern Poverty Law Center (SPLC) says 250 new nativist groups have formed since April 2005, when the first Minutemen Civil Defense vigilante border patrol announced itself. The SPLC also cites anti-immigrant sentiment as one of the primary reasons for an increase in the number of hate groups in the United States—up 50 percent in 2008 to 926; even FBI statistics, which are conservative by most accounts, show that hate crimes against Latinos rose 40 percent in the four years between 2003 and 2007 (Holthouse 2009). Obama was correct, again, in listing "guns" in his litany.

The connections between religion, politics, immigration, and violence are not always clear-cut and certainly not always fully acknowledged, but they are often present and palpable. For example, in terms of religion and politics, Dobbs lamented on his news show the erosion of church-state separation, saying, "[W]e have precious little protection against the political adventurism of all manner of churches and religious organizations." Yet he appeared as a guest on the weekly news radio show of the influential conservative Christian group the Family Research Council (FRC). Here he admitted that his real problem is with *liberal* religious groups arguing for amnesty for undocumented immigrants: "My problem is the political direction those churches, especially Catholics, are taking in pushing for amnesty and not border security." The FRC president, Tony Perkins, and Dobbs lambasted Los

Angeles Cardinal Roger Mahony, a staunch proponent of immigrant rights. Perkins took issue with Mahony's interpretation of the Bible, especially his belief that people of faith should care for the "stranger among us." Said Perkins, "The stranger has to abide by the laws . . . there's no mandate for Christians to welcome the illegal stranger." And Dobbs responded: "I wish the good cardinal would call you for counsel on scripture."[4]

Although they purport to be a secular group, FAIR has connections to both the religious right and to white supremacist groups, according to the SPLC. Local governments such as the Altoona city council do not often acknowledge the involvement of FAIR—until pressed—or the religious influence. It is partly my purpose here to reveal the manner in which members of the Christian right infiltrate local politics in the interest of identifying a group of Outsiders when, in fact, it is they who are often the outsiders to the community. Immigration has become a hot issue for the Christian right, perhaps more important than same-sex marriage and abortion in providing a platform for their pro-family, law-and-order agenda. Perkins opened the FRC's special conference on immigration in 2005 with this remark: "At question today is, do we have an immigration policy that is serving to strengthen the cultural fabric of our nation, which has a great influence on the family? The answer is no. We must get this right" (quoted in Zaitchik 2006: 1). "Getting it right" means deportation: more than 90 percent of FRC members polled favored immediate expulsion of undocumented immigrants.

As Perkins's and Dobbs's reference to Cardinal Mahony indicates, a fairly powerful faith-based voice has emerged in the immigration debates, one that might be called the religious progressives, an ecumenical, loosely organized network that has launched a critique—sometimes a radical critique—of the underlying causes of immigration as well as the injustices many migrants encounter in the United States. Drawing on the stories of refugees in the Bible, religious activists call for welcoming the migrant as "the stranger among us," dissolving the boundary between outsider and citizen and producing a notion of community that is much more diasporic and loosely bounded than the family values crowd. The movement draws on the tenets of liberation theology and the tradition of theologians such as Virgilio Elizondo, who sees Jesus as a mestizo and a relentless border crosser who expected his followers to become migrants as well. This kind of diasporic faith disregards national borders in the belief that spirituality transcends the limited construction of the nation-state. The religious left rejects the "rule of law" as the highest authority, believing rather that the primary responsibility of Christians is to alleviate suffering, leading some denominations to give sanctuary in their churches to undocumented people in danger of deportation. Theirs is not an otherworldly practice; it speaks to particular social injustices perpetrated by the U.S government and requires that any legislation take those injustices into account. And the movement is not just Christian. A new, ecumenical Sanctuary Movement has formed, building on the 1980s practice of granting refuge to Central Americans fleeing U.S.-funded wars; this coalition includes Roman Catholic, Lutheran, Presbyterian, Union of Reform Judaism, American Friends Service Committee, Evangelical Christian, Sikh, and Muslim members.[5]

Dobbs and the local ordinance campaigns reveal what Miranda Joseph calls the "slippage from civic republicanism to fundamentalist Christianity, from commitment to community to submission to god" (Joseph 2002: 7). They share a vision of the ideal community, the heart and soul of the nation: an all-white town, grounded in the history of Manifest Destiny and the white Anglo-Saxon Protestant heritage that conservatives extol. Christianity can be masked in appeals to community and nationalism, which is Dobbs's news persona, but, as Joseph notes, these "national formations tend to depend on mythic origin stories, on narratives that aim to restore some imagined historical community as timeless" (Joseph 2002: xx). For many communities, such as Hazleton and Altoona, the myths of origin erase previous cycles of xenophobia and anti-Catholic sentiment, often against the very groups, such as Italians, who are now leading the anti-immigrant charge. Scapegoating today's immigrants is easier than acknowledging that the problem is globalization and a national economy that no longer needs the railroad or the steel industry to prosper. As such, "community" advocates seek recourse in nostalgia for a time when they were an integral part of a nation whose members all looked like they did.

Altoona's Preemptive Ordinance

"What does this ordinance mean for the soul of our city? It's this kind of law that really could call into question our humanity."

As he speaks, Father Luke Robertson, head of Catholic Charities in Altoona, gestures outside his offices to the main business street. "Last year, there were three drive-by shootings within a mile of this office," he says. "People are angry about the loss of jobs, the increasing crime rate, the influx of drugs. But the vast majority of crimes are committed by Anglos."[6] Latino migrants, he says, are the scapegoats for economic decline. Much of Altoona's downtown is shuttered. The city has been struggling for years to recover from the death of the railroad industry that at one point made it the second-largest city in Pennsylvania.

On a side street, nearly nestled under a railroad bridge, the United Veterans Association club serves as a space of nostalgia for the working-class man. The white working-class man.

The sign on the door reads, "Attention: This is a Members Only club. Current card must be presented for admittance to club." On August 28, 2005, Miguel Padilla, not a member, was denied entrance to the United Veterans Association club in Altoona. Incensed, he went to his car, got his gun, and returned to the club. He shot and killed three men: Alfred Mignogna, the bar owner; Fred Rickabaugh, the bouncer; and Stephen Heiss, a patron and off-duty security guard. Padilla, twenty-six years old, was an undocumented Mexican who had lived in the United States—mainly in the nearby town of Gallitzen—since he was nine. He received the death penalty on September 14, 2006. On October 23, 2006, the Altoona City Council passed the Undocumented Alien Control Ordinance, which is similar to Hazleton's measure insofar as it imposes fines on landlords who rent to and employers who hire undocumented people.

The murder seemed to confirm for local residents what national anti-immigrant groups had been saying: that "illegal aliens" destroy the fabric of American culture with drugs and violence, that Mexicans in particular do not fit in and become perpetual Outsiders to truly American communities. Consider this comment from a "Pennsylvania reader" that appears on the Web site VDARE.com under the headline "A Pennsylvania Resident Says a Mexican Alien Has Terrorized Her Community."[7] The woman says that after seeing a photo of Padilla in the newspaper, her "eyes were immediately drawn to the huge tattoo covering the right side of his neck and 'Mexico' emblazoned on this evil person. He has lived, illegally, in the USA since he was nine, but obviously his allegiance is to the south. So much for assimilation!" The reader holds then-President George W. Bush "morally responsible" for failure to enforce immigration laws. Hers is a more extreme statement of a popular opinion: one poll showed that almost two-thirds of Pennsylvanians would support laws similar to Hazleton's in their communities (D. Brown 2006). The reader's comment also illustrates a common conservative sentiment used to justify opposition to immigrants: their refusal to assimilate. While the invocation of assimilation suggests that the United States is willing to accept newcomers who try to blend in, the rhetoric also indicates the extreme skepticism that integration will occur, revealing a biological notion of essential racial differences that trumps invocations of cultural assimilation. Padilla's violent, even "terrorist," act reveals his intrinsic difference—read, criminal tendencies—even though, as Father Luke notes, the vast majority of crimes in Altoona are committed by Anglos.

Unlike Hazleton, Altoona has very few Latina/o residents; according to the 2010 census, the city counted 609 Latinos, just 1.3 percent of its total 46,320. Even Steven A. Camarota, director of research for the Center for Immigration Studies, a think tank that favors tougher immigration laws, was quoted in the *New York Times* as saying, "If you were to look for the area of the fewest immigrant settlements in the country, you would look to south central Pennsylvania. There just aren't many immigrants—legal or illegal—around Altoona because there aren't many jobs" (quoted in Hamill 2006).

So why pass the ordinance? Joe Rieker, city council member, said, "We wanted to stay ahead of the curve." The Federation for American Immigration Reform (FAIR) helped Altoona write its ordinance; its spokesman, Ira Mehlman, said the passage in Altoona was an indication of the town's frustration with the federal government's lack of immigration enforcement. Yet as Bishop Joseph V. Adamec of the local Catholic diocese warned, the ordinance could actually drive away business: "They're not going to build here if we aren't welcoming" (quoted in Hamill 2006).

Altoona appears nostalgic for a certain story about its past, when immigrants were white Europeans and jobs were plentiful. The town was founded in 1849 by the Pennsylvania Railroad, a company owned by Philadelphia industrialists who financed the building of a trans-Pennsylvanian railroad linking Philadelphia and Pittsburgh. Altoona was the critical junction, perfectly situated as a repair site for trains before they made the climb over the Allegheny Plateau. The area was also rich in timber and iron deposits. Labor was needed to build the railroad, and the town welcomed immigrants from England, Germany, Ireland, and Italy. By the 1920s, Altoona was the state's second largest city, after Philadelphia, and the hub of new railroad-design technology, like the observation car and illuminated electrical lights. The railroad industry employed 16,000 people, and there were other industries as well: a silk mill, timber mill, and large brickyard. By 1930, however, the industry—and the city—began its decline.[8]

At roughly the same time, the Ku Klux Klan established itself in Altoona as a major presence; the city had the largest single klavern in the state in 1925, with 2,805 members. The county, Blair, had seven klaverns with 4,500 members out of a total population of 140,000 (Jenkins 1997: 71). As was true throughout the northern United States, much of the Klan resurgence in Pennsylvania was based on anti-immigrant, anti-Catholic (often conjoined) biases. According to religious historian Philip Jenkins, Klan members were driven by a "Protestant nativism" that "was commonly a vehicle for the populist expression of underlying social and political grievances, focused chiefly on rapid social change and a perceived decline of moral values" (70). In Altoona in the mid-1920s, the Protestant English and German inhabitants focused their animosity on the more recently arrived Irish and Italian Catholic immigrants, who were coming at the very moment that the town's economic successes began to wane. This tension also characterized the Hazleton region, another Klan stronghold, where established Protestant groups such as the Welsh clashed with Catholic Irish, Polish, Slovaks, and Italians who came to work in the anthracite mines (Jenkins 1997: 73).

The current anti-immigrant movement is based on a perverse rewriting of this history, for the ancestors of the very people who were discriminated against are now leading the anti-immigrant movement. Then Hazleton Mayor Barletta, for example, is the great-grandson of Italian immigrants. Altoona entered a downturn around 1930 after decades of high immigration rates, fomenting xenophobia and Klan activity; in the 1980s, an economic downturn sparked by deindustrialization combined with growing numbers of immigrants laid the groundwork for a new anti-immigrant movement.

Today's xenophobia is driven by fear that globalization has made any kind of local control impossible. Altoona will never again be the boomtown it once was, and because the city finds it hard to live without that dream, it looks for a scapegoat: the handful of Latino residents who, despite the fact that they represent no economic threat, *seem* to represent the forces of globalization (racial and ethnic diversity) that have destroyed local economies. The response is something geographers call "jumping scale," considered "a political strategy for dealing with forces that originate from varying scales of power. Normally, this implies local places negotiating extralocal forces, often global in nature, in order to have some control over how those forces will affect the locale" (Gallaher 2004: 188). In the globalized economy, says geographer Colin Flint, "formerly privileged groups (white workers) can no longer count on the borders of the state and the nation to secure their privilege—diaspora creates fears of a deterritorialized world. Their economic privilege is threatened as is their racial privilege" (Flint 2004: 170). The response, says Flint, "has been to promote 'cultural and biological purity in answer to the corrosive effects of differentiation manifested, above all, in the presence of postcolonial peoples—always out of place—at the hub of the old imperial networks" (170).

The Hazleton ordinance has generated racist epithets and threats based on this belief that brown-skinned people are "out of place" in the United States. A New Jersey–based Ku Klux Klan group sent a letter to Barletta saying they supported his efforts and telling him of their plans to hold a rally in Hazleton, which Barletta rejected, acting outraged that the Klan thought he would welcome them. Yet Dr. Agapito Lopez, a Hazleton resident and one of the most outspoken critics of the ordinance, testified in the federal trial that he had received hate mail saying, "We think you and Anna [his wife] ought to think twice before you speak." Another letter read, "if its [sic] brown, flush it down," next to a caricature of a Mexican men wearing a sombrero with the phrase "subhuman spic scum" written on it. My own review of various blog sites regarding the case turned up frequent racist and xenophobic comments, such as this one:

> I am hard pressed as to why any person in their sane mind would protest to the city of Hazletown [sic]. The illegals have no rights and should not have the ACLU [American Civil Liberties Union] protecting them and ACLU then writing off the expense for their taxes. Next if they wish they can take care of the bast**ds & not make me. The illegal not the legal are draining our country just like a knife to the throat drains the life out of a living animal. They need to be shot when caught the second time in our country, no ifs, ands, and buts. Jail is too good for them as that cost me even more. I am a Christian I think but even a Christian has to have some defense against any illegal thing or person. The best of good byes from Austin, TX and Frank Bowers (posted by frankbowers at 6:35 p.m., March 14, 2007).

In the name of Christianity, this blogger justifies murder for those who breach the borders of the nation.

There is not much distance between Bowers's dehumanization of immigrants and the characterization by Barletta and others in city hall of immigrants as criminals and even terrorists. Because they come from "outside the nation," they are perceived to operate outside the law and thus represent a threat to law-abiding citizens. In the Dobbs's town forum, Barletta said he was trying to "protect the people of Hazleton" from gangs and referred to the MS-13 gang, a Los Angeles–based Salvadoran gang. At a hearing on immigration in Philadelphia, he claimed that immigrants have "terrorized" the city, such that "Senior citizens are afraid to walk the street" (Rightwingwatch .org, July 14, 2006). The ordinance itself declares that "illegal immigration leads to higher crime rates." This claim was convincingly contested at the trial by Rubén Raumbaut, a sociologist from the University of California, Irvine, who showed that in the same period in which immigration has grown exponentially, crime rates in the United States have been decreasing: burglary rates have stabilized, in 2005 theft rates reached the lowest level ever recorded, and motor vehicle theft rates leveled off after 2000. In Hazleton, police records obtained by the ACLU show that undocumented immigrants were only involved in about twenty of the more than 8,500 crimes committed there since 2001; of the 428 "violent crimes" defined as such by the city, undocumented immigrants were responsible for less than five. During questioning by ACLU lawyer Witold Walczak at the trial on the ordinance's constitutionality, Barletta was forced to admit that he had no evidence of an immigrant crime wave: "When you have violent crimes committed, it takes away and chews at our quality of life. I don't need numbers. . . . The people in my city don't need numbers" (Rightwingwatch.org, March 16, 2007).

Even though Barletta rejected the KKK's support, there is an ideological overlap insofar as both entities are engaged in a construction of insiders and outsiders based on narrowly construed notions of citizenship and community belonging. For the KKK, of course, that means racial and religious hierarchies. The city of Hazleton insists that its ordinance is not based on race but rather on legal status. Yet at the town forum, Barletta was hard-pressed to explain how the legislation would not lead to racial profiling and discrimination against all people perceived to be "foreign," as happened to Agapito Lopez. Because of this discrimination, many Latinas/os have left Hazleton, making the effects similar to those endorsed by the KKK: an Anglo population in control because people of color are afraid to live in the town.

The ordinances allow for the mainstreaming of white supremacist views, a process facilitated by the Internet. As Abby Ferber, a scholar of the white supremacist movement, says:

> It is increasingly difficult to tell who is or is not a member of the movement. Indeed, traditional notions of "membership" are becoming outdated. The movement's goals of spreading white-supremacist ideology and encouraging violent acts designed to provoke a race war no longer require building groups with large membership rosters. With the Internet providing the primary means of communication and facilitating a sense of identity and community among previously isolated pockets of people around the world, it may be time to rethink what constitutes the "movement." (Ferber 2004: 7)

True to Ferber's assessment, the city ordinance movement, according to Mark Potok of the Southern Poverty Law Center, began when a San Bernardino, California, resident named Joseph Turner began a Save Our State (SOS) campaign, saying that his goal was to save California from turning into a "Third World cesspool of illegal immigrants." Turner failed to get enough signatures to force a vote in San Bernardino, but he persisted by advertising his plan on the radio and sending e-mails to city officials throughout the country. SOS rallies have attracted neo-Nazis, says Potok, and Turner has done nothing to turn them away. Barletta modeled his ordinance on Turner's.[9]

Furthermore, Turner was hired by FAIR; this group was founded in 1978 by John H. Tanton, who the SPLC identifies as the founder of the modern anti-immigration movement and the "puppeteer" behind thirteen anti-immigrant groups. Although FAIR disclaims any ties to white supremacist groups, the SPLC has documented numerous links. For example, FAIR received $1.2 million between 1985 and 1994 from the Pioneer Fund, which subsidizes studies of a so-called connection between race and intelligence, and it has worked with the racist Council of Conservative Citizens (Beirich n.d.). An SPLC investigation into Tanton's private papers, archived at the Bentley Historical Library at the University of Michigan, revealed quotes such as this one: "I've come to the point of view that for European-American society and culture to persist requires a European-American majority, and a clear one at that." The papers in the Bentley Library also show that Tanton has connections to Holocaust deniers and former Klan lawyers ("Intelligence Files" n.d.).

Population control becomes another way to sound the alarm about the loss of white control in the face of a growing Latino population, as Rajani Bhatia argues in her analysis of the nativist tendencies of environmental movements. Similar to the conservatives cited previously, nativists in the movement also speak of "culture" rather than "race" as the "primary category of division between people" (Bhatia 2004: 212); they critique "cultures" that they say are contributing to overpopulation of the planet. Despite differing in many ways from conservative politicians, their critique converges insofar as they position immigrant groups with high birthrates as a threat to the more restrained "native" population. Perhaps the most infamous example of this conservative position of late has been Harvard Professor Samuel Huntington, who says he is concerned about the large numbers of Latinos, especially their "high fertility rate." He describes the dangers Latinos represent to the Anglo-Protestant traditions that for him define this country: their refusal to assimilate, their retention of Spanish, and their physical closeness to Mexico. "Will the United States remain a country with a single national language and a core Anglo-Protestant culture? By ignoring this question, Americans acquiesce to their eventual transformation into two peoples with two cultures (Anglo and Hispanic) and two languages (English and Spanish)" (Huntington 2004).

Segments of the Christian right have joined forces with many anti-immigrant groups. According to the SPLC, a group called the Secure Border Coalition has formed, "where the religious right meets and meshes with the extreme end of anti-immigrant politics." It includes Phyllis Schlafly's Eagle Forum, Lou Sheldon's Traditional Values Coalition, Howard Phillips's Conservative Caucus, and Bishop Harry R. Jackson's Hope Christian Ministries. The right-wing political groups in the border coalition include English First, the American Council for Immigration Reform, the Center for Immigration Studies, and the Minutemen. In June 2006, the coalition issued a statement opposing all amnesty and guest-worker programs, vowing to oppose candidates who are soft on border security and calling for a near freeze on legal immigration.

Within the Secure Borders Coalition, alliances are being cemented. According to the SPLC, Chris Simcox, a Minuteman leader, put his contingent "under the wing of Alan Keyes' Declaration Alliance, a group dedicated to overturning *Roe v. Wade* that believes in a 'founding mandate to freely and publicly acknowledge the authority of the Creator God.'" And Schlafly's Eagle Forum featured Jim Gilchrist, another Minuteman leader, at the annual Eagle Forum Conference in 2006.[10] Schlafly has said the amnesty and guest-worker programs are "immoral" and argued in her newsletter that the Christian thing to do is "erect a fence and double our border agents in order to stop the drugs, the smuggling racket, the diseases, and the crimes" (quoted in Zaitchik 2006).

In these alliances, the borders between religion and the law are eroded. Belief in "God" is used as legitimation by groups who claim that the law is not being enforced and who see themselves as the necessary enforcers of a Christian nation. If the U.S. government cannot do an adequate job of policing the borders, they are happy to step in and do it themselves; the alliance between the Minutemen and the Eagle Forum represents a kind of Christian vigilantism aimed at purging the nation of "undesirable elements." Ultimately, it *is* the threat of the "brown-skinned hordes" that motivates the religious right; for them, brown people cannot assimilate, no more so than blacks can, no matter their cultural practices, because they are fundamentally and intrinsically strangers to the U.S. nation. Gary Bauer, president of the Christian fundamentalist group American Values, argued in an opinion piece in *USA Today* that "[h]yphenated Americans put other countries and affiliations first, and they drive a wedge into the heart of 'one nation'" (quoted in Zaitchik 2006). Thomas Fleming, president of the Rockford Institute, which has Christian inclinations, said at a 2006 institute conference (where Republican Sen. John Cornyn of Texas gave the keynote speech) that "the cultural ambience aspect of [the immigration debate] is the only one that interests me." In the Rockford Institute's magazine, he said, "Whatever we may say in public, most of us do not much like Mexicans, whom we regard as too irrational, too violent, too passionate" (quoted in Zaitchik 2006).

Who is the stranger among us? Who is "us"? Miguel Padilla was not a stranger to the Altoona community. "He's one of us," Catholic Archdiocese Bishop Joseph V. Ademac told the *New York Times* (quoted in Hamill 2006). "The one who did it, he came here when he was a boy and went to our schools. He didn't come here already formed." Ademac's is not just a message of inclusion; it goes beyond tolerance to question the effects of Christian intolerance. The violence, he suggests, belongs to the community where Padilla was raised and perhaps mistreated due to his status as Other. Bishop Ademac disarticulates the links between family, community, nation, and religion that undergird the anti-immigrant ordinances. Like others on the religious left, he calls for an expansive concept of community that undermines the very notion of "us" and "them" and questions the validity of a law that rests on that division.

The Strangers among Us

Jesus, according to some interpretations, was radically opposed to family values. He told his potential followers, "If anyone comes to me and does not hate his father and his mother, his wife and children, his brothers and sisters—yes, even his own life—he cannot be my disciple" (Luke 14:26). Slavoj Žižek interprets this passage as the essence of agape, which, as described by Saint Paul, is "the key intermediary term between faith and hope: it is love itself that enjoins us to 'unplug' from the organic community into which we were born" (Žižek 2000: 121). Agape requires us to forsake the easy kind of love that depends on predictable ties, like the familial and national allegiances invoked by the Christian right. Rather, says Žižek,

> As every true Christian knows, love is the *work* of love—the hard and arduous work of repeated "uncoupling," in which, again and again, we have to disengage from the inertia that constrains us to identify with the particular order we were born into. Through the Christian work of compassionate love, we discern in what was hitherto a disturbing foreign body, tolerated and even modestly supported by us so that we were not too bothered by it, a subject, with its crushed dreams and desires—it is *this* Christian heritage of "uncoupling" that is threatened by today's "fundamentalisms," especially when they proclaim themselves Christians. (Žižek 2000: 129)

"Uncoupling" requires one to work against the tendency to premise community on family and familiarity and rather demands that one see in each needy person a subject like any other, one with "crushed dreams and desires." This project requires as well an uncoupling from the law, which, as do the ordinances, works to maintain homogeneity in the name of "order." In keeping with this notion of agape, the Altoona diocese has decided to not to recognize the authority of the anti-immigrant ordinance, which criminalizes social-service assistance to undocumented people. Father Robertson of Altoona argues that at times the law needs to be disregarded:

> The Catholic Charity policy is to serve people regardless of who they are or where they come from. . . . [O]bviously, we can't have a governmental body telling us what to do. This isn't just a legal question. It's also a spiritual issue. The Gospel mandate to help the poor is not negotiable just because the state says we can't do it. The church needs to be on the side of the poor. I don't care if they're documented or undocumented.

He invokes the history of church opposition to slavery and racism despite their governmental sanction: "When the church finds itself to be in conflict with the state, sooner or later you're going to find yourself in conflict with the law. When people [in the parish] ask us 'Are you telling us to disobey the law?' I say yes, some laws are unjust and we've got to oppose them."

The Altoona church's response is consistent with other Catholic dioceses, including Los Angeles, where Cardinal Roger Mahony has been a strong proponent of immigrant rights. In 2006, Mahony said he would instruct priests and others working in the Archdiocese of Los Angeles to disregard provisions of House bill 4437, which criminalized humanitarian assistance to undocumented persons. Mahony's call is credited with helping spark the formation of a New Sanctuary Movement, the coalition of faith-based groups that began meeting in January 2007 to advocate for immigrant rights.[11]

These religious dissidents not only present an alternative to Christian fundamentalism but also to the discourse of inclusion that characterizes liberal support for immigration reform. For example, in his speech in El Paso, Texas, in May 2011, President Obama began by celebrating the United States as a "nation of immigrants." He then argued that one of the primary reasons for immigration reform is to benefit the middle class:

> So one way to strengthen the middle class in America is to reform the immigration system so that there is no longer a massive underground economy that exploits a cheap source of labor while depressing wages for everybody else. I want incomes for middle-class families to rise again. I want prosperity in this country to be widely shared. I want everybody to be able to reach that American dream. And that's why immigration reform is an economic imperative.[12]

Obama thus appeals to Latinos on the basis of their inclusion in a multicultural United States while also managing the anxieties of a wider audience whose primary concern is their own economic well-being. The Latino immigrant is welcomed and managed through the intertwined discourses of diversity and legalization, the latter of which is offered by a benevolent government. As Wendy Brown argues, "tolerance is a practice for managing a dangerous, foreign, or exotic difference that also demands its incorporation, thus sustaining the threatening entity . . . what is tolerated remains distinct even as it is incorporated" (W. Brown 2005: 27–28). .

In a more radical articulation, the religious left undermines the notion of liberal tolerance in which the dominant, nationally homogenous "us" welcomes the multicultural stranger as Other. In this view, Jesus deconstructs the very categories of native and stranger, for in his parable about giving food to the hungry, water to the thirsty, clothing to the naked, and generally welcoming the stranger, it turns out that *he* is the stranger, already living among the people. On Judgment Day, goes the story, Jesus will welcome all those gathered on his right hand into the Kingdom of God, for, as he tells them, when he was hungry, thirsty, naked, and in prison, they cared for him. These people, however, are surprised by Jesus' words:

> Lord, when was it that we saw you hungry and gave you food, or thirsty and gave you something to drink? And when was it that we saw you a stranger and welcomed you, or naked and gave you clothing? And when was it that we saw you sick or in prison and visited you? And the king will answer them, "Truly I tell you, just as you did it to one of the least of these who are members of my family, you did it to me." (Matthew 25:37–40)

Those on Jesus' left hand are not so fortunate, for they rejected the stranger, not realizing that the stranger was actually Jesus himself. In damning them to hell, Jesus admonishes, "Truly I tell you, just as you did not do it to one of the least of these, you did not do it to me" (Matthew 24:45). In a masterful move, Jesus illustrates not only the predictable point about how power operates to preserve privilege when it excludes the Other but also the less obvious point about how helping the Other usually includes an ulterior motive (such as securing cheap labor, which relies on the retention of the Other as included Other, or simply appearing tolerant because of one's inclusive politics). That's why those who helped the stranger without knowing he/she was Jesus are deserving of salvation. Thus the Gospel represents a third option—neither rejection nor inclusion on the basis of difference—but one in which the humble are rewarded simply for being generous without regard to material gain or recognition. Their reward is to live in a world where the notion of "stranger" does not exist.

That is not this world, however, and religious activists have also addressed current material realities shaping immigration. They are not afraid to point to the root causes of immigration, critique the U.S. government for its economic greed and political corruption, and defend the rights of people to migrate for survival over the need to police national borders. As an example of this, I turn to a document produced at a conference of Catholic bishops from the United States and Mexico, "Strangers No Longer: Together on the Journey of Hope." The document is a call to action; in it, the bishops express their concern that "civil and church structures" are not meeting the needs of the migrant community and that responding to this lack is imperative: "We judge ourselves as a community of faith by the way we treat the most vulnerable among us. . . . We invite Catholics and persons of good will in both nations to exercise their faith and to use their resources and gifts to truly welcome the stranger among us" (U.S. Conference of Catholic Bishops 2003: 2).

The bishops acknowledge a common history of migration that defines the Americas. They also point to a "common faith in Jesus Christ" that "moves us to search for ways that favor a spirit of solidarity," suggesting, unlike Samuel Huntington, that they are not invested in fostering Protestant-Catholic divisions. Though they exclude other faiths in their invocation of Jesus, they appeal to all "persons of good will," suggesting a lack of judgment about faiths. Unlike those who use this common immigrant history to judge newcomers who don't immediately succeed, the bishops point to the differences in power that shaped colonization, genocide, and slavery and that continue to shape immigration today, producing discrepancies that force Mexicans to migrate for economic survival. The way to resolve the "immigration debate" is to address these economic disparities—then Mexicans may not want to come to the United States: "Catholic teaching also states that the root causes of migration—poverty, injustice, religious intolerance, armed conflicts—must be addressed so that migrants can remain in their homeland and support their families" (U.S. Conference of Catholic Bishops 2003: 4).

Specific causes of some of these injustices are named. For example, the bishops point out the contradiction in government policy that calls, on the one hand, for free trade and, on the other hand, for barriers to the movement of people. They name the North American Free Trade Agreement (NAFTA) as an example of the failure of these policies, saying that it has "harmed small businesses in Mexico," prompting people to have to seek jobs across the border. The bishops recognize that many Mexicans do not want to leave their country, thus dismantling the myth of the United States as a land of opportunity. In so doing, they offer a more complex notion of migration—not as a free choice for which one must then bear the responsibility for "breaking the law" but rather as a limited choice shaped by economic and political reasons that are beyond any one individual's control.

Given their role in producing these economic disparities, the United States has a particular obligation to welcome immigrants, an obligation that transcends the need to protect national borders. While recognizing the right of nations to control their borders, the bishops quote an encyclical by Pope Pius XII to argue that "this right is not absolute," since "the needs of immigrants must be measured against the needs of the receiving countries" (U.S. Conference of Catholic Bishops 2003: 5). In the case of the United States and Mexico, the receiving country, being the wealthier one, has the moral duty: "The Church recognizes the right of sovereign nations to control their territories but rejects such control when it is exerted merely for the purpose of acquiring additional wealth. More powerful economic nations, which have the ability to protect and feed their residents, have a stronger obligation to accommodate migration flows" (U.S. Conference of Catholic Bishops 2003: 5). Thus the bishops also provide an answer to the debates about whether immigrants hurt the economy, suggesting the U.S. economy can and should integrate migrant workers, and that if it can open its borders in the interest of free trade and material gain, it can also open its borders in the interest of helping the people harmed by those free-trade policies.

If people cannot feed themselves and their families in their homelands, they have a right to migrate, say the bishops, providing a radical justification for breaking national law that is based on Jesus' life: "Catholic teaching has a long and rich tradition in defending the right to migrate. Based on the life and teachings of Jesus, the Church's teaching has provided the basis for the development of basic principles regarding the right to migrate for those attempting to exercise their God-given human rights" (U.S. Conference of Catholic Bishops 2003: 4).

The bishops' definition of community transcends the narrow borders of nationalism; to belong to "God's household" is to belong to a diasporic community. They reject xenophobia as the basis of community: welcoming the stranger, making him/her part of the community, leads to a "conversion of mind and heart" and a "renewed spirit of communion" that helps "confront attitudes of cultural superiority, indifference, and racism; accepting migrants not as foreboding aliens, terrorists, or economic threats, but rather as persons with dignity and rights, revealing the presence of Christ; and recognizing migrants as bearers of deep cultural values and faith traditions" (U.S. Conference of Catholic Bishops 2003: 6). In other words, the values that generally get associated with the "Heartland," such as hard work, family, and faith, are actually not inherently conservative or white; rather, they are carried with various peoples across borders as they constitute and reconstitute places to call home.

Notes

1. Both the Clinton and McCain campaigns called Obama's comments elitist. Obama apologized for his choice of words but stuck by his assertion that people are bitter and have a right to be frustrated about the economy. Obama quotes taken from Foxnews.com, Friday, April 11, 2008.

2. Perhaps the most infamous of these laws, SB 1070 in Arizona, passed in April 2010, made the failure to carry immigration documents a crime and gave the police broad power to detain anyone suspected of being in the country illegally. An Arizona federal district court and the U.S. Ninth Circuit Court of Appeals ruled that certain provisions of Arizona's law usurp federal immigration enforcement efforts.

In June 2012, the U.S. Supreme Court struck down three major aspects of Arizona's immigrant law, but it upheld the fourth, which requires police officers to review the immigration status of any detainee they suspect of being in the United States illegally.

3. In July 2007, the Hazleton ordinance was declared unconstitutional in federal court. The lawsuit was brought on behalf of Hazleton residents, landlords, and business owners by the American Civil Liberties Union (ACLU), the ACLU of Pennsylvania, the Puerto Rican Legal Defense and Education Fund, the Community Justice Project, and the law firm of Cozen O'Connor. In issuing his opinion, Judge James M. Munley wrote: "We cannot say clearly enough that persons who enter this country without legal authorization are not stripped immediately of all their rights because of this single act. . . . The United States Supreme Court has consistently interpreted [the Fourteenth Amendment] to apply to all people present in the United States, whether they were born here, immigrated here through legal means, or violated federal law to enter the country" (http://www.aclu.org). In 2008, the city of Hazleton lost their appeal of Judge Munley's ruling when it was upheld by the Third Circuit Court of Appeals in 2010. However, a 2011 U.S. Supreme Court ruling vacated the circuit court's ruling, and the case as of October 2012 was back in the Third Circuit Court for another hearing

4. These comments were made on the Family Research Council's Washington Watch Weekly Radio show on June 9, 2007.

5. See the New Sanctuary Movement Web site, http://www.newsanctuarymovement.org.

6. Information gathered during a personal interview on March 2, 2007.

7. "A Pennsylvania Resident Says a Mexican Alien Has Terrorized Her Community," VDARE.com, December 4, 2006, http://www.vdare.com/letters/a-pennsylvania-reader-says-a-mexican-alien-has-terrorized-her-community (September 26, 2012).

8. For this history, I am indebted to Kevin Zalanowski, author of the unpublished manuscript "Altoona, Pennsylvania: An Ethnic Study from 1880–1920."

9. Personal interview with Potok, May 7, 2007.

10. The Minutemen have been riven by internal conflict; Gilchrist's contingent did not join the Secure Borders Coalition.

11. The movement locates itself in the tradition of the Sanctuary Movement of the 1980s, which focused on Central American refugees fleeing political persecution and denied asylum in the United States.

12. The full text of the speech is available from the White House Press Office at http://www.whitehouse.gov/the-press-office/2011/05/10/remarks-president-comprehensive-immigration-reform-el-paso-texas (accessed November 8, 2012).

Works Cited

American Civil Liberties Union. 2007. "Federal Trial over Hazleton, PA's Anti-Immigrant Ordinances Concludes." March 22. http://www.aclu.org/immigrants-rights/federal-trial-over-hazleton-pa%E2%80%99s-anti-immigrant-ordinances-concludes (November 8, 2012).

Beirich, Heidi. n.d. "The Anti-Immigrant Movement." Southern Poverty Law Center. http://www.splcenter.org/get-informed/intelligence-files/ideology/anti-immigrant/the-anti-immigrant-movement (accessed November 8, 2012).

Bhatia, Rajani. 2004. "Green or Brown? White Nativist Environmental Movements." In *Home-Grown Hate: Gender and Organized Racism,* ed. Abby L. Ferber, 205–26. New York: Routledge.

Brown, David M. 2006. "Pa. Pool Finds Support for Local Immigration Laws." *Pittsburgh Tribune-Review,* October 23.

Brown, Wendy. 2005. *States of Injury.* New Brunswick, N.J.: Princeton University Press.

Ferber, Abby L. 2004. "Introduction." In *Home-Grown Hate: Gender and Organized Racism,* ed. Abby L. Ferber, 1–18. New York: Routledge.

Flint, Colin. 2004. "United States Hegemony and the Construction of Racial Hatreds: The Agency of Hate Groups and the Changing World Political Map." In *Spaces of Hate: Geographies of Discrimination and Intolerance in the U.S.A.,* ed. Colin Flint, 165–82. New York: Routledge.

Gallaher, Carolyn. 2004. "Mainstreaming the Militia." In *Spaces of Hate: Geographies of Discrimination and Intolerance in the U.S.A.,* ed. Colin Flint, 183–208. New York: Routledge.

Hamill, Sean D. 2006. "Altoona, with No Immigrant Problem, Decides to Solve It." *New York Times,* December 7.

Holthouse, David. 2009. "926 Hate Groups Active in 2008: Number of Hate Groups Tops 900." Intelligence Report, Southern Poverty Law Center. http://www.splcenter.org/get-informed/intelligence-report/browse-all-issues/2009/spring/the-year-in-hate (accessed November 8, 2012).

Huntington, Samuel P. 2004. "The Hispanic Challenge." *Foreign Policy,* March 1. http://www.foreignpolicy.com/articles/2004/03/01/the_hispanic__challenge (accessed September 26, 2012).

"Intelligence Files: John Tanton." n.d. Southern Poverty Law Center. http://www.splcenter.org/get-informed/intelligence-files/profiles/john-tanton (accessed November 8, 2012).

Jenkins, Philip. 1997. *Hoods and Shirts: The Extreme Right in Pennsylvania, 1925–1950.* Chapel Hill: University of North Carolina Press.

Joseph, Miranda. 2002. *Against the Romance of Community.* Minneapolis: University of Minnesota Press.

Lochhead, Carolyn. 2006. "Immigration Debate Splits Christian Right." *San Francisco Chronicle,* April 28, A1.

New Oxford Annotated Bible. 2010. Michael D. Coogan, ed. Oxford: Oxford University Press.

Rumbaut, Rubén G. 2007. "Report on the City of Hazleton's Premise, in the Illegal Immigration Relief Act Ordinance, that Illegal Immigrants Contribute to Higher Crime Rates." Unpublished document presented at federal court hearing, March.

U.S. Conference of Catholic Bishops. 2003. "Strangers No Longer: Together on the Journey of Hope." "A Pastoral Letter Concerning Migration from the

Catholic Bishops of Mexico and the United States, United States Conference of Catholic Bishops," January 22. http://www.usccb.org/issues-and-action/human-life-and-dignity/immigration/strangers-no-longer-together-on-the-journey-of-hope.cfm (accessed September 26, 2012).

Zaitchik, Alexander. 2006. "Family Research Council Poll Shows Many Conservative Christians Hardlined against Illegal Immigration." *Southern Poverty Law Center Intelligence Report* no. 124 (Winter). http://www.splcenter.org/get-informed/intelligence-report/browse-all-issues/2006/winter/christian-nativism (accessed November 8, 2012).

Zalanowski, Kevin. 2001. "Altoona, Pennsylvania: An Ethnic Study from 1880–1920." Unpublished paper, Schreyer Honors College, Pennsylvania State University.

Žižek, Slavoj. 2000. *The Fragile Absolute, or Why Is the Christian Legacy Worth Fighting For?* London: Verso.

PART VI

Demographics

CHAPTER 11

Latin American Migrations to the U.S. Heartland

Demographic and Economic Activity in Six Heartland States, 2000–2007

SCOTT CARTER

Introduction

Latin American migrations away from traditional growth states to regions such as the U.S. Heartland have been dubbed "new destinations" (Zúñiga and Hernández-León 2005). The forces, both demographic and economic, behind this most recent of immigrations is an amalgam involving local communities in vastly different parts of the world being thrust together by the forces of globalization. The problem is quite complex, and no answer can be postulated without a deep understanding of the various inter- and intraconnections between the movement of people in one direction and a movement of capital in the other (Kwong 1997; Sassen 1988, 1995). Certainly since the passage of the North American Free Trade Agreement (NAFTA) and the opening of commodity trade and capital flows (*not* labor flows) between the United States, Canada, and Mexico, the United States especially has seen an influx of undocumented immigrants displaced by the importation of cheaper U.S.-produced agricultural commodities into Mexico. The local market for the goods produced by many people in rural Mexico and Central America (and all over the world) simply evaporated once the effects of NAFTA began to make themselves felt throughout the countryside.

At the same time, communities in the United States were also becoming victims to the winds of globalization. Factories in local communities closed down and were either relocated to countries such as Mexico and other localities or their former function was contracted out to the low-cost manufacturing mecca of China. The power of labor unions had for many years been crushed in the reforms of the Ronald Reagan–Margaret Thatcher era in the early 1980s, and in recent years, many working- and middle-class Americans began to see the "good life" erode before their eyes. Such is the context of the recent Latin American migrations. Displaced peoples from rural communities with little history of migration northward came to regions of the United States in search of work to what in many ways were displaced American communities, displaced in the context that what had been the norm only a few years earlier was now gone.

This chapter presents empirical evidence on the demographic and economic impact of Latin American migrations to the six core Heartland states of Arkansas (AR), Iowa (IA), Kansas (KS), Missouri (MO), Nebraska (NE), and Oklahoma (OK); hereafter referred to collectively as the Heartland 6 (HL6). The findings presented here are consistent with literature on the recent immigrations: although remaining small in terms of the actual number of Hispanics in these states, the rates of growth especially of the foreign-born component are both relatively high and on an upward trajectory from 2000 to 2007. Put simply, the Heartland has become increasingly a "new destination" for Latin American migrations.

Presenting these findings in some detail is the purpose of the present chapter, which is broken down into a demographic section and an economic section. In the initial demographic portion, the performance of the HL6 will be compared against that of the traditional growth states vis-à-vis Latin American migrations, specifically those of California (CA), Florida (FL), Illinois (IL), New Jersey (NJ), New York (NY), and Texas (TX), hereafter referred to collectively as the traditional growth 6 (TG6). This allows for a broader understanding of recent movements in Latin American migrations by comparison of the respective growth rates and other indicators of these two state clusters. The subsequent economic portion of the essay will concentrate in the main on labor-market indicators, per capita income measures, and income distribution in the face of the demographic flows presented. Here, especially, the impact of gender will be explicit.

Demographic Analysis

The data used in this study comes from three separate U.S. government sources. The most highly used data comes from the U.S Census American Community Survey (ACS) Annual Supplements. This data contains a large number of demographic and economic variables broken down according to ethnicity and citizenship status for each state. Note that the undocumented are *not* specifically singled out for measurement, although according to Passel (2006) the lion's share of the undocumented is captured in noncitizen foreign-born measures. Also used in this study are rates of unemployment and labor force participation rates from the Bureau of Labor Statistics (BLS), which again are broken down according to ethnicity, although with nowhere near the detail of the ACS. Last, state economic-growth indicators and the sectoral classification schema according to the North American Industry Classification System (NAICS) at the two-digit level are utilized from the Bureau of Economic Analysis (BEA).

The time span of this study covers the years 2000 through 2007. It is important to note that concerned here are the patterns evident prior to the recession of 2008. The overall impact of the 2008 recession on Latin American migrations to the Heartland remains to be studied, but whatever the eventual trajectory that emerges out of the current crisis, it will have its departure point the patterns resultant from the first seven years of the twenty-first century.

The basic data used in the demographic portion of this study are the respective state, region, and national tallies of (i) the total population, (ii) the Hispanic population, and (iii) the foreign-born portion of the Hispanic population, which we define as follows:

$(N_i)_t$ = Total (non-Hispanic plus Hispanic) population in
  region i in year t

$(N_i^h)_t$ = Total Hispanic population in region i in year t

$(N_i^{FBh})_t$ = Total foreign-born Hispanic population in region i in year t

Each of these measures are subsets of the other; thus the total population $(N_i)_t$ is the sum of the total non-Hispanic population plus the total Hispanic population $(N_i^h)_t$. The total Hispanic population $(N_i^h)_t$ is itself the sum of the non-foreign-born and the foreign-born Hispanics $(N_i^{FBh})_t$. Non-foreign-born Hispanics are of course U.S. citizens ("natives"). The foreign-born comprise naturalized citizens as well as nonnaturalized immigrants, the latter referred to in this study as *non-U.S. citizen Hispanics*. The non-U.S. citizen Hispanic population can be further broken down into documented ("legal") and undocumented ("illegal"); thus it is from this pool of the population that estimates of the undocumented emanate (see Passel 2006). The noncitizen foreign-born Hispanic population represents the wave of recent arrivals. As indicated, it is from this pool that the undocumented belong. Passel (2006) estimates that 87 percent of the undocumented are accounted for in this reported population. This means that there is on average a 13 percent undercounting in the official census of the foreign-born. To ascertain the diffusion of Hispanics throughout the United States as a whole in comparison to the diffusion of the total population as a whole, figures 11.1 and 11.2

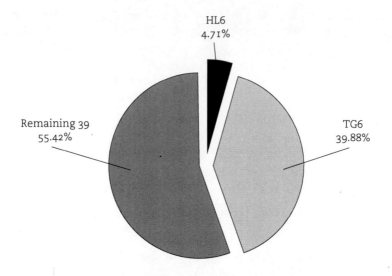

Figure 11.1. Concentration of total population, average for 2000–2007

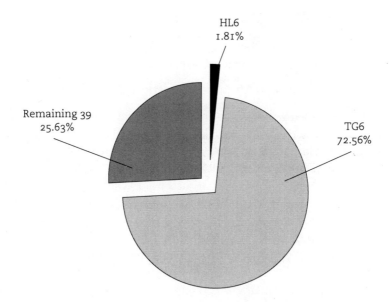

Figure 11.2. Concentration of Hispanic population, average for 2000–2007

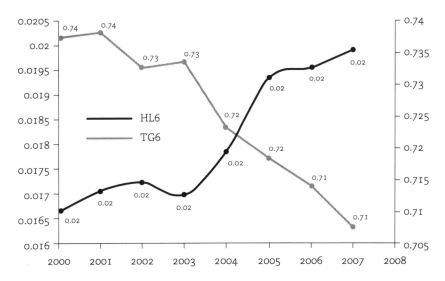

Figure 11.3. Trajectory of Hispanic concentration in HL6 and TG6 (ACS)

show the relative concentrations in these data of the respective populations in the HL6, the TG6, and the remaining thirty-nine states for the average years 2000–2007.

The pie charts express the percentages in each state cluster that constitute both the total population and the Hispanic population. Comparing the two pie charts shows that the HL6 states make up a much smaller percentage of both the total population and the Hispanic population, although relatively fewer Hispanics appear in the HL6. Also seen from this comparison is the fact that Hispanics overwhelmingly populate the TG6 states as compared to the total. Turning to the Hispanic population, presence in the HL6 remains the relatively small portion of only 1.81 percent of all the Hispanics nationwide. The vast majority reside in the TG6 states (72.56 percent), with the remaining thirty-nine states accounting for the difference (25.63 percent). To see the trend in the rate of growth, consider the trajectory of the concentration of Hispanics for the HL6 and the TG6, depicted in figure 11.3:

From figure 11.3 it can be seen that the change in the Hispanic concentration in the HL6 increased from 1.67 percent in 2000 to 1.99 percent in 2007, a percent change of positive 19.55 percent and that of the TG6 for the same years decreased from 73.74 percent in 2000 to 70.75 percent in 2007, a percent change of negative 4.05 percent. This reveals that although constituting less than 2 percent of the total Hispanic population, the rates at which the Hispanic presence grew in the HL6 dwarf those of the other regions. Appendix B considers in more detail the percentage of Hispanics out of the total populations of the United States as a whole (USA) and in the two state clusters (TG6 and HL6).

Foreign-Born

It is useful to consider the extent to which the Hispanic population are foreign-born as well as the portion of those that remain noncitizens, the latter portion being a proxy for more recent migrations. To express these relations, three specific population shares are constructed and presented. The first is the share of Hispanics in each state cluster and nationwide as a percentage of the total population per state cluster. These data are referred to as the *inter-share* of Hispanics to the total population and are denoted by the Greek letter *eta* (η) defined for region i as:

$$\eta_i = \frac{(N_i^h)}{(N_i)} = \left(\frac{\text{total Hispanic population}}{\text{total population}} \right)_{\text{region } i} \tag{1}$$

The inter-share in equation (1) shows the ratio of Hispanics to the total population in the region. It is dubbed "inter" to denote the fact that it relates the Hispanic population to that of the total (Hispanic plus non-Hispanic) population per region.

But there is another measure that warrants consideration, namely the relationship among Hispanics only. This measure is referred to as the *intra-share* of Hispanics, two of which are calculated for the present study. The first is the intra-share of foreign-born Hispanics to total Hispanics and the second is the intra-share of noncitizen foreign-born Hispanics to that of the foreign-born. These ratios are defined for region i as follows:

$$\eta_i^h = \frac{(N^{FBh})}{(N_i^h)} = \left(\frac{\text{total foreign-born Hispanic population}}{\text{total Hispanic population}} \right)_{\text{region } i} \tag{2.1}$$

$$\eta_i^{FBh} = \frac{(N^{\text{noncitizen } FBh})}{(N_i^{FBh})} = \left(\frac{\text{total noncitizen foreign-born Hispanic population}}{\text{total foreign-born Hispanic population}} \right)_{\text{region } i} \tag{2.2}$$

The intra-share in ratio (2.1) shows the concentration of foreign-born Hispanics to the total Hispanic population per region, and ratio (2.2) shows the concentration of noncitizen foreign-born Hispanics to the total foreign-born population of Hispanics. Both of these intra-measures are proxies of the relative concentration of recent immigration. They are dubbed "intra" to denote the fact that they relate different elements of the Hispanic popu-

Table 11.1. Relative population shares (ACS): average 2000–2007 (%)

	(1) $\eta_i = \dfrac{(N_i^h)}{(N_i)}$	(2) $\eta_i^h = \dfrac{(N^{FBh})}{(N_i^h)}$	(3) $\eta_i^{FBh} = \dfrac{(N^{noncitizen\,FBh})}{(N_i^{FBh})}$
USA	13.99	42.42	70.68
HL6	4.97	39.04	78.07
KS	7.27	33.03	79.16
NE	6.57	39.61	77.67
OK	6.10	40.00	79.87
AR	4.05	50.66	85.69
IA	3.39	36.61	77.40
MO	2.43	34.38	68.63
TG6	22.12	47.46	66.35
CA	34.66	42.20	72.28
TX	34.59	32.76	75.03
FL	18.86	61.94	58.74
NY	16.03	52.00	58.80
NJ	14.74	50.40	62.06
IL	13.86	45.45	71.19

lation among themselves. Table 11.1 shows averages of the three ratios for the regions relevant to the present study, sorted by descending values of the relative inter-shares (column 1):

The first column of table 11.1 reproduces for the 2000–2007 average period. The relative size of the Hispanic population in the HL6 is small in terms of the total population of those regions as evidenced by the inter-share in column (1). Each of the HL6 states falls far below the national average of 13.99 percent. The converse is true of the TG6, where, except for Illinois, each state in this cluster evidences a Hispanic population greater than the national average. The Hispanic presence in the Heartland 6 is still dwarfed by that of the traditional growth states; this is the small slice out of the national pie shown in figure 11.2. The 2000–2007 average inter-share population ratios are depicted in figure 11.4:

As can be discerned from figure 11.3, the Hispanic population in the HL6 states remains relatively small in comparison to the TG6 and the national average. Consider next the intra-share ratio of foreign-born Hispanics to the total Hispanic population per state and region shown in column 2 of table 11.1. These data are depicted in figure 11.5:

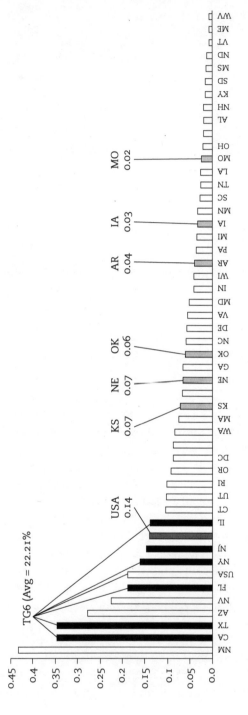

Figure 11.4. Relative inter-shares of Hispanics to the total population in each state (2000–2007 average; ACS data)

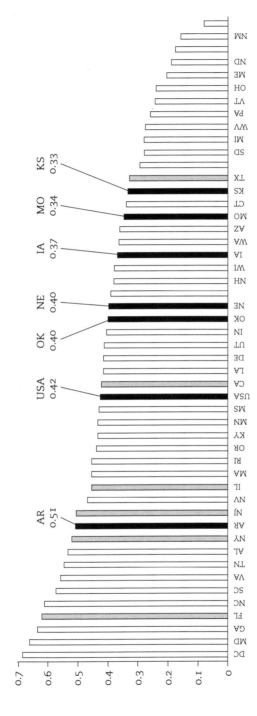

Figure 11.5. Relative intra-shares of foreign-born Hispanics to the total Hispanic population in each state (2000–2007 average; ACS data)

Figure 11.5 shows that on average (2000–2007) 42.42 percent of all His-panics in the United States are foreign-born. Of that, the HL6 states except Arkansas still lag behind the national average, whereas only California and Texas from the TG6 lag behind the national average.

Considering the third intra-share measure, specifically the intra-share of the noncitizen foreign-born Hispanics to total foreign-born Hispanics shown in column 3 of table 11.1, the results are striking, as seen in figure 11.6: Here five of the HL6 states have a noncitizen foreign-born intra-ratio greater than both the national average as well as the TG6. This is taken as evidence of increased immigration by noncitizen Hispanics away from tra-ditional growth states to the Heartland, the Southeast, and the Northwest. Figure 11.5 in a very simple manner posits the main thesis that the recent Latin American migrations to the U.S. Heartland consist in the main of the noncitizen foreign-born.

Convergence Analysis

It is of interest to consider the patterns in Hispanic presence for the HL6 as a whole. Here we engage in what is referred to as *convergence analysis*. The basic premise of convergence analysis is to measure the extent to which the Hispanic presence in the six Heartland states becomes increasingly similar. Thus as the percentages of Latinos among and between the different states begin to become more similar, we would say that this presence is *converging* among those states. There are two basic methods used to ascertain whether convergence would occur. The first involves a ratio (fraction) of what in statistics are called the first two *moments of a distribution*. These two mo-ments are (i) the mean, or average value of the data series, and (ii) that data series' standard deviation. The first moment measures the center of gravity of the data and the second measures the dispersion about that center. The smaller the standard deviation, the closer is each statistic to its mean value (and thus the "thinner the tail"). The ratio of convergence, called the *coef-ficient of variation* (cv), is simply the fraction of the standard deviation (σ) to the mean (μ):

$$cv = \frac{\text{standard deviation of a data series}}{\text{mean of that data series}} = \frac{\sigma}{\mu} \tag{3}$$

If the coefficient of variation decreases over time, then that is an indication that the dispersion of the series relative to its mean is decreasing. And with decreased dispersion we have a situation in which the data series become increasingly convergent: a decreased coefficient of variation is an indication

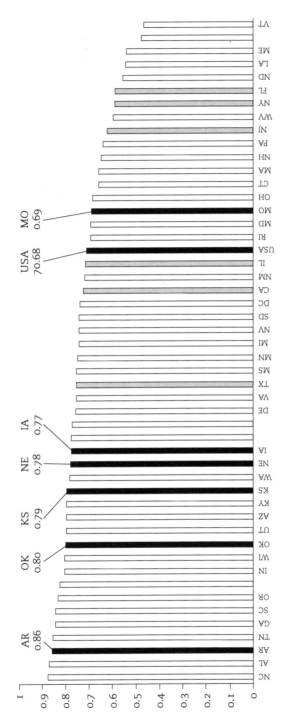

Figure 11.6. Relative intra-shares of noncitizen foreign-born Hispanic population in each state (2000–2007 average; ACS data)

of convergence in the data series considered. In figure 11.7, we show the coefficient of variation for the percentage of Latinos in each state's annual population.

From figure 11.7 we clearly see that there is convergence in the percentage of Latinos in each of the states under consideration, which becomes especially pronounced after 2003. This is taken as an indication that the patterns of Latino presence are becoming increasingly similar for these states, an observation that seems consistent with much of the literature on Latino migration to the "new destinations" (Durand, Massey, and Capoferro 2005; Bump, Lowell, and Pettersen 2005).

This method of measuring convergence is referred to as *sigma convergence,* named after the Greek letter sigma (σ) that is commonly used in statistics to refer to standard deviation, as in equation (3). A second method commonly used to ascertain convergence is referred to as *beta convergence,* so named after the "beta" coefficient of a simple regression equation. To ascertain this measure of convergence, the initial value of a data series—in this case Latino percentage of the population in the year 2000—is regressed against the growth rate of that series for the entirety of the years in question. The basic regression equation would look something like the following:

$$(\% \text{ Latinos in population})_{2000} = \alpha + \beta \text{ (average growth rate of \% of Latinos in population)} + \varepsilon \qquad (4)$$

The key here is the sign of the beta coefficient: a negative sign would mean that *larger* percentages of Latinos in the population in the year 2000

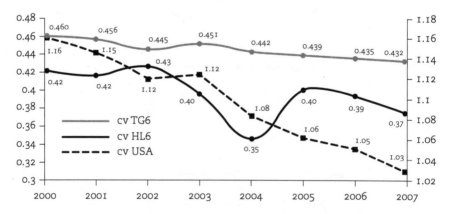

Figure 11.7. Coefficient of variation in percentage of Hispanics from three regions

are associated with *smaller* rates of growth in that variable: thus what were initially large differences in the initial year between Latino percentages of population become increasingly smaller as time moves forward, that is to say the series converge. Figure 11.8 shows beta convergence in percentages of Latinos in the population:

To better see these trends in convergent Latino/Hispanic demographics for the region in question, consider the Theil diversity index. This index belongs to the general category of measurements of "evenness" of the spatial segregation among various groups (McKibben and Faust 2004: 118). The particular form of the index employed is that found in Durand, Massey, and Capoferro (2005: 4) given by the following equation:

$$E = \frac{-\sum_{i=1}^{n} p_i \ln(p_i)}{\ln (n)} \times 100 \tag{5}$$

where p_i = percentage of the Latino/Hispanic population in state i and n = number of states, which in this case is six (thus the denominator is the natural log of 6 = 1.792). The index is bounded by a minimum value of zero and a maximum value of 100, where "minimum diversity occurs when all people are concentrated in one category and maximum diversity occurs when each category contains exactly the same number of people" (Durand, Massey, and Capoferro 2005: 4). Table 11.2 contains the percentage of Latinos/Hispanics out of the total for the ten midwestern states under consideration:

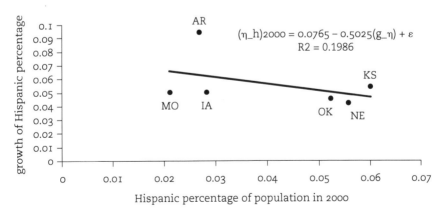

Figure 11.8. Beta convergence in percentage of Hispanic population in HL6, 2000–2007

Table 11.2. Latino/Hispanic population as a percentage of HL6 (MW 10)

	2000	2001	2002	2003	2004	2005	2006	2007
AR	10.10%	12.02%	12.10%	12.50%	13.61%	13.27%	13.51%	13.59%
IA	11.60%	11.25%	11.45%	11.27%	12.12%	11.09%	11.04%	11.10%
KS	22.74%	23.66%	24.11%	22.66%	18.62%	23.44%	23.09%	22.52%
MO	16.69%	15.54%	14.76%	15.90%	16.64%	15.58%	15.72%	16.40%
NE	13.47%	13.03%	13.30%	13.33%	13.69%	12.81%	12.72%	12.29%
OK	25.41%	24.51%	24.27%	24.34%	25.33%	23.81%	23.92%	24.10%
Total HL6	100.00%	100.00%	100.00%	100.00%	100.00%	100.00%	100.00%	100.00%
Theil Diversity Index	96.84	97.16	97.17	97.52	98.15	97.48	97.53	97.56

Source: Census Bureau American Community Survey.

Shown in the bottom row is the calculated Theil diversity index, also re-produced visually in figure 11.9:

As can be seen from the table and graph, the Hispanic diversity remained relatively high throughout the region as a whole, increasing up to 2004 and then tapering off and returning to the 2003 level.

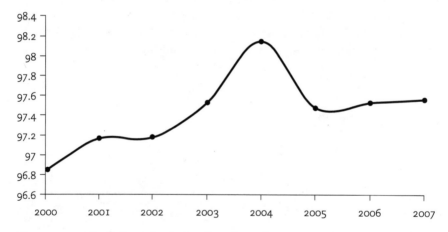

Figure 11.9. Theil diversity index for Hispanic presence in HL6

National Level

Table 11.3 shows the average inter-share Hispanic population ratio depicted in figure 11.3 as well as the average growth rate of this ratio for each state. This particular table sorts in descending order the average percentage.

Table 11.3. Average percentage of Hispanics per state and corresponding average rate of growth sorted by percent

State	Average percentage	Growth rate of percentage	State	Average percentage	Growth rate of percentage
USA	13.99%	4.56%	NC	4.73%	5.71%
NM	42.21%	0.72%	VA	4.52%	5.18%
TG6: CA	32.60%	1.49%	MD	4.33%	5.40%
TG6: TX	32.26%	1.56%	IN	3.56%	4.65%
AZ	25.32%	2.27%	WI	3.53%	4.46%
NV	19.83%	3.38%	MI	3.19%	3.15%
CO	17.13%	2.12%	PA	3.14%	5.00%
TG6: FL	16.88%	2.83%	HL6: IA	2.82%	5.01%
TG6: NY	15.10%	1.15%	HL6: AR	2.67%	9.45%
TG6: NJ	13.36%	2.50%	MN	2.63%	5.80%
TG6: IL	12.49%	2.54%	LA	2.34%	4.13%
CT	9.41%	2.89%	SC	2.34%	6.81%
UT	9.01%	3.60%	TN	2.25%	6.07%
RI	8.76%	3.57%	HL6: MO	2.11%	5.07%
DC	8.12%	0.37%	OH	1.92%	3.52%
OR	8.05%	3.90%	NH	1.72%	5.20%
ID	7.86%	3.19%	AL	1.70%	5.99%
WA	7.51%	3.26%	MT	1.46%	8.64%
MA	6.73%	2.78%	KY	1.34%	6.49%
WY	6.42%	1.34%	SD	1.28%	6.91%
HL6: KS	5.99%	5.40%	MS	1.21%	5.70%
NE	5.57%	4.18%	ND	0.80%	9.09%
GA	5.35%	5.08%	VT	0.70%	8.81%
HL6: OK	5.23%	4.54%	ME	0.59%	9.42%
DE	4.83%	4.23%	WV	0.57%	8.88%

The TG6 and HL6 states have been offset to allow for easier interpretation. The table shows the national average percentage of Hispanics as 13.99 percent and the average rate of growth of 4.56 percent. Gateway states such as New Mexico, California, and Texas have larger shares of Latinos in their populations, whereas states such as Vermont, Maine, and West Virginia having the lowest such shares. However, as an indication of the diffusion of Latinos throughout the country, notice that the rates of growth of the percentage of Latinos in population in the traditionally underrepresented states are actually *higher* than those in the traditionally gateway states.

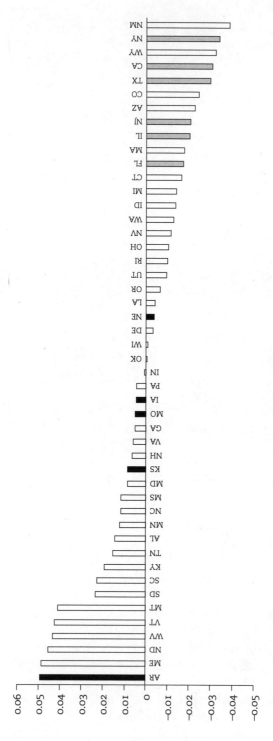

Figure 11.10. Deviation per state to national average of growth rates of Hispanic interpopulation shares (ACS)

The deviation in the growth rates of Hispanics out of total population for each state as compared to the national average is shown in figure 11.10: states with the lowest percentage of Hispanics are among those with the highest rate of growth in that ratio, and states with the highest percentage of Hispanics have the lowest rate of growth. This can be expressed in the beta convergence graph for every state in figures 11.11 and 11.12.

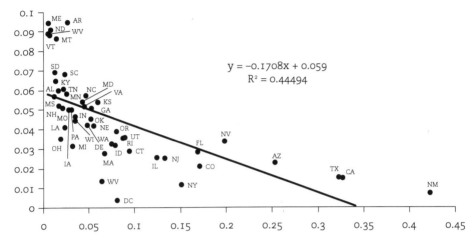

Figure 11.11. Beta convergence in inter-Hispanic shares: 48 states

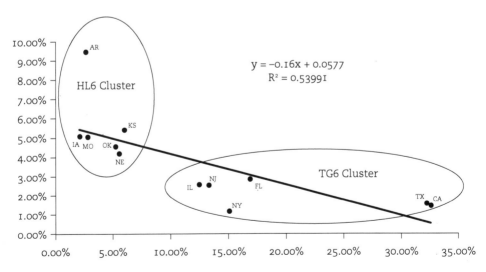

Figure 11.12. Beta convergence in inter-Hispanic shares: HL6 and TG6 clusters

Economic Activity of Hispanics in HL6

The total population is defined as the sum of people who do *not* participate in the civilian labor force (CLF), such as minors, homemakers, and the retired, and those who do participate in the CLF:

Total population = non-CLF + CLF

The labor force participation rates (LFPR) are defined as the percentage of population that participates in the civilian labor force (CLF):

$$LFPR = \frac{CLF}{population} \qquad (6)$$

Table 11.4 reports the LFPR data for the Heartland 6 and the traditional growth 6 with data taken from the Bureau of Labor Statistics (BLS) for the years 1999 to 2008. Table 11.4 shows that the HL6 experienced across-the-board greater degrees of labor force participation as compared to the United States and the TG6. Figure 11.13 shows the average labor force participation rates for the United States, the TG6, and the HL6 across the 2000–2007 time period.

Hispanics in the HL6 participated in the labor force in the largest proportion, and Hispanics in the TG6 participated in the labor force at a rate slightly above the national average. When the respective regions are differenced by the national total, this result can express the HL6's across-the-board experience of a significantly larger portion of its Hispanic population actively participating in the labor force than that of the TG6.

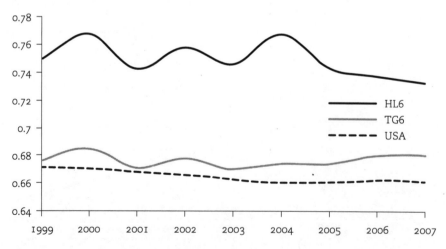

Figure 11.13. Labor force participation rates for United States, HL6, and TG6 Hispanics (BLS)

Table 11.4. Labor force participation rates for Hispanics in HL6 and TG6 (BLS)

LFPR USA	1999	2000	2001	2002	2003	2004	2005	2006	2007	Average
USA	0.671	0.671	0.668	0.666	0.662	0.660	0.660	0.662	0.661	0.664

LFPR HL6	1999	2000	2001	2002	2003	2004	2005	2006	2007	Average
AR		0.786	0.791	0.778	0.735	0.729	0.750	0.752	0.781	0.749
IA			0.697	0.721	0.729	0.800	0.767	0.775	0.750	0.752
KS	0.75	0.753	0.692	0.730	0.785	0.789	0.726	0.756	0.788	0.738
MO			0.746	0.800	0.729	0.782	0.778	0.712	0.622	0.754
NE	0.784	0.759	0.769	0.786	0.750	0.785	0.734	0.704	0.713	0.735
OK	0.712	0.776	0.758	0.735	0.750	0.722	0.704	0.722	0.739	0.748
HL6	0.749	0.768	0.742	0.758	0.746	0.768	0.743	0.737	0.732	0.763

LFPR TG6	1999	2000	2001	2002	2003	2004	2005	2006	2007	Average
CA	0.682	0.687	0.689	0.698	0.681	0.679	0.676	0.684	0.691	0.682
FL	0.662	0.654	0.661	0.651	0.640	0.653	0.662	0.675	0.686	0.683
IL	0.743	0.741	0.731	0.740	0.717	0.693	0.702	0.723	0.712	0.743
NJ	0.707	0.715	0.686	0.684	0.699	0.722	0.726	0.706	0.710	0.723
NY	0.595	0.627	0.591	0.619	0.614	0.633	0.613	0.622	0.615	0.612
TX	0.670	0.684	0.667	0.674	0.668	0.664	0.666	0.669	0.665	0.662
TG6	0.676	0.685	0.671	0.678	0.670	0.674	0.674	0.680	0.680	0.684

Table 11.4. Continued

LFPR HL6	1999–2003	2004–2008	LFPR TG6	1999–2003	2004–2008
AR	0.772	0.753	CA	0.687	0.683
IA	0.716	0.773	FL	0.654	0.669
KS	0.742	0.765	IL	0.734	0.708
MO	0.758	0.724	NJ	0.698	0.716
NE	0.770	0.734	NY	0.609	0.621
OK	0.746	0.722	TX	0.673	0.666
HL6	0.753	0.745	TG6	0.676	0.677

	1999–2003	2004–2008
USA	0.667617	0.660583

Note that the employment data in tables 11.4 and 11.5 include the years 1999 and 2008 in contrast with the demographic data.

Unemployment Rates for Hispanics

The rate of unemployment is derived from the civilian labor force. Specifically, it is defined as the ratio of the unemployed members of the CLF divided by the total CLF:

$$U_L = \frac{(CLF)_{unemployed}}{(CLF)_{total}} \tag{7}$$

Table 11.5 reports the unemployment rates for the United States, the HL6 and the TG6 with data from the Bureau of Labor Statistics. Table 11.5 shows that the HL6 experienced across-the-board greater degrees of unemployment as compared to the United States and the TG6. Figure 11.14 shows unemployment rates for Hispanics for the United States, the TG6, and the HL6 across the 1999–2008 time period.

Hispanics in both the HL6 and TG6 experience greater rates of unemployment compared to the national average. When the respective regions are differenced by the national total, this result can express the TG6 and HL6 larger portion of its Hispanic population unemployed.

Consider now a comparison of the unemployment rates for Hispanics against those of the total (Hispanic and non-Hispanic), which shows that in both the HL6 and the TG6 Hispanics were across the board more unemployed than the total populations in each state cluster.

In terms of presence in the labor force, it is shown that on average that Hispanics on the whole have a greater rate of labor force participation *and* a greater rate of unemployment. This is especially pronounced in the HL6 states for the labor force participation rate; put simply, Hispanics in this region on the whole actively participated in the labor force 7 percent to 10 percent more than the national average and only slightly less than their Hispanic counterparts in the TG6. It can be conjectured that Hispanics in the HL6 came to the region in search of work.

Conclusion

In this chapter descriptive patterns of demographic presence and economic performance of Hispanics in six core Heartland states have been presented. What emerges out of the data is a strong tendency toward diffusion of Latin American migrations throughout the United States. The demographic growth rates are much higher in new destinations such as the Heartland, and this has caused a tremendous amount of change in those regions. What also emerges out the data is the fact that Hispanics came to the HL6 in search of employ-

Table 11.5. Unemployment rates for the United States and HL6, TG6 Hispanics (BLS)

U, USA	1999	2000	2001	2002	2003	2004	2005	2006	2007	2008
USA	4.22%	3.97%	4.74%	5.78%	5.99%	5.54%	5.08%	4.61%	4.61%	5.82%

Heartland 6	1999	2000	2001	2002	2003	2004	2005	2006	2007	2008
AR	n/a	6.06%	2.94%	7.14%	8.00%	5.88%	3.33%	5.26%	6.67%	4.55%
IA	n/a	n/a	6.52%	8.06%	7.14%	7.81%	7.58%	4.35%	4.17%	7.69%
KS	1.96%	4.48%	6.76%	7.87%	7.14%	6.98%	9.09%	5.56%	4.63%	8.00%
MO	n/a	n/a	8.51%	8.93%	6.41%	7.22%	3.30%	7.59%	8.20%	8.22%
NE	5.00%	7.32%	5.00%	9.09%	10.53%	8.06%	4.35%	4.35%	4.84%	5.00%
OK	3.85%	3.95%	4.17%	5.56%	6.41%	4.29%	7.37%	6.59%	5.68%	9.09%
HL6	3.60%	5.45%	5.65%	7.77%	7.61%	6.71%	5.84%	5.62%	5.70%	7.09%

Traditional growth 6	1999	2000	2001	2002	2003	2004	2005	2006	2007	2008
CA	6.99%	6.49%	7.11%	7.89%	7.41%	8.16%	6.44%	5.65%	6.41%	9.37%
FL	5.21%	4.76%	6.74%	6.76%	6.52%	4.96%	4.32%	3.43%	4.78%	7.34%
IL	5.49%	4.68%	7.73%	8.32%	9.17%	6.38%	7.06%	5.59%	5.66%	6.64%
NJ	5.56%	4.63%	5.96%	7.73%	8.15%	4.51%	4.85%	6.37%	5.88%	6.48%
NY	8.40%	6.92%	6.60%	8.67%	8.94%	7.75%	6.54%	5.73%	6.53%	6.71%
TX	6.23%	4.97%	5.53%	7.17%	7.60%	6.49%	5.94%	4.63%	4.50%	5.61%
TG6	6.31%	5.41%	6.61%	7.76%	7.96%	6.37%	5.86%	5.23%	5.63%	7.03%

Table 11.5. Continued

UL HL6	1999–2003	2004–2008	UL TG6	1999–2003	2004–2008
AR	6.04%	5.14%	CA	7.18%	7.20%
IA	7.24%	6.32%	FL	6.00%	4.97%
KS	5.64%	6.85%	IL	7.08%	6.27%
MO	7.95%	6.90%	NJ	6.40%	5.62%
NE	7.39%	5.32%	NY	7.91%	6.65%
OK	4.79%	6.60%	TX	6.30%	5.43%
HL6	6.02%	6.19%	TG6	6.81%	6.02%

	1999–2003	2004–2008
USA	4.94%	5.13%

	1999	2000	2001	2002	2003	2004	2005	2006	2007	2008
UL_H_HL6	3.60%	5.45%	5.65%	7.77%	7.61%	6.71%	5.84%	5.62%	5.70%	7.09%
UL_HL6	3.29%	3.38%	4.07%	4.69%	5.21%	5.07%	4.79%	4.18%	4.33%	4.45%
UL_H_TG6	6.31%	5.41%	6.61%	7.76%	7.96%	6.37%	5.86%	5.23%	5.63%	7.03%
UL_TG6	4.62%	4.24%	4.90%	6.16%	6.25%	5.59%	4.89%	4.44%	4.60%	5.92%
UL_USA	4.22%	3.97%	4.74%	5.78%	5.99%	5.54%	5.08%	4.61%	4.61%	5.82%

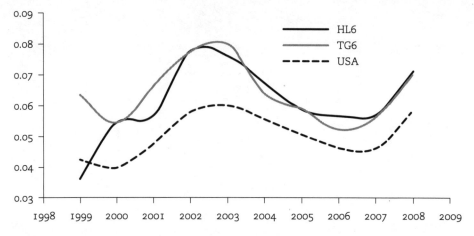

Figure 11.14. Unemployment rates for United States, HL6, and TG6 Hispanics (BLS)

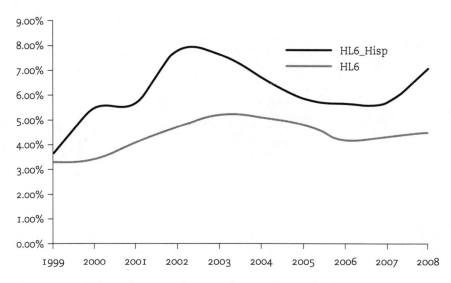

Figure 11.15. Hispanic vs. total unemployment rates in HL6

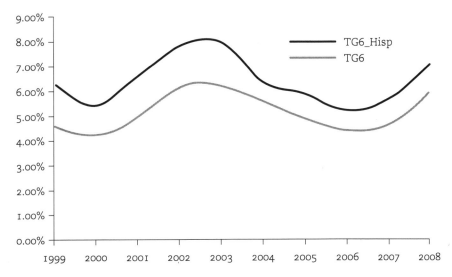

Figure 11.16. Hispanic vs. total unemployment rates in TG6

ment. Labor force participation rates for Hispanics in the region were indeed very high even if the actual rate at which Hispanics were unemployed was higher as well. This indicates that when out of a job, Hispanics in the region were still in search of employment. The income distribution measures also show that Hispanics remain on the lower end of that distribution.

Appendixes

The Appendixes appear on the following pages.

Appendix A: Raw Demographic Data for the United States, HL6, and TG6

	2000	2001	2002	2003	2004	2005	2006	2007
U.S.								
Total population	271,859,935	275,213,476	278,226,624	281,058,168	283,828,530	286,498,255	297,442,934	299,654,293
Hispanic population	34,365,405	36,090,675	37,759,550	39,074,812	40,332,125	41,741,161	44,115,116	45,283,826
Foreign-born Hispanics	15,379,242	16,130,863	17,267,905	17,517,840	15,839,559	16,755,063	17,696,178	18,047,141
Naturalized Hispanic (stock)	4,700,652	4,929,500	5,337,966	5,408,880	4,434,914	4,698,601	4,857,782	5,076,531
Non-U.S. citizen Hispanic	10,678,590	11,201,363	11,929,939	12,108,960	11,404,645	12,056,462	12,838,396	12,970,610
HL6								
Total population	13,026,839	13,059,768	13,158,855	13,216,132	13,289,206	13,367,060	13,904,575	13,990,728
Hispanic population	572,184	615,305	650,929	663,339	720,066	807,421	862,673	901,389
Foreign-born Hispanics	194,917	247,892	248,617	263,599	268,120	330,071	357,916	372,603
Naturalized Hispanic (stock)	48,468	49,784	49,128	45,376	52,390	58,086	69,260	75,056
Non-U.S. citizen Hispanic	146,449	198,108	199,489	218,223	215,730	271,985	288,656	297,547
AR								
Total population	2,599,492	2,618,137	2,634,848	2,650,062	2,675,872	2,701,431	2,810,872	2,834,797
Hispanic population	69,344	87,579	92,400	98,628	117,568	126,932	138,283	146,542
Foreign-born Hispanics	32,354	47,246	48,922	50,223	60,247	63,443	68,602	73,266
Naturalized Hispanic (stock)	7,038	5,709	6,600	3,860	10,380	6,178	11,287	11,746
Non-U.S. citizen Hispanic	25,316	41,537	42,322	46,363	49,867	57,265	57,315	61,520
IA								
Total population	2,822,155	2,818,957	2,832,392	2,839,868	2,851,165	2,862,541	2,982,085	2,988,047
Hispanic population	79,637	81,958	87,447	88,869	104,688	106,052	112,987	119,716
Foreign-born Hispanics	25,741	29,087	34,331	37,058	26,762	41,605	42,831	49,548
Naturalized Hispanic (stock)	5,148	6,852	8,649	5,414	8,839	8,208	9,735	10,867
Non-U.S. citizen Hispanic	20,593	22,235	25,682	31,644	17,923	33,397	33,096	38,681

KS								
Total population	2,775,997	2,764,075	2,662,616	2,653,454	2,641,747	2,634,122	2,612,636	2,606,468
Hispanic population	242,787	236,351	224,152	160,808	178,727	184,148	172,339	156,191
Foreign-born Hispanics	92,508	92,229	82,130	55,254	59,011	51,053	53,739	37,839
Naturalized Hispanic (stock)	18,577	20,552	18,052	9,688	15,952	8,348	9,669	8,877
Non-U.S. citizen Hispanic	73,931	71,677	64,078	45,566	43,059	42,705	44,070	28,962
MO								
Total population	5,878,415	5,842,713	5,631,910	5,586,114	5,534,753	5,505,963	5,467,596	5,433,153
Hispanic population	176,878	160,898	148,994	143,729	125,406	112,698	113,203	114,615
Foreign-born Hispanics	60,652	51,774	56,185	41,761	43,278	45,158	39,065	37,517
Naturalized Hispanic (stock)	14,215	12,495	15,732	13,401	19,366	11,326	15,828	12,349
Non-U.S. citizen Hispanic	46,437	39,279	40,453	28,360	23,912	33,832	23,237	25,168
NE								
Total population	1,774,571	1,768,331	1,706,976	1,696,513	1,687,661	1,677,978	1,662,378	1,660,445
Hispanic population	132,477	130,230	122,518	118,227	105,122	101,573	94,904	92,506
Foreign-born Hispanics	54,257	55,628	53,859	43,929	38,258	35,635	40,946	34,679
Naturalized Hispanic (stock)	14,366	9,826	11,304	9,376	7,495	11,185	9,349	6,360
Non-U.S. citizen Hispanic	39891	45802	42555	34,553	30,763	24,450	31,597	28,319
OK								
Total population	3,617,316	3,579,212	3,433,496	3,412,202	3,396,794	3,379,515	3,347,660	3,338,279
Hispanic population	259,867	244,822	227,767	218,775	191,993	185,361	178,525	174,506
Foreign-born Hispanics	103,024	98,626	89,034	81,928	79,049	78,676	76,874	64,304
Naturalized Hispanic (stock)	19,500	17,860	14,344	14,107	12,655	14,346	18,205	21,045
Non-U.S. citizen Hispanic	83,524	80,766	74,690	67,821	66,394	64,330	58,669	43,259

Appendix A: Continued

TG6

Total population	107,649,075	109,336,491	111,072,950	112,189,980	113,485,726	114,548,497	118,917,934	119,545,035
Hispanic population	25,340,525	26,643,315	27,667,546	28,666,818	29,170,983	29,981,561	31,494,990	32,037,878
Foreign-born Hispanics	11,859,471	12,314,560	13,030,077	13,174,684	11,668,231	12,193,292	12,773,038	12,970,837
Naturalized Hispanic (stock)	3,809,770	3,999,573	4,306,657	4,365,690	3,576,709	3,724,859	3,844,733	3,999,771
Non-U.S. citizen Hispanic	8,049,701	8,314,987	8,723,420	8,808,994	8,091,522	8,468,433	8,928,305	8,971,066

CA

Total population	33,051,894	33,681,509	34,292,871	34,650,690	35,055,227	35,278,768	36,457,549	36,553,215
Hispanic population	10,773,995	11,334,407	11,647,324	11,980,884	12,246,122	12,523,379	13,074,155	13,220,888
Foreign-born Hispanics	4,713,117	4,823,227	5,081,362	5,031,695	5,080,515	5,201,526	5,390,489	5,472,178
Naturalized Hispanic (stock)	1,257,114	1,302,267	1,374,588	1,404,880	1,394,550	1,487,571	1,520,381	1,579,781
Non-U.S. citizen Hispanic	3,456,003	3,520,960	3,706,774	3,626,815	3,685,965	3,713,955	3,870,108	3,892,397

FL

Total population	15,593,433	16,007,098	16,318,656	16,618,145	16,990,183	17,382,511	18,089,889	18,251,243
Hispanic population	2,632,946	2,815,847	2,969,016	3,108,578	3,250,768	3,414,414	3,642,989	3,757,424
Foreign-born Hispanics	1,923,472	2,043,007	2,126,380	2,167,859	1,707,175	1,781,596	1,903,010	1,938,508
Naturalized Hispanic (stock)	785,408	828,928	907,033	923,279	703,718	730,594	772,880	786,120
Non-U.S. citizen Hispanic	1,138,064	1,214,079	1,219,347	1,244,580	1,003,457	1,051,002	1,130,130	1,152,388

IL

Total population	12,097,512	12,160,474	12,279,027	12,328,721	12,390,521	12,440,351	12,831,970	12,852,548
Hispanic population	1,510,869	1,573,733	1,663,514	1,694,185	1,739,870	1,804,619	1,888,439	1,917,420
Foreign-born Hispanics	694,726	753,780	794,449	795,581	771,225	789,340	824,545	829,272
Naturalized Hispanic (stock)	205,334	206,859	233,529	238,446	222,401	221,792	233,492	239,384
Non-U.S. citizen Hispanic	489,392	546,921	560,920	557,135	548,824	567,548	591,053	589,888

NJ

Total population	8,219,529	8,289,599	8,395,357	8,444,076	8,503,294	8,521,427	8,724,560	8,685,920
Hispanic population	1,097,815	1,140,886	1,198,470	1,234,632	1,274,500	1,307,412	1,364,699	1,382,029
Foreign-born Hispanics	598,509	645,424	667,160	706,113	540,687	581,153	646,166	621,932
Naturalized Hispanic (stock)	247,006	253,707	262,947	255,554	211,842	210,694	217,229	238,015
Non-U.S. citizen Hispanic	351,503	391,717	404,213	450,559	328,845	370,459	428,937	383,917

NY

Total population	18,395,996	18,433,370	18,571,545	18,600,527	18,634,337	18,655,275	19,306,183	19,297,729
Hispanic population	2,778,191	2,895,976	2,997,676	3,034,125	3,003,572	3,028,658	3,139,590	3,159,732
Foreign-born Hispanics	1,805,146	1,787,031	1,949,104	1,941,420	1,146,410	1,225,021	1,276,988	1,295,975
Naturalized Hispanic (stock)	742,765	827,334	891,473	907,138	449,383	443,536	465,875	489,707
Non-U.S. citizen Hispanic	1,062,381	959,697	1,057,631	1,034,282	697,027	781,485	811,113	806,268

TX

Total population	20,290,711	20,764,441	21,215,494	21,547,821	21,912,164	22,270,165	23,507,783	23,904,380
Hispanic population	6,546,709	6,882,466	7,191,546	7,614,414	7,656,151	7,903,079	8,385,118	8,600,385
Foreign-born Hispanics	2,124,501	2,262,091	2,411,622	2,532,016	2,422,219	2,614,656	2,731,840	2,812,972
Naturalized Hispanic (stock)	572,143	580,478	637,087	636,393	594,815	630,672	634,876	666,764
Non-U.S. citizen Hispanic	1,552,358	1,681,613	1,774,535	1,895,623	1,827,404	1,983,984	2,096,964	2,146,208

(Source: U.S. Census American Community Survey)

Appendix B: Hispanic Population per State Cluster as a Percentage of Total Population: 2000-2007 (%)

	2000	2001	2002	2003	2004	2005	2006	2007
U.S. Hispanic to total U.S. population	12.64	13.11	13.57	13.90	14.21	14.57	14.83	15.11
TG6 Hispanic to total TG6 population	23.54	24.37	24.91	25.55	25.71	26.17	26.49	26.80
HL6 Hispanic to total HL6 population	4.39	4.71	4.95	5.02	5.42	6.04	6.20	6.44

Period Averages	2000–2003	2004–2007
US Hispanic to total U.S. population	13.31	14.68
TG6 Hispanic to total TG6 population	24.59	26.29
HL6 Hispanic to total HL6 population	4.77	6.03

Source: U.S. Census American Community Survey.

Figure A. Percentage of Hispanics in total population for the United States, TG6, and HL6: period averages. The figure shows the basic trend that although a relatively small percentage of the total population, the rate of growth of Hispanics in the HL6 increased at a rate over 26 percent compared to that of 10.3 percent in the nation as a whole and 6.9 percent in the TG6. Put simply, although remaining only a small slice of the Hispanic pie, the growth rates of Hispanics in the "new destinations" of the HL6 more than double those of the nation and are almost four times those of the TG6 states. Source: U.S. Census American Community Survey.

Appendix C: Poverty Rates of Hispanics by Age (%): HL6, TG6, United States

Minors	2000	2001	2002	2003	2004	2005	2006	2007	Average
U.S.	28.86	27.44	28.34	28.40	28.60	29.09	28.04	27.47	28.28
AR	38.00	23.17	34.07	35.46	28.90	30.74	34.85	38.41	32.95
IA	19.61	13.40	34.19	19.80	17.97	31.30	32.03	30.51	24.85
KS	24.17	20.08	44.62	23.26	29.27	29.97	28.47	32.19	29.01
MO	27.71	31.12	27.55	14.46	18.02	28.44	31.71	28.32	25.92
NE	16.27	32.72	32.04	30.07	32.17	29.99	26.50	28.33	28.51
OK	23.78	36.27	24.45	33.64	32.66	35.93	37.48	39.60	32.98
HL6	24.92	26.13	32.82	26.11	26.50	31.06	31.84	32.89	29.04
CA	28.19	25.79	26.92	26.14	26.95	26.28	25.12	23.65	26.13
FL	23.71	23.76	21.79	22.91	22.84	22.27	20.65	21.10	22.38
IL	18.37	19.36	18.97	19.59	19.46	22.17	23.00	21.00	20.24
NJ	19.21	22.36	17.40	23.70	19.44	23.70	22.43	20.82	21.13
NY	34.50	34.23	33.45	34.69	33.94	33.99	33.53	32.94	33.91
TX	34.43	32.00	34.43	34.37	35.37	36.11	33.74	33.01	34.18
TG6	26.40	26.25	25.49	26.90	26.33	27.42	26.41	25.42	26.33

18 to 64	2000	2001	2002	2003	2004	2005	2006	2007	Average
U.S.	18.42	17.62	17.91	18.41	18.49	18.79	17.95	17.15	18.09
AR	23.91	19.53	29.24	19.82	24.31	20.93	22.92	22.18	22.86
IA	15.34	7.72	29.13	8.90	13.56	22.87	19.60	19.31	17.05
KS	15.34	7.72	29.13	8.90	13.56	22.87	19.60	19.31	17.05
MO	12.75	17.47	12.51	16.52	10.77	16.04	22.57	16.93	15.69
NE	17.82	16.77	21.15	22.78	21.35	18.04	17.69	19.06	19.33
OK	18.05	24.04	20.20	21.15	19.47	21.81	24.45	22.03	21.40
HL6	17.20	15.54	23.56	16.34	17.17	20.43	21.14	19.80	18.90
CA	18.52	16.08	17.00	16.76	16.96	16.76	16.01	14.83	16.61
FL	16.03	15.06	15.07	15.00	14.30	14.81	13.92	13.12	14.66
IL	13.14	12.45	13.04	12.63	13.34	15.33	14.62	12.97	13.44
NJ	11.61	15.48	11.01	15.91	13.90	14.73	13.37	13.39	13.67
NY	20.02	21.93	18.73	19.92	21.96	20.55	20.87	20.14	20.51
TX	21.08	20.01	22.20	22.38	22.98	23.37	21.01	20.05	21.64
TG6	16.73	16.83	16.17	17.10	17.24	17.59	16.63	15.75	16.76

65+									
U.S.	19.39	20.15	19.79	20.52	19.92	20.83	19.72	18.54	19.86
AR	23.56	36.77	0.00	18.23	13.88	17.56	19.07	22.92	19.00
IA	2.79	13.33	14.69	7.71	19.16	17.06	20.24	10.07	13.13
KS	2.79	13.33	14.69	7.71	19.16	17.06	20.24	10.07	13.13
MO	0.00	9.52	16.76	15.19	27.04	7.35	16.93	9.34	12.77
NE	10.66	31.87	15.93	23.46	5.74	14.03	12.90	26.04	17.58
OK	16.64	50.07	14.02	20.67	0.00	16.43	18.00	21.25	19.64
HL6	9.40	25.82	12.68	15.50	14.16	14.92	17.90	16.62	15.87
CA	14.40	13.48	11.33	12.22	12.22	13.26	13.88	12.50	12.91
FL	22.99	20.29	22.43	21.72	23.15	21.99	21.89	20.34	21.85
IL	12.84	19.29	15.62	12.29	13.72	16.07	17.34	13.94	15.14
NJ	22.81	18.62	26.35	20.44	26.36	27.02	21.34	19.97	22.86
NY	24.74	24.90	30.49	35.84	30.93	31.28	26.59	25.02	28.72
TX	22.96	26.04	26.44	28.11	25.84	27.31	25.42	24.08	25.77
TG6	20.12	20.44	22.11	21.77	22.03	22.82	21.08	19.31	21.21

(Source: U.S. Census American Community Survey)

Appendix D: Gender by Income of Hispanics (%): HL6, TG6, United States

	U.S. Male							
	2000	2001	2002	2003	2004	2005	2006	2007
$1 to $2,499 or less	0.14%	0.08%	·0.17%	0.12%	0.13%	0.11%	0.11%	0.11%
$2,500 to $4,999	0.32%	0.14%	0.19%	0.14%	0.21%	0.20%	0.13%	0.13%
$5,000 to $7,499	1.37%	1.43%	1.09%	0.96%	1.05%	1.05%	0.92%	0.87%
$7,500 to $9,999	2.51%	2.41%	1.74%	1.61%	1.63%	1.44%	1.23%	1.05%
$10,000 to $12,499	9.52%	8.15%	6.65%	6.12%	5.63%	5.84%	5.03%	4.55%
$12,500 to $14,999	7.35%	5.62%	5.50%	5.23%	5.18%	5.15%	4.52%	4.12%
$15,000 to $17,499	10.28%	9.28%	10.01%	9.76%	9.54%	8.19%	8.60%	7.83%
$17,500 to $19,999	6.51%	7.11%	6.52%	6.40%	6.37%	6.14%	6.60%	5.97%
$20,000 to $22,499	8.65%	9.94%	9.60%	9.69%	9.68%	8.96%	9.26%	9.37%
$22,500 to $24,999	5.96%	5.47%	5.56%	5.32%	5.32%	6.12%	6.01%	5.74%
$25,000 to $29,999	11.17%	11.30%	11.12%	12.21%	11.29%	11.28%	11.60%	11.46%
$30,000 to $34,999	9.20%	9.31%	9.69%	9.59%	9.40%	9.58%	9.40%	9.94%
$35,000 to $39,999	6.23%	6.98%	6.56%	6.78%	6.94%	7.22%	7.28%	7.37%
$40,000 to $44,999	5.22%	5.53%	5.85%	5.77%	5.92%	6.36%	6.29%	6.43%
$45,000 to $49,999	3.38%	3.44%	3.87%	4.06%	4.31%	4.22%	4.27%	4.35%
$50,000 to $54,999	2.96%	3.38%	4.03%	3.96%	3.96%	4.04%	4.21%	4.51%
$55,000 to $64,999	3.62%	3.80%	4.31%	4.39%	4.39%	4.55%	4.66%	5.16%
$65,000 to $74,999	1.89%	2.30%	2.45%	2.30%	3.03%	3.03%	3.01% .	3.35%
$75,000 to $99,999	1.86%	2.23%	2.58%	3.11%	3.15%	3.31%	3.51%	4.04%
$100,000 or more	1.86%	2.11%	2.51%	2.50%	2.87%	3.20%	3.35%	3.66%

	U.S. Female							
	2000	2001	2002	2003	2004	2005	2006	2007
$1 to $2,499 or less	0.26%	0.29%	0.18%	0.19%	0.22%	0.19%	0.21%	0.17%
$2,500 to $4,999	0.39%	0.54%	0.32%	0.38%	0.33%	0.37%	0.41%	0.35%
$5,000 to $7,499	2.86%	2.36%	2.12%	2.09%	1.26%	1.76%	1.67%	1.45%
$7,500 to $9,999	4.45%	3.97%	3.16%	3.06%	2.39%	2.65%	2.33%	2.00%
$10,000 to $12,499	13.70%	11.23%	11.12%	10.21%	9.03%	8.76%	8.25%	7.37%
$12,500 to $14,999	7.65%	7.76%	7.25%	7.80%	7.48%	6.96%	6.86%	6.36%
$15,000 to $17,499	10.76%	10.56%	10.64%	10.90%	10.25%	9.20%	9.65%	9.95%
$17,500 to $19,999	7.12%	7.27%	6.69%	6.55%	6.27%	6.80%	6.54%	6.36%
$20,000 to $22,499	8.67%	9.37%	9.19%	9.26%	9.46%	8.37%	8.97%	9.16%
$22,500 to $24,999	6.24%	5.49%	5.25%	5.00%	5.40%	6.35%	5.72%	5.59%
$25,000 to $29,999	10.76%	10.61%	10.92%	11.06%	10.78%	11.00%	10.90%	10.86%
$30,000 to $34,999	8.39%	9.12%	8.96%	9.08%	9.56%	9.28%	9.43%	9.75%
$35,000 to $39,999	4.98%	5.72%	5.94%	6.33%	6.72%	6.80%	6.75%	6.50%
$40,000 to $44,999	4.04%	4.10%	5.02%	5.03%	5.68%	5.67%	5.55%	5.79%
$45,000 to $49,999	2.44%	2.83%	3.14%	2.94%	3.73%	3.47%	3.56%	3.78%
$50,000 to $54,999	2.05%	2.33%	2.83%	2.68%	2.93%	2.94%	3.11%	3.41%
$55,000 to $64,999	2.01%	2.65%	2.72%	2.93%	3.50%	3.57%	3.77%	3.97%
$65,000 to $74,999	1.28%	1.46%	1.65%	1.63%	1.97%	2.22%	2.10%	2.58%
$75,000 to $99,999	1.28%	1.36%	1.81%	1.71%	1.87%	2.16%	2.53%	2.68%
$100,000 or more	0.67%	0.99%	1.08%	1.17%	1.16%	1.51%	1.70%	1.92%

	2000	2001	2002	2003	2004	2005	2006	2007
				HL6 Male				
$1 to $2,499 or less	0.00%	0.05%	0.16%	0.67%	0.84%	0.13%	0.08%	0.22%
$2,500 to $4,999	0.20%	0.00%	0.00%	0.30%	0.00%	0.52%	0.08%	0.08%
$5,000 to $7,499	0.47%	1.04%	0.11%	0.69%	0.99%	1.12%	1.20%	0.96%
$7,500 to $9,999	0.34%	3.17%	0.43%	0.76%	1.86%	1.86%	0.80%	0.84%
$10,000 to $12,499	12.36%	6.25%	5.02%	2.33%	8.54%	5.39%	5.02%	5.59%
$12,500 to $14,999	6.81%	3.69%	2.82%	1.64%	5.52%	6.52%	3.84%	4.25%
$15,000 to $17,499	10.78%	10.11%	9.11%	3.74%	5.93%	9.26%	9.97%	8.33%
$17,500 to $19,999	8.86%	8.86%	8.67%	3.25%	13.65%	8.71%	8.47%	7.21%
$20,000 to $22,499	9.32%	9.83%	13.27%	6.59%	9.09%	10.17%	11.58%	10.64%
$22,500 to $24,999	6.93%	4.23%	8.31%	3.98%	4.53%	8.03%	8.20%	8.24%
$25,000 to $29,999	12.91%	10.35%	12.07%	9.33%	14.73%	12.67%	14.76%	14.94%
$30,000 to $34,999	8.32%	13.42%	12.01%	11.13%	8.14%	8.89%	10.24%	10.19%
$35,000 to $39,999	6.79%	9.17%	4.93%	8.90%	10.09%	7.08%	5.57%	5.74%
$40,000 to $44,999	4.49%	3.77%	6.98%	8.99%	2.63%	4.18%	4.70%	5.30%
$45,000 to $49,999	2.15%	2.61%	3.60%	6.10%	2.57%	2.41%	3.87%	3.34%
$50,000 to $54,999	2.66%	3.39%	3.76%	6.92%	3.11%	2.60%	3.10%	3.53%
$55,000 to $64,999	2.93%	3.05%	3.81%	7.48%	2.37%	3.80%	2.60%	4.20%
$65,000 to $74,999	1.58%	3.55%	1.55%	4.43%	2.19%	2.03%	1.98%	2.13%
$75,000 to $99,999	1.43%	2.23%	1.14%	6.18%	2.52%	2.42%	1.90%	2.34%
$100,000 or more	0.65%	1.25%	2.26%	6.58%	0.69%	2.23%	2.03%	1.94%
				HL6 Female				
$1 to $2,499 or less	0.46%	0.00%	0.26%	0.39%	0.00%	0.00%	0.11%	0.23%
$2,500 to $4,999	0.19%	0.23%	0.26%	0.36%	0.08%	0.83%	0.47%	0.34%
$5,000 to $7,499	1.66%	2.51%	2.41%	1.35%	0.58%	1.72%	1.94%	2.83%
$7,500 to $9,999	6.08%	1.50%	1.89%	1.75%	1.50%	2.46%	2.70%	2.33%
$10,000 to $12,499	8.87%	10.32%	10.07%	4.90%	6.04%	11.81%	5.87%	7.53%
$12,500 to $14,999	8.57%	8.71%	8.52%	4.14%	9.24%	7.88%	8.69%	8.33%
$15,000 to $17,499	10.90%	12.23%	11.79%	7.31%	14.23%	9.27%	11.52%	10.04%
$17,500 to $19,999	10.15%	8.45%	10.10%	6.43%	7.20%	12.21%	9.26%	8.54%
$20,000 to $22;499	10.83%	12.07%	11.17%	10.13%	11.55%	10.91%	9.67%	12.13%
$22,500 to $24,999	8.53%	5.65%	5.87%	5.90%	8.23%	9.34%	6.99%	8.25%
$25,000 to $29,999	9.67%	9.19%	10.12%	13.72%	13.14%	10.96%	13.00%	10.65%
$30,000 to $34,999	9.15%	9.09%	10.79%	10.88%	10.58%	7.13%	9.20%	10.23%
$35,000 to $39,999	3.91%	11.78%	1.91%	8.64%	6.11%	3.37%	5.02%	4.49%
$40,000 to $44,999	6.46%	2.09%	3.55%	7.05%	4.18%	3.36%	5.45%	3.96%
$45,000 to $49,999	1.52%	3.38%	2.55%	3.91%	2.12%	1.12%	2.86%	2.26%
$50,000 to $54,999	2.40%	0.09%	2.07%	3.43%	1.49%	1.71%	1.63%	2.18%
$55,000 to $64,999	0.09%	0.72%	2.15%	3.81%	1.24%	3.14%	2.47%	2.39%
$65,000 to $74,999	0.28%	0.76%	1.83%	1.89%	1.15%	1.03%	1.51%	1.55%
$75,000 to $99,999	0.04%	0.50%	2.12%	2.45%	1.29%	0.95%	0.89%	0.86%
$100,000 or more	0.24%	0.72%	0.58%	1.55%	0.04%	0.79%	0.77%	0.88%

Appendix D: Continued

	TG6 Male							
	2000	2001	2002	2003	2004	2005	2006	2007
$1 to $2,499 or less	0.16%	0.05%	0.14%	0.29%	0.14%	0.11%	0.08%	0.08%
$2,500 to $4,999	0.39%	0.15%	0.15%	0.15%	0.25%	0.20%	0.14%	0.13%
$5,000 to $7,499	1.48%	1.49%	1.04%	0.53%	1.09%	1.01%	0.88%	0.86%
$7,500 to $9,999	2.74%	2.50%	1.65%	0.52%	1.64%	1.48%	1.23%	1.03%
$10,000 to $12,499	9.77%	8.89%	6.87%	1.68%	5.93%	5.90%	5.03%	4.59%
$12,500 to $14,999	7.35%	5.78%	5.83%	1.15%	5.29%	5.28%	4.61%	4.23%
$15,000 to $17,499	10.60%	8.82%	10.12%	2.31%	9.19%	8.09%	8.58%	7.71%
$17,500 to $19,999	6.45%	6.89%	6.32%	1.73%	6.10%	5.94%	6.55%	5.96%
$20,000 to $22,499	8.36%	9.65%	9.45%	3.70%	9.58%	8.57%	8.86%	9.12%
$22,500 to $24,999	5.94%	5.39%	5.40%	2.24%	4.78%	5.85%	5.92%	5.51%
$25,000 to $29,999	10.68%	10.94%	10.84%	6.53%	10.97%	11.10%	11.02%	10.96%
$30,000 to $34,999	8.82%	9.31%	9.35%	7.79%	9.46%	9.33%	9.25%	9.78%
$35,000 to $39,999	6.00%	7.05%	6.64%	7.02%	6.94%	7.25%	7.39%	7.37%
$40,000 to $44,999	5.53%	5.75%	5.76%	8.08%	5.92%	6.56%	6.41%	6.48%
$45,000 to $49,999	3.28%	3.43%	4.06%	5.66%	4.46%	4.34%	4.41%	4.51%
$50,000 to $54,999	2.92%	3.41%	4.06%	7.66%	4.12%	4.19%	4.37%	4.66%
$55,000 to $64,999	3.86%	3.79%	4.44%	9.40%	4.64%	4.78%	4.91%	5.31%
$65,000 to $74,999	1.86%	2.26%	2.62%	7.17%	3.13%	3.15%	3.14%	3.62%
$75,000 to $99,999	1.83%	2.30%	2.58%	11.12%	3.29%	3.52%	3.70%	4.24%
$100,000 or more	1.97%	2.15%	2.65%	15.30%	3.07%	3.36%	3.51%	3.84%

	TG6 Female							
	2000	2001	2002	2003	2004	2005	2006	2007
$1 to $2,499 or less	0.21%	0.28%	0.16%	0.26%	0.27%	0.21%	0.19%	0.15%
$2,500 to $4,999	0.48%	0.51%	0.37%	0.25%	0.24%	0.39%	0.40%	0.37%
$5,000 to $7,499	3.06%	2.60%	2.12%	0.82%	1.21%	1.77%	1.63%	1.48%
$7,500 to $9,999	4.89%	4.30%	3.32%	1.04%	2.54%	2.81%	2.39%	2.02%
$10,000 to $12,499	14.46%	11.70%	11.55%	3.40%	9.45%	8.92%	8.81%	7.58%
$12,500 to $14,999	7.80%	8.05%	7.15%	2.63%	7.79%	6.92%	7.03%	6.50%
$15,000 to $17,499	10.21%	10.51%	10.88%	4.07%	10.30%	9.21%	9.34%	10.17%
$17,500 to $19,999	6.74%	6.62%	6.37%	3.54%	6.06%	6.58%	6.37%	6.05%
$20,000 to $22,499	7.86%	8.88%	8.58%	6.47%	8.88%	8.13%	8.82%	8.65%
$22,500 to $24,999	5.91%	5.18%	4.94%	4.06%	5.23%	5.91%	5.53%	5.38%
$25,000 to $29,999	10.83%	10.51%	10.74%	10.40%	10.29%	10.61%	10.40%	10.60%
$30,000 to $34,999	8.10%	9.31%	8.94%	11.25%	9.71%	9.16%	9.32%	9.59%
$35,000 to $39,999	5.11%	5.57%	5.95%	9.18%	6.51%	6.91%	6.88%	6.50%
$40,000 to $44,999	4.28%	3.98%	5.07%	8.30%	5.84%	5.90%	5.67%	5.95%
$45,000 to $49,999	2.48%	3.07%	3.25%	5.83%	3.89%	3.72%	3.63%	3.95%
$50,000 to $54,999	2.22%	2.40%	2.96%	5.88%	2.99%	3.00%	3.27%	3.53%
$55,000 to $64,999	1.99%	2.54%	2.79%	6.74%	3.72%	3.65%	3.89%	4.08%
$65,000 to $74,999	1.39%	1.57%	1.73%	4.70%	2.04%	2.40%	2.12%	2.70%
$75,000 to $99,999	1.35%	1.38%	1.99%	5.84%	1.91%	2.29%	2.64%	2.79%
$100,000 or more	0.63%	1.06%	1.16%	5.33%	1.12%	1.52%	1.66%	1.99%

(Source: U.S. Census American Community Survey)

Works Cited

Bump, Micah N., B. Lindsay Lowell, and Silje Pettersen. 2005. "The Growth and Population Characteristics of Immigrants and Minorities in America's New Settlement States." In *Beyond the Gateway: Immigrants in a Changing America*, ed. Elżbieta M. Godździak and Susan F. Martin. New York: Lexington Books.

Durand, Jorge, Douglas S. Massey, and Chiara Capoferro. 2005. "The New Geography of Mexican Immigration." In *New Destinations: Mexican Immigration in the United States*, ed. Víctor Zúñiga and Hernández-León. New York: Russell Sage Foundation.

Kwong, Peter. 1997. *Forbidden Workers: Illegal Chinese Immigrants and American Labor.* New York: New Press.

McKibben, Jerome N., and Kimberly A. Faust. 2004. "Population Distribution—Classification of Residence." In *The Methods and Materials of Demography*, 2nd ed., ed. Jacob. S. Siegel and David. A. Swanson. San Diego: Elsevier Academic Press.

Passel, Jeffrey. 2006. *Unauthorized Migrants in the United States: Estimates, Methods, and Characteristics.* Organization of Economic Cooperation and Development (OECD); Social, Employment and Migration Working Paper No. 57.

Sassen, Saskia. 1988. *The Mobility of Labor and Capital: A Study in International Investment and Labor Flow.* New York: Cambridge University Press.

Sassen, Saskia. 1995. "On Concentration and Centrality in the Global City." In *World Cities in a World System*, ed. Paul L. Knox and Peter J. Taylor. Cambridge: Cambridge University Press.

Zúñiga, Víctor, and Rubén Hernández-León, eds. 2005. *New Destinations: Mexican Immigration in the United States.* New York: Russell Sage Foundation.

Conclusion

Latin American Migrations to the U.S. Heartland: Reshaping Communities, Redrawing Boundaries

LINDA ALLEGRO AND
ANDREW GRANT WOOD

I don't need a passport to walk on this earth
Anywhere I go 'cause I was made of this earth
I'm born of this earth, I breathe of this earth
And even with the pain I believe in this earth.
—Michael Franti, "Hello Bonjour"

Why, in this era of free trade, digital revolution, and globalization, is the movement of people so regulated? Money, goods, and services are encouraged to circulate freely in the world economy, but workers—those who by and large produce wealth—are not. Instead, they face strict limitations, especially when considering transnational possibilities. The discrepancies of the neoliberal ideology that profess free markets, democracy, and freedom but simultaneously erect barriers and police the movement of people through detention and deportation strategies have resulted in a stark paradox of our time. Global migrations everywhere, including to the U.S. heartland, are witnessing similar processes of exclusion as new incursions of capitalist development make their way to still more remote and distant places.

Our collective endeavor here means to encourage the reshaping of communities and the redrawing of boundaries as we rethink the study of the Americas. Moving beyond nation-state constructs—those containers of citizenship and fixed borders—this volume offers new meanings of place and belonging. It aims to challenge powerful hegemonic discourses that separate the peoples of the Americas where distinctions are drawn out and lives appear in seemingly unconnected ways. The rhetorical construct of the "clash of civilizations" frames that difference where commonalities between peoples are incongruous and diversity insurmountable. Even academics are complicit as we have inherited a way to operationalize social study that often reinforces difference.

Perhaps not surprisingly, anti-immigrant sentiment today is directed at Latin Americans living in the United States (both undocumented and legal residents alike) in a misguided effort to assign blame for a host of economic and political troubles. Influential contemporary pundits presently lead a calculated xenophobic campaign that turns the poorest, most desperate laborers into criminalized scapegoats. Hunted now by an assortment of local and state vigilante lawmen casually deputized as federal immigration-enforcement agents, all people of apparently "Hispanic" descent are today generally determined to be guilty of unauthorized human traffic until otherwise proved innocent. This is the pervasive racist and ethnic profiling of our time.

Yet contrary to the diatribes of so many ill-informed "experts" and those who invite millions of television, Internet, and archconservative Sunday-morning audiences to buy into their ideology of hate, it is not "foreigners" and people of color who are depressing wages and costing jobs but corporate decision makers themselves who exploit the laboring classes in their zeal to maximize profits. As has so often been the case in the past, politicians who self-righteously claim that immigration is "out of control" in public forums hypocritically also work hand in glove with corporate interests to ensure that a ready supply of undocumented workers is always available at a moment's notice. Consciously creating a climate of social anxiety, suspicion, and fear, elites clearly play both sides of the immigration debate to their own advantage. They rail about the Mexican poor who—yes, often in economic desperation—violate immigration law. Yet these influence peddlers say little against their hidebound brethren, the unscrupulous corporations, businesses, and related interests that hire the undocumented with impunity. How infrequently we hear in the corporate media of entire industries (such as agribusiness, meatpacking, construction, certain service and manufacturing operations) that consistently avail themselves to the cheapest available labor. Yet it is not just the modern-day white-collar criminals who are to blame; in fact, it is all of us who, residing in the United States, have long been complicit in a quid pro quo agreement between lawmakers and corporate giants. They arrange for and manage underpaid and overworked labor, and we enjoy the smiley face "cheap stuff," whether it be food, clothing, or other mass-produced goods.

This is not to say that Latin Americans are unwilling to work for low (by U.S. standards) wages. Having talked with and read about dozens of Mexican taxi drivers, restaurant employees, construction workers, landscapers, nannies, musicians, and others over the years who have lived for a time in the United States before returning to their home country, we find it quite understandable that able-bodied individuals respond to economic opportunities in the United States. They know full well, as do the people who hire them, that if they get caught without proper documentation, they will probably get deported. They also know that they can probably mount another clandestine trip across the border and, before long, another laboring stint. Even with barbed wire, border patrols, and the latest and greatest in electronic surveillance in force, U.S. officials simply cannot fully control the movement of a population determined to find a way to survive in the face of an ever-globalizing economy. Why not migrate when a significantly better-paying job and the associated opportunities afforded such a position may await on the other side? Clearly, hemispheric elites prefer to maintain the distinction between "free" trade and "nonfree" labor.

We see commonality across the Americas. In fact, many of the migrants who reshape workplaces, neighborhoods, local politics, and communities come to the U.S. Heartland from similarly structured places in Mexico, El Salvador, Guatemala, and elsewhere. As people from diverse backgrounds are brought together by globalization, a common commitment to family, work, cultural values, and faith can be observed. Our experience reveals that the Heartland is more than conservative politics, xenophobia, and empty-minded consumerism. As with neoliberal restructuring in Latin America, we see a much similar process unfolding in the United States in which dispossession, unemployment, and increasing inequality now threaten the fabric of society.

Heartland America, like so many other places, is suffering under the yoke of global corporate rule. By highlighting the negative impact of neoliberalism, we aim to encourage further comparative, transnational analysis. We need to replace racist constructions of "us *versus* them" (such as Anglos against people of color/foreign nationals) with more economically grounded understandings of "us standing up to them" (the vast majority of ordinary people challenging economic and political elites).

Much of our research underscores the role of labor in defining our commonalities. Tracking the contributions of farmworkers in Idaho, Nebraska, North Carolina, Iowa, and elsewhere, our volume's case studies examine the enormous obstacles and often violent conditions Latin American farmworkers endure in their work experiences in the United States. Up against wage theft, worker injury, harsh living conditions, and discrimination, a context of labor exploitation is revealed in many of the case studies of the Heartland. Often these very conditions are not much different from abusive practices and socioeconomic relations of work in the home nations of migrants. As migrants enter areas in the U.S. Heartland, they may not be aware of the local restructuring that has taken place in which corporate agriculture has taken over family farms and mom-and-pop businesses have folded, making way for big-box stores. This kind of global restructuring has caused local populations everywhere to be displaced and dispersed, including in the all too familiar ghost-town imaginary of the region. In the studies of Oklahoma, Arkansas, and North Carolina, our contributors track the way government policies, changing legal-status markers, and shadowy labor recruitment practices position corporate enterprises in advantageous positions at the expense of labor protections. It is our intention to call attention to labor relations and practices rather than to emphasize the "immigrants contribute to the economy" narrative that strips workers of a sense of their human dignity.

We draw attention to the reprehensible notion of "deportability" that continues to instill fear in the hearts of those who live in the shadows. The prevailing policy response for managing the movement of workers under global restructuring is to strengthen and enforce policing strategies. From the uprooting of Salvadoran migrants under threats of deportation in Arkansas, to Immigrations and Customs Enforcement raids of meat-processing plants in Iowa, to routine traffic-stop sweeps in Oklahoma, contemporary undocumented migrants and their families live under a constant threat of detention and deportation. Through the use of ethnography, narratives, and oral histories, contributors here offer voices to those swept up in the deportation industry as a way to humanize the story. The revolving door of detention, deportation, and reentry has not only failed in assuaging the undocumented but has created deep cleavages and wedges within communities where individuals question the "legal" status of others and in so doing heighten their distrust, preventing more cooperative models from developing. And yet sanctuary sites such as local schools and churches respond with their own autonomous strategies for protecting and solving the crises before them.

Stories of people banding together to organize labor, strengthening community-based institutions, offering sympathetic media coverage of immigrant families coping with deportation, and telling tales of everyday individuals who fight hate and discrimination in small towns in Pennsylvania, Kansas, Idaho, and Nebraska demonstrate the power of collection action. In these moments we find evidence of unity and cooperation. In turn, we call upon the people of the Americas to leave behind past antagonisms and instead work in good faith to realize cooperative, critical class connections. It is the right thing to do.

Contributors

LINDA ALLEGRO is a lecturer in the Department of Political Science at Oklahoma State University. Her publications appear in *Latin American Perspectives, Red State, Centro: The Journal of Puerto Rican Studies,* and *Latino America: A State by State Encyclopedia.* She hosted a cultural segment called "Huellas Hispanas" on a local Spanish-language cable station in Tulsa, Oklahoma, and is engaged in immigrant and worker advocacy. She calls herself trilocal, living between Miami Beach, Tulsa, and Nicaragua.

Independent historian **TISA M. ANDERS** earned her PhD in religion and social change at the University of Denver/Iliff School of Theology. She is currently CEO/founder of Writing the World, LLC. Anders specializes in agricultural history, nineteenth-century U.S. reform movements, and oral history. Publications include "L. Maria Child: One Woman's Spiritual Journey in Nineteenth Century America" (Swedenborg Foundation, in progress); two chapters with coauthor Rosa Cobos on gender and migration in the edited collections: "Gender and Rural Migration: Realities, Conflict and Change," Glenda Tibe Bonifacio, ed. (Routledge, in progress) and "Farming across Borders: Selections on Transnational Agricultural History in the North American West," Sterling Evans, ed., Connecting the Greater West series (Texas A&M University Press, in progress); and "Junius Groves," an encyclopedia entry in the online African American and African history encyclopedia BlackPast.org (http://www.BlackPast.Org, 2008). Anders grew up in Western Nebraska and retains strong, current ties to the area. She thus brings an insider focus to her topic.

SCOTT CARTER is associate professor of economics at the University of Tulsa. He has published in the *Journal of Post Keynesian Economics,* the *Journal of the History of Economic Thought,* the *Review of Political Economy,* and the *American Journal of Economics and Sociology.* His interest in the connection between immigration and labor struggles began in the mid-1990s in New York City's Chinatown through organizing with the Chinese Staff and Workers Association and its executive director, Wing Lam. In addition to immigration issues, his research interests include labor economics, theories of growth and distribution, heterodox theory and pedagogy, and original archival research on the Cambridge, England, economist Piero Sraffa. He is also a member of the Steering Committee of the Union of Radical Political Economics (URPE).

CAITLIN DIDIER is a cultural anthropologist and small business owner in Columbus, Ohio. Her research focuses on the development and maintenance of ethnic identity in Postville, Iowa, a rural meatpacking town that has undergone rapid social, religious, and economic change. She centers her research on the impact of globalization and the social, economic, and political policies that affect immigrant integration in the United States. Her other research interests lie in the area of new religious movements and the strategies employed by members of those movements to address problems that plague their communities. Caitlin is currently finishing her PhD through the University of Kansas and is a part-time instructor at Denison University.

MIRANDA CADY HALLETT holds a position as assistant professor of anthropology at Otterbein University in Columbus, Ohio. Miranda completed a PhD in cultural anthropology in 2009 from Cornell University. Her dissertation, "Disappeared Subjects: Migration, Legality, and the Neoliberal State," analyzes the precarious legal condition of many transnational migrants as the construction, through law, of racialized hierarchies that serve neoliberal production regimes. Recent publications include a 2011 article in *Urban Anthropology* on Salvadoran activism for diasporic voting rights and a 2012 piece in the journal *Latino Studies* entitled "Better Than White Trash," looking at the discursive boundary work Latinos in Arkansas use to make moral claims of belonging. Miranda has conducted research on Salvadoran communities since 1998 and on transnational migration into the rural South and Midwest since 2004, and her current research project focuses on insights into transformations of statehood in the era of neoliberal globalization, based on ethnographic interviews from 2005 to the present with officials in Salvadoran government offices. In addition to her scholarly pursuits, Miranda is also an engaged public anthropologist with a history of activism and collaboration with social movements such as migrants' rights and the workers' center movement in the United States.

EDMUND "TED" HAMANN is an associate professor in the Department of Teaching, Learning, and Teacher Education at the University of Nebraska–Lincoln (UNL). He earned his PhD in education from the University of Pennsylvania in 1999 and his master's degree in anthropology in 1995 from the University of Kansas. He is author of *Education in the New Latino Diaspora* (Ablex Press, 2002; with Stanton Wortham and Enrique Murillo), *The Educational Welcome of Latinos in the New South* (Praeger, 2003), *Alumnos Transnacionales: Las Escuelas Mexicanas Frente a la Globalización* (with Víctor Zúñiga and Juan Sánchez García), and more than forty chapters and peer-reviewed articles on reconciling school reform with school responsiveness to transnational newcomers (including English learners). He is also involved in other education policy and practice issues.

ALBERT IAROI, a PhD student in sociology at Kansas State University, has a bachelor's degree in journalism and a master's degree in Eastern European contemporary history from Babes-Bolyai University in Romania. His areas of interest include rural and international development, environmental and natural resource studies—particularly regarding alternative fuels—and internal and international migration. He is also interested in the social, economic, and environmental impacts of biofuels development in small rural communities in the Midwest. His dissertation research is focused on ethanol production in rural Kansas.

ERROL D. JONES, a native of Utah, is professor emeritus in the History Department at Boise State University located in Boise, the capital of Idaho. Jones joined the faculty of Boise State University in 1982 after teaching in universities in Texas, Utah, Mexico, and Brazil. Trained in Latin American history, he specialized in the history of Mexico upon arriving at Boise State. From 1997 to 2006, he taught a course on Latinos in the United States and continues to do research and publish on the history of Latinos in Idaho. His most recent publications in this area are "A Long Struggle: Mexican Farmworkers in Idaho, 1918–1935," with Kathleen R. Hodges in *Memory, Community, and Activism: Mexican Migration and Labor in the Pacific Northwest,* edited by Jerry and Gilbert Garcia (2005); "The Shooting of Pedro Rodriguez," *Idaho Yesterdays* (2005); and the chapter on Idaho in *Latino America: A State by State Encyclopedia,* edited by Mark Overmeyer-Velazquez, 2 vols. (2008); he also served as guest editor and author of *Idaho Landscapes: La Cultura Mexicana* (2011).

JANE JUFFER is associate professor of English and Feminist, Gender, and Sexuality Studies at Cornell University. She is the author of two books, *At Home with Pornography: Women, Sex, and Everyday Life* and *Single Mother: The Emergence of the Domestic Intellectual,* both with New York University Press, as well as various articles in the field of Latino/a cultural studies. Her book *Intimacy across Borders: Race, Religion, and Migration in the U.S. Midwest* is forthcoming in spring 2013 with Temple University Press.

LÁSZLÓ J. KULCSÁR is an associate professor of sociology and former director of the Kansas Population Center. His field of expertise is social demography and regional development, with a particular emphasis on migration, urbanization, and spatial inequalities. He does research on population dynamics and social change in rural areas, focusing on two major trends: aging and the impact of natural resource use. Dr. Kulcsár participates in a National Science Foundation funded interdisciplinary research program that ties population projections to system-level ecological and land-use change and the transforming rural landscape in the Great Plains. He also studies the social and demographic transformation of Eastern Europe from a historical perspective, but with a particular emphasis on the postsocialist period. Dr. Kulcsár teaches courses on social and spatial inequalities, population dynamics, aging, immigration, and sociological methodology.

Dr. **JENELLE REEVES** is an associate professor in the Department of Teaching, Learning, and Teacher Education at the University of Nebraska–Lincoln where she is an English as a second language (ESL) teacher educator. Herself a former high school ESL teacher in Niigata, Japan, and university ESL teacher in Chuncheon, Korea, and Seattle, Washington, Jenelle's research focuses on ESL teachers' learning and development as viewed from a sociocultural perspective. Jenelle conducts ethnographic research with teachers in newly linguistically diverse schools in midwestern and southern U.S. states, including Nebraska, Alabama, and Tennessee. Teachers' construction of their teaching identities, the development of teachers' linguistic knowledge for teaching, and teachers' learning through the use of scripted materials are topics that have emerged from her research. Her work is published in *Linguistics and Education, TESOL Quarterly, Teaching and Teacher Education, Journal of Educational Research,* and *Journal of Latino- Latin American Studies,* among other professional journals. Jenelle is currently investigating the experiences of Anglo, monolingual teachers in rural Nebraska schools and communities that are experiencing rapid demographic change.

JENNIFER F. REYNOLDS is an associate professor of anthropology at the University of South Carolina and a core member of the Latin American, Latino/a, and Caribbean Studies Program and the interdepartmental program in linguistics. She is a linguistic anthropologist who examines the relationship(s) between quotidian discourse practices and social reproduction. Her current research is a longitudinal study of Guatemalan indigenous youth and their families' experiences as they cross multiple borders, assume new identities, and restructure familial relationships in different receiving contexts within transnational circuits of migration. She has published in *American Anthropologist, Anthropological Quarterly, Journal of Linguistic Anthropology, Pragmatics,* and *Reading Research Quarterly,* among other professional journals and edited book volumes.

SANDY SMITH-NONINI, PhD, author of *Healing the Body Politic: El Salvador's Popular Struggle for Health Rights—From Civil War to Neoliberal Peace* (Rutgers University Press, 2010), is research assistant professor of anthropology at the University of North Carolina at Chapel Hill. She was assistant professor of anthropology at Elon University from 2000 to 2005. Smith-Nonini helped found a multiyear project supported by the Unitarian-Universalist Funding Program to educate North Carolinians about farm labor issues, and she received a Mellon Sawyer postdoctoral award for research on farm labor activism. She received her PhD from the University of North Carolina at Chapel Hill in 1998 and has done research and authored several book chapters and journal articles on the politics of resurgent tuberculosis epidemics and on community health in El Salvador. She was a 2006–2007 Richard Carley Hunt Fellow with the Wenner Gren Foundation and is a former recipient of the Peter K. New Prize from the Society for Applied Anthropology.

ANDREW GRANT WOOD is Stanley Rutland Professor of American History at the University of Tulsa. He is author of *Revolution in the Street: Women, Workers and Urban Protest in Veracruz, 1870–1927* (SR Books/Rowman and Littlefield, 2001) and *Agustín Lara: A Cultural Biography* (Oxford University Press, 2014). He is also editor of *The U.S.–Mexico Border: An Encyclopedia of Culture and Politics* (Greenwood Publishing Group, 2008) and *On the Border: Society and Culture between the U.S. and Mexico* (SR Books/Rowman and Littlefield, 2004) and coeditor (with Alejandra Bronfman) of *Sound, Media and Culture in Latin America and the Caribbean* (University of Pittsburgh Press, 2012) and (with Dina Berger) *Holiday in Mexico: Essays on Tourism and Tourist Encounters* (Duke University Press, 2010). He was born in Montreal, Canada.

Index

THE WORKING CLASS IN AMERICAN HISTORY

Worker City, Company Town: Iron and Cotton-Worker Protest in Troy and Cohoes,
New York, 1855–84   *Daniel J. Walkowitz*

Life, Work, and Rebellion in the Coal Fields: The Southern West Virginia Miners,
1880–1922   *David Alan Corbin*

Women and American Socialism, 1870–1920   *Mari Jo Buhle*

Lives of Their Own: Blacks, Italians, and Poles in Pittsburgh, 1900–1960
John Bodnar, Roger Simon, and Michael P. Weber

Working-Class America: Essays on Labor, Community, and American Society
Edited by Michael H. Frisch and Daniel J. Walkowitz

Eugene V. Debs: Citizen and Socialist   *Nick Salvatore*

American Labor and Immigration History, 1877–1920s: Recent European Research
Edited by Dirk Hoerder

Workingmen's Democracy: The Knights of Labor and American Politics   *Leon Fink*

The Electrical Workers: A History of Labor at General Electric and
Westinghouse, 1923–60   *Ronald W. Schatz*

The Mechanics of Baltimore: Workers and Politics in the Age of Revolution,
1763–1812   *Charles G. Steffen*

The Practice of Solidarity: American Hat Finishers in the Nineteenth Century
David Bensman

The Labor History Reader   *Edited by Daniel J. Leab*

Solidarity and Fragmentation: Working People and Class Consciousness
in Detroit, 1875–1900   *Richard Oestreicher*

Counter Cultures: Saleswomen, Managers, and Customers in American
Department Stores, 1890–1940   *Susan Porter Benson*

The New England Working Class and the New Labor History   *Edited by
Herbert G. Gutman and Donald H. Bell*

Labor Leaders in America   *Edited by Melvyn Dubofsky and Warren Van Tine*

Barons of Labor: The San Francisco Building Trades and Union Power
in the Progressive Era   *Michael Kazin*

Gender at Work: The Dynamics of Job Segregation by Sex during World War II
Ruth Milkman

Once a Cigar Maker: Men, Women, and Work Culture in American Cigar
Factories, 1900–1919   *Patricia A. Cooper*

A Generation of Boomers: The Pattern of Railroad Labor Conflict in
Nineteenth-Century America   *Shelton Stromquist*

Work and Community in the Jungle: Chicago's Packinghouse Workers,
1894–1922   *James R. Barrett*

Workers, Managers, and Welfare Capitalism: The Shoeworkers and Tanners of
Endicott Johnson, 1890–1950   *Gerald Zahavi*

Men, Women, and Work: Class, Gender, and Protest in the New England
Shoe Industry, 1780–1910   *Mary Blewett*

Workers on the Waterfront: Seamen, Longshoremen, and Unionism in the 1930s
Bruce Nelson

German Workers in Chicago: A Documentary History of Working-Class Culture
from 1850 to World War I   *Edited by Hartmut Keil and John B. Jentz*

The University of Illinois Press
is a founding member of the
Association of American University Presses.

University of Illinois Press
1325 South Oak Street
Champaign, IL 61820-6903
www.press.uillinois.edu